W. Drott

A superb treatment of the Kingdom of God —

On Mk 4: 2-20 see pp. 15 el. "eyes see not," etc

Excellent breakdown of Mk, Q, L, M : the characteristics
of each.

THE TEACHING OF JESUS

The
TEACHING OF JESUS

STUDIES OF
ITS FORM AND
CONTENT

by

T. W. MANSON, D.D., D.LITT.

*Rylands Professor of Biblical Criticism and Exegesis,
in the University of Manchester; Fellow of
the British Academy*

CAMBRIDGE
AT THE UNIVERSITY PRESS
1955

PUBLISHED BY
THE SYNDICS OF THE CAMBRIDGE UNIVERSITY PRESS

London Office: Bentley House, N.W. 1
American Branch: New York

Agents for Canada, India, and Pakistan: Macmillan

First Edition 1931
Second Edition 1935
Reprinted 1939
1943
1945
1948
1951
1955

First printed in Great Britain at the University Press, Cambridge
Reprinted by offset-litho by Percy Lund Humphries & Co. Ltd

CONTENTS

PART I
PRELIMINARY QUESTIONS

PART II
THE CONTENTS OF THE TEACHING

PREFACE

THE present work, as I have tried to make clear in the title, does not pretend to be a complete and exhaustive treatment of its subject. Neither is it a collection of detached essays. It is a set of studies which are linked together by two main ideas. One is that the substance of the Gospel 'is neither a dogmatic system nor an ethical code, but a Person and a Life'.[1] The other is that the key to the New Testament is the notion of the 'saving Remnant'. In the light of these two ideas it seems possible to see light clearly and to understand much in the teaching of Jesus that would otherwise remain obscure.

The book has grown out of the technical studies described in Chapter I (pp. 15–21). My original plan was to publish the results of these studies *simpliciter*, and to leave it to others to draw their own conclusions: and I prepared a first chapter somewhat after the style of what now appears as Appendix I, but much more elaborate and detailed. This I showed to Principal Oman and Professor Anderson Scott. Both agreed that the results were interesting, and both advised me that it would be better if their implications could be drawn out more fully. This I have attempted to do. In the process more and more of my material has been absorbed in the text, and the Appendices have been correspondingly reduced. From first to last the work has occupied the greater part of my leisure time during the past five years. Its publication now is made possible by the generosity of the Syndics of the Press.

[1] Lightfoot, *Commentary on Philippians*, Preface to 1st edition (end).

The nature of these studies is such that my time has had to be spent in close application to the details of the Synoptic Gospels rather than in wide reading of books about them: and consequently my largest debt is to Moulton and Geden, and Hatch and Redpath. Huck's excellent *Synopse der drei ersten Evangelien* (5th ed.) has also been in constant use. Two other works demand special acknowledgement: the great Commentary of Strack and Billerbeck, and Canon Streeter's invaluable book, *The Four Gospels*. I have taken Canon Streeter's 'Four-document hypothesis' seriously and used it in my own investigations. These, for what they are worth, seem to me to confirm it in essentials. Where I am conscious of borrowing from other works the fact is acknowledged in the footnotes.

I have also to record with gratitude the help which I have received at all stages in the preparation and production of this book. Principal Oman and Professor Anderson Scott gave valuable advice and encouragement at the point where such things were most needed. Professor A. A. Bevan, Professor P. S. Noble and Mr C. P. T. Winckworth kindly allowed me to consult them on special points. Professor J. M. Creed read the typescript and, by his suggestions, enabled me to make some considerable improvements in detail. My friend the Rev. J. R. Coates, of the Selly Oak Colleges, Birmingham, read the whole of the text, partly in proof and partly in manuscript, and made many valuable suggestions. My principal creditors are three: the Rev. E. W. Philip, M.A., who read the whole work in manuscript and again in proof, checked the biblical references, and made many important criticisms and suggestions; the Rev. P. L. Hedley, B.D., who performed like services when the book was in proof; and my wife, who prepared the whole of the typescript for the Press. The vigilance of Mr Philip and Mr Hedley has availed to clarify many obscurities in my writing and to ensure accuracy in the references. For any blemishes that remain the responsibility must be laid at my door. Finally I have to thank the officials and craftsmen of the Press for their unfailing skill and kindness.

T. W. MANSON

FALSTONE MANSE
NORTHUMBERLAND

August 1931

PREFACE TO THE SECOND EDITION

The demand, which has come sooner than I expected, for a second edition of my book gives me an opportunity of acknowledging the kindness with which it has been received by reviewers and readers alike. It has not been possible to carry out any extensive revision of the text; nor, indeed, is there any important change that I should care to make. I have, however, added a few notes, which will be found on pp. 330–333.

T.W.M.

OXFORD
June 1935

LIST OF ABBREVIATIONS

B.D.B. Brown, Driver and Briggs, *Hebrew and English Lexicon of the Old Testament.*

G.J.V. Schürer, *Geschichte des Jüdischen Volkes im Zeitalter Jesu Christi.* 4th edition.

H.B.N.T. Lietzmann (editor), *Handbuch zum Neuen Testament.*

I.C.C. *International Critical Commentary.*

J.T.S. *Journal of Theological Studies.*

K.A.T. Schrader, *Die Keilinschriften und das Alte Testament.* 3rd edition by Zimmern and Winckler.

K.H.C. Marti (editor), *Kurzer Hand-Commentar zum Alten Testament* (1897–1904).

L.O.T. Driver, *Introduction to the Literature of the Old Testament.* 9th edition.

N.H.W.B. Levy, *Neuhebräisches u. Chaldäisches Wörterbuch über die Talmudim u. Midraschim.*

S.B. Strack and Billerbeck, *Kommentar zum Neuen Testament aus Talmud u. Midrasch* (1922–1928).

S.N.T. *Die Schriften des Neuen Testaments.* 3rd edition.

U.A.C. Meyer, *Ursprung u. Anfänge des Christentums.*

References to the Old Testament, unless otherwise stated, are to the 2nd edition of Kittel's *Biblia Hebraica*: those to the New Testament are to the text of Westcott and Hort. Citations of the LXX version follow the chapter and verse division in Swete's manual edition.

Ch 1 — Taking <u>Mark</u> as the original document of the life & works of Jesus, Manson judges the other sources by it. It has the most reliable chronology of Jesus ideas and events. There are 4 Gospel sources: Mk, M, L, & Q. Mk is narrative, Q is sayings & stories, L is parables & popular aphorisms, M is didactic & Rabbinic.

Problem: getting back to best texts of Gospels, then correlating the evidence of the sources for the utterance closest to Christ's made in Aramaic; then the problem of interpretation.

Manson says to understand Jesus you cannot separate the developmt of His life from the development of His teaching & ideas. Two periods here: Before & after Peter's Confession. Manson's clues in Mark: Jesus use of terms 'Kingdom of God' and 'Son of Man'. Finally: a hermeneutical key: The 3 audiences

PART I.
PRELIMINARY QUESTIONS

Ch 2 — In Mark 'Son of Man' is used Messianically after Peter's Confession; also only then does Jesus use 'father'. Before Con. Kingdom is 'at hand'? AC— has come in Him & is to be entered. Prepared for K. by insight, repentance, trust. After by believing in Him. Jesus — Son of Man.

Q — the Semetic original, oracles, short addresses, dialogues. Jesus here is Prophet. Used for propaganda, careful not to offend Jews. No narration, no Passion story. Emphasize Jesus teaching.

   To Jews that: if they reject Jesus they cast away their birthright.
                 The invitation then is open to Gentiles
                 Disciples — stand fast in your faith

M — Jewish — gospel here is new law, best wine in old wineskins. Here the emphasis is on community & its 'rule'— ie the Teaching of Jesus. Severe with proud Pharisees. Jesus here a Rabbi

L — oral tradition culled from common people. Gospel for underdog. Ht. He is friend of Poor.

Ch 3 — The language: Jesus spoke to the people in Aramaic; to scribes in Rabbinic Hebrew.
   The Poetry: good section pp. 51 ff.
   Parable: not mere stories, but maxims: proverbs of two types: a. personal example to warn or give example; b) Principle of God & govt — a both ethical type character "concrete universal". a — To arouse conscience b — To teach. — a Parable has two meanings.

            Note on Lk 11^{20}

Chapter I

INTRODUCTION: PROBLEMS AND METHODS

THE study of the teaching of Jesus has close affinities with two of the main branches of modern theological investigation, for, on the one hand, no attempt to write the life of Jesus, or even to sketch his likeness, could be considered complete without some account of his words: and, on the other, any work on New Testament Theology must necessarily take as its foundation the Theology of the Founder of Christianity. The study of the teaching of our Lord is a branch both of Biblical History and of Biblical Theology. These two disciplines are essentially modern: they were begotten by the Reformation, though they did not actually come to birth until the eighteenth century. In principle they were already present when Luther transformed faith from the mere acceptance of ecclesiastical dogma into a personal living trust in God through Jesus Christ. This transformation necessarily involved a change of method in dealing with Scripture, particularly the Gospel narrative, even though the extent of the change was not fully realised until a later date.

It has been said that the Reformation merely set up one infallibility in place of another, merely substituted an infallible Bible for an infallible Church. If this charge were true, it would be a serious matter: for it would be no real emancipation at all, which freed the plain man from the bondage of Scholastic metaphysics merely to deliver him into an equally rigorous servitude to a new Scholasticism made by philologists and rabbinical exegetes. Faith would still be a *fides implicita*, an assent to the uncomprehended—only instead of being the intention to believe what the Church believes, it would become the intention to believe what the scholars think. All that would happen

paper Pope

would be a change from the tyranny of the Church to the tyranny of the School.

But so far as such a result did follow from the Reformation it has to be said that it was due to a failure to grasp in its completeness the cardinal principle of the Reformation: and this failure in its turn was due to the influence of prejudices and prepossessions carried over from the pre-Reformation era. From such prepossessions Luther himself was not free, his frank criticisms of some books of the Bible notwithstanding,[1] and his followers continued to use the Scriptures in the old way, as a *dossier* of proof-texts (the so-called *dicta probantia*) for new doctrinal constructions.

Only towards the end of the eighteenth century was the right of Scripture to say something on its own account, and not merely to be called in to ratify the decisions of Oecumenical Councils or Assemblies of Protestant Divines, openly proclaimed by Gabler.[2] From that time onwards Biblical Theology came into its own as a discipline whose object is simply to set down in as orderly a fashion as possible what doctrines are, as a matter of fact, taught in the Scriptures. The Theology of the New Testament forms an obvious division of the whole: and within New Testament Theology the teaching of Jesus takes of right the leading place.

A parallel development took place in the study of the life of Jesus. From the earliest times to the end of the eighteenth century, such Lives of Jesus as were written were composed not as historical works but as treatises for edification. So long as the essential truth concerning the Lord was given by doctrinal formulae, the Gospel narratives could only serve to embellish the figure provided by those formulae. The work of Reimarus[3] and his successors

---

[1] For a collection of these cf. P. Smith, *The Life and Letters of Martin Luther*, ch. XXIII.

[2] *De justo discrimine theologiae biblicae et dogmaticae*, 1787.

[3] In some matters—rationalisation of the Gospel miracles for example—Reimarus merely followed the English Deists in forcing a philosophical theory on to the Gospel narrative. His true originality comes out only when he treats the Gospels as historical documents and endeavours to place the events recorded in them in their historical context.

changed all that and effected a Copernican revolution in this branch of theological enquiry. What was implicit in the Reformation was brought out into the light of day: this namely, that if Christ be in truth the centre of Christianity, then the formulation of the faith must be made to conform to Christ and not Christ to the formulation. Hitherto the portrait of the Master had been painted to fit into the frame provided ready-made by the creeds and confessions: now it began to appear that the proper procedure is to paint the portrait first and then make a frame to fit it. The dangers of this method are obvious. One was that the biographers of Jesus would find in the Gospels just what they were looking for, that to the Rationalists he would be a Rationalist, that, in fact, every man would make Christ in his own idealised image. Another was that every man would bring with him his own general view of God, man, and the world, in a word, that in place of the one Procrustes-bed of dogma every biographer would produce a bed of his own devising on to which the 'historical Jesus' would somehow be fitted. This was and still is a real danger; but it is one which must be faced. For theology to-day there is no possible line of retreat, and the only way of safety is to go forward in the face of dangers, in the faith that the truth as it is in Jesus will disclose itself like all other truth to patient enquiry and religious insight.

The study of the teaching of Jesus is thus of vital importance both to New Testament Theology, of which it is the kernel, and to the study of the life of Jesus, a life in which, more than in any other, word and deed are united in indissoluble harmony. But the study of the teaching has an independent interest of its own and a definite task of its own, namely, that we use every resource we possess of knowledge of historical imagination, and of religious insight to the one end of transporting ourselves back into the centre of the greatest crisis of the world's history, to look as it were through the eyes of Jesus and to see God and man, heaven and earth, life and death, as he saw them, and to

find, if we may, in that vision something which will
satisfy the whole man in mind and heart and will. Thus
stated the task seems simple enough. We only realise its
magnitude and the difficulties that lie in the way when we
consider that it has fascinated—and more often than not
baffled—some of the acutest and best-equipped of theological
enquirers over something like a century and a half, and
that to-day the results which may be considered to be
firmly established stand in sadly small proportion to the
labour expended.

Some of the difficulties lie on the surface for anyone who
reads the Gospels with care: others have only been brought
to light during the course of research, and the doubts and
fears aroused by them have hardly passed beyond the
narrow circle of learned debate. Typical of the former
group is the problem raised by the Fourth Gospel: of the
latter the controversy concerning the 'Son of Man'.

The material for our study is contained in the four
canonical Gospels. And at the outset a difficulty presents
itself. The first three Gospels immediately group themselves
together, while the Fourth stands alone. 'The modern
student cannot but feel that to turn from the Synoptics to
the Fourth Gospel is to breathe another atmosphere, to be
transported to another world.'[1] So it comes about that the
very Gospel which seemed to Calvin to be the key to the
other three[2] has to be set apart as a special and highly
complex problem on its own account. This fact is the
justification for confining the present work to what is contained in the Synoptic record. Does not use John

But even the Synoptic Gospels present problems of their
own, though many of these have been solved or are on the
way to a solution. First and foremost is the question of the
relation of the three accounts to one another. It is now

[1] H. Latimer Jackson, *The Problem of the Fourth Gospel*, p. 82. Chapter v of
this work contains a convenient summary of the points of difference.
[2] 'Dicere soleo, hoc Evangelium clavem esse, quae aliis intellegendis
januam aperiat'—*Argumentum in Ev. Ioannis*.

generally admitted that certain main results of the study of this problem are firmly established: and these may be briefly summarised at this point.

(a) Mark is prior to both Matthew and Luke: and the two latter have borrowed freely from Mark. Between them they reproduce the whole of Mark with the exception of some 31 verses.[1] Nine-tenths of Mark is transcribed in Matthew and rather more than half of Mark in Luke. The position is thus that 'Matthew may be regarded as an enlarged edition of Mark; Luke is an independent work incorporating considerable portions of Mark'.[2]

(b) Where Matthew and Luke have matter in common which does not appear in Mark (about 200 verses), they are both dependent on a source now lost (usually referred to as Q).[3]

(c) The subtraction of Marcan and Q material from Matthew leaves a residue of matter peculiar to that Gospel: and the same is the case with Luke. The analysis of the three Gospels thus leads to the differentiation of four main sources of information designated by the symbols Mk, Q, M, and L. Mk is our second Gospel: Q is the lost document which lies behind the matter common to Matthew and Luke: and M and L stand for the sources of matter peculiar to Matthew and Luke respectively. For the story of how these sources have been combined to produce the Synoptic Gospels reference may be made to works dealing specifically with the Synoptic Problem.[4] What is important for our present purpose is that we have to deal not simply with three canonical Gospels but with four documents which perhaps represent the Gospel tradition as it was current in four leading Churches of the Apostolic age.

[1] Streeter, *The Four Gospels*, p. 195, where the list is given.

[2] Streeter, *op. cit.*, p. 151.

[3] A list of non-Marcan parallels in Matthew and Luke is given in Streeter, *op. cit.*, p. 197. His reconstruction of Q containing additional matter found only in Luke runs to 272 verses and is given in the same work, p. 291.

[4] E.g. Streeter, *op. cit.*

Canon Streeter[1] suggests the connexion of Mk with Rome, Q (in its Greek dress) with Antioch, M with Jerusalem, and L with Caesarea. One of our Gospels—Mark—corresponds with the document Mk, but the other two are composite works, Matthew being built up out of the elements Mk + Q + M, and Luke out of Q + L + Mk.

These considerations determine the first task in such an enquiry as the present—to get behind the Gospels to the sources embodied in them. It is this fact which gives to Mark the pre-eminent position which it rightly has: for Mark is not only a Gospel, it is a source for Matthew and Luke. From this, two conclusions follow immediately. First, that where Mark is the source of Matthew and Luke we have the evidence of one witness only—Mark. That of Matthew and Luke becomes, as it were, hearsay, and cannot add any weight to what is already embodied in Mark. The second conclusion is that no variation from Mark in their versions of Marcan matter can affect the testimony of Mark. The copies cannot be used to check the original: rather Mark can and must be used to check the other two. By a comparison of Mark with the Matthaean and Lucan versions of Mark we can gain valuable information about the editorial methods and personal idiosyncrasies of St Matthew and St Luke,[2] which may be of service when we have to attempt the restoration of documents which have survived only in their pages.

But even if we could, by some fortunate discovery, be presented with the documents Q, M, and L to set along-side the Mark which we do possess, we should still have the largest and most difficult part of the task before us. For, even in their present condition, it is obvious that there are differences between them quite as striking as their general agreement. A single example will show what is meant. In Mk. xiii we are given a picture of the last things. The

[1] *Op. cit.*, pp. 223–235.
[2] I use St Mark, St Matthew, etc., to indicate the Evangelists; Mark, Matthew, etc., to indicate the books.

Mark: Warnings
Q: Surprise attack

prophecy of the destruction of the Temple (*v.* 2) leads up
to a description of the premonitory signs of the end: wars
and rumours of wars, persecution of the disciples, utter
desolation in Judaea, the rise of false Messiahs and false   *Contrast*
prophets, signs in heaven, 'and then (*v.* 26) they shall see   *of*
the Son of Man coming with clouds with much power and   *2ed advent*
glory'.   Compare this with the account in Q (Lk. xvii.   *in Mk. & Q*
22–37) where the day of the Son of Man is likened success-
ively to lightning, the Deluge, and the destruction of
Sodom.[1]   In the one case the final act in the drama is
preceded by a host of premonitory signs, and the parable of
the Fig Tree (Mk. xiii. 28 f.) makes it clear that these signs   *Warnings*
will be an indication that the end is very near even though
nobody can tell the exact time of its coming. When we turn
to Q we find the end conceived as a bolt from the blue,   *No warning*
something that comes without warning and bursts into the
daily routine of the world as utterly unexpected as the
crashing chords that open the Seventh Symphony.

Instances could easily be multiplied, but one is enough to
show that the evidence offered by our documents needs to
be carefully weighed and sifted. We have, in fact, to
realise that just as there is a personal equation, of which we
must take account, in the work of St Matthew or St Luke, so
there is probably a personal equation in the work of the
writers of the original sources. The whole Synoptic Problem
arises out of the simple fact that the closest verbal agreements and the strangest verbal differences stand side by
side in the parallel columns of a synopsis of the Gospels.
But suppose that problem solved, we should forthwith have
on our hands another of the same kind. We could do with
our four documents what we have already done with our
three Gospels—arrange them in parallel columns. We
could set the Marcan account of the preaching of John
alongside that of Q; we could do the same in other cases,
that of the Parousia cited above, for example. Then we
should have a problem similar in kind to that of the restora-

[1] A similar view is presented in I Thess. v. 1–3.

tion of Q, except that we should not be in search of a lost
document but rather trying to recover from the different
witnesses the actual sayings and doings of the Lord.

Here, again, a single example will suffice. The saying of
Jesus concerning the unforgivable sin is contained in Mk.
iii. 28 f. The Q version of the same saying is given in Mt.
xii. 32 and Lk. xii. 10. The task of the Synoptic critic is to
restore, so far as he can, the original Greek text lying
behind Matthew and Luke. If we suppose this accomplished, the next step is to place the recovered Q alongside
Mk and attempt to recover, not a document, but the words
of Jesus himself; to get behind the primary written records
to the spoken word.

At this point a new problem—the linguistic—arises. Up
to this point we are dealing with Greek Gospels, and, in
two cases at least, with Greek sources. Mark lies before us
in Greek: and the amount of verbal agreement between
Matthew and Luke makes it certain that Q lay before them
in Greek also. But the mother-tongue of our Lord and the
Apostles was not Greek but Galilean Aramaic,[1] so that,
even if we could push the analysis of the Greek evidence to
its farthest limit, we should be left with the hazardous
enterprise of retranslation[2] in order to get back to the
ipsissima verba of Jesus; and, at the end, we should have no
certainty that anything more than an Aramaic Targum of
the Greek had been produced. More than that, it may be
questioned whether the result would be worth the labour

[1] I say 'mother-tongue' rather than 'language' in order not to prejudge
the question whether any of our Lord's words were uttered in some other
dialect than Aramaic. It seems not impossible that some of his words may
have been spoken in the language which is preserved in the Mishnah and the
older Midrashim. The disputes with Scribes and Pharisees occur to one in
this connexion, for it is just in such contexts that we find words and phrases
which go most naturally into the Scholastic Hebrew. I have no doubt that
this language was spoken and regularly used in learned debate (cf. Moore,
Judaism, 1. 99 f.) and it would not be surprising if Jesus knew and used it in
his controversies with the scholars. For a fuller discussion of this question see
Chapter III.

[2] For essays in retranslation see Dalman, *The Words of Jesus* and *Jesus-
Jeshua,* and Burney, *The Poetry of our Lord.*

involved. Our ultimate aim is to comprehend the thought
of Jesus, and this fact sets strict limits to the profitable use
of retranslation. There are many cases where the meaning
of the Master is perfectly clear in the Greek or, for that
matter, in the Authorised Version: in such cases there is
little, if anything, to be gained by adding another version
to those already existing. In other instances, however,
retranslation clears up obscurities in the Greek or explains
differences between the documents. For example the
saying, Mt. viii. 20 = Lk. ix. 58 (Q): 'The foxes have
holes and the birds of the air have nests, but the Son of
Man has nowhere to lay his head'. Retranslation could
add nothing to our understanding of the first half; but the
moment we put the second part back into Aramaic we are
brought face to face with one of the most baffling problems
of interpretation of the teaching—the meaning of the
phrase 'Son of Man'. Similarly in the case of the saying
about the unforgivable sin cited above, it is by retransla-
tion that the clue is found for the harmonisation of Mk *then the best regard) ipsissima verba —*
and Q. *First, back to the Words —? then the Problem of Meaning remains. —*

 All that has been said up to this point has to do with what
are essentially preliminary investigations. Could we
imagine the whole programme successfully carried out, we
should be in possession of a true text of the recorded
sayings and doings of Jesus, but the task of comprehending
them would still lie before us with all its own peculiar
difficulties. And it must be admitted that if we were to
adhere strictly to the programme, the ultimate goal—the
comprehension of the teaching—would recede into the far
distant future. This programme, however, represents only
the logical order of investigation. Theoretically the correct
procedure is (1) textual criticism and recovery of the true
text of the Gospels; (2) Synoptic criticism and recovery of
the original sources used by the Evangelists; (3) comparison
of the sources and recovery of the primary tradition concerning Jesus; (4) study and interpretation of this material.
But in practice these stages of the enquiry are not suc-

cessive but concurrent. If we had to wait till the last manuscript had been collated and the final definitive edition of the Gospels published, we might wait for ever. Moreover Synoptic criticism can go a long way towards its goal even with a text that is not perfect: and, what is still more important, progress in one branch of the investigation can assist enquiry in another. Synoptic criticism can cast valuable light on textual problems, and exegesis is involved in the decision of all higher critical questions. An advance on any part of this battle-front affects the whole situation and prepares the way for an advance all along the line.

The special problems connected with the interpretation of the teaching arise partly from the form in which the tradition has been handed down and partly from the nature of some of the leading conceptions employed by Jesus. We have no connected treatise on theology composed by our Lord. We have not even a Life of Jesus. Apart from a few fragments of doubtful value all that has come down to us is a biographical sketch by St Mark; a collection of parables and sayings on various occasions forming the document Q, which is preserved more or less intact in Matthew and Luke; and the two collections of sayings and narratives which we call M and L. Even if we give the shortest possible duration to the ministry, there are still great stretches of it where no detailed record of our Lord's doings has been preserved; and it is certain that many a spoken word has gone the same way into oblivion. The material is woefully scanty both for the life and for the teaching.

Again, a study of Mark shows that there are changes of emphasis, emergence of new ideas and dropping of old ones during the ministry—a development of the teaching which proceeds *pari passu* with the unfolding of the drama of the life. This fact compels the assumption that one of the first steps toward the understanding of the teaching will be to fit it as far as possible into the framework of the life of

Jesus. The mission of Jesus, like the careers of many of the great masters in music and literature, falls into periods.

The most obvious and striking division is that marked by Peter's Confession. It has long been recognised that this event marks a turning-point in the life of our Lord; what is perhaps not so clearly realised is that it marks the close of one period and the beginning of another in the teaching. It is possible to draw up a list of important terms, key-words, that make their first appearance in the recorded utterances of Jesus after this event, and another list of words that form part of the vocabulary of his teaching before the Confession and afterwards recede into the background or disappear altogether. An example of the former group is the phrase 'Son of Man' (excluding cases where it means simply 'man'). Whatever may be the sense which Jesus attached to the phrase in his special use of it, it seems certain that he did not make use of it before Peter's Confession.[1] To the latter category belong, among others, those words which imply a demand for understanding on the part of Christ's hearers: e.g. ἀσύνετος, βλέπω and γινώσκω where insight is in question, νοέω, συνίημι, and the saying 'He that hath ears to hear, let him hear'. It is not necessary at this stage to multiply instances: it is enough to note that the turning-point in the life marks also a turning-point in the teaching and that the teaching as a whole can only be fully understood in the context of the life as a whole.

This is a point of no little importance. It is possible, for instance, to study profitably such a work as the *Ethics* of Spinoza even though we know nothing about the author: the prophecy of Amos is intelligible to us and we know next to nothing about Amos. With the teaching of Jesus it is different. The life interprets the teaching and the teaching the life: and it is surely not without significance that the opening words of St Mark's Gospel, ἀρχὴ τοῦ εὐαγγελίου

---

[1] This particular case has been noticed and discussed by Dalman, *Words of Jesus* (E.T.), pp. 258–264.

'Ιησοῦ Χριστοῦ, are the preface not to a theological treatise or a book of pious meditations but to a biography.

A second set of special problems in the interpretation of the teaching arises out of the use by Jesus of certain leading conceptions. The result is that in our records we are constantly coming across words and phrases which are, as it were, the technical terms of the teaching. Such, for example, are 'Kingdom of God' and 'Son of Man'. On the precise meaning which we assign to terms such as these will depend in a large measure our conception of the teaching as a whole. In a matter of this sort extreme cases are instructive. To-day we may read in the morning paper that a political leader or a popular novelist has given it as his considered opinion that the essence of Christianity lies in the ethics of the Sermon on the Mount. To-morrow, as likely as not, we shall learn from the same source that a small company of ardent believers is assembled somewhere to await the imminent end of the world. The orthodox may dismiss these phenomena as heresy, or superstition, or what they will. But in truth they are the manifestation of divergent interpretations of the term 'Kingdom of God'. They represent the liberal, rational, evolutionary interpretation and the eschatological, catastrophic interpretation respectively, pushed to their extreme limits.

It is easy enough to trace the scriptural pedigree of such strange creeds. The one goes back through Mt. v–vii to the great prophets of the eighth century B.C., all interpreted in a religio-ethical humanitarian sense; the other goes through Mt. xxiv, xxv, supplemented by the Johannine Apocalypse, back to the Book of Daniel.

Moreover, these extreme views have their counterparts in the more sober scholarly criticism of the Gospel record. If the ideas of Mt. v–vii be taken as the supreme standard for the interpretation of the life and teaching of Jesus, it is obvious that we shall arrive at a result very different from that which ensues from taking Mt. xxiv f. as the norm. And this is what has in fact happened. The student at the present

Two views of Jesus: X

time has to choose between the religio-ethical humanitarian and the eschatological view of the Gospels. On the
one view, Jesus becomes the pattern religious and social
reformer; on the other a mistaken enthusiast. On the one
view, the Crucifixion is a gross miscarriage of justice comparable to the death of Socrates; on the other it is something which Jesus deliberately sought as part of his
mission.[1] On the one view the subsequent history of the
Church is the story of the failure either to understand or to
live up to the religio-ethical ideal put forward by the
prophet of Nazareth; on the other it is essentially the
triumph of a mistake made by Jesus in believing that he
was the Son of Man spoken of in Daniel and Enoch.

The vital question, then, is whether these two alter-
natives exhaust all the possibilities of the case. It is
difficult to be satisfied with either the liberal or the
apocalyptic portrait of Jesus, though, of the two, the
apocalyptic is farthest removed from being a mere lay
figure. Moreover, both views have their difficulties. The
one has to get rid of the Son of Man and the thirteenth
chapter of Mark; the other has to reduce large portions of
the teaching to the position of 'interim-ethic'.[2] There is a
prima facie case for a fresh investigation of all the material:
and one of the leading problems in any such enquiry will
be to discover the sense in which Jesus used such terms as = *The clue*
'Kingdom of God' and 'Son of Man'. ← *says Manson*
The importance of the factor of date—before or after *to Jesus teaching is these 2 terms.*
Peter's Confession—has been indicated above. There is
another factor, that of audience, which seems to demand
more attention than it has hitherto received. To the neglect
of this, as it seems to me, important factor many causes
have contributed. So long as the New Testament was
regarded as a mere collection of proof-texts for dogmatic

[1] So for example Schweitzer, *Quest of the Historical Jesus*, p. 389: 'Towards
Passover, therefore, Jesus sets out for Jerusalem, solely in order to die there'.
[2] There is also the suspicion that if the eschatological view is to be taken
really seriously, large parts of the ministry must partake of the same 'interim'
nature—a prelude to something which did not come off.

purposes, there was no occasion to consider closely the
particular circumstances in which the eternal truths were
published to the world. They were seen, not as branches of
the tree of life each with its own individuality, each alive
and adapted to its surroundings, but as props and girders
ready hewn and trimmed to support this or that doctrinal
edifice. Again, when the interest in the Gospels became
historical rather than dogmatic, the instinct remained to
find in the mind of Jesus some simple formula—ethical or
eschatological or what not—and to trace the working of it
in all his utterances. Jesus must be consistent: he must
have the same message in much the same terms for everyone. Above all he must be a popular teacher whom the
common people hear gladly, because his message is so
simple that all can understand it. As an ethical teacher
'he contends for the weightier matters in the law, for the
common morality which sees its aim in the furtherance of
the well-being of others, and which commends itself at
once to the heart of everyone'.[1] The religion of Jesus,
which is carefully distinguished from the religion about
Jesus, comes in the last resort to be a few simple axioms
about the fatherhood of God and the brotherhood of man.
All is perfectly easy of comprehension by rich and poor,
learned and unlearned, young and old. The parable is a
pedagogic device to make these ultimate simplicities
simpler still and Mk. iv. 11 f. is dismissed as the dogmatic
pedantry of a later age. All too readily we paint for ourselves a Renanesque portrait of Jesus purveying a 'religion
without tears' to an eager and admiring multitude.[2]

But while the religion of Jesus is undeniably simple, it is

[1] Wellhausen, *History of Israel and Judah*, p. 224. Cf. E. Meyer, *Ursprung
und Anfänge des Christentums*, II. 431: 'So ist die Ethik Jesu in der Tat nichts
anderes als eine Umsetzung des kategorischen Imperativs in ein praktisches
Gebot: "Handle so dass die Maxime deines Willens jederzeit zugleich als das
Prinzip einer allgemeinen Gesetzgebung gelten könne"'.

[2] So, for example, Bousset says (*Jesus* (E.T.), p. 33), 'we have only to
remember how large a part was played in his public ministry by *plain,
homely teaching*, and how in his parables *he cares only for what is simple, clear, and
didactic*'. The italics are mine. See also pp. 36 f. of the same work.

not therefore to be regarded as easy of comprehension.[1] *On understanding Jesus' teachings.*
Those who have the childlike spirit may come directly to
the heart of it; but for the most of mankind its ultimate
simplicity can only be grasped after a stern spiritual
discipline. It is the pure in heart, and they only, who may
see God: and only when the eye is single can the whole
body be full of light. Jesus himself emphasises the fact that
the gate is strait and the way narrow that leads to life:
and it is doubtless out of his own bitter experience that he
adds—'and few there be that find it'.

These considerations prepare us for the fact, which careful analysis of the Synoptic record reveals: that there is not
one uniform strain of teaching delivered to all and sundry
alike, but that there are three distinct and readily dis- *X 1 mpt*
tinguishable streams. Jesus has one way of dealing with the
Scribes and Pharisees, another for the multitudes and yet
another for his intimate disciples. This fact stands out
clearly in Mark. That it is obscured in Matthew and, in a
lesser degree, in Luke is due to the manner of composition
of these two Gospels. When critical methods are applied to
them and their sources disentangled, it is found that these
sources support in a large measure the conclusion drawn
from the study of Mark.[2] *3 matter messages : 3 methods*

We can go even farther and find in the Synoptic record
not merely three strains of teaching but three manners of *X*
address or teaching methods, determined by the personal
relation between the teacher and the audience.

Perhaps the most clearly marked case is the relation
between Jesus and the Scribes and Pharisees. Here from the
very beginning the attitude towards Jesus is critical and
increasingly hostile. This determines the form of the
teaching so far as the Scribes and Pharisees are audience:
it is polemic. Jesus carries the war into the enemy's
territory and answers their criticism of his teaching by

---

[1] In like manner throughout the Scriptures salvation is free—but never
cheap.
[2] See below, Chapters IV–VI, for proof in detail of this statement.

devastating attacks on their system. Jesus meets the Jewish teachers on their own ground. It is even possible that he used the language of the Rabbinical schools[1] and fought them with their own weapons. The passages that record his controversy with them are readily distinguishable from the remainder of his utterances by their tone, to a certain extent by their vocabulary, and by the nature of the matters discussed. Indeed most serious students of the Gospels will have no difficulty in recognising that the passages, where Jesus speaks to the religious teachers of his day, form a class apart with characteristics all their own.

The distinction between the polemical utterances of Jesus and the rest of his teaching is clear: what is less obvious but much more important is the line to be drawn between his public addresses and the private instruction of his intimate followers. Whatever the saying in Mk. iv. 11 f. may mean,[2] it is at least clear that the words 'Unto you is given the mystery of the Kingdom of God: but unto them that are without, all things are done in parables' imply that our Lord had in mind two classes of hearers and two methods of teaching. To the same effect is the record in *vv.* 33 f.: 'And with many such parables spake he the word unto them, as they were able to hear it: and without a parable spake he not unto them: but privately to his disciples he expounded all things'.

The significance of teaching by parables I have attempted to explain below.[3] Here it is sufficient to notice that Jesus, according to the earliest Gospel, has two methods of instruction: that when he speaks to the mass of the people he always uses parable—and 'parable' in the Gospels has a much wider connotation than 'illustrative anecdote'— and that in intimate conversation with his disciples he is prepared to reveal much more—all that is signified by 'mystery of the Kingdom of God'—than he will utter in

[1] Considerations which favour this hypothesis are advanced in Chapter III, section 1.

[2] An explanation of this difficult saying is offered below, pp. 74–80.

[3] In Chapter III, section 3.

public preaching. It may also be noted that this division is confirmed by other texts, and that there are indications that Jesus himself regarded this reserve as a temporary measure. We may adduce Mt. x. 26 f. = Lk. xii. 2 f. (Q), where it is affirmed that there is nothing hidden that shall not be revealed; that what is said in darkness shall be heard in light, and that what is whispered in the ear is to be proclaimed from the housetops. The same idea is expressed in Mk. iv. 22 = Lk. viii. 17.

i.e. Eventually the esoteric shall become the Evangel.

What it seems to amount to is this, that both as to matter and method the teaching of Jesus is conditioned by the nature of the audience. The blank opposition of the religious authorities is met by Jesus with destructive criticism of their systems. The crowds, again, are indeed curious and to a certain extent interested in this new teacher; but their interest is apt to be focused on wonderful cures of bodily ailments rather than on the things of the spirit. The alleged 'fickleness' of the multitude is less impressive when we realise that they were never attached in any serious fashion to Jesus and never had any real grasp of his message. The Fourth Evangelist has doubtless the more correct view of all the circumstances when he makes our Lord say to the people (vi. 26), 'Ye seek me, not because ye saw signs, but because ye ate of the loaves, and were filled'. The disciples form the third class of hearers. To them Jesus gives his confidence and speaks without reserve. In some way they must have commended themselves to him as worthy of receiving the secret of the Kingdom. Perhaps it was that they showed some signs of that insight and understanding for which in the earlier part of the ministry Jesus is always seeking.

the Church

At all events there is a *prima facie* case for a detailed examination of the teaching with particular reference to the nature of the audience in each case. A single example will suffice to show how the method may be applied.

In Mk. vii. 1–23 we find three short speeches—*vv.* 6–13, 14–16, and 17–23—all arising out of one incident—the

eating with unwashed hands. Of these the first is addressed
to the Scribes and Pharisees, the second to the general
public, and the third is spoken privately to the disciples.
The first is sharply distinguished from the other two in
tone, style, and matter: it is impatient, it contains legal
terms, and it discusses a legal question. The second is an
epigram.[1] The third is the explanation of the whole matter.
The two last contain words—σύνετε, ἀσύνετοι, νοεῖτε—
which seem to be characteristic of the period before
Peter's Confession.

The question at once arises whether it is not possible by
examining all the teaching on these lines to draw general
conclusions which will help us to a better understanding of
the mind of Jesus.

The necessary procedure is to mark in different colours
all the utterances of Jesus recorded in Mark, distinguishing
between polemical speeches, words spoken to the disciples,
and words spoken to the general public or to individuals
who are neither disciples nor opponents. This leaves (a) the
prayers, which on examination turn out to be closely
allied to the speeches to the disciples, and (b) the words
spoken in exorcizing demons. The same can be done with
the other two Gospels.[2] Here the only new sayings not
covered by the classification are the replies to the Tempter,
which consist mainly of quotation from the Old Testament.

The next step is to work through the vocabulary of the
sayings in a concordance marking every important word so
as to indicate the nature of the audience in each case where
the word is used. If we do this, certain interesting results
at once emerge. We get a list of important words and
phrases peculiar to the addresses to the disciples, another
list of words which occur only in polemical passages, and a
third shorter list of words peculiar to matter addressed to
the public at large. For the sake of brevity we may refer to

---

[1] παραβολή (v. 17).
[2] In composite discourses, such as the Sermon on the Mount, it is not
always possible to determine to what class a saying belongs.

the group of <u>polemical</u> utterances as <u>P,</u> those addressed to the <u>disciples</u> as <u>D,</u> and those spoken to the <u>general public</u> as <u>G,</u> so long as it is understood that D, P, and G are not documents but merely classes of sayings.

We have then three lists of what might be called the key-words of D, G and P. There are also three shorter lists of words which are common to two of the three groups—D and P, D and G, G and P—and, of course, a large residue of words common to all three. These six lists, with notes on the usage of the words, will be found in the Appendix to the present work.

We can now deal with each list separately and set down, as it were, <u>the life history of each word as it occurs in the teaching.</u> We can note the occurrences in each of the four documents Mk, Q, M, and L so far as we are able to identify them. We can also take account of the date when a word first appears in the teaching or when it drops out.[1]

This in outline is the process which has been carried out in the research which underlies this book. The result is in the lists and observations collected in the Appendix. The object of the following chapters will be to apply the information gained by this method to the elucidation of the main problems already sketched in this introduction.

[1] For a specimen 'biography'—in this case 'Son of Man'—see Chapter VII.

Can a sermon combine all 3? Each section of a sermon should have a pithy epigram, perhaps with wit & humor that reaches the crowd — Some barb, satire & sharp argument that meet the critic & objectors, preferable to show the weakness of that belief that opposes the one taught in Bible — But the bulk with explanation & application for the Beloved.

BC — He was Prophet & Teacher Messiah — "Teacher of Righteousness"

AC — He was Suffering Servant Messiah — & King of the Kingdom.

Chapter II

THE SOURCES

MARK

SINCE the Gospels came to be studied as historical documents rather than as mere treatises for edification, the work of St Mark has emerged from a long period of unmerited neglect. to take its place as a primary authority for the life and teaching of Jesus. The preeminent position which is assigned to this document by modern scholars is no new thing: it is the original standing restored. For if the conclusions reached by students of the Synoptic Problem are correct. Mark enjoyed in the days when the Gospels first came into being a reputation very similar to that which it has to-day. 'The Gospel according to Matthew is *a fresh edition of Mark*, revised, rearranged, and enriched with new material; the Gospel according to Luke is *a new historical work*, made by combining parts of Mark with parts of other documents.'[1] This means that out of all the available material our First Evangelist chose Mark as the foundation of his work and that St Luke at least chose it as a trustworthy document out of the several accounts with which he was acquainted. If Canon Streeter's Proto-Luke hypothesis is sound, we can go even farther and say that St Luke found it necessary to revise and enlarge his earlier work in order to admit a new source which he recognised as a first-rate authority.

For this high repute of Mark in the earliest days of Gospel-writing the most probable reason is to be found in the statement of Papias of Hierapolis,[2] derived ultimately from the Elder John, that this Gospel embodies the

---

[1] Burkitt, *Earliest Sources for the Life of Jesus* (1922), p. 97.
[2] Eusebius, *H.E.* III. xxxix. 15. Translated Streeter, *The Four Gospels*, p. 17.

teaching of Peter which St Mark had heard while serving the great Apostle in the capacity of interpreter.[1] The place given by St Matthew and St Luke to Mark is easily understood if they knew that it was really the testimony of Peter which lay before them. And if we also can believe this, it must make Mark for us what it was for them—an authority of the first rank. There is nothing inherently improbable in the story of Papias: and study of the Gospel reveals details which strongly suggest that it is the 'record, objectively stated, of the experience of an eye-witness, an intimate companion of Jesus throughout His Ministry'.[2]

On one point Papias, or his informant, is critical of Mark. He tells us that St Mark 'wrote down accurately everything that he remembered, without however recording in order what was either said or done by Christ'. The impression which Papias seems to wish his readers to carry away is that St Mark was in possession of a collection of anecdotes concerning the career of Jesus; that these anecdotes were not derived from a connected narrative but picked up haphazard in the course of listening to Peter's teaching; and that later St Mark fitted them together into a Gospel and in doing so got some at least in the wrong order. It may well be, as Canon Streeter has suggested,[3] that this charge of inaccuracy in order is made in the interests of the Fourth Gospel, which has an order in violent conflict with that of Mark.

However that may be, it can at least be said that on the whole the order of events in Mark makes a plain straightforward story. Moreover this general impression is confirmed, so far as the teaching is concerned, by a close

---

[1] Ἑρμηνευτής. The Syriac version of Eusebius (ed. Wright and McLean) renders this word by ܡܬܪܓܡܢܐ a distant relative of our English word 'dragoman'. I incline to the view that the position held by St Mark was one which combined the duties of a private secretary and an *aide-de-camp*. The word used by Papias *may* mean something like this. Cf. C. H. Turner in *A New Commentary on Holy Scripture*, N.T., p. 44 *a*.

[2] C. H. Turner, *loc. cit.*, p. 45 *b*; cf. 48 *b*. Cf. Ed. Meyer, *Ursprung und Anfänge des Christentums*, I. 238.

[3] *The Four Gospels*, p. 20.

But perhaps Mark preserves more chronology than ideas -- not of events, but of ideas. ✗

Son of Man ✗ (Matt.)

Mark:

Father B. ✗ (Matt.)

verbal analysis. When we come to examine important words and phrases closely, we find in Mark a certain consistency and order in the way in which they make their appearance or drop into the background: and this order and consistency suggest, if they do not compel, the inference that Mark gives the teaching in something very like the original order.

This feature is most clearly marked in the case of the two periods which are separated by Peter's Confession. For example, the term 'Son of Man' occurs fourteen times in Mark. Two cases fall before Peter's Confession (Mk. ii. 10, 28) and these are just the two cases where a non-Messianic interpretation is possible. Further, both are in sayings which belong to the P class. Of the twelve instances in the second period all are D with one exception (Mk. xiv. 62, P) which is a quotation from Daniel. Contrast this with what we find in Matthew and Luke. Matthew has eight cases before Peter's Confession—four from Q (Mt. viii. 20; xi. 19; xii. 32, 40), three from M (x. 23; xiii. 37, 41) and one of his own devising (xvi. 13). Four of them he assigns to D, two to G, and two to P. Luke places two occurrences in the first period, both from Q (vi. 22; vii. 34); the first is in the Lucan 'Sermon' and the second is G. For the period after Peter's Confession Matthew has the phrase only in D contexts, Luke has three G cases and the remainder are D. This means that in the case of 'Son of Man' Mark presents us with a clear and simple set of data of which we may seek an explanation. His witness is that Jesus uses the term in its special Messianic sense only after Peter's Confession and only in sayings addressed to his disciples. The evidence of Matthew and Luke is by comparison confused and indecisive.

The same phenomenon may be observed in the case of the name 'Father' for God. The evidence bearing on this point is collected and discussed below (in Chapter iv). Here it is enough to point out that according to Mark Jesus uses 'Father' as a name for God only in the period subse-

The Kingdom came i e at time between Peters Confession + Transfiguration.

quent to Peter's Confession.[1] In Matthew, on the other
hand, 'Father', 'Father in heaven', 'heavenly Father'
are scattered indiscriminately throughout the Gospel.

Again, with reference to the Kingdom of God there is a *Kingdom.*
certain definiteness of usage observable in Mark. In the *C.*
first part of the ministry Jesus is represented as speaking of
the Kingdom as something which is at hand: in the later
period it is something into which men may enter.[2] In this *It has come i.e.*
case also the evidence of Matthew and Luke lacks the
clearness and simplicity which are found in Mark: and
Matthew is the chief sinner in this respect.

It is not necessary to multiply instances. Those given are
enough to show that Mark in comparison with Matthew *th Marks*
and Luke has a very clear and decided 'order' in which *order*
developments in the teaching proceed *pari passu* with the
march of events in the life of Jesus. This order is obscured
in the other Synoptics partly because they are compilations,
partly because of editorial modifications of the sources used
by St Matthew and St Luke.

It is a highly significant fact that, when we eliminate the
editorial work of St Matthew and St Luke and analyse
their Gospels into sources, the sources are found to give a
large measure of support to Mark. That Mark is right in his *XX*
account of our Lord's use of the name 'Father' for God and
of his manner of speaking of the Kingdom of God is confirmed by Q and L, though not by Matthew and Luke.
This fact is a very clear hint that any profitable investiga- *X =*
tion of the life and teaching of Jesus must work more and
more with the four Synoptic sources, Mk, Q, M, L, rather
than with the three Synoptic Gospels. It is true that there
must always be a certain amount of risk in analysing
Matthew and Luke into their component elements; but

---

[1] I am of the opinion that the same thing can be shown to be true—or, at
any rate, as probable as such things can be—in the case of Q (see below,
pp. 95 f.), and also in the case of L (below, p. 98).
[2] For evidence and discussion see below, Chapter v. Here again I think
that Q is found to support Mark: and the genuine L passages point to the
same conclusion.

this risk can be, and often is, greatly exaggerated. In any case it is a risk that must be taken: and it may be hoped that, as the methods of study and analysis become more refined, the risk will grow proportionately less.

What is clear at the present stage is that, as against Matthew and Luke, Mark shows a distinct order of development both in the main events of the life of Jesus and in the emergence of the leading conceptions in his teaching. As between these three Gospels it is not a case of preferring Mark's order to that of Matthew or Luke. It is a case of Mark's order or none at all. Secondly, if we compare sources rather than Gospels it appears that Mk has considerable support in the most important points from Q. This is shown in detail in Chapters IV–VII of the present work. Finally, as compared with the other sources, Mk possesses this enormous advantage that it lies before us substantially in the form in which it was used in the composition of Matthew and Luke, and not as a more or less hypothetical reconstruction.

On all these grounds the primary importance of Mark can and should be maintained. If the criticism of Papias means that Mark's order is not the correct order of events in the life and teaching of Jesus, the answer is that investigation tends to show that the charge is unfounded, so far, at all events, as the main outlines of the Marcan story are concerned. In the account of the teaching Mark has an order which is, in the main, clear and intelligible: and when we find it confirmed in important particulars by Q and L we have good grounds for believing that it is the correct order.

It is true that if we had only the Marcan account of the teaching we should miss much that is of inestimable value—the Sermon on the Mount, the Prodigal Son, the Talents, and much else. We have in Mark only an outline and we have to apply to the other sources for fuller information at almost every point. But—and this is the crux of the matter—it is an outline which we can trust: and if we

Mk is base —
Lk - matt build on it!
add to it.

THE SOURCES   27

wish to frame a comprehensive picture of the teaching as a
whole, as it developed during the course of the ministry,
it is this Marcan outline which we must make the foundation.

Q good or characteristics of Q

In Eusebius[1] we find a quotation from Papias stating
that 'Matthew composed the oracles (τὰ λόγια) in the
Hebrew language, and each one interpreted them as he
was able'. This obviously cannot refer to the First Gospel,
which is essentially a Greek work based on Greek sources, of
which Mark is one. It is, however, possible that what is
meant is the document which we now call Q. Doubtless Q
lay before St Matthew and St Luke in a Greek dress—the
verbal agreement in many places is too close to be mere
coincidence; but the differences between the Matthaean
and Lucan versions suggest a Semitic original behind the
Greek. The most striking example is Wellhausen's reconciliation of Mt. xxiii. 26 with Lk. xi. 41 by perceiving that
δότε ἐλεημοσύνην in Luke is an easy mistranslation of an
Aramaic original rightly rendered by καθάρισον in
Matthew. There are other cases where it is not necessary to
suppose mistranslation on the part of either Evangelist,
but where the divergences between Matthew and Luke
may be regarded as different renderings of the same
Semitic original. In Mt. xxiv. 27 = Lk. xvii. 24, for
example, Matthew has φαίνεται where Luke has λάμπει.
In the Greek versions of Daniel xii. 3 the same thing
occurs: φανοῦσιν LXX, λάμψουσιν Theodotion—both
going back to the original יַזְהִרוּ. In the next verse, Mt.
xxiv. 28 = Lk. xvii. 37, Matthew has πτῶμα where Luke
has σῶμα. Here again in Num. xiv. 33 Aquila and Theodotion have πτώματα, Symmachus σώματα (LXX κῶλα),
going back to the Hebrew פִּגְרֵיכֶם. The hypothesis of a
Semitic original for Q will go some way at any rate
towards explaining the differences in Matthew and Luke.

[1] *H.E.* III. xxxix. 16.

If this Semitic original of Q is the document or embodies the document referred to by Papias, then Q will challenge comparison with Mark as a source of Apostolic origin. In any case, to have been embodied in Matthew and Luke, it must be a document which came into existence about the same time as Mark and enjoyed a repute similar to that of Mark. In modern times some scholars would assign to it an even earlier date and a higher reputation than they would give to Mark.

So far as we can gauge its general character from the remains preserved in Matthew and Luke, Q appears to be a document of a very different type from Mark. If it is the Logia document spoken of by Papias, it must be admitted that the name is apt, for it consists almost entirely of detached oracles, short addresses and scraps of dialogue. The great bulk of this matter consists of religious and ethical teaching, and that of a kind to make it a useful work for propaganda purposes. Professor Burkitt has pointed out[1] that Justin Martyr in his *Apology* addressed to the Roman Emperor derives nine-tenths of his examples of the ethical teaching of Christ from Q:[2] Nor is this the only side of the matter. The analysis of the teaching into D, G, and P groups reveals the striking fact that the proportion of polemical matter is lower in Q than in any other of our four documents. The proportions are shown in the following table:

	D	G	P
Mk	53.5 %	23.0 %	23.5 %
Q	52.4	36.9	10.7
M	66.3	8.4	25.3
L	26.6	34.9	38.5

If we may take Mark as the standard, we find that Q is abnormally low in the P class of saying, M in the G class,

[1] *Earliest Sources for the Life of Jesus*, p. 44.

[2] We may add that the story of the Centurion of Capernaum (Mt. viii. 5–13; Lk. vii. 1–10), the denunciation of the Galilean cities (Mt. xi. 21 ff., Lk. x. 13 ff.) and the declaration against sign-seeking (Mt. xii. 38–42; Lk. xi. 29–32) all contain a tacit *invitation* to the Gentiles.

and L in the D class. These facts call for comment: and
in the case of Q, which concerns us here, the explanation
would seem to be that the work was designed to avoid, as
far as possible, offending Jewish susceptibilities. Even the
most polemical passage in Q—the speech against Pharisaism (Lk. xi. 37–52; parallels in Mt. xxiii)—is not without
parallels in the Rabbinic writings,[1] where it is clearly
recognised that there are Pharisees *and* Pharisees.

Closely connected with this small proportion of polemic
in Q is the question whether Q contained an account of the
Passion, which perhaps more than anything else would be
to the Jews a stumbling-block and to the Greeks foolishness.
This question must, I think, be answered in the negative.
The main argument in support of this answer is of course
the fact that in the Passion story as recorded in Matthew
and Luke we find no agreements against Mark that are of
any consequence. To this fact may be added the consideration that on the whole the tendency of Q is to avoid any
reference to the matter. In Mark the impending sufferings
of the Son of Man are announced on three separate
occasions: in Q, on the other hand, when killing or
persecution is in question, it is the prophets who are the
victims or the disciples as the successors of the prophets. In
this respect Q is curiously akin to the Epistle of James,
with which at other points it has affinities.[2]

But the question whether Q contained an account of the
Passion is also linked with the question whether Q contained any narrative at all. If the latter be answered in the
negative, then the former will automatically be answered

---

[1] Cf. Strack-Billerbeck, *Kommentar*, iv. 336–9.

[2] As a simple and strictly objective test I take the illustrative references to
the Synoptic Gospels in the Commentary on James by Windisch (*Handbuch z.
N.T.*) The assumption is that the commentator will choose for this purpose
the text which comes closest in thought or terminology to the passage on
which he is commenting. For Windisch the figures are: References to Mk 9,
to Q 35, to M 14, to L 4. Hollmann and Bousset in *Die Schriften des N.T.*
draw 50 per cent. of their illustrative quotations—and those the most important—from Q. I am glad to find that the affinity of Q and the Epistle of
James is maintained by Professor B. W. Bacon, *The Story of Jesus*, p. 37.

in the negative also. Did Q then contain any narrative? The moment the question is asked the story of the Centurion of Capernaum springs to the mind. But the examination of this passage in Matthew and Luke reveals the curious fact that agreement between the two Gospels begins where the dialogue begins and ends where it ends.

Mt. viii 5–8 *a*, 13 (R.V.)	Lk. vii. 1–6, 10 (R.V.)
And when he was entered into Capernaum, there came unto him a centurion, beseeching him, and saying, Lord, my servant lieth in the house sick of the palsy, grievously tormented. And he saith unto him, I will come and heal him. And the centurion answered and said, Lord, I am not worthy etc....	After he had ended all his sayings in the ears of the people, he entered into Capernaum. And a certain centurion's servant, who was dear unto him, was sick and at the point of death. And when he heard concerning Jesus, he sent unto him elders of the Jews, asking him that he would come and save his servant. And they, when they came to Jesus, besought him earnestly, saying, He is worthy that thou shouldest do this for him: for he loveth our nation, and himself built us our synagogue. And Jesus went with them. And when he was now not far from the house, the centurion sent friends to him, saying unto him, Lord, trouble not thyself: for I am not worthy etc....
v. 13. And Jesus said unto the centurion, Go thy way; as thou hast believed, so be it done unto thee. And the servant was healed in that hour.	*v.* 10. And they that were sent, returning to the house, found the servant whole.

The only points on which there is agreement are 'entered into Capernaum' (but cf. Mk. ii. 1 and parallels) and 'centurion' ('servant' is a translation of παῖς in Matthew and δοῦλος in Luke). The inference is, I think, obvious. These matters were not recorded in Q. What is more, we can leave them out and begin our story in some such way as this: 'A certain centurion said to Jesus: Lord, I am not worthy that thou shouldest come under my roof, etc.' It is obvious from what the centurion says that the servant is ill: and this is the only fact that is required to make the conversation intelligible. Moreover, when the narrative portions are removed the real point of the anecdote

becomes clear—namely the saying of Jesus: 'I have not
found so great faith, no, not in Israel';[1] and the Roman
centurion takes his place along with the folk of Tyre and
Sidon, the men of Nineveh, and the Queen of Sheba in the
company of Gentiles who by repentance or faith or zeal
for wisdom put the chosen people to shame.[2] The conclusion would seem to be that what stood in Q was simply the
dialogue between Jesus and the centurion and that each
Evangelist has filled in the narrative details to the best of
his information.

If we now turn to other Q passages recorded in Matthew
and Luke, we find the same thing repeated. Real agreement between the two Gospels begins and ends with the
spoken words. The inference is that Q contained no
narratives and therefore no Passion story.[3]

If there was no account of the Passion in Q, the question
arises how much of the ministry was covered by the
document. As this question is bound up with that of the
original order of the Q matter the two points may be considered together. Canon Streeter has shown good grounds
for believing that the original order of Q is best preserved
in Luke:[4] and if we take the Lucan order, it would seem
that Q stops just short of the Passion story. It is in fact
possible on this order to establish a rough kind of parallelism between Mark and Q—at least at the beginning and

---

[1] Cf. Harnack, *Sprüche und Reden Jesu* (1907), p. 146; Meyer, *Ursprung und Anfänge des Christentums*, I. 225; Streeter, *The Four Gospels*, p. 233.

[2] It is doubtless a mere coincidence, but nevertheless suggestive, that Q has these four examples of Gentile people contrasted with Israel to the dis-advantage of the latter—Tyre and Sidon in the north, Nineveh in the east, Sheba in the south, and Rome in the west—and also the saying (Lk. xiii. 29), 'They shall come from east and west and north and south and sit down in the Kingdom of God', which in Matthew is appended to the con-versation with the centurion.

[3] I am inclined to think that St Luke derived the introductory matter, which he prefixes to Q passages, from the same source that provided him with what we call L, i.e. oral tradition. It would be a case of taking a Q passage to someone likely to know and asking, When, where, and why was this said by Jesus? St Luke might quite easily have a copy of Q when he was at Caesarea, A.D. 56–58.

[4] *The Four Gospels*, ch. X.

end of the documents. Both begin with the preaching of
John the Baptist followed by the Baptism[1] and Temptation. Thereafter they seem to separate, only to come together again in the discourse against Pharisaism and the
announcement of the coming of the Kingdom in power.
For what lies between the Temptation and the discourse
against Pharisaism, it is much more difficult to trace any
parallelism. The Beelzebub controversy, the mission charge,
and the declaration against sign-seeking, however, occur
in both documents, though not in the same order. Q has
(a) mission charge..., (b) Beelzebub controversy...,
(c) declaration against sign-seeking: Mark gives these in
the order (b) (a) (c).

At two other points of importance it is just possible that
we may have a connection between Mark and Q. It may be
that the saying in Lk. x. 21 f. belongs to the time of Peter's
Confession. It has some points of contact with Mt. xvi.
17 (M).[2]

Mt. xvi. 17 (M)	Lk. x. 21 = Mt. xi. 25 (Q)
Blessed art thou, Simon bar Jona, for flesh and blood hath not revealed it to thee, but my Father in heaven.	I thank thee, Father, Lord of heaven and earth, that thou hast hid these things from the wise and prudent, and revealed them to babes.

The second case is still more conjectural. It concerns
Lk. x. 23 f., which, I venture to suggest, may belong to the
context of the Transfiguration. Lk. x. 24: 'I say unto you
that many prophets and kings [Mt, just men][3] desired to
see the things that you see, and did not see them, and to
hear the things that you hear, and did not hear them'
implies something seen and heard of a specially memorable
nature: and the Transfiguration will certainly bear this
description. It would be curious if these two great

---

[1] If, as seems probable, Q contained something about the Baptism.

[2] Cf. J. Weiss in *N.T. Studien für Georg Heinrici*, pp. 126 f.

[3] This is a curious variant. Is it an editorial effort on the part of one of the
Evangelists (presumably S. Matthew; cf. Mt. x. 41), or does it presuppose a
variation of translation? If the latter I can only suggest a confusion of יְשָׁרִים
and שָׁרִים or Aram. ישריא and שריא.

occasions had passed by without leaving some trace in Q:·
and there seems to be no context where these two sayings
would fit in better. The other points where Mk and Q
have matter in common do not concern us at this stage.

Taking Q as it stands in Luke the impression that it
makes as a whole is fairly simple and straightforward. It
begins by linking the work of Jesus with that of John the
Baptist. After some account of the preaching of John there
followed the Baptism (probably) and the Temptation.
We pass at once to the first account of the preaching of
Jesus. Appended to this is the story of the centurion,
where, besides the commendation of the Gentile's faith, we
may note a certain disappointment at the response from
Israel. After the question of John the Baptist and the
testimony of Jesus to John comes a second appeal to the
people, this time by means of the disciples, to whom the
charge is given. Here again the seed seems to fall on
barren ground, for the next item is the condemnation of
the Galilean cities for their indifference, coupled with the
statement that if the same chance had been given to
Tyre and Sidon, the response would have been different.
The Doxology, 'I thank thee, Father', and the saying to
the disciples (Lk. x. 23 f.) I take to refer to Peter's Confession and the Transfiguration. The next point which can
be connected with the life of Jesus would appear to be the
charge of casting out demons by the aid of Beelzebub and
the answer to that charge, followed by a declaration against
sign-seeking, again with an appeal to Gentile examples of
repentance and thirst for wisdom. Jesus now turns upon
his opponents in the discourse against Pharisaism and
passes on to give warning of the approaching Parousia. In
this concluding set of sayings occurs the statement that the
Gentiles will precede the Jews into the Kingdom.

Q is thus a record of the teaching of Jesus: that, we may
be sure, is just what it set out to be. But through the utterances it is, I think, possible to trace the vague outline of a
story—the story of the rejection of the teaching, the in-

difference of the people at large, the open hostility of their religious leaders. But neither indifference nor hostility can prevent the coming of the Kingdom; they can only hinder a man from entering it. If we may speak of the purpose of the document, it seems to be threefold: an exhortation to those who are disciples to stand fast in their faith, a warning to Jews that "in rejecting Jesus they will cast away their birthright," and an invitation to Gentiles to share in the good things of the Kingdom.

M

Anyone who comes straight from the study of Mk or Q to read the matter peculiar to Matthew is at once conscious of breathing a different atmosphere, an atmosphere which can only be described as Jewish. We feel that we are on Palestinian soil and in the midst of a Jewish-Christian community. The Gospel is not something to be sharply contrasted with the Law; it is itself a new Law or a new edition of the old. The Gospel is not the new wine that bursts the old wineskins: it is an *aqua vitae* distilled out of the old wine—more easily handled and more potent.

The proportions of D, G, and P matter in M as contrasted with Mk are instructive—D: Mk 53.5 per cent., M 66.3 per cent.; G: Mk 23 per cent., M 8.4 per cent.; P: Mk 23.5 per cent., M 25.3 per cent. That is, the proportion of polemic in Mk and M is about the same; but whereas in Mk little more than half of the total teaching is D, in M, D has two-thirds; and while almost a quarter of Mk's teaching matter is devoted to the general public, M has less than a tenth.[1] The Christian community is already in some sense a school and discipleship has become much the same thing as membership of this school.[2] The members are

[1] These figures for M are not absolute, since, owing to St Matthew's habit of piling up material into discourses, many verses (especially in the Sermon on the Mount) cannot be definitely assigned to D, G, or P. But one may reasonably expect that the proportions will hold in the main.

[2] So much so that if all that we knew of the teaching of Jesus were what is given in M, we should be inclined to posit a בית ישוע to set alongside the בית שמאי and בית הלל.

Emphasis in Mt on Disciples - teaching - school - new law et.
moved from focus on Jesus as in Mk. To his teachings; the
rules for the community of learners et.

THE SOURCES   35

all scholars under one Teacher and at the same time a
fellowship of brethren with one Father in Heaven,[1] yet the
assembly (ἐκκλησία) has certain judicial and legislative
powers.[2] We have travelled a long way from Mk and Q.

This community is the salt of the earth and the light of
the world. They are to shine so that by their good deeds
men may be induced to give glory to God. They are
provided in the Sermon with a new law of morals, covering
such matters as murder, adultery, divorce, oaths, and the
lex talionis; and new rules for the religious observances of
almsgiving, prayer, and fasting. They have a missionary
task; but it is, in the first instance at least, only to Israel
(Mt. x. 5 *b*–8, 23).

Under this rule and engaged in this mission, the community awaits the coming of a new age and the end of the
present order. Between this age and the new lies the
Judgement, which is a very simple affair, involving no
more than the separation of two classes who, at that stage,
are already distinct and recognisable for what they are,
though at present they may not be so easily distinguished.
This is the burden of the parables of the Wheat and Tares,
the Dragnet, the Marriage Feast (second parable: Mt.
xxii. 11–14[3]), the Wise and Foolish Virgins, and the description of the Judgement (Mt. xxv. 31–46). It is implied that
those who do live by the rule and bring forth fruit will
find themselves on the right side of the Judge on the great
Day. On the other side stand those who in their immersion

---

[1] Mt. xxiii. 8–10. The school is also a חבורה.

[2] Mt. xviii. 17 f. The ἐκκλησία performs the functions of a בית דין.

[3] That Mt. xxii. 11–14 is the end of a parable which has lost its beginning
is clear. Canon Streeter has pointed out that as it stands it makes no sense:
'How could the man, just swept in from the highways, be expected to have
on a wedding garment?' (*The Four Gospels*, p. 243 n. 2). Mt. xxii. 11–14 is
curiously like the latter part of a Rabbinic parable preserved in *Shabbath*,
153 *a*, and *Midrash Eccl.* IX. 8, and attributed to R. Johanan b. Zakkai (ob. c.
A.D. 80). In this parable a king issues an invitation without specifying a
fixed time. When the summons comes the wise are found prepared and the
foolish unprepared, and dealt with accordingly. This parable is translated in
Strack-Billerbeck, I. 878 f., and (with explanation) in Gossel, *Was ist und was
enthält der Talmud?* (1907), pp. 64 f. See further Detached Note B at end of
Chapter III below.

in worldly cares have neglected the invitation (first
parable of the Marriage Feast: Mt. xxii. 1–10) and those
whose religion is a pretence, who make a great outward
show of piety to which nothing within corresponds
(parable of the Two Sons, Mt. xxi. 28–32).

We are not left in any doubt as to who are compre-
hended in this last class: they are the Scribes and Pharisees.
And here we may note the curious fact that this document,
which, of all our sources, shows by far the greatest respect
for the Law (Mt. v. 17, 19 f.) and even for the oral
tradition (Mt. xxiii. 1 f.), at the same time displays by far
the greatest animus against the Scribes and Pharisees. The
terms of the indictment in M are far more bitter than anything we can find in Mk or Q: so much so that the very
violence of the abuse, contrasted with the greater restraint
shown in the other sources, raises the suspicion that there is
more here than Jesus said.

Two other characteristics of M deserve mention. In the
footnote on Mt. xxii. 11–14 attention has been drawn to a
Rabbinic parable which it closely resembles. This is not an
isolated case; for one of the most striking features of this
source is the way in which close parallels to much that is
contained in it can be found in the Rabbinical literature.
Mt. v. 7—'Blessed are the merciful for they shall obtain
mercy'; Shabbath, 151 *b* and elsewhere, 'He who has
mercy on his fellow-men receives mercy from Heaven'.
Similarly Mt. v. 28–30 is thoroughly Jewish, with numerous
close parallels in Talmud and Midrash.[1] Mt. v. 37, 'Let
your word be yea, yea, and nay, nay', can be compared
with the saying, 'Let your "Yea" be righteous and your
"Nay" righteous'.[2] Along with this similarity in thought
goes a striking similarity of diction. In all the sources we
find words and phrases of the Rabbinic vocabulary; but in
Mk, Q and L they occur in the place where we expect them,
in polemical passages. In M, on the other hand, these

---

[1] Cf. G. F. Moore, *Judaism*, II. 267 ff.
[2] *Sifra* on Lev. xix. 36 (ed. Weiss, 91 *b*). Cf. Jas. v. 12.

"M" is a new Rabbenism. 1. Teaching 2. Community 3. Rabbinic 4. Jewish 5. Baptist

technical terms are found in all kinds of discourse whether D, G, or P. From D contexts we may note $\delta\acute{\epsilon}\omega$ = אסר and $\lambda\acute{u}\omega$ = התיר, $\sigma\grave{\alpha}\rho\xi\ \kappa\alpha\grave{\iota}\ \alpha\tilde{\iota}\mu\alpha$ = בשר ודם. In a G passage $\zeta\upsilon\gamma\acute{o}s$ is used exactly like עול in such expressions as עול תורה and עול מלכות שמים—the yoke of the Gospel is contrasted with the yoke of the Law; but the term is retained. Perhaps the most striking example of all is the use in Matthew of the phrase 'Father in heaven', on which Professor Moore remarks that it 'is peculiar to the rabbinical sources, which represent normative Judaism, in distinction from the sects or circles that produced the apocalyptic literature (in which, indeed, the thought of God as father has very little place), and from Hellenistic Judaism, so far at least as this may be legitimately inferred from Philo. In the New Testament it is found only in the Gospel of Matthew in which the Palestinian impress is much stronger on both thought and expression than in the others'.[1]

The other peculiarity of M which excites notice is the close connection of much of the teaching in it with that of John the Baptist. This again holds of both thought and expression. In the Sermon on the Mount, Mt. vii. 19, 'Every tree which does not produce good fruit is cut down and cast into the fire', is a reproduction of the saying of John in Mt. iii. 10 = Lk. iii. 9. Again the parables of the Wheat and Tares (Mt. xiii. 24–30, 36–43), of the Dragnet (xiii. 47–50), of the Sheep and Goats (xxv. 31–46), and perhaps also of the Ten Virgins (xxv. 1–13) and of the Marriage Feast (xxii. 11–14) are all of them just variations, more or less elaborate, on the theme of John the Baptist—wheat and chaff (Mt. iii. 12 = Lk. iii. 17). From the mouth of John comes the phrase $\gamma\epsilon\nu\nu\acute{\eta}\mu\alpha\tau\alpha$ $\grave{\epsilon}\chi\iota\delta\nu\tilde{\omega}\nu$ (Mt. iii. 7 = Lk. iii. 7) which reappears in Mt. xii. 34; xxiii. 33 and nowhere else in the New Testament.

These considerations show that M is a source which must be used with the utmost caution. It is of course quite con-

[1] Op. cit., II. 204 f.

ceivable that there should be parallels between the teaching of Jesus and the fine and truly spiritual teaching contained in the Rabbinical literature. It is also not by any means impossible that some of the preaching of John should have been taken up by Jesus. What is not conceivable is that the same person should have said to the Scribes and Pharisees: 'You stultify the commandment of God in order to keep your tradition'[1] and to his disciples and the people: 'The Scribes and Pharisees sit in Moses' seat: all things therefore that they tell you do and keep'.[2] These sayings are in flat contradiction: and, of the two, the former is on every ground the more likely to be authentic. Similarly, in the case of John, the saying of Jesus: 'I tell you, of them that are born of women there has not risen a greater than John the Baptist: yet the least in the Kingdom of God is greater than he',[3] has no meaning unless Jesus himself had something more to give than the best that John could offer. This does not mean that because a saying or a parable of Jesus in M can be paralleled from the Talmud or from John the Baptist, it is therefore not genuine. It only means that it is to be regarded with reserve and weighed against what we learn of the teaching of Jesus from our other sources.

Yet even after we have made allowance for all doubtful cases, there remains in M a considerable body of teaching whose authenticity there seems no good reason to doubt. To this category belong the parables of the Hidden Treasure, the Pearl of Great Price, the Labourers in the Vineyard, and the Two Sons, besides much in the Sermon on the Mount, such sayings as Mt. x. 25 b; xi. 28 ff.; xviii. 3 f., 10, and the like. These and other similar sayings we may accept with a good deal of confidence; but, on the whole, the testimony of M must be regarded as inferior in value to that of Mk and Q and can only be admitted after the strictest examination.

---

[1] Mk. vii. 9; cf. the whole passage, vii. 6–13.
[2] Mt. xxiii. 2 f.   [3] Mt. xi. 11 = Lk. vii. 28.

L

In the *Hibbert Journal* for October 1921 Canon Streeter propounded a hypothesis which he has since restated with much additional material in *The Four Gospels* (1924) *"Luke"* ch. VIII. The essential part of this theory is that the Third Gospel came into existence in two stages. The first stage was the compilation of a document, which Streeter calls Proto-Luke, compounded of the elements Q + L. Later this work was enlarged by the addition of the Infancy narratives and the insertion of extracts from Mark. The history of St Luke's Gospel, according to Streeter, runs like this.[1] 'Luke during the two years he was at Caesarea */U* in the company of Paul made good use of his opportunities of collecting information and made copious notes. Later on, probably not till after the death of Paul, a copy of Q came his way,[2] and on the basis of this and his own notes he composed Proto-Luke as a Gospel for the use of the Church in the place where he was then living. Still later a copy of Mark came his way, and he then produced the second and enlarged edition of his Gospel that has come down to us.'

The importance of this conclusion lies in the fact that it is possible to restore with a fair amount of probability the document Proto-Luke, and from what we otherwise know of the editorial methods of the Third Evangelist, to analyse it, again with a fair amount of probability, into its constituent elements Q and L. According to Streeter[3] the following passages are most probably to be 'assigned to Proto-Luke: Lk. iii. 1–iv. 30; v. 1–11; vi. 14–16; vi. 20–viii. 3; ix. 51–xviii. 14; xix. 1–27; xix. 37–44; xxi. 18, 34–36; xxii. 14 to the end of the Gospel, except for the verses derived from Mark, the identification of which is very problematical'. This composite document forms a little Gospel of about the same extent as Mark. If we now

---

[1] *The Four Gospels*, pp. 218 f.

[2] But see above, p. 31. St Luke may have had a copy of Q while he was gathering the material we call L.

[3] *Op. cit.*, p. 222.

"L"

subtract from this all the matter which can probably be assigned to Q, we are left with the source L, the main contents of which may be summarised as follows:[1] (part of John's preaching), arrest of John, genealogy of Jesus, (return to Nazareth), inaugural sermon and rejection in Nazareth, call of the first disciples, list of Apostles restoration of a widow's son at Nain, anointing of Jesus in Simon's house, account of the women who ministered to Jesus, (inhospitality of the Samaritans), the sending forth of the seventy, (return of the seventy), discussion as to the chief commandment, parable of the Good Samaritan, story of Mary and Martha, Lord's Prayer, parable of the Importunate Householder, parable of the Rich Fool, Pilate's victims a call to repentance, parable of the Barren Fig Tree, healing of a woman on the Sabbath, cure of a man with dropsy on the Sabbath, discourse on table manners and choice of guests, parables of the Great Feast, of Building a Tower, of an Embassy before Battle, of Lost Sheep, Lost Coin, Prodigal Son, and Dishonest Steward, saying on Pharisaic pride, parable of Dives and Lazarus, saying on the rewards of service, cure of the lepers, parables of the Unjust Judge and the Importunate Widow, and of the Pharisee and the Publican, story of Zacchaeus, jubilation at entry of Jesus into Jerusalem, prophecy of the destruction of the city, sayings concerning the coming of the Day of the Son of Man, narratives of the Last Supper, arrest and trial of Jesus, the Crucifixion, death, and burial of Jesus, the empty grave, Resurrection appearances and the Ascension.

The first thing that arrests attention is the strong contrast between this and Q. Q consists almost entirely of sayings, with very little of parable and no narrative: L, on the other hand, has many stories, many parables, and in comparison very few detached sayings. This fact at once suggests that here, if anywhere, we have to do with oral tradition. These stories are just the things that would

[1] Brackets indicate that it is doubtful whether the passage enclosed should be assigned to Q or L.

imprint themselves indelibly on the memory; just the kind
of thing that St Luke would be likely to pick up during his
stay in Caesarea; and, we may add, just the kind of thing
he would be most likely to wish to preserve in writing, for
St Luke, more than any other New Testament writer,
loves a good story.

Another striking characteristic of this source is revealed
by the analysis of its contents according to the audience.
The proportions are: D 26.6 per cent., G 34.9 per cent.,
P 38.5 per cent. Compared with Mk's D 53.5 per cent.,
G 23 per cent., P 23.5 per cent., L has an unusually low
proportion of matter assigned to the disciples as hearers:
and the G and P sections are proportionately enlarged.
This again is explicable on the supposition that St Luke
gathered a mass of oral traditions at Caesarea. We have
here collected the things that Jesus said to the common
people or in their hearing, and this collection makes up
about three-quarters of the spoken words of Jesus as
recorded in this source. The remaining quarter assigned to
D may represent what St Luke gathered from disciples of
the Lord, or it may embody sayings addressed to the
disciples when others were present.

The percentage of P sayings is higher in L than in any
other of our sources: Mk has 23.5 per cent., Q 10.7 per
cent., M 25.3 per cent., and L 38.5 per cent. It has, however, to be noted that the character of the polemical
matter is different in L. There is argument on points of
law, such as the observance of the Sabbath, just as in the
other sources; but in place of the open denunciations which
we find in them, we have in L the subtler method of rebuke
by means of parables such as those of the Lost Sheep, the
Lost Coin and the Prodigal Son. The indictment of the
Pharisees is not in the main directed at their casuistry, as in
Mk, or the hypocrisy of some of them, as in M, but rather
at the pride and exclusiveness of their attitude to the
common people. The charge is not so much that they make
a fence about the Law as that they make a fence about

themselves, that they trust in themselves that they are
righteous and despise others.[1] Elsewhere in our sources the
contrast is drawn between the simple principles that lie at
the foundations of the Law and the scribal refinements that
may even stultify the Law, or between the lavish display of
the outward forms of piety and the lack of real religion on
the part of some at least of the Pharisees. In L the sharp
contrast is between Pharisee and publican, between the
elder brother and the prodigal. It is the cry of the '*Am
ha-ares* that finds utterance here.

All these facts point in one direction and each helps to
explain the others. We have in L the result of selection—the
unconscious selection made by ordinary people. The
things that for them were memorable were the things that
touched their own lives, their needs, their difficulties, their
sins. And so L is the Gospel of the under-dog, the poor,
the despised, the outcast, and the sinner. Its message is not
to Jew or Gentile specially but to man simply as man. The
greater part of it might be regarded as commentary on the
text 'They that are whole have no need of the physician,
but they that are sick. I am not come to call the righteous
but sinners'.[2] This source is universal in its appeal just
because it speaks to man as man: and it is characteristic
that whereas Matthew carries the genealogy of Jesus
back to Abraham, Luke goes farther and carries it to
Adam.

It is a noticeable feature of L that it lays great stress on
the kindliness and sympathy of Jesus in his dealings with
the poor and the outcast. Here also we have matter that
would linger long in popular memory; and it is not surprising that such stories should have been preserved when
the chief actor in them was one who received from his
critics—and apparently accepted with pride—the title
'the friend of publicans and sinners'[3]. The portrait of
Jesus which is sketched in L is one which tallies well with

[1] Lk. xviii. 9.   [2] Mk. ii. 17
[3] Lk. vii. 34 = Mt. xi. 19 (Q).

that description, though the friendship offered is an article of a very different kind from that imagined by the first coiners of the phrase.

We may thus accept L for what it is, the record of specially memorable sayings and doings of Jesus. This record we owe to the diligence and care of Luke, the companion of St Paul, who had ample opportunity to make such a collection, and, it would seem, used his opportunities with singular zeal and discretion. The result of his labours is to present an aspect of the character and teaching of the Master which we could ill afford to miss, an aspect which does not conflict with what we learn from Mk or Q but supplements those sources. The material provided by L may be largely derived from oral tradition; but it is none the worse for that: for parables are just the kind of teaching that would be most likely to be preserved accurately in that medium. So far as the teaching of Jesus is concerned we may take what L offers with good confidence that it represents authentic utterances of Jesus substantially as he gave them to his hearers.

CONCLUSION

The conclusion to be drawn from this discussion is that we have in the Synoptic record four sources for the teaching of our Lord. Of these Mk, representing the reminiscences of Peter, takes the leading place and supplies the framework which we must use. As supplements to what we have in Mk, we can use Q and L with confidence and, with greater reserve, M. Each source has its own peculiarities. Mk is a simple objective record of word and deed: Q is דברי ישוע—the words of Jesus—a collection of the oracles of the Lord modelled on the prophetic books of the Old Testament: L is a selection of interesting and memorable stories about Jesus and striking parables from his teaching: M is an attempt to make a 'new' Law by combining the teaching of Jesus with the Law of Moses. In Q Jesus is the Prophet; in M the Rabbi, however unorthodox; in L he is

What does this do with the Deity of Christ — since Mk. emphasizes the Man — unless 'Son of Man' be a title of Deity.

44

THE SOURCES

one who fulfils the prophecy in Isaiah lxi. 1 f. and lviii. 6:
'The Spirit of the Lord is upon me because he has anointed
me to bring good news to the poor, he has sent me to
proclaim liberty to the captives and restoration of sight to
the blind, to set at liberty those that are oppressed, to
proclaim the year of the favour of the Lord'. In Mk he is
all this and something more—something which lies hidden
in the enigmatic title 'the Son of Man'. Q, M, and L
emphasise different aspects of our Lord's life and teaching
to such a degree that we might almost call Q a Gospel for
the votaries of ethical religion pure and simple, M a Gospel
for ecclesiastics, and L a Gospel for evangelists and
missioners. These are rash generalisations and not to be
pressed too hard; but they serve to convey the general
impression made by these three sources. And it is just
because Q, M, and L make each a single and simple impression that they stand, in a manner, apart from Mk.
They simplify by what they omit. Mk on the other hand
is obscure and difficult—and the most important of them
all—just because it presents a picture of the whole personality of Jesus and reveals him as someone greater than can
be measured by any of our ordinary standards. It is
St Mark's portrait before which we must stand. We may fill
in the details of his sketch from our other sources; but if we
desire to keep the picture true to the life we must keep the
outline which Mk presents.

Chapter III

FORMAL CHARACTERISTICS OF THE TEACHING

1. LANGUAGE

THE linguistic problem raised by the Synoptic Gospels involves three distinct questions: (1) What was the language in which the Gospels were composed? (2) What is the original language of the sources which lie behind the Gospels? (3) Seeing that the Gospels all record speeches and dialogues, in what language were these utterances spoken? It is the third of these questions that most closely concerns us in the present enquiry. As to the first, it is now definitely answered, so far as Matthew and Luke are concerned, by the fact that both Gospels make use of our Greek Mark. They are therefore to be regarded as Greek compositions. Mark is still generally regarded as a Greek work, though Wellhausen argued for Aramaic[1] and, more recently, Dr P.-L. Couchoud thinks of this Gospel as originally composed in Latin.[2] The second question is more difficult. Seeing that the 'Ur-Marcus' theory is now discredited, there is no longer any reason to suppose that the source Mk differed in any important respect from our Mark: and consequently any conclusion reached as to the original language of the Gospel will hold of it *qua* source. If Q be the document referred to by Papias, it follows that it was originally composed in a Semitic dialect—probably Aramaic—and we have already seen that there are some grounds, apart from the testimony of Papias, for supposing this to be the case.[3] With regard to M and L we are left largely to conjecture. If I am right in supposing that L is a collection of oral traditions made by

[1] *Einleitung*, §§ 2 f.
[2] Cf. *J.T.S.* July 1928, pp. 375–381; Oct. 1928, pp. 47–51.
[3] *Supra*, p. 27.

St Luke and first committed to writing by him, it will be probable that the original language of L *as a written document* was Greek. The strongly Judaistic character of M suggests, though it does not necessitate, a Semitic original, while the phraseology often reminds one of the Hebrew of the Mishnah and the early Midrashim rather than the Aramaic vernacular.

However these questions may be answered, the really important problem for the present enquiry is the third: In what language did Jesus speak to his disciples and to the common people, in what language did he discuss with the Scribes and Pharisees? Thanks very largely to the labours of Dalman[1] this problem is now, in principle, solved: Aramaic was the mother-tongue of Jesus and his disciples and the great mass of the people." It was, of course, not the only language in use in Palestine in the days of our Lord: besides Aramaic there were three other tongues—Latin, the official language of the Roman army of occupation; Greek, the language of the official administration and of international commerce; and the Hebrew of the Rabbinical schools, the language of the learned Jews. It is possible that Jesus had some acquaintance with Greek; but there is no good reason to suppose that any part of his teaching was delivered in that language. The only occasion when he may perhaps have spoken in Greek is in the trial before Pilate, less probably in the conversation with the Syro-Phoenician woman (Mk. vii. 24–30).[2] Latin may be regarded as out of the question. There remains the Hebrew of the Rabbis (לשון חכמים), as distinguished from the classical Hebrew of the Old Testament (לשון תורה), which was in the time of Christ a dead language used only for liturgical purposes or in the study.

The Hebrew of the Rabbis is the language of the Mishnah

---

[1] *Grammatik des Jüdisch-palästinischen Aramäisch*, 2nd ed. 1905; *Die Worte Jesu I*, 1898 (E.T. *The Words of Jesus*, 1902); *Jesus-Jeschua*, 1922 (E.T. *Jesus-Jeschua*, 1929).

[2] Dalman, *Jesus-Jeschua*, pp. 5 f.

and the earliest Midrashim. It is, as Professor Moore well
describes it, 'a Hebrew with characteristic peculiarities of
its own which distinguish it sharply from that of even the
latest books of the Old Testament. The Jews were fully
aware of the difference, and call one "the language of the
Bible", the other "the language of scholars". The latter is
neither simply a degenerate Hebrew whose idiom was
disintegrated by the influence of the Aramaic vernacular,
nor is it an artificial language, a kind of academic jargon.
*It is a scholastic language, which has its roots not only in biblical
Hebrew but in living speech,* and was developed and adapted
to serve as a medium for technical definition and discussion. Classical Hebrew owes its charm to the wealth of
its diction and the subtlety of its syntax, neither of which
excellences is conducive to the juristic precision which the
schools of the Law aimed at. Their idiom, on the other
hand, is admirably fitted to their purpose, *and it may fairly
be inferred that it had had a long evolution in the schools before it
attained the stage in which we have our first acquaintance with it'.*[1]
I have quoted the passage at length because it gives the
authority of this distinguished scholar to two important
propositions: first that Rabbinical Hebrew was a real
language, used it may be in a limited circle and for a
special purpose, but still used in the full sense of the word:
and second that it had a history that goes much farther
back than the dates of the earliest documents in which it is
used, that is, that it was a spoken language for generations
before the compilation of the earliest Mishnah or Midrash.

Granted this, we are entitled to say that it was in use in
the time of Christ as the language of learned debate: and
the question arises whether there is any evidence that he
was acquainted with it and made use of it. Both parts of
this question can, in my opinion, be answered in the affirmative. In favour of the view that Jesus was conversant
with the language of the schools the following grounds may
be advanced: (*a*) As his quotations from the Old Testa-

[1] *Judaism*, I. 99 f. The italics are mine.

ment show, his knowledge of the Hebrew Scriptures was both extensive and profound.[1] Anyone who had the acquaintance with the language of the Scripture shown by these quotations would have little difficulty with the language of the scholars. (*b*) He is addressed as διδάσκαλε (= Rabbi)[2] not only by his own disciples (Mk. iv. 38; ix. 38, etc.) or by members of the public (Mk. ix. 17) but by the learned themselves (Mk. xii. 14, 32). This suggests that they recognised him as a competent scholar who could meet them on their own ground. (*c*) In the earlier part of the ministry he is reported as teaching *in the synagogue*. We are certainly told that his teaching differed from that of the Scribes; but the possibility of taking up an attitude different from or hostile to that of the Scribes implies an acquaintance with their methods. Moreover if, as seems probable, the teaching in the synagogue consisted in expounding and applying the synagogue lessons for the day and formed part of the regular order of service, it seems unlikely that anyone would be called on to carry out this duty who was not considered to have some qualification for the task. (*d*) We have a story of Jesus at the age of twelve sitting among the Teachers (ἐν μέσῳ τῶν διδασκάλων—Rabbis) in Jerusalem. If there is any reliance to be placed on this story—and there is nothing improbable about it[3]—we must ask what happened in the intervening eighteen years before the be-

[1] The eighty-seven quotations by Jesus from the O.T. which are recorded in our four sources are distributed as follows: Mk 37, Q 12, M 28, L 10. They cover all five books of the Law; in the second division of the Hebrew Canon the only books not cited are Joshua, Judges, II Samuel, Amos, Obadiah, Nahum, Habakkuk, and Haggai: in the Hagiographa we have quotations from Psalms, Job and Daniel. The distribution of the quotations by audience is: D 38 (41), G 19 (16), P 16, quotations in the Sermon on the Mount not definitely assignable 14. See further Detached Note A at end of this chapter.
[2] Cf. Strack-Billerbeck on Mt. xxiii. 7.
[3] Any incredibility that attaches to the story is largely the creation of Western imagination, which, seizing on the 'twelve years of age', has made of Jesus in this incident an infant prodigy, and forgotten that twelve in Palestine is equivalent to something more like seventeen or eighteen in the West. The addition to *Aboth* (Taylor, 2nd ed., p. 97), entitled 'The Ages of Man', runs: 'At five years old, Scripture: at ten years, Mishnah: at thirteen, the Commandments', i.e. full responsibility.

Jesus from 12.30 Training as a rabbi

ginning of the ministry. Is it not likely that much of this time was spent in the continuation of just such studies as these? The strong condemnation of the scribal refinements of the Law at least suggests that Jesus had tried the method thoroughly and found it wanting. (*e*) The fact that Jesus was brought up in a humble household and to manual labour does not tell against his being a scholar in the Jewish sense. Many of the most distinguished ornaments of Rabbinical scholarship were men of humble origin who supported themselves and their families by manual labour while prosecuting their studies in the schools of the Law.[1]

There is thus a *prima facie* case for supposing that Jesus knew and could use the language of the schools: is there any positive evidence in the records for the theory that he actually made use of it? Naturally the place where we should expect it to be employed, if it were employed at all, would be in controversy with the learned. To the mass of the people, as to his own disciples, the antecedent probability is that he would speak in Aramaic—the language which they understood and, for most of them, the only language which they could understand. Where the actual words of Jesus have been recorded as spoken to simple unlearned people, they are Aramaic: ταλειθά κούμ (Mk. v. 41 : G); ἐφφαθά (Mk. vii. 34: G). But when we turn from the D and G sections of the teaching to P, we find a difference which suggests the employment of Rabbinic Hebrew rather than Aramaic. The most striking instance is Mk. vii. 1–23, which contains utterances all bearing upon the same matter —ritual purity and true purity—addressed to three distinct audiences: P, G, and D. The P section (*vv.* 6–13) contains three quotations from the Old Testament, numerous technical terms, and one word transliterated—κορβάν in *v.* 11. And κορβάν is the exact equivalent of the Rabbinic קרבן in the Mishnah *Nedarim*, I. 2, etc.[2] The inference one

---

[1] Cf. Schürer, *G.J.V.*[4] II. 379; Taylor, *Sayings of the Jewish Fathers*, p. 20 n. 26.

[2] Cf. Dalman, *Grammatik*[2], p. 174 n. 3.

should draw is that this discussion was probably carried on in the school language: and this conclusion is strengthened somewhat by Mk. vii. 14: 'And recalling the crowd he said to them',[1] which suggests that what had been going on between him and the Scribes and Pharisees was something in which the crowd had no part, presumably because they could not follow the discussion.

We may say then that Aramaic was the language which came most naturally to the tongue of Jesus. It is the language of his prayers,[2] the language in which he spoke to ordinary folks who came to him with their troubles, and the language in which he delivered his message to the people and his teaching to the disciples. On the other hand it seems not improbable that in discussion and dispute with the Jewish scholars he may have employed the language, as he certainly used the exegetical methods and terminology, of the Rabbinical schools.

2. POETIC FORM

The eighteenth century, which saw in Germany the first attempts at a Biblical Theology and the beginnings of the study of the life of Jesus on strictly historical lines, saw also in France and England the first serious application of the methods of literary criticism to the books of the Bible. In France Astruc laid the foundations of the documentary analysis of the Pentateuch: in England Lowth was investigating the characteristic forms of Hebrew poetry.[3] Lowth's great and fruitful discovery was embodied in two words: *parallelismus membrorum*. Lowth himself defines it thus:[4]

[1] καὶ προσκαλεσάμενος πάλιν τὸν ὄχλον κ.τ.λ.

[2] On this point 'Abba' (Mk. xiv. 36) is decisive. The question whether the words of Ps. xxii. 1 in Mk. xv. 34 were spoken in Hebrew or Aramaic is still undecided: and just because this is an O.T. quotation it hardly affects the main issue how it is decided. For recent arguments that the quotation was made in Hebrew see C. H. Turner in *J.T.S.* Oct. 1927, p. 12; and Dalman, *Jesus-Jeschua*, p. 185.

[3] *De Sacra Poesi Hebraeorum Praelectiones Academicae*, 1753; *Isaiah, a new Translation*, 1778.

[4] *Isaiah*, ed. 3, p. xiv, quoted by G. B. Gray, *The Forms of Hebrew Poetry*, pp. 48 f.

'The correspondence of one verse, or line, with another, I call parallelism. When a proposition is delivered, and a second is subjoined to it, or drawn under it, equivalent, or contrasted with it, in sense; or similar to it in the form of grammatical construction; these I call parallel lines, and the words or phrases, answering one to another in the corresponding lines, parallel terms. Parallel lines may be reduced to three sorts: parallels synonymous, parallels antithetic and parallels synthetic'. Examples of this parallelism are:

Synonymous:

> The heavens | declare | the glory of God;
> And the firmament | showeth | his handywork.
> > (Ps. xix. 2.)

Antithetic:

> The memory | of the just | is blessed;
> But the name | of the wicked | shall rot.
> > (Prov. x. 7.)

Synthetic:

> I waited patiently for the Lord
> And he inclined unto me and heard my cry.
> > (Ps. xl. 2.)

Besides this feature of parallelism it is possible to distinguish in Hebrew poetry certain regular rhythmic structures depending on the number of stressed syllables to a line. There are lines with four, three and, more rarely, two stresses; and there is the characteristic Kinah or dirge form, which gains its peculiarly haunting effect by the alternation of members of three and two stresses. The use of rhyme is infrequent in the Old Testament. 'There is, however, a class of ancient Hebrew poetry in which the use of rhyme was probably a favourite device, namely, the popular poetry of the relatively uncultured.'[1]

This brief digression into the Old Testament sphere is rendered necessary by the fact that the researches of the

---

[1] C. F. Burney, *The Poetry of Our Lord*, p. 148.

late Professor Burney have shown convincingly that all the formal elements of Hebrew poetry—parallelism, rhythm, and rhyme—are present in the discourses of Jesus. Of the many examples given in Burney's book it is not necessary to quote more than one or two. For parallelism the following will suffice:

Synonymous:

There is nothing hid | that shall not be made manifest,
Nor secret | that shall not come to light.

(Mk. iv. 22.)

Love your enemies,
Do good to your haters,
Bless your cursers,
Pray for your persecutors.
(Lk. vi. 27, 28; Mt. v. 44: Q.)

Antithetic:

He that would save | his life | shall lose it:
But he that shall lose | his life |...shall save it.
(Mk. viii. 35.)

There is no good tree | producing | corrupt fruit,
Nor yet a corrupt tree | producing | good fruit.
(Lk. vi. 43; Mt. vii. 17: Q.)

Synthetic:

I came to cast fire upon the earth;
And what will I, if it be already kindled?
(Lk. xii. 49.)

To these three varieties of parallelism Burney adds a fourth, which he calls step-parallelism, 'in which a second line takes up a thought contained in the first line, and, repeating it, makes it as it were a step upwards for the development of a further thought, which is commonly the climax of the whole'.[1] An example of this form is:

He that receiveth this child in my name *receiveth me*;
And he that receiveth me, | receiveth him that sent me.
(Mk. ix. 37.)[2]

[1] *Op. cit.*, p. 90.
[2] The italics indicate the repeated member which serves as a step: and the vertical line stands before the climax.

The detection of rhythm in our Lord's utterances depends
to a large extent on retranslation into Aramaic: the
detection of rhyme is of course impossible without retranslation. For examples of these reference may be made
to Burney's work cited above, where these matters are
treated in detail and the necessary retranslations attempted.

The fact that many utterances of Jesus are cast in poetic
form is of course very important, in one direction especially.
The recovery of the true text of these utterances in cases
where divergent versions lie before us can frequently be
helped by observing which of them best preserves the
parallelism or rhythm or even rhyme. Such a test must be
applied with caution—many rash acts have been committed
in Old Testament criticism *metri causa*—but within its
limits the test of poetic form is a useful one. For example a
comparison of Mk. viii. 17, 18 with Mt. xvi. 9 leaves little
doubt as to which is the more original: and the same thing
holds of Lk. vi. 27, 28 compared with Mt. v. 44 (Q). In
both cases we have to deal with one of the favourite
practices of the first Evangelist, abbreviation, which he
carries out even at the expense of poetic form.

In the brief sketch given above the largest stress is laid
on the phenomenon of parallelism, because it is such a
marked feature in the poetry of the Old Testament and the
Gospels. It would be, I think, possible to go much farther
than this and to bring all the marks of poetic form under
the one head of parallelism. For, after all, rhyme and
rhythm are just a kind of external parallelism, a recurrence
of similar sound groups or of similar collocations of
accented and unaccented syllables. What we call rhyme and
rhythm are just parallelisms of sound: and what Lowth
calls parallelism is just the rhyming of ideas or parallelism
of sense. So that parallelism, rhythm or metrical structure
and rhyme are not utterly separate poetical devices, but
manifestations in different ways, in different media, of one
principle of poetic composition. This principle of recurrence with variation whether of ideas or sounds, is

Use poetry in preaching too --
& learn to use the parallelisms like Jesus.

what distinguishes poetry from prose, which, on the other hand, is characterised by its linear structure.

On this view parallelism may be conceived as confined to the smallest external points of end rhyme or assonance; it may be expanded to mean the recurrence with variations of metrical structures such as the hexameter, or stress systems as in English blank verse; or again it may be taken as the recurrence, with variation, of thought groups of a simple character capable of being expressed in three or four words as in Hebrew poetry. A still greater extension of the phenomenon of parallelism, and one which has not so far as I am aware been noticed as such, is to be found in the words of Jesus. Here the parallelism covers not single clauses containing each one simple idea, but still larger aggregates each of which contains many clauses. In these cases the aggregates are parallel wholes, and the constituent clauses form the parallel members. As an example of this compound parallelism we may take the passage Lk. xvii, 26–30:

I. And as it happened in the days of Noah,   (*a*)
   So shall it be in the days of the Son of Man: (*b*)
      They ate, they drank,   (*c* 1)
      They married, they gave in marriage   (*c* 2)
   Till the day when Noah went into the ark   (*d*)
   And the Deluge came and destroyed them all.   (*e*)

II. Likewise as it happened in the days of Lot: (*a*)
      They ate, they drank,   (*c* 1)
      They bought, they sold,   (*c* 2)
      They planted, they built,   (*c* 3)
   But, in the day when Lot went forth from Sodom,   (*d*)
   Fire and brimstone rained from heaven and destroyed
      them all.   (*e*)
   Just so shall it be in the day when the Son of Man is
      revealed.   (*b*)

Here the parallelism of structure can be represented schematically:

I. *a*, *b*, *c* 1, *c* 2,   *d*, *e*.
II. *a*,   *c* 1, *c* 2, *c* 3, *d*, *e*, *b*.

So also Lk. xi. 31, 32:

I. The queen of the South shall rise in the Judgement
with the men of this generation and con-
demn them,   (a)
For she came from the ends of the earth to hear the
wisdom of Solomon   (b)
And lo, a greater than Solomon is here.   (c)

II. The men of Nineveh shall rise in the Judgement with
this generation and condemn it,   (a)
For they repented at the preaching of Jonah   (b)
And lo, a greater than Jonah is here.   (c)

Here the parallelism of clauses can be represented quite
simply:

I. *a, b, c.*
II. *a, b, c.*

Other examples of the same kind of structure are: Mk. ii.
21, 22, New Patch on old Garment, New Wine in old
Wineskins; ix. 43–48, hand, foot, eye to be sacrificed;
from Q: besides the two cases quoted above, Lk. xii.
24–28 = Mt. vi. 26–30, birds of the air, lilies of the field;
Lk. xiii. 18–21 = Mt. xiii. 31–33, Mustard Seed, Leaven;
Lk. x. 13–15 = Mt. xi. 21–23, Chorazin and Bethsaida,
Capernaum; from L: Lk. iv. 25–27, Elijah, Elisha; xiii.
2–5, Pilate's victims, those killed by the fall of the tower of
Siloam; xiv. 28–33, Building a Tower, Going to War;
xv. 4–10, Lost Sheep, Lost Coin (perhaps we should add
11–32, Lost Son); from M: Mt. xiii. 44–46, Hidden
Treasure, Pearl of Great Price; xxiii. 16–21, swearing by
the Temple, swearing by the altar.

In all these cases the device of parallelism is pushed to its
extreme limits. We have passed beyond the parallelism of
single lines, though this is present, to the parallelism of
whole strophes or oracles, a form which produces an effect
of singular intensity and dramatic power. The two
examples quoted above come burdened with a sense of
utter finality: it is as though we heard the very voice of

Destiny or the pronouncements of that court from which there is no appeal.

Yet the same poetic form can be used to produce impressions of quite a different kind. Nowhere has the belief in God's fatherly care been more beautifully or more forcibly stated than in Lk. xii. 24–28 = Mt. vi. 26–30 (Q):

I. Consider the ravens,	(*a*)
They do not sow or reap;	(*b* 1)
They have no barn or storehouse;	(*b* 2)
And God feeds them:	(*d*)
How much better are you than the birds!	(*f*)
II. Consider the lilies, how they grow:	(*a*)
They do not toil or spin;	(*b*)
Yet I tell you that not even Solomon in all his	
glory was arrayed like one of these.	(*c*)
But if God so clothe the grass	(*d*)
Which to-day is in the field	(*e* 1)
And to-morrow is cast into the oven;	(*e* 2)
How much more you, oh ye of little faith?	(*f*)

Schematically:

I   *a*, *b* 1, *b* 2,   *d*,   *f*.
II. *a*, *b*,   *c*, *d*, *e* 1, *e* 2, *f*.

Still another note is sounded in the twin parables of the Lost Sheep and the Lost Coin, and another in the Mustard Seed and Leaven. This form can cover the widest possible range of ideas and emotions: and on whatever theme it is employed it gives to the presentation an emotional intensity that could hardly otherwise be achieved. We have seen that all the customary devices of Hebrew poetic style are to be found in the discourses of Jesus. Perhaps we should regard this strophic parallelism as the most distinctive characteristic of his poetry and his special contribution to the forms of poetry in general.[1]

[1] It is much to be desired that in editions of the text of the Gospels, whether Greek or English, the poetical pieces should be printed as such. A beginning has been made by Dr James Moffatt in *The New Testament, a new translation*: and there seems to be no good reason why the same thing should not be done in printing the Greek text.

3. PARABLE

In all the teaching of Jesus there is no feature more striking than his parables. Whether we consider them in themselves, or according to their influence in human life, they are unique. They have supplied inspiration to poets, artists, moralists: much of the current coin of our common speech—'good Samaritan', 'hiding one's light under a bushel', 'talents'—is drawn direct from this treasury. Most curious of all, whole volumes have been written in exposition of compositions whose meaning is supposed to be obvious.

Apart from the interpretation of individual parables, two questions require discussion at this stage. (1) What is a parable, and which among the utterances of Jesus belong to this class? (2) On what principle or principles did he make use of this form of teaching?

One of the chief obstacles to a proper understanding of the parables of Jesus is an unconscious assumption which most people make with regard to the nature of parables. Coming to the study of the Gospels, as most of us do, with a long course of Church services behind us, we tend to think of the parables which occur in the teaching of Jesus as something akin to the 'illustrations' used in sermons. This supposition is fortified by examination of the definitions of παραβολή given by the classical writers on rhetoric. The *locus classicus* for the Western notion of παραβολή is Aristotle, *Rhetoric*, II. xx. 2–4, where Cope comments as follows: 'παραβολή is *juxtaposition*, setting one thing *by the side* of another for the purpose of *comparison* and "illustration"; taking analogous or parallel cases; it is the argument from analogy, ἄν τις δύνηται ὅμοιον ὁρᾶν, § 7. A good instance of παραβολή in this sense occurs *Pol.* II. 5, 1264 *b* 4, where Plato is said to derive a παραβολή or analogy, ἐκ τῶν θηρίων (i.e. dogs), to prove that the pursuits and occupations of men and women should be the same...Aristotle distinguishes parable *in general* from fable by this; that the former depicts *human* relations (in which the N.T. parable coincides with it); it *invents* analogous cases, which are not *historical*, but always such as *might* be so; always probable, and corresponding with what actually occurs in real life. The fable is *pure fiction*, and its essential characteristic is, that it invests beasts, birds, plants, and even things inanimate with the attributes of humanity'.

Now it is obvious that if this be the true nature of parable, then every parable should be itself crystal clear. If its object be simply to illuminate the obscure or to carry conviction to an audience unable to follow a long chain of abstract reasoning, then it must itself be simple and convincing. With this agrees the statement of Eustathius[1] that a parable ought always to be more readily intelligible than that which it is intended to illustrate: and that a vice in parables is the use of the unknown and the unfamiliar. In other words the parable should be a road to the truth so simple and straightforward that the wayfaring man, though a fool, cannot err therein. It is the concrete example that happily lights up the general principle, or the well-chosen analogy by which things that are seen and temporal are made to reflect the things that are unseen and eternal.

Such is the general idea of parable which a mind trained in Western ways of thought will bring to the parables of the Bible. And it will not be denied that, up to a certain point, this notion is adequate. There are parables which can be taken as concrete instances meant to illuminate a general principle: the Good Samaritan is such a case. There are others where an analogy drawn from human affairs is put forward as an indication of conditions in the heavenly places: as when the story of the Lost Sheep[2] in L is made to suggest that there is more joy in heaven over one sinner who

---

[1] Eustathius, *ad Il.* A, p. 176, cited by Cope, II. 198, ὀφείλει πάντως γνωριμώτερον εἶναι τοῦ δι' ὃ παρείληπται. κακία γὰρ παραβολῆς τὸ ἄγνωστον καὶ ἀσύνηθες.

[2] Lk. xv. 4–7.

repents than over ninety-nine just persons who do not need
to repent.[1]

It is, however, speedily evident, when we come to
examine the parables in the Synoptic Gospels, that this
idea of parable will <u>not</u> serve to cover all the examples
there that bear the name: nor will it square with some of
the things that are said about parables. Under the first
head we note such sayings as 'Physician, heal thyself'
(Lk. iv. 23: L) or 'Not that which enters a man defiles him,
but that which comes out' (Mk. vii. 15). <u>These we should
hardly reckon as parables, yet they are explicitly so called
in the records.</u> Under the second head come such utterances as Mk. iv. 11 f. addressed to the disciples: 'To you is
given the secret of the Kingdom of God; but to those outside
all things come in parables, that seeing they may see and
not perceive, and hearing they may hear and not understand, lest they should turn and obtain forgiveness'. This
hard saying seems to be a flat contradiction of all that we
commonly suppose to be the object of parabolic teaching.
And so it is, so long as we are content with the notion of
parable which we obtain from classical theories of rhetoric.
Either we must explain away or reject such sayings as Mk.
iv. 11 f.[2] or we must revise our notions of what a parable is
and what it is intended to do. If we choose the latter
course, the obvious place to begin our enquiry is not with
the rhetoricians of the West but with the Old Testament.

The word παραβολή is regularly used in the LXX to
render the Hebrew noun *māshāl* or the verb *māshal*. The

---

[1] The use of παραβολή in Heb. ix. 9; xi. 19 (the only occurrences in N.T.
outside the Synoptic Gospels) is an elaborate and somewhat artificial
extension of this: it is the kind of thing that St Paul would call ἀλληγορία.
Cf. Gal. iv. 21–31.

[2] This alternative is chosen by many modern scholars: e.g. Bousset
(*Jesus*, E.T., p. 42), who describes Mk. iv. 11 as 'preposterous' and dismisses
it as 'the dogmatic pedantry of a later age'; Jülicher, cf. art. 'Parables' in
Enc. Bib. col. 3564; Menzies; Montefiore, 'The conception of 11 and 12 is
Pauline' (*The Synoptic Gospels*[1], I. 124); J. Weiss-W. Bousset in *Die Schriften des
N.T.*[3], I. 110 ff.

Aramaic equivalent of *māshāl* is *m͏ᵉthal*, det. *mathlā*: and so the Targums and the Peshitta commonly render the Hebrew. The term *māshāl* has a very wide range of meanings: and, what is most striking, only in a very small minority of the O.T. cases does it connote what we understand by parable. In Hebrew literature the name is given to the following classes of saying: brief sentences of popular wisdom, ethical maxims, proverbs in general. Examples of this are: 'Is Saul also among the prophets?' (I Sam. x. 12); 'From the wicked comes forth wickedness'—*Anglice* 'What can you expect from a pig but a grunt?' (I Sam. xxiv. 14); 'Like mother, like daughter' (Ezek. xvi. 44); 'The fathers have eaten sour grapes and the children's teeth are set on edge' (Ezek. xviii. 2); besides any number of cases in the Book of Proverbs and in Ecclesiasticus. Many of these sayings are cast in poetic form, usually as couplets in antithetic parallelism. In I Kings v. 12 (M.T., iv. 28 LXX) we are told that Solomon composed 3000 specimens of the *māshāl* and 5000[1] odes (*shîr*), where the distinction is between gnomic and lyric poetry.[2] Some sayings of this sort involve a comparison, e.g. 'As vinegar to the teeth, and as smoke to the eyes, so the sluggard to them that send him' (Prov. x. 26) or 'As a jewel of gold in a swine's snout, so is a fair woman which is without discretion' (*ib.* xi. 22); but the majority of these terse epigrammatic sayings are just what we should call proverbs or aphorisms rather than parables. Yet in the O.T. such sayings fall under the head of *māshāl*: and their equivalents in the Gospels are reckoned among the παραβολαί. The saying (Lk. iv. 23: L) 'Physician, heal thyself', which is explicitly described as a parable—πάντως ἐρεῖτέ μοι τὴν παραβολὴν ταύτην—corresponds exactly with the examples from the O.T. cited above. It is a piece of popular pro-

---

[1] Taking the reading of LXX.

[2] Skinner in Century Bible, *ad loc*. Wildeboer in *Kurzer Handkommentar* to Prov. i. 6 maintains that מָשָׁל is the opposite of שִׁיר. They are the two forms of metrical composition in Hebrew: מָשָׁל that which was meant to be spoken, שִׁיר that which was destined to be sung.

verbial wisdom "found not only in the Gospel but in Jewish, Greek, and Latin sources.[1] Again the saying in Mk. vii. 15 is a sentence of ethical wisdom similar to many of the sayings in the Book of Proverbs and, like them, cast in the form of a couplet whose two lines stand in antithetic parallelism:

There is nothing from outside entering into a man which can defile him;
But the things which proceed out of a man are the things which defile a man.

Such sayings as these in the Hebrew Scriptures and in the Gospels are the generalisation of wide experience or deep insight crystallised in the form of aphorisms. They are general statements, even though they be put in a pointed and sometimes personal manner. The great bulk of them would admit of being put into strict logical form as universal affirmative or negative propositions.

The second use of *māshāl* in Hebrew writings has no parallel in the words of Jesus. This use covers all the cases where the word may be rendered in English by 'byword'. Examples are to be found in Deut. xxviii. 37; Ps. xliv. 15; lxix. 12; Jer. xxiv. 9; Ezek. xiv. 8. In these cases a particular is held up as an example, usually to contempt and obloquy. From the nature of the case it is commonly Israel that is so marked out as a shocking example, or what in Scotland would be called an 'awfu' warning'. An extension and elaboration of this use is to be found in the *māshāl* as 'taunt-song', e.g. in Mic. ii. 4; Hab. ii. 6; Is. xiv. 4. The underlying notion of the 'taunt-song' is the same as that of the 'byword': the only real difference would seem to be in the degree of elaboration in the working out. As stated above there is no clear case in the words of Jesus of anything corresponding to these uses of *māshāl*. The nearest approach to it in the Gospels would perhaps be found in the words of the mockers at the

---

[1] *Gen. R.* 23 (ed. Theodor, p. 225); Eur. *Fragm.* 1086; Cicero, *Ep. ad Fam.* IV. 5. 5.

Crucifixion: 'He saved others; himself he cannot save' (Mk. xv. 31).[1]

A perplexing group of cases of the use of *māshāl* in the O.T. is Num. xxiii. 7, 18; xxiv. 3, 15, 20, 21, 23, all in the story of Balaam, where the oracles of the prophet are introduced by the formula וישא משלו; and again in Job xxvii. 1 and xxix. 1, where we have ויוסף איוב שאת משלו. Along with these may be reckoned Ps. lxxviii. 2. It is difficult to see just why the name *māshāl* should be applied to these discourses. In Job xxix. 1, in view of what follows in chapters xxix and xxx, we may perhaps regard *māshāl* as equivalent to taunt-song. These chapters will then represent the climax of Job's speeches: and it may be taken as significant of the depth of his humiliation and woe that he should utter a taunt-song in which he is both author and subject. Psalm lxxviii may be taken as an attempt to read history in the light of popular proverbial wisdom such as is embodied in *vv.* 7 and 8. The oracles of Balaam contain a number of similes and this may be the reason for the name *māshāl* prefixed to them.

In all these cases, which form the vast majority of the Old Testament examples, there is nothing corresponding at all closely to what we are accustomed to call a parable. We may indeed detect in some of them the germ out of which a parable, in our sense of the word, might be developed; but it is, at the best, only a germ. There are, however, in the Old Testament, a few cases which are really similar to the parables which we find in the Gospels. Nine examples can properly be called parables: and two would be more accurately described as fables. To the latter class belong Jotham's account of the Trees choosing

---

[1] The singling out of particular individuals, classes, or peoples as examples, i.e. the making of 'bywords', is not peculiar to Scripture. The names of Don Juan, Pandarus, de Sade, Oedipus have all been used as bywords for types of immorality; Bluebeard for a certain kind of murderer; Jew or Aberdonian is made, often very unjustly, a synonym for 'mean', and so on. The principle which governs the selection of such types is the same as that which underlies the *māshāl* in the cases considered above.

a King (Jud. ix. 7–15) and the fable of the Thistle and the Cedar (II Kings xiv. 9). The parables properly so called are:

The Ewe Lamb	(II Sam. xii. 1–14)
The Two Brethren and the Avengers of blood	(II Sam. xiv. 1–11)
The Escaped Prisoner	(I Kings xx. 35–40)
The Vineyard and Grapes	(Is. v. 1–7)
The Eagles and the Vine	(Ezek. xvii. 3–10)
The Lion Whelps	(Ezek. xix. 2–9)
The Vine	(Ezek. xix. 10–14)
The Forest Fire	(Ezek. xxi. 1–5)
The Seething Pot	(Ezek. xxiv. 3–5)

The first thing which arrests attention about these is that only two of them are explicitly called parables: the Eagles and the Vine, and the Forest Fire, both of which come from Ezekiel. The same thing holds of the Gospel parables, where not more than twenty-two of the utterances of Jesus are described as parables; and of these only four sayings— the Sower, the Mustard Seed, the Fig Tree (all in Mk), and 'Physician, heal thyself' (L)—are actually called parables by Jesus himself. This suggests that it is only by stretching a point that these stories are called parables at all: and we have to ask what is the thread that connects these 'parables' with the sayings in the Old Testament, which are properly and regularly gathered under the name *māshāl*.

If we turn to our nine specimens from the O.T. we find that they fall into two classes, the basis of distinction being whether the parable is directed *ad hominem* or *ad rem*. Clear examples of the first sort are the three cases from the historical books. The story of the Ewe Lamb is deliberately intended to arouse the conscience of David and convict him of his sin. In the parables of Ezekiel, on the other hand, the story told is the shadow of coming events, which the prophet by virtue of his insight into God's ways is able to foresee. In Isaiah's song of the Vineyard these two aspects are combined: it is at once a prick to the conscience of the people and a warning of approaching doom. By the aid of this distinction it is now possible to connect the two types of parable with the two main varieties of *māshāl* considered above: the parable *ad hominem* corresponding to the *māshāl* as 'byword', and the parable *ad rem* to the *māshāl* as a sentence of popular wisdom. In the 'byword' a particular case is selected by popular fancy out of the common experience and held up as a type of one way of life and its consequences: in the parable *ad hominem* the same thing is done, except that the typical case is not found but created for its purpose by the parabolist. In the 'byword' the example chosen as the type of conduct is matter of fact—a real person or people or class; in the parable the example is a work of art, a piece of fiction invented or inspired to serve as a typical case. Again in the proverbial wisdom of the ancients the result of wide and age-long observation of human experience is crystallised in aphorisms which describe in universal form the relations of character and life and destiny. When prophetic vision is added to human sagacity we get the parable *ad rem*. Here the inductions from human experience, which produce proverbs, give place to deductions from the divine nature. The connections between character and conduct, life and destiny are not merely observed uniformities of nature but decrees of Providence. The element of comparison, which is found in some of the proverbial sayings, is taken up and elaborated in the new development; but the elaboration is subsidiary to the main purpose; it serves merely to prepare the mind to receive the general truth which governs the whole matter. All the details in the parable of the Vineyard are steps to the climax which is a perfectly general proposition—destruction of the worthless—conceived as a divine law dominating the course of events.

The recognition of these facts carries with it a conclusion of great importance, which has a bearing on such difficult passages as Mk. iv. 11, 12. This is that every real parable is significant in two ways. It has its own meaning as a story

Double Meaning

and a further meaning—and this is the important thing—
by application to persons or events or both together. It is
possible for a hearer to follow and appreciate the former
meaning without having the slightest inkling of the latter.
Thus in the parable of the Ewe Lamb, David is able to
understand every detail of the story and to pronounce
judgement on the principal actor in it in all good faith. It
is only the dramatic pronouncement of the prophet, 'Thou
art the man', that first brings home to him the application
of the story. Similarly in Ezek. xxi. 5 we have the complaint of the prophet that the people accuse him of speaking
in parables.[1] The reference is to the parable of the Forest
Fire and Ezekiel is thereupon commissioned to give the
meaning of the parable (Ezek. xxi. 6–10). It is clear from
these and other cases that a parable may be perfectly
intelligible in itself while its application is hidden from the
hearers.

The conception of parable which we take from the Old
Testament to the Gospels will then be somewhat as follows.
A parable is a literary creation in narrative form designed
either to portray a type of character for warning or example
or to embody a principle of God's governance of the world
and men. It may partake of both natures. In logical
terminology it might almost be called a concrete universal.
The immediate object of the story is to be intelligible and
interesting in itself; but its ultimate aim is either to
stimulate the conscience, or to awaken religious insight in
the hearers, or both together. In other words it has to
make God and himself real to a man: so real that he is
forthwith moved to genuine repentance and faith. It is
emphatically not a mere sermon illustration for the
purpose of stating some abstract proposition of ethics or
theology in a simple pictorial form for the benefit of the
unlearned: it is the word of God itself 'quick and powerful
and sharper than any two-edged sword, piercing even to
the dividing asunder of soul and spirit and of the joints and

הֲלֹא מְמַשֵּׁל מְשָׁלִים הוּא [1]

marrow, a discerner of the thoughts and intents of the heart'. Further it depends for its effectiveness not primarily on its excellence as an illustration, as we are so prone to imagine, but on the responsiveness of those to whom it is addressed. The power of Nathan's parable lies not in the story itself, though that is sufficiently apt, but in the spontaneous moral indignation of David: and it is on that moral response to the story that everything subsequently hinges. The seeing eye and the hearing ear and the understanding heart are essential if the parable is to do its proper work.

With these things in mind we can now turn to the parables recorded in the Gospels: and we begin with lists of the parables in the four sources. There will, of course, be difference of opinion as to some items in the lists: it is not always easy to say whether a particular saying is to be regarded as a parable or simply as a figurative way of speaking. To some the lists will seem to include too much: from another point of view they might be considerably enlarged. They do, however, include all the sayings that are usually reckoned as parables: and they provide a sufficiently representative collection of material for the purposes of this discussion. An asterisk indicates that the word παραβολή is actually used by the Evangelist to describe the saying: the obelus indicates that it is so designated by Jesus himself. Brackets indicate some doubt as to whether the saying should be reckoned a parable or not.

Mk

ii. 17	(The Whole and the Sick)	(P)
19 f.	Children of the Bridechamber[2]	(P)[1]
21	New Patch on Old Garment* RL	(P)
22	New Wine in Old Wineskins	(P)
iii. 24–26	Divided Kingdom or House*[2]	(P)
27	Strong Man armed*[2]	(P)

[1] Includes disciples of John the Baptist.
[2] Also in Q.

OF THE TEACHING

67

iv.	3–9	The Sower*†	(G)
	21	Light under a Bushel[1]	(D)
	24	(Measure for Measure)[1]	(D)
	26–29	Seed growing of itself	(D)
	30–32	Mustard Seed†[1]	(D?)
vii.	14 f.	What defiles a Man*	(G)
	27	(Children's Bread to Dogs)	(G)
viii.	15	(Leaven of Pharisees and Herod)	(D)
ix.	49 f.	Fire and Salt[1]	(D)
xii.	1–11	Vineyard*	(P)
xiii.	28 f.	Fig Tree†	(D)
	34–37	Absent Householder	(D)

Q (Streeter's Reconstruction: *The Four Gospels*, p. 291)

Lk. vi.	38	(Measure for Measure)[2,3]	
	39	Blind leading Blind* RL?[3]	
	41 f.	Mote and Beam[3]	
	43–45	Tree and Fruit[3]	
	47–49	Wise and Foolish Builders[3]	
vii.	31–35	Children in the Marketplace	(G)
ix.	58	(Foxes have Holes)	(G)
x.	2	Harvest and Labourers	(D)
xi.	11 f.	Stone for Bread, etc.	(D)
	17	Divided Kingdom or House[2]	(P)
	21 f.	Strong Man armed[2]	(P)
	33	Light under a Bushel[2]	(G)
	39–41	Cleansing outside of Cup	(P)
xii.	35–38	Lord returning from Marriage Feast	(D)
	39	Householder whose House is broken into* RL?	(D)
	42–46	Faithful and Unfaithful Stewards	(D)
	47 f.	(Servants who know or do not know)	(D)
xiii.	18 f.	Mustard Seed* RMT[2]	(G)
	20 f.	Leaven* RMT	(G)
	24–30	The Shut Door	(D?)
xiv.	34 f.	Salt[2]	(G)
xvi.	13	(Servant and Two Masters)	(D)
xix.	11–27	Pounds* RL (= Talents in Mt.)	(D)

[1] Also in Q.
[2] Also in Mk.
[3] From Luke's Sermon on the Plain.

5-2

M

Mt. v.	14	City on a Hill	(D?)
	vii. 6	(Holy Things and Pearls)	
	xii. 11 f.	(Sheep fallen into a Pit)	(P)
	xiii. 24–30	Wheat and Tares*	(G)
	44	Hidden Treasure[1]	(D)
	45 f.	Pearl of Great Price[1]	(D)
	47–50	Dragnet[1]	(D)
	52	Householder with New and Old Things[1]	(D)
	xv. 13	(Tree not rightly planted)	(D)
	xvii. 25	(Tribute of Earthly Kings)	(D)
	xviii. 12–14	Lost Sheep[2]	(D)
	23–35	Unmerciful Steward	(D)
	xx. 1–16	Labourers in the Vineyard	(D)
	xxi. 28–31	The Two Sons† (cf. xxi. 33: ἄλλην π.)	(P)
	xxii. 1–10	Marriage Feast, I*[2]	(P)
	11–14	Marriage Feast, II*	(P)
	xxv. 1–12	Ten Virgins	(D)

L

Lk. iv.	23	'Physician, heal thyself'†	(G)
	vii. 40–43	Two Debtors	(P)
	x. 30–37	Good Samaritan	(P)
	xi. 5–9	Importunate Householder	(D)
	xii. 16–21	The Rich Fool*	(G)
	xiii. 6–9	Unfruitful Fig Tree*	(G)
	xiv. 7–11	Places at Table*	(G)
	16–24	Great Feast[3]	(G)
	xv. 3–7	Lost Sheep *[3]	(P)
	8–10	Lost Coin	(P)
	11–32	Lost Son	(P)
	xvi. 1–8	Unjust Steward	(D)
	19–31	Dives and Lazarus	(P)
	xvii. 7–10	From Field to Kitchen	(D)
	xviii. 1–8	Unjust Judge and Importunate Widow*	(D)
	9–14	Pharisee and Publican*	(P)

[1] Cf. Mt. xiii. 53.
[2] Also in L.
[3] Also in M.

After allowing for doublets there is a total of <u>sixty-five</u> parables. Before embarking on a consideration of the parables themselves we may note the characteristic ways in which the Evangelists introduce them. A good example of the different usages is in Mk. xii. 1 and parallels:

Mk. xii. 1, καὶ ἤρξατο αὐτοῖς ἐν παραβολαῖς λαλεῖν.

Mt. xxi. 33, ἄλλην παραβολὴν ἀκούσατε.

Lk. xx. 9, ἤρξατο δὲ πρὸς τὸν λαὸν λέγειν τὴν παραβολὴν ταύτην.

The normal formula in Mark is 'he spoke ἐν παραβολαῖς αὐτοῖς'; in Matthew again the usual form is 'he said (delivered) παραβολὴν αὐτοῖς'; in Luke, 'he spoke παραβολὴν πρὸς αὐτούς'. We cannot be certain that the word παραβολή stood in Q: in the four cases where Q material has an introductory formula, the formula is, in my judgement, to be regarded as the work of the Evangelist. In the two cases in Mt. xiii. 31, 33 the form is typically Matthaean: and the same holds good of one example at least from Luke: xix. 11 introducing the parable of the Pounds. Lk. vi. 39, εἶπεν δὲ καὶ παραβολὴν αὐτοῖς, is singular in having the dative in place of the usual πρός with acc. In no case do Matthew and Luke agree in applying the word to a saying of Jesus. We may therefore regard these four cases as editorial work: and they are marked RMT or RL in the list accordingly. There remains Lk. xii. 41, which forms the transition from one Q parable to another. The transition is peculiar to Luke (cf. Mt. xxiv. 43–51) and probably to be marked RL also. This case and the introduction to the parable of the Pounds (Lk. xix. 11) are evidence in favour of the view that St Luke had a copy of Q before he began collecting the material which we call L: and that what Canon Streeter calls Proto-Luke was made by combining L with St Luke's *annotated* copy of Q, the notes being derived from the same source that provided L, oral tradition.

The parables themselves can be divided into two main groups, the principle of division being the same as in the case of the O.T. parables. That is, <u>they present either a</u> type of human conduct or a <u>principle of God's govern-</u>

1.
ad hominer

2.
ad rem

ment of the world. In the former case the primary appeal is to the conscience, in the latter to the religious insight and faith of the hearers. In some cases both features are present in the same parable, though even in these cases one side is usually predominant. It will be convenient to consider these different classes of parables separately.

(a) *The Parable as an ethical type.*   Type A

Examples of this kind of parable are: the Vineyard (Mk); Wise and Foolish Builders, Faithful and Unfaithful Stewards, the Pounds (Talents), from Q; the Two Sons, the Ten Virgins (M); the Two Debtors, the Good Samaritan, the Rich Fool, the Pharisee and the Publican (L); and a good many more. The characteristic feature of this sort of parable is that a certain kind of conduct is sketched in the most vivid colours and held up before the audience. They are expected to apply the story to their own lives either as an example or as a warning. The warning note is clear and unmistakable in the parables of the Vineyard and the Rich Fool. More usually, however, in the parables of Jesus two types are contrasted in the one story and the burden of choice laid on the hearers. This is the case with most of the examples noted above. There are no half-tones; but all is drawn in the sharpest contrast of black and white. What is set before us is not duties and privileges about which we may haggle and bargain, seeking the minimum that will satisfy the requirements of a law, or devising extenuating circumstances that will excuse us from obeying it, or again defining its terms to suit our own convenience; but rather living characters between which we must choose. There are a dozen ways in which we may evade the commandment 'Thou shalt love thy neighbour as thyself'. We may point out that we cannot control our feelings; we may define neighbour in half a hundred different ways, any one of which will enable us to escape from the commandment. But there is no escaping from the Good Samaritan and his opposites in the parable. Once we have seen them fairly and squarely the real issue is before us in a form in which we cannot evade it: and to the 'Go thou and do likewise' of Jesus there is not, nor can be, any answer.

In several cases, the direct appeal to the conscience which this kind of parable makes is further emphasised by Jesus by means of a question appended to the story. Thus in the parable of the Vineyard, the narrative is followed by the query 'What will the lord of the vineyard do?' — Similarly in the parable of the Two Sons, 'Which of the two did the will of his father?'; of the Two Debtors (Lk. vii. 42), 'Which of them will love him most?'; and in the parable of the Good Samaritan, 'Which of these three seems to you to have been neighbour to him that fell among the thieves?' Or the question may be prefixed to the parable: 'Who is the faithful and prudent steward?' (Lk. xii. 42). Or the question stated or implied may be explicitly answered: the Rich Fool—'So is everyone that layeth up treasure for himself and is not rich toward God'; Pharisee and Publican—'This man went down to his house justified rather than the other'. Further cases of the same kind can readily be found.

In all these and similar cases the object of the parable is to work through the imagination and understanding of the hearers in order to arouse the conscience, and the real goal of parabolic teaching is not attained unless the conscience is aroused, unless, confronted by the story of the Rich Fool for example, conscience says, 'Thou art the man', or by the Good Samaritan, 'This is what thou must be'. Doubtless there were many who enjoyed listening to the parables—the 'Prodigal Son' has been classed with the finest short stories in the world—but merely to take pleasure in them as stories was not enough. Others in a way understood them. Certain of those who heard the parable of the Vineyard realised that it was directed at them (Mk. xii. 12); but their understanding only served to inflame their resentment: it did not in any real sense touch the conscience. The seed fell on barren ground and produced no fruit. On the other hand there were not wanting those who laid these sayings to heart and pondered over them. The mere fact that they have been preserved, some of them in more than one line of tradition, would prove that, apart from any other evidence. But there was also the circle of people who were sufficiently responsive to want further instruction and who for that very reason were worthy and capable of receiving it. In them was fulfilled the saying: 'To him that hath shall be given and he shall have abundance'.

Type B

(b) *The Parable as exhibiting some aspect of God's rule.*

As such I should reckon among others: the Seed growing of itself, the Mustard Seed, the Fig Tree (Mk); the Bread and Stone, Mustard Seed, Leaven (Q); Wheat and Tares, Hidden Treasure, Pearl of Great Price, Labourers in the Vineyard (M); the Importunate Householder, Unfruitful Fig Tree, Lost Sheep, Lost Coin, Prodigal Son (in part), the Unjust Judge and the Importunate Widow (L). In these cases some natural phenomenon or human relation is used to suggest or symbolise a religious truth. The primary appeal is thus to the faith and insight of the hearers. The best we know or can imagine is an indication of what we should believe concerning God. Thus in one important respect the teaching of Jesus on these matters differs from modern apologetics. He is not concerned to demonstrate that God exists, but rather to show the nature of the God whose existence is common ground for him and his audience. His aim is not to make God an article of faith but the object of faith. We are often concerned to make God probable to men; he set out to make God real to them. It is this fact that makes parable the inevitable form in which the teaching of Jesus on the nature and ways of God should be delivered.

It is in connection with parables of this kind that we must be most careful to guard ourselves against the assumption, all too readily made by minds trained in Western modes of thought, that the parable is an easy substitute for philosophical or theological argument, a simple rhetorical device by which minds incapable of sustained thought may be led to conclusions, which could otherwise be reached as the result of elaborate trains of reasoning. To suppose anything of the sort is to misapprehend the whole nature of parables. The business of philosophy is systematic reflection on experience as a whole: that of the philosophy of religion and of theology is systematic reflection on that part of our experience which we specifically call religious. Such reflection may lead to certain conclusions concerning the existence and nature of God and similar matters: and, if it be desired to popularise these conclusions, they may be stated in some simple form with illustrative examples drawn from ordinary life. But such illustrations will not be parables in the sense that the parables of the New Testament are parables. They are merely the embellishment of something else, namely the chain of logical reasoning; they are the sugar-coating on the theological pill. The true parable, on the other hand, is not an illustration to help one through a theological discussion; it is rather a mode of religious experience. It belongs to the same order of things as altar and sacrifice, prayer, the prophetic vision, and the like. It is a *datum* for theology, not a by-product. It is a way in which religious faith is attained and, so far as it can be, transmitted from one person to another. It is not a crutch for limping intellects, but a spur to religious insight: its object is not to provide simple theological instruction, but to produce living religious faith.

The moment this fact is grasped a number of peculiarities and difficulties about the parabolic teaching of Jesus can be explained. For example the passage Lk. xi. 9–13 (Q) runs as follows:

And I say unto you,

> Ask and it shall be given you,
> Seek and ye shall find,

Knock and it shall be opened to you.
For every asker receiveth,
And the seeker findeth,
And to the knocker it shall be opened.

And what father among you if his son ask for a fish will give him instead of a fish a serpent? Or if he ask for an egg will give him a scorpion? If you then, bad as you are, know how to give good gifts to your children, how much more will the Father from heaven give the holy spirit to those who ask him?[1]

Two features about this call for comment. First, the parable proper follows on a practical precept, an exhortation to prayer. That is, its object is to be understood in the light of this fact. It sets out to induce the frame of mind in which prayer will seem the most natural and inevitable thing in the world. How is that object attained? First by the parable itself and more particularly by the conclusion drawn from it. This conclusion contains the second of the features that are noteworthy: the words πόσφ μᾶλλον 'how much more', which represent the well-known Rabbinical formula *kal wāhōmer*, the argument *a fortiori*. Now this is the nerve of the whole matter. The 'how much more' is the transition from experience to faith. What in effect the parable does is to take human experience at its highest levels—in this case the natural affection of parent for child—and make this the jumping-off place for the adventure of faith. It says: take the best you know; God is all that—and more. And this procedure can be paralleled from other parables of this sort. Considered thus a parable shows at once just what are the demands which it makes on those who hear or read it. It requires first the insight which will perceive what really are the highest values in life; and then the faith to project these values into the unseen and eternal, to find in them a reflection of God himself.

It is along these lines that we may look with some con-

[1] The translation follows Westcott and Hort's text. For the present purpose the variants need not be considered, since they do not affect the argument one way or the other. The version in Mt. vii. 7–11 is to the same effect with minor variations, which again do not affect the present argument.

fidence for the solution of the difficulty raised by the perplexing passage Mk. iv. 2–20, particularly *vv.* 10–14. These verses present *the* problem so far as the parabolic teaching of Jesus is concerned and, so long as we hold to our common notion of parable, the problem is insoluble by any method short of the blue pencil.

And when he was alone, those who were about him along with the Twelve asked him (about) the parables. And he said to them: To you the secret of the Kingdom of God is given; but to those who are outside all things come in parables, that

Seeing they may see and not perceive
And hearing they may hear and not understand
Lest at any time they should turn and it be forgiven them.
And he said to them, You do not know this parable? and how will you know all the parables?[1]

Then follows the interpretation of the parable of the Sower. Later in the same chapter (*vv.* 33 f.) we read that 'in many such parables he spake the word to them as they were able to hear: and without a parable he did not speak to them, and privately he explained all things to his disciples'.[2]

This much-discussed passage begins by making a division: ὑμῖν...ἐκείνοις δὲ τοῖς ἔξω. The former class are already defined as οἱ περὶ αὐτὸν σὺν τοῖς δώδεκα, i.e. his followers[3] along with the Twelve. This we may take to

---

[1] καὶ ὅτε ἐγένετο κατὰ μόνας, ἠρώτων αὐτὸν οἱ περὶ αὐτὸν σὺν τοῖς δώδεκα τὰς παραβολάς. καὶ ἔλεγεν αὐτοῖς Ὑμῖν τὸ μυστήριον δέδοται τῆς βασιλείας τοῦ θεοῦ· ἐκείνοις δὲ τοῖς ἔξω ἐν παραβολαῖς τὰ πάντα γίνεται, ἵνα

βλέποντες βλέπωσι καὶ μὴ ἴδωσιν,
καὶ ἀκούοντες ἀκούωσι καὶ μὴ συνίωσιν,
μήποτε ἐπιστρέψωσιν καὶ ἀφεθῇ αὐτοῖς.

καὶ λέγει αὐτοῖς Οὐκ οἴδατε τὴν παραβολὴν ταύτην, καὶ πῶς πάσας τὰς παραβολὰς γνώσεσθε;

[2] καὶ τοιαύταις παραβολαῖς πολλαῖς ἐλάλει αὐτοῖς τὸν λόγον, καθὼς ἠδύναντο ἀκούειν· χωρὶς δὲ παραβολῆς οὐκ ἐλάλει αὐτοῖς, κατ' ἰδίαν δὲ τοῖς ἰδίοις μαθηταῖς ἐπέλυεν πάντα.

[3] This use of οἱ περί with acc. of the person is especially common in II Macc. in the sense of 'followers', 'partisans', 'retinue' of someone. The Syriac version (ed. de Lagarde) usually renders it by ܗܘܐ ܐܝܬ ܠܡܠܐ ܚܡܪ or ܕܝܠܗ. In Mk. iv. 10 the Old Syriac (ed. Burkitt) has ܬܠܡܝܕܘܗܝ simply for οἱ περὶ αὐτὸν σὺν τοῖς ιβ'. The Peshitta renders οἱ περὶ αὐτόν by ܗܢܘܢ ܕܥܡܗ.

mean those whom Jesus himself had called and a further
group of people who had attached themselves to him. With
this class is contrasted the other class who are outside. To
the inner circle is given the secret of the Kingdom of God,
to the others only parables. The most obvious question to
ask at this stage is how the two classes are divided: what is
it that places a man in the one class rather than the other?
In view of what has been said above on the nature of
parables, there can be only one answer to this question. It
is the man himself who places himself in one category or
another, and that simply by the response which he makes
to the parables. Those in whom religious insight and faith
are awakened by the hearing of parables press into the
inner circle for more. Once more the saying applies: 'To
him that hath shall be given'. The parable is in practice a
test: and the response of a man to it is what determines
whether he shall ever get beyond it to the secret of the
Kingdom.

We are now brought face to face with the chief difficulty of the passage: ἵνα βλέποντες... ἀφεθῇ αὐτοῖς. The
stumblingblock here is the ἵνα. As the text stands it can
only mean that the object, or at any rate the result, of
parabolic teaching is to prevent insight, understanding,
repentance, and forgiveness. "On any interpretation of
parable this is simply absurd." If parables had this object or
result, that in itself would be the strongest possible argument against making use of them, and would make it
impossible to imagine why Jesus should have employed
such a way of delivering his teaching. The solution of the
difficulty is to be sought in two directions. The first clue
is the parable of the Sower itself. Commentators have
pointed out that vv. 11, 12 are really an intrusion between
the parable and its interpretation: and the step from
'intrusion' to 'interpolation' is easily made. But the
intrusion of this saying is perfectly natural, if, as I believe,
the 'Sower' is a parable about parabolic teaching. 'The
sower sows the word' (v. 14): 'and in many such parables

he spake the word to them' (*v*. 33). Now the one thing that is clear in the parable is that the result of the sowing depends, not on the seed, but on the kind of ground in which it lodges. In other words the efficacy of parables depends, not on the parables, but on the character of the hearers. The object of sowing is not to prevent growth and fruition but rather to see whether anything will grow and give fruit. Granted this, it will follow that the inner circle in *v*. 11 represent the good ground which brings forth fruit; while those outside correspond to the ground which, for various reasons, produces nothing.

The second clue lies in the fact that the quotation from Is. vi. 9 f. ends with the words καὶ ἀφεθῇ αὐτοῖς, departing from LXX καὶ ἰάσομαι αὐτούς, and the Hebrew וְרָפָא לוֹ, and agreeing with the Targum וישתביק להון. This suggests that the last part of the quotation is given in what was the accepted version for synagogue purposes, a version which later was incorporated in the written Targum. It also stamps the saying as Palestinian in origin and thus creates a strong presumption in favour of its authenticity. If we now turn to the beginning of the quotation we find that in the Targum it runs as follows:[1]

ואמר איזיל ותימר לעמא הדין דשמעין משמע ולא מסתכלין וחזן מיחזא ולא ידעין :

And he said: Go and speak to this people who hear indeed and do not understand, and see indeed but do not know.

Turned into Greek this would be:

καὶ εἶπεν Πορεύθητι καὶ εἰπὸν τῷ λαῷ τούτῳ οἱ
ἀκούοντες ἀκούουσι καὶ οὐ συνίουσιν
καὶ βλέποντες βλέπουσιν καὶ οὐκ οἴδασιν.

Here again the quotation in Mark agrees with the Targum against both the Hebrew and the LXX in putting the verbs in the third person rather than the second. The chief point of difference is that the Marcan form gives final

[1] Ed. P. de Lagarde, p. 230.

clauses where the Targum has relative clauses. Now in Aramaic the particle ד, which is used in the Targum here, can be used to introduce either a relative or a final clause: it can mean either οἵ or ἵνα. The conclusion to be drawn is, I think, that the form in which the words were spoken by Jesus approximated to what we find in the Targum, and that the Marcan version rests on a misunderstanding of the Aramaic due mainly to the ambiguity of the particle ד. We may conjecture that what Jesus said was:

not in order that

To you is given the secret of the Kingdom of God; but all things come in parables to those outside who

> See indeed but do not know
> And hear indeed but do not understand
> Lest they should repent and receive forgiveness[1]

put the initiative on them.

where the last words would seem to mean: 'For if they did, they would repent and receive forgiveness'.

In support of this interpretation one other point may be mentioned. If the object of the quotation were to show that parabolic teaching was calculated to harden the hearts of the hearers, it is curious that the words in Is. vi. 9 f. which would most strongly suggest this are precisely those which are omitted in Mark: 'Make the heart of this people fat and make their ears heavy, and shut their eyes, lest they see with their eyes and hear with their ears, and understand with their heart'. These would surely be more apt to the purpose than what we actually have in Mark: and it seems to me significant that they are *not* quoted. With the omission of these words the conjunction דילמא is left in the air: and at once two possibilities emerge. Either it may be taken in the sense suggested above, in which case it will appear that the real cause of the blindness of those outside is that they do not wish to repent and be forgiven: 'a deadly self-satisfaction is the real hindrance to the efficacy of parabolic teaching.' Or, though this seems to me less probable, we may place a full stop after 'understand' and

[1] Cf. Is. xlii. 18–20.

take דילמא in its other sense of 'perhaps'. The last words
would then express a hope that the unresponsiveness of these
people will yet be overcome—'Perhaps they may yet repent'.

If it be objected that this interpretation of the passage
makes Jesus do violence to the Old Testament text, the
answer is that this passage is a piece of Haggadah and that
the passage from Isaiah is not cited as a proof-text but as an
illustration. Further, it is not cited in the original but in
the current Aramaic version, which, as we have already
seen, departs from the Hebrew in several important
particulars. And it may be added that Jewish practice
permitted and approved a much greater freedom in the
use of the Scriptures when quoted in Haggadah than
would be allowable when strict interpretation of the Law
was in question. Anyone who is familiar with the feats of
exegesis performed in the homiletic Midrashim will find
nothing startling in this case. We may conclude then that
the text as it stands in v. 12 rests on a misunderstanding of
what Jesus really said and that the true sense of his words
would be given by a text running somewhat as follows:

ἐκείνοις δὲ τοῖς ἔξω ἐν παραβολαῖς τὰ πάντα γίνεται, οἳ βλέποντες
βλέπουσι καὶ οὐκ οἴδασιν, καὶ ἀκούοντες ἀκούουσι καὶ οὐ συνίουσιν, μή
ποτε ἐπιστρέψωσιν καὶ ἀφεθῇ αὐτοῖς.[1]

The passage will then be in complete agreement with what
we learn elsewhere in the Synoptic Gospels about the nature
and object of teaching in parables. It will be clear that the
purpose of parables is not to harden the hearts of the
hearers, but that it is the hardness of heart of the hearers
that defeats the purpose of parables. The quotation from
Isaiah is not introduced by Jesus to explain the purpose of

---

[1] This represents an Aramaic original which would be somewhat as
follows: דחזן מיחזא ולא ידעין ושמעין משמע ולא מסתכלין דילמא יתובון
וישתביק להון :
which has been misunderstood as if it were: דיחזון מיחזא ולא ידעון וישמעון
משמע ולא יסתכלון דילמא יתובון וישתביק להון :
thus producing the text which stands in Mark.

teaching in parables, but to illustrate what is meant by `οἱ ἔξω`: it is in fact a definition of the sort of character which prevents a man from becoming one of those to whom the secret of the Kingdom is given, a description in language borrowed from the Jewish Bible of those people who did not produce the things for which Jesus was constantly seeking—insight, repentance, and faith.

(*c*) *Parables which combine the characteristics of both* (*a*) *and* (*b*).

There remain, in addition to the kinds of parable discussed above under (*a*) and (*b*), a number of parables which combine in the one story an ethical type and a principle of the divine government. This class includes some of the elaborate examples such as: the Vineyard (Mk); the Pounds (Talents) (Q); the Unmerciful Steward (M); the Unfruitful Fig Tree, the Great Feast, the Prodigal Son (L). In these cases some feature of God's dealings is compared or contrasted with typical human conduct. In the parable of the Prodigal Son the divine attitude to the repentant sinner is contrasted with the human in the figures of the father and the elder brother respectively. In the parable of the Vineyard God's long forbearance is contrasted with human obstinacy and unresponsiveness. It is in such cases as these that the art of making parables reaches its highest point, and the parable itself makes its biggest appeal, speaking both to the moral and the religious side of human nature, and bringing into one vivid picture the deepest needs and highest hopes of men and women, and their complete satisfaction in God.

So we can answer the two questions proposed at the beginning of this section. A parable is a picture in words of some piece of human experience, actual or imagined. As such it is a work of art. Further, this picture portrays either an ethical type for our admiration or reprobation, or some principle of the rule of God in the world, or it does both things at once. That is to say it embodies the moral insight and the religious experience of its creator. Its object is to awaken these things in those to whom it is addressed, to pierce through the husk of self-satisfaction and worldly cares and interests to the essential man, to arouse the slumbering conscience, to turn the affections from things that change and pass to things that have the quality of eternity, to induce repentance and faith. In actual working, then, every true parable is a call to a better life and a deeper trust in God, which things are but the Godward and manward sides of a true religion, the obverse and reverse of the one medal. For its effectiveness the parable requires a certain responsiveness on the part of those who hear it: and this response, in practice, separates those who may go farther from the others who make no advance. The parable becomes a kind of test which determines who shall be disciples.

Such is the nature of the parable as we find it in the teaching of Jesus, and such are the principles on which he made use of parabolic teaching. He made many parables, long and short, in many moods, addressed to all kinds of people; scribes and lawyers, his own disciples, the great multitudes. Yet all are governed by a single purpose—to show, directly or indirectly, what God is and what man may become, and to show these things in a way that will reach men's hearts if it is possible to reach them at all. And, when we come to think of it, the greatest and most effective parable of them all is his own life.

DETACHED NOTE A

On Mt. xii. 28; Lk. xi. 20 (Q)

Mt. xii. 28: εἰ δὲ ἐν πνεύματι θεοῦ ἐγὼ ἐκβάλλω τὰ δαιμόνια, ἄρα ἔφθασεν ἐφ᾿ ὑμᾶς ἡ βασιλεία τοῦ θεοῦ.

Lk. xi. 20. The same with the substitution of δακτύλῳ for πνεύματι.

This case first excites interest on account of this one striking difference in the midst of a word-for-word agreement between the two Evangelists. The problem is to account for the difference and to determine which of the two variants is to be regarded as the original. What stood in the document which St Matthew and St Luke are obviously copying here? Instinctively one looks first for a possible Aramaic original which might be mistranslated; but no such word presents itself: and we have to explore the second possibility, that one or other of the Evangelists has revised the Greek text which lay before him. The result of this enquiry is to make it practically certain that the original reading is δακτύλῳ and that πνεύματι in Matthew is an editorial modification. For this conclusion the following reasons may be advanced:

(a) πνεῦμα is a favourite word with St Luke. If it stood in the text of Q which lay before him, it is difficult to see why he should have altered it.[1]

(b) A reason—the desire to remove an anthropomorphism—can be suggested for the change of δακτύλῳ to πνεύματι; but no really convincing reason can be given for the opposite change.

(c) The reading δακτύλῳ involves a direct reference to Ex. viii. 15 in the Hebrew. In Ex. viii the narrative is occupied with the plagues of Egypt. Concerning the first two plagues we are told that the magicians by their enchantments were able to duplicate them; the third plague however proved to be beyond their power. 'And the magicians did so with their enchantments to bring forth lice, but they could not: and there were lice upon man, and upon beast. Then the magicians said unto Pharaoh, This is the finger of God.' Commenting on this passage the Midrash (*Ex. R.* § 10, end) remarks: 'When the magicians saw that they could not produce the lice, they

---

[1] The remarks of Harnack on this point (*Sprüche und Reden Jesu*, p. 20) are not convincing.

recognised immediately that the happenings (the plagues) were the work of God and not the work of demons'. What is meant here is plain enough. The magicians had reproduced two of the miracles successfully and that by the agency of demons.[1] There came a point, however, when the demons could not do any more: and the magicians were constrained to recognise the finger of God in the matter. Their point of view is perfectly simple: 'This thing is impossible to the demons, therefore it must be the work of God'. The argument by which Jesus refutes the charge of being in league with Beelzebub to cast out the demons, runs the same course. He first shows that the thing which he is doing is something which demons cannot reasonably be expected to do. That is the obvious sense of the parable of the Divided Kingdom and the Divided House. Dog does not eat dog. If then the demons are out of the question, his opponents will be constrained to say as the Egyptian magicians said: אצבע אלהים הוא—it is the finger of God. And if it is the finger of God, then ἔφθασεν ἐφ᾽ ὑμᾶς ἡ βασιλεία τοῦ θεοῦ.

These considerations seem to me to be conclusive in favour of the originality of the Lucan version of the saying: and the words δακτύλῳ θεοῦ should be printed in the Greek text in the special type reserved for quotations from the Old Testament.

The passage is also interesting as showing that our Lord's acquaintance with the Hebrew Bible was not only wide, as has been noted above (pp. 47 ff.), but also very intimate and detailed; and that so far as the specialised knowledge of the sacred text was concerned he was well able to meet the scholars on their own ground.

DETACHED NOTE B

The Parable of the Wedding Feast (Mt. xxii. 1–14)

It has been pointed out already[2] that this passage is composite, verses 1–10 forming one parable, and 11–14 the conclusion of another whose beginning has been lost. In the present note I wish to draw attention to some peculiarities of the former passage.

[1] Cf. Blau, *Das Altjüdische Zauberwesen*[2], p. 15.
[2] See above, p. 35 n. 3.

First it has certain points of contact with the parable of the Great Feast in Lk. xiv. 16–24. The matter common to the two versions may be summarised as follows: A person makes a feast and issues invitations. When the feast is ready he sends his servant (Mt servants) to tell the guests that the feast is ready. The guests however decline to come, having business elsewhere. Thereupon the host, being justly annoyed, sends out to bring in all and sundry and the house is filled.

Now this skeleton outline is a single complete story in itself, and all that is added to it in the Lucan version is just a filling in of detail whereby the story may be made more vivid and lifelike. In the account in Matthew, however, this is not the case. There a number of new features are introduced, which have no parallel in Luke, which moreover are not essential to the narrative at all. The feast is a wedding feast given by a king for his son. After the guests have gone about their own affairs 'the remainder' set about the king's servants, maltreat and kill them. The king is angry and sends his armies, destroys those murderers and burns their city. In the ordinary way we might explain these phenomena as due to the Matthaean version of the parable having been transmitted along a different line of tradition from the Lucan; but this explanation will not answer in the present case for the following reasons:

(*a*) The version of the parable in Matthew agrees in all essentials with that in Luke. It is not a different version so much as an abbreviation of the same story which is given fully in Luke.

(*b*) The details which are peculiar to Matthew are not merely unessential to the story: they are a positive intrusion, and in some cases where they enter they make nonsense of the parable. The most glaring instance is in *v.* 7 where the king furnishes a military expedition and executes summary vengeance on the murderers and their city. Then (*v.* 8) as if nothing had happened he resumes the arrangements for the feast. The feast was ready in *v.* 4 and it is still ready in *v.* 8, though during the interval the servants have been murdered, an army mobilised, and military operations carried out against the murderers. Again who are οἱ λοιποί in *v.* 6? They appear from nowhere merely for the purpose of maltreating and slaying the messengers. Further, it is noteworthy that two messages are sent to the guests, against one in Luke: and that, on the other hand, the twofold mission of the servants in Luke to bring the people from the streets is reduced in Matthew to a single errand.

We conclude that the extra items introduced into the Matthaean version have nothing to do with the parable at all. The question then arises: Are they editorial additions? This is the opinion of Wellhausen with regard to *vv.* 6, 7, which he takes to have been written after A.D. 70 and to refer to the destruction of Jerusalem. There is, however, another possibility, which is at least worth considering: that the parable in Matthew is a conflation of the parable of the Great Feast with another parable now lost. We may gather from what we have in Matthew the rough outline of this second story. It concerns a king who made a marriage feast for his son. He sends servants to call the guests to the feast. The guests instead of responding to the invitation turn on the messengers, maltreat and kill them. Then the king sends out his armies and visits the guilty with exemplary punishments. If this reconstruction is correct, it at once appears that we have here the remains of a parable akin to that of the Vineyard which immediately precedes this passage in Matthew.[1]

Two points may be mentioned which favour such a hypothesis and carry it still farther: (a) the introductory formula is remarkable: καὶ ἀποκριθεὶς ὁ Ἰησοῦς πάλιν εἶπεν ἐν παραβολαῖς αὐτοῖς λέγων. As has been noted above εἶπεν ἐν παραβολαῖς αὐτοῖς is a phrase which is characteristic of Mark. What we should expect from Matthew would be an introduction like ἄλλην παραβολὴν ἀκούσατε or ἄλλην παραβολὴν παρέθηκεν αὐτοῖς. The presence of this typical Marcan formula prompts the conjecture—admittedly a rash one—that some such parable as this may have stood originally in Mark and still have been there when the other two Synoptic Gospels were written. In that case St Matthew will have conflated it with the parable of the Great Feast: St Luke on the other hand will, according to his usual custom, have omitted it, seeing that he already had the parable of the Great Feast in another context. We know that the second Gospel did as a matter of fact suffer mutilation at the end; and it is not outside the bounds of possibility that a portion may have been lost at this point. The parable of the Vineyard in Mark certainly ends very abruptly with the quotation from Ps. cxviii. 22 f., the gap being filled differently in Matthew and Luke.

[1] Cf. Harnack, *Sprüche und Reden Jesu*, p. 83. His opinion is that St Matthew has conflated a parable akin to that of the Vineyard with the parable of the Great Feast. It should be added that the argument of the present note was completely worked out before I was aware of Harnack's conclusion.

(*b*) However this may be, there is the fact that it was a favourite device of Jesus to duplicate sayings. Attention has been drawn to this above:[1] and it would not be at all surprising that the parable of the Vineyard should have a companion piece, conveying the same lesson in a different form.

In matters of this sort certainty is probably not attainable; but the hypothesis outlined above seems worth examining, in view of what we know otherwise about the tendency of Matthew to conflate sources.

[1] Pp. 54 ff. Cf. also an essay by v. Dobschütz: *Paarung u. Dreiung in der Evangelischen Überlieferung* in the Heinrici *Festschrift*.

PART II

THE CONTENTS OF THE TEACHING

Ch 4 — God is Father in O.T. — but not in physical sense. Israel is His son by adoption — He chose her — & thus real father who expects devotion & obedience in return for care & love. Former in Greek! later Hebrew? No Three nations failure — moves from national — to personal remnant. His children: not those who ought to obey, but those who do. To Jesus it was not adoption, but a sacred & solemn relationship. Spoken A.C. & only to disciples, only remnant would understand. ∴ the truth is only for those who experience it.

Chapter IV

GOD AS FATHER

'THAT was not first which is spiritual, but that which is natural: and afterwards that which is spiritual.' The notion of a divine parentage for nations, clans, or individuals, was common enough in the ancient world, and that not merely as figure of speech but as a statement of physical fact. Clans and nations, families and individuals traced their descent back to a divine ancestor, who was supposed to be in literal truth their progenitor. Whether or not this crude idea was ever entertained by the Semitic peoples in general or by the Hebrews in particular[1], it is already a more spiritual conception which meets us in the Old Testament. The few passages where a divine parentage might be understood in the physical sense are all cases where heathen or idolatrous cults are in question.[2] The paternal relation of Jehovah to Israel is not at all conceived in physical terms.[3]

When once the crude idea of physical generation has been put on one side, the idea that God is the Father of a nation or an individual may be conceived in two ways, corresponding to the two aspects of the relation of father to

[1] The evidence for the existence of this belief among the Semitic peoples is collected by Robertson Smith: *Rel. Sem.* (1894), Lecture II, especially pp. 39–51. He draws from it the conclusion stated above. The evidence is re-examined by Lagrange (*Études sur les Religions Sémitiques* (1903), pp. 109–118), who is not prepared to accept the conclusions of Robertson Smith with regard to the Semitic peoples, but maintains that 'les noms religieux baby-loniens à frappe individuelle remontent à la plus haute antiquité que nous puissions atteindre, et qu'ils sont un indice sérieux que la parenté n'était pas entendue dans le sens naturel' (p. 118). Cf. also E. Meyer, *Ursprung und Anfänge des Christentums*, II. 437 f., G. R. Driver in *The Psalmists*, pp. 156, 161.

[2] Num. xxi. 29: Moabites as sons and daughters of Chemosh; Jer. ii. 27: idolaters say to a stock, 'Thou art my father', and to a stone, 'Thou hast brought me forth'; Mal. ii. 11: a heathen woman is called 'the daughter of a strange god'.

[3] Cf. Weiss-Bousset in *Die Schriften des N.T.*,[3] i. 76 f.; Dalman, *Words of Jesus*, pp. 272 f.

Jesus thought of God as Father thru blood.
Jesus! Paul – thru His spiritual Covenant! adoption

child in the human sphere, which we call <u>paternity</u> and fatherhood. That is to say, the earthly father may be thought of primarily as the person responsible for the existence of his child or as responsible for the welfare of the child: in the former case the link between father and son is one of <u>origin</u>, the tie is the natural tie of blood; in the latter the link is one of mutual responsibilities and obligations, the tie is the moral tie of respect and affection. Ideally of course these two sides co-exist; but it is not necessary that they should do so in every case. There are fathers—unnatural ones—whose only claim to the title is the biological; as there are adoptive fathers who fulfil all the moral obligations of fatherhood to children with whom they have no direct blood tie at all. Thus the conception of fatherhood, which we entertain, will depend on which of these two aspects we put in the foreground: and this holds both of our ideas of earthly fatherhood and heavenly. When the word 'Father' is used as a name for God, it means primarily either that God is the *fons et origo* of human life, the Father of our spirits, or that he watches over and cares for men and women in a manner analogous to the parental care of a good earthly father. The former is typical of <u>Greek</u> thought, the latter is characteristic of Hebrew, Jewish, and Christian utterances.

Thus in the *Timaeus* (28 c), Plato speaking of God says, 'To find the maker and father of this universe is a hard task; and, when you have found him, it is impossible to speak of him before all people'.[1] With this we may compare the speech recorded in Acts xvii, which might almost be taken as a sermon with the passage from Plato as its text. This address, as far as the end of *v.* 29 at any rate, is obviously designed to discover a *point d'appui* for the Gospel message in Greek modes of thought: and it also has a quotation, this time from the poet <u>Aratus of Soli</u> (*c.* 270 B.C.): τοῦ γὰρ καὶ γένος ἐσμέν—'For we also are his off-

It's in the 2nd sense that every O.T. sees God the Father.

IMPt / God as Cov. maker.

yes – so in our mind when we speak of God's 'Fatherhood'.

IU

Acts 17

---

[1] This passage is translated and discussed by Burnet, *Greek Philosophy*, Pt I, *Thales to Plato*, pp. 337 f.

spring'. So also in the Hymn to Zeus by Cleanthes (300–220 B.C.) we find ἐκ σοῦ γὰρ γένος ἐσμέν. In such passages as these God is thought of as Father in the sense that he is the origin of all things, including human life; in him we live and move and have our being. The crude myth of physical generation is passed over, and in its place we have a philosophical theory which makes God not the first ancestor of human beings but the ultimate ground of their existence. This mode of thought can easily pass, and often does, into Pantheism: and the transition is easy to make unless, along with the conception of the Fatherhood of God as an explanation of the origin of things and people, there is also held the conception of that Fatherhood as a moral tie, a fatherly love and care on the one side and a filial devotion and obedience on the other.

It is this latter aspect of the divine Fatherhood which is most strongly emphasised in Hebrew, Jewish, and Christian thought. In the Old Testament, God is the Father of Israel in the sense that he is the founder and creator of the nation (Deut. xxxii. 6; Is. lxiii. 16; Mal. ii. 10). This creation, however, is to be understood in a different sense from that in the *Timaeus*. The reference in the O.T. is to a particular historical event in the deliverance of the people from Egypt. Thus the act by which Jehovah becomes the Father of Israel is to be thought of as adoption rather than creation. He is the creator of all the peoples; but Israel is in a special sense his son (Hos. xi. 1), even his firstborn (Ex. iv. 22; Jer. xxxi. 9). This initial act, by which Jehovah becomes in the special sense the Father of Israel, is the beginning of a long history of his dealings with the nation. By these dealings he clearly shows himself as Father in the second sense. His constant care for Israel is likened to the nurture and upbringing of a child by his father (Deut. i. 31; viii. 5; Is. i. 2). On the part of Israel it is expected that this divine favour will find a response in filial love and obedience (Deut. xiv. 1; Jer. iii. 19; Mal. i. 6); and the failure of Israel as a whole to produce these answering

tokens leads eventually to a certain restriction of the idea
of God's Fatherhood. God comes to be the Father of the
God-fearing and the righteous in Israel rather than of
Israel as a whole (Ps. ciii. 13; Mal. iii. 17). This change is
most marked in the post-canonical literature (Wisd. Sol. ii.
16, 18; v. 5; Jub. i. 24 f.; Ps. Sol. xiii. 8; xvii. 30; xviii. 4);
and while it is in one way a restriction of the Fatherhood of
God, it yet contains the germ of a greater universality.
The relation is in process of passing from the national and
particular to become something individual and universal.[1]
The line of development is: Israel—the righteous in
Israel—the righteous anywhere; and the extent to which
the relation had already become a personal one before the
Christian era is shown by such a mode of address to God as
Ecclus. xxiii. 1—κύριε, πάτερ καὶ δέσποτα ζωῆς μου,
repeated in xxiii. 4 with the substitution of θεέ for δέσποτα.[2]

In early Judaism[3] we find the Fatherhood of God
prominent in doctrine and piety: it is a common theme of
Rabbinic teaching, and 'Father' is a common mode of
address in prayer. One of the products of Jewish piety in
this period is the name 'Father in heaven' for God, a
phrase which also meets us in Matthew. This name is
always used in a personal way, 'Our Father who is in
heaven' or with some other possessive pronoun.[4] In the
oldest prayers in the Jewish liturgy 'Our Father' is found
as a form of address to God; for example in the Ahabah
prayer, which according to the late Dr Abrahams probably
belonged already to the service of the Temple (before
A.D. 70), we have the petition: 'Our Father, our King,...
be gracious unto us and teach us. Our Father, merciful
Father, ever compassionate, have mercy upon us'.[5]

[1] Cf. Schürer, G.J.V.[4] II. 646 ff. 'Der ethische Faktor tritt in den Vorder-
grund und der nationale zurück'.
[2] Cf. III Macc. vi. 2–4, 8; Wisd. ii. 16.
[3] Cf. G. F. Moore, Judaism, II. 201–211; A. Lukyn Williams in J.T.S. Oct.
1929, pp. 42–47.
[4] Moore, op. cit. II. 202.
[5] Singer, Authorised Daily Prayer Book, p. 39. Abrahams, Companion to the
Daily Prayer Book, p. xlix.

In the Rabbinical literature the Fatherhood of God is
conceived as an ethical relation between God and Israel:
and just as in the Old Testament we find a wider and a
narrower view, so in the teaching of the Rabbis we find
those who maintain that all Israelites are the sons of God—
foolish sons, untrustworthy sons, vicious sons maybe, yet
nevertheless sons;[1] and those who hold that sonship is in
some way conditioned by the character of the individual
or the nation.[2] Where the whole of the Hebrew Bible was
accepted as the standard of faith and duty, it was possible
to find arguments and proof-texts for either view.

Many fine and noble thoughts of the Rabbis centre
round the doctrine of the Fatherhood and all that it implies of duty and privilege. The historic deliverances of
Israel by God are like the watchful care of a Father: and so
in times of difficulty and even of despair, like those that
followed the destruction of the Temple, there is but one
answer to the question: whom have we to lean upon?—
Our Father who is in heaven.[3] On man's side again
filial duty and love are things to be emphasised. The will
of God is the will of the Father: 'Be strong as a leopard and
swift as an eagle and fleet as a gazelle and brave as a lion to
do the will of thy Father who is in heaven'.[4] When Jews
are persecuted and even put to death for keeping the Law,
their sacrifice makes them beloved by their Father in
heaven. When they repent it is to their Father that they
return. Such utterances as these stand in need of no commendation: they commend themselves.

Enough has been said to show that when Jesus spoke of
God as Father he was not presenting a new and revolu-
tionary doctrine for men's acceptance; but rather taking
up into his teaching something that had been part of the
faith of prophets, psalmists, and sages for centuries before:
and something, it must be added, which has carried on an

[1] E.g. R. Meir.
[2] R. Judah b. Ilai. Cf. Moore, *op. cit.* II. 203.
[3] E.g. *Soṭa*, ix. 15 (R. Eliezer, c. A.D. 90).
[4] R. Judah b. Tema, *Aboth*, v. 20.

independent existence in Judaism up to the present day.
Yet, although the doctrine was neither a novel thing nor
yet peculiar to Christianity, it did become one of the central
things in the new faith and that at a very early date. It has
been well said that 'a religion may call God by several
names, but there are titles for God without which it would
not be itself, and for Christianity the supreme title is that of
"Father"'.[1] Moreover, one has only to read the New
Testament to realise that 'the Father' was not a mere
article in a creed or just a title for God, but a burning
conviction, a spiritual experience which gave new meaning
and value to life, and brought new peace and joy to
human hearts. Such a passage as Rom. viii. 12–39 reveals
in a way that cannot be mistaken the transforming power
of this vision of God as our Father. St Paul writes here—
and elsewhere—as a new man to new men living in a new
world. The question is at once posed: What did Jesus do to
this old belief in the Fatherhood of God to give it such
power and influence over the lives of men? For an answer
to this question we turn first to the use of the name
'Father' for God in the teaching. The occurrences of the
word are shown in the following tables. The letters in
brackets indicate the nature of the audience: D = disciples, G = the general public, P means that the word is
used in dispute with opponents; Pr = prayer, and S
indicates that the occurrence is in the Sermon on the
Mount (Mt) or the Sermon on the Plain (Lk).

Mark

viii. 38 (D + G) = Mt. xvi. 27 (D) = Lk. ix. 26 (D + G):
His Father (of the Son of Man).
xi. 25 (D); cf. Mt. vi. 14 (S):
Your Father in heaven.
xiii. 32 (D) = Mt. xxiv. 36 (D):
The Father.
xiv. 36 (Pr) = Mt. xxvi. 39 (Pr) = Lk. xxii. 42 (Pr):
Abba, Father (Mt: my Father; Lk: Father).

Mk. xi. 26 is rejected on textual grounds.

[1] J. Moffatt, *The Theology of the Gospels*, p. 99.

In Mark all the cases of the use of the name 'Father' for))
God fall after Peter's Confession. One is in prayer to God,
two are in sayings addressed to the disciples, and the fourth
case is in a saying addressed primarily to the disciples,
though others are present.

Q (Streeter's reconstruction)

LUKE vi. 35 (S):	MATTHEW v. 45 (S):
The Most High (ὕψιστος).	Your Father in heaven.
vi. 36 (S):	v. 48 (S):
Your Father.	Your heavenly Father.
x. 21 (Pr):	xi. 25 f. (Pr):
Father (twice).	Father (twice).
x. 22 (D):	xi. 27 (D):
My Father.	My Father.
x. 22 (D):	xi. 27 (D):
The Father (twice).	The Father (twice).
xi. 13 (D):	vii. 11 (S):
The Father.	Your Father in heaven.
xii. 6 (D):	x. 29 (D):
God.	Your Father.
xii. 8 (D):	x. 32 (D):
The Angels of God.	My Father in heaven.
xii. 9 (D):	x. 33 (D):
The Angels of God.	My Father in heaven.
xii. 12 (D):	x. 20 (D):
The Holy Spirit.	The Spirit of your Father.
xii. 24 (D):	vi. 26 (S);
God.	Your heavenly Father.
xii. 30 (D):	vi. 32 (S):
Your Father.	Your heavenly Father.
xii. 32 (D):	No parallel in Mt.
Your Father.	
——	? vii. 21 (S):
	My Father in heaven.
	(cf. Lk. vi. 46).

In eight cases Matthew and Luke agree in having the word
'Father'. Luke never has it against Matthew; but in six
instances Matthew has the word where Luke in the parallel
has some other expression. All of these are dealt with by

Harnack[1] except Lk. xii. 12: Mt. x. 20; and the only case
in which he prefers the Matthaean reading to the Lucan is
Mt. v. 45: Lk. vi. 35. A decision in such cases as these is a
difficult and delicate matter; but a comparison of Mt. xii.
50 with Mk. iii. 35; Mt. xx. 23 with Mk. x. 40; Mt. xxvi.
29 with Mk. xiv. 25 inclines one to prefer the readings in
Luke to those in Matthew. It is evident that 'Father',
'heavenly Father', and especially 'Father in heaven', are
favourite words with the First Evangelist, and that he was
apt to insert them in his text even when some other expression was used in his sources. We may therefore confine
ourselves to those passages where the reading 'Father' is
confirmed by Luke. Of these one occurs in the Lucan
Sermon (Lk. vi. 36), two are in a prayer (Lk. x. 21 *bis*), the
remaining five examples (Lk. x. 22 *ter*; xi. 13, xii. 30) are
all in D contexts. Lk. xii. 32 is D and Mt. vii. 21 is in the
Sermon on the Mount. Further, if we accept the Lucan
order of Q matter as the original order, all the cases except
one (Lk. vi. 36: S)[2] occur after Peter's Confession, thus
agreeing with what we find in Mark. This conclusion is
confirmed if I am right in supposing that the passage
Lk. x. 21 f. dates from that event. Our two primary
authorities Mk and Q thus agree in their testimony that
Jesus speaks of 'the Father' or 'my Father' or 'your
Father' only in his prayers or in conversation with his
disciples, and that only in the period subsequent to Peter's
Confession. This curious fact calls for explanation which
will be attempted later in this chapter. We may now turn
to our other two sources.

M

Mt. v. 16 (S): Your Father in heaven (cf. Lk. xi. 33: G).
vi. 1 (S): Your Father in heaven.
vi. 4, 6 (S): Thy Father who sees in secret.
vi. 6 (S): Thy Father in secret.
vi. 8 (S): Your Father (cf. Lk. xii. 30: D = Mt. vi. 32: Q).

---

[1] *Sprüche u. Reden Jesu* (1907).
[2] In a composite discourse.

vi. 9 (S) : Our Father in heaven (cf. Lk. xi. 2 : D; 'Father': L).
vi. 14 (S) : Your heavenly Father (cf. Mk. xi. 25: D).
vi. 15 (S) : Your Father.
vi. 18 (S) : Thy Father in secret.
vi. 18 (S) : Thy Father who sees in secret.
xiii. 43 (D) : The Kingdom of their Father.
xv. 13 (D) : My heavenly Father.
xvi. 17 (D) : My Father in heaven.
xviii. 10 (D) : My Father in heaven.
xviii. 14 (D) : My Father in heaven.
xviii. 19 (D) : My Father in heaven.
xviii. 35 (D) : My heavenly Father.
xxiii. 9 (D) : One is your Father, the heavenly.
xxv. 34 (D) : Blessed of my Father.
xxv. [41 (D) : My Father (but the text is very doubtful)].
xxvi. 42 (Pr) : My Father (cf. Mk. xiv. 36 (Pr) and parallels).
xxvi. 53 (D) : My Father.
xxviii. 19 (D) : The Father.[1]

The first thing that strikes us in this table is that almost half of the cases in M are in the Sermon on the Mount: and as that is a composite discourse, we are left very largely in the dark as to where the sayings should properly be placed in the teaching. In one or two instances, however, we have a control over Matthew by the fact that a similar saying occurs in Mark or Luke: and in those cases we find that the non-Matthaean context is generally D (the only exception is Lk. xi. 33, not a close parallel) and always later than Peter's Confession. Mt. xiii. 43 is suspect as soon as we compare Mt. xxvi. 29 with Mk. xiv. 25 and observe that 'the Kingdom of my Father' in Matthew is an editorial modification of 'the Kingdom of God' in Mark. This may well be the case here also. Mt. xv. 12–14 is an anecdote which has been inserted in its present place by St Matthew. As it stands it is in the middle of a passage from Mark where it merely serves to interrupt the story. It may belong anywhere. The remaining instances of the word in M conform to the rule established for Mk and Q : they are all spoken

---

[1] It is noteworthy that in M '*my* Father' belongs to the period after Peter's Confession.

either in prayer or to the disciples: and they all occur after Peter's Confession.

There remain three cases in Matthew: xii. 50; xx. 23; xxvi. 29. These are all editorial modifications of what is given in Mark, and should be left out of account altogether. The symbol for them is not M but R<small>MT</small>.

L

Lk. ii. 49 (Parents): My Father.
xi. 2 (D): Father (cf. Mt. vi. 9).
xxii. 29 (D): My Father.
xxiii. 34 (Pr): Father.
xxiii. 46 (Pr) · Father.
xxiv. 49 (D): My Father.

These again, with the exception of ii. 49, conform to the rule.

The result of this detailed examination of all four sources is to justify the general conclusion, suggested by Mk and Q, that Jesus rarely if ever spoke directly of God as Father except to his disciples and that he began to speak to them in this way only after Peter's Confession. It can hardly be an accident that three of our four sources are practically unanimous on these two points: and that the fourth (M) is open on other grounds to grave suspicion in the cases where it offers facts at variance with this conclusion. If the conclusion is, as I believe, correct, it is a matter that calls urgently for explanation.

In order, however, to complete the present survey it is necessary to consider some cases where the doctrine of the Fatherhood of God is implied rather than expressly stated: namely, the four parables Mk. xii. 1–11; Mt. vii. 9 f. = Lk. xi. 11 f. (Q); Mt. xxi. 28–31 (M); and Lk. xv. 11–32 (L). All these are subsequent to Peter's Confession. That from Q is the parable of the Son asking his Father for Bread: and the verses immediately preceding and following show how 'father' in the parable is to be understood. This parable is addressed to the disciples, according to Luke.

The other three are all in polemical passages, and in all it is clear that the father in the parable is intended to represent God. Further, two of them emphasise two points which are favourite themes in the teaching of the Rabbis[1]—the duty of filial obedience to God and God's readiness to forgive the repentant sinner. In both, moreover, there is an accusation express or implied that Jesus found his opponents unwilling or unable to live up to their own standards. In the parable of the Two Sons the rebuke is open: in the Prodigal Son the elder brother is brought in as a type of the kind of Pharisaism which Jesus condemns, in contrast to the picture of God presented by the father in the parable. The parable of the Vineyard will be dealt with later.

Such are the facts. We have now to attempt to estimate their significance. It is clear at the outset that the dominating place taken by the doctrine of the Fatherhood of God in Christian thought and faith is due not so much to what is directly given by the Synoptic Gospels as to what is found in other books of the New Testament. This can be shown most easily by statistics.

I. *Use of the name 'Father' for God by Jesus.*

Mk 4; Q 8 or 9; M 23 at the outside; L 6; John 107.

II. *Use of the name in other books of the N.T.*

Acts 3; Pauline Epistles 39; Pastoral Epistles 3; Hebrews 2; James 3; I Peter 3; II Peter 1; I and II John 16; Jude 1; Revelation 4.

It is the Johannine writings primarily which have made 'Father' the natural name of God for Christian people. The Sermon on the Mount, too, with seventeen cases of the word concentrated in three chapters—and those much read—has also had a large influence in making the idea of God's Fatherhood familiar. The comparatively high figure for the Pauline Epistles is less striking when we consider their bulk in comparison with, say, I and II John. The New Testament writings which put the Fatherhood of

[1] See above, p. 93.

God into the forefront of the Christian message are the
Gospels of Matthew and John and the Johannine Epistles.
On the other hand, the idea *is* present in the other books
and in the teaching of Jesus as given by our four sources in
the Synoptic Gospels.

Now we find that in the seven cases where Matthew has
the word 'Father' for God in matter taken from Mark,
three of them are cases where he has substituted 'Father'
for another expression in Mk. The same thing holds for Q.
In six cases out of fourteen the name Father seems not to
be taken from Q, but substituted in Matthew for something
else in Q. The tendency of the First Evangelist is thus to
emphasise the doctrine even at the expense of literal
accuracy in reporting the sayings of Jesus. We see the same
tendency operating much more powerfully in John. The
conclusion to be drawn is that these writers were en-
deavouring to bring into the foreground something which
they perceived to be of far more vital import than would
appear from such documents as Mk and Q. If Mk and Q
be taken as the standard by which other witnesses are to be
judged, then it must be admitted that Matthew and John
are abnormal in their use of the name 'Father'. Two lines
of explanation are possible. Either the constant emphasis
on the divine Fatherhood is an intrusion, an addition of
extraneous matter to the genuine teaching of Jesus; or it is
an attempt to bring out clearly what appeared to these
writers to be of the essence of the Gospel. The fact that the
Fatherhood of God is attested as an essential element in the
Gospel by all the New Testament documents compels us to
adopt the latter alternative. Matthew and John do not
introduce, so far as the Fatherhood of God is concerned, a
new doctrine; they rather proclaim from the housetops
what, in the more primitive documents, is whispered in the
ear. We may, if we choose, call it interpretation rather
than strict history, or exaggeration of one feature in the
teaching of Jesus; but it is interpretation of something that
is given and exaggeration of something real.

If this be the true explanation of the facts, the conclusion follows that in the Early Church it was recognised
that 'the Father' meant a great deal more in the life and
teaching of Jesus than would appear from the limited use
of the name in Mk and Q. We may thus assume as a
working hypothesis that there is, so to speak, artistic
justification for the procedure followed in Matthew and
John, while maintaining that Mk and Q are the more
accurate records from the point of view of scientific
history. The question then becomes one of finding an
explanation of the reticence of Jesus on a matter of vital
importance. Matthew and John suggest, rightly as I think,
that the Fatherhood of God is one of the keys to the Gospel:
our primary authorities, Mk and Q, again I think rightly,
show on the part of Jesus a disinclination to speak of the
matter at all except during the latest period of the ministry,
and then only to a limited circle of hearers. Is there any
explanation which will cover both sets of facts?

Put in the bluntest form: Why this extraordinary reserve
on the part of Jesus in speaking about what was after
all a theological commonplace? the question practically
answers itself. The Fatherhood of God was not a theological
commonplace for Jesus. We can only begin to understand
what it was for him when we realise that his true humanity
involved a genuine religious experience, that his temptations
or his prayers were as real as ours. It is, unfortunately, very
easy to lose sight of this vitally important fact. We are so
accustomed, and rightly, to make Jesus the object of
religion that we become apt to forget that in our earliest
records he is portrayed not as the object of religion but as a
religious man. Or, at another extreme, we think of him as
a religious teacher, a purveyor of sound religious and moral
instruction to the world at large. As if the things that he
really desired to impart could be conveyed in the form of
dissertations on theology and ethics! On the one view,
the Fatherhood of God becomes a special metaphysical
relation between God and Jesus, and the issue of the matter

Was to Jesus not a teacher but an experience of God. He "God as Father

is in centuries of theological dispute, much of it logomachy of the barrenest kind. On the other view, we reduce the Fatherhood to a theological commonplace, stated perhaps more eloquently or more forcibly by Jesus than by other people, but essentially nothing more than could be got from the Jewish teachers. We create difficulties for ourselves by reading into the words of Jesus the dogmatic theories of a later age or by reducing his burning thoughts to the dead level of average religious ideas.

But these two ways of dealing with the Fatherhood of God in the teaching of Jesus do not exhaust the possibilities of interpretation; nor, indeed, is either of them a probable way of discovering what 'the Father' meant to him. There is yet another way of approaching these sayings, and one which will bear a good deal of exploration. We know from the Synoptic record that Jesus prayed to God and that in the Garden of Gethsemane he prayed with the most intense earnestness. These facts alone are sufficient to justify us in the belief that he passed through a religious experience comparable in kind with that of men and women: and if that belief be well founded the question at once arises whether the Fatherhood of God was not the core of the experience. The hypothesis to be considered is then somewhat as follows: Jesus did not preach in public about the Fatherhood of God, but occasionally spoke privately about it to his closest friends and followers. For them he made God the Father real, not by argument or by much speaking, but because it was obvious that the Father was the supreme reality in his own life. The former of these two propositions is matter of fact: and the evidence for it is given above. The latter may be justified by a consideration of the narratives and sayings in which the idea of God's Fatherhood is given directly or implied.

The experience of God as Father dominates the whole ministry of Jesus from the Baptism to the Crucifixion: that is, it fills the whole period for which we have certain and detailed information. What lies before the Baptism we can

only conjecture: our knowledge of the religious experience
of Jesus begins at the moment when he comes up out of
Jordan, and sees the heavens opened and the Spirit like a
dove descending upon him: and hears a voice from heaven,
'Thou art my beloved Son, in thee I am well pleased'.[1]
Thus at the very beginning of the ministry we are shown an
experience on the part of Jesus which involves the relation
of son to father between Jesus and God. The Marcan
account makes it clear that it was Jesus himself, and he
alone, who saw the vision and heard the voice: and if that
be so, it will follow that this account derives ultimately
from the Master himself.

The place of this experience as a prelude to the active
work of the ministry inevitably calls to mind the inaugural
visions which take a similar place in the lives of the great
prophets of the Old Testament. But on one very important
point there is a wide difference. The inaugural vision of the
prophet is essentially a commission: it accredits the
prophet as God's representative to the people. To Isaiah
comes the question: 'Whom shall I send and who will go
for us?' (Is. vi. 8). To Jeremiah God says:

'Lo, I put my word in thy mouth:
See, I put thee in charge this day
Over the nations and over the kingdoms
To pluck up and to pull down, to build and to plant'.[2]

Amos tells us: 'Jehovah said to me: Go, prophesy to my
people Israel' (Am. vii. 15). In all these cases the vision
and the voice are a call to action: the prophet receives a
message and a mission. With the vision and the voice at the
Baptism the case is otherwise: Jesus receives an assurance,
the essence of which is contained in the declaration: 'Thou
art my Son'. What is given here is not a task to be performed or a message to be delivered, but a status and a
relation. At the very outset it is indicated that the central

---

[1] Mk. i. 10 f. In the Q version the voice says: 'Thou art my Son, this day
have I begotten thee'. Cf. Streeter, *The Four Gospels*, pp. 143, 188, 276.

[2] Jer. i. 9 f. Trans. Skinner: *Prophecy and Religion*, p. 26.

thing in his ministry will be what he *is* rather than what he *says*. As the ministry continues the message becomes plainer and the task more obvious; but both message and task are still conditioned by the primary fact of sonship.

That Jesus was fully aware of the difference between the prophets and himself is indicated in the words spoken by him concerning John the Baptist (Mt. xi. 11–13 = Lk. vii. 28; xvi. 16: Q). There it is clearly shown that John is the last and greatest representative of the old order and that, with the advent of Jesus, a new order is inaugurated.

The difference is brought out still more clearly in the parable of the Vineyard (Mk. xii. 1–11 and parallels). In this parable Jesus distinguishes himself as the Son from the prophets, who appear in the story as the servants of God (cf. Am. iii. 7). Moreover the words 'They will reverence my son' imply that the Son is more than a messenger. He is rather, as the husbandmen perceive, the heir. If this parable is genuine—and the criticism that rejects it will be capable of getting rid of anything in the Gospels—it can only mean that Jesus claimed to stand in a special relation to God, a relation which he himself chooses to describe as that of Son to Father: and the real question which we have to face is how this relation is to be understood.

Once again, in the prayer in Gethsemane,[1] the Father appears as the supreme reality in the life of Jesus, the will

---

[1] Mk. xiv. 35 f. The arguments by which it is sought to prove that the words of the prayer are not authentic are extremely unconvincing. They hinge on two main points: the distance of Jesus from the chosen three and the fact that they fell asleep. To make the former at all effective the μικρόν of Mk. xiv. 35 has to be stretched beyond what is reasonable. The latter has no force unless we make the supposition, whose absurdity is evident as soon as it is made, that all three companions of Jesus composed themselves to slumber as soon as he took the first step away from them and were already sound asleep when he began to pray. The supposition, put forward by Weiss-Bousset (*S.N.T.* i. 206) as the most natural, that Jesus prayed in silence is not to be entertained until it is first shown on independent grounds that the account in Mark is unreliable: and no good reason has yet been advanced for supposing this to be the case. On the contrary, the text of Mark leaves us perfectly free to believe that Jesus remained within hearing of his three companions; that he prayed aloud, at the beginning of his prayer, if not throughout; and that one or other of the disciples heard what was said before sleep overtook them.

of the Father is the dominating factor in the life of the Son.
And in the prayer this absolute trust in the Father and
complete obedience to his will overcome the natural
shrinking from the approaching ordeal. Not only so, but
they steel his resolution to face the last extremity not merely
of physical suffering but also of unmerited contempt and
hatred; to endure the insolent triumph of the priestly
cabal, the calm and calculated unscrupulousness of
Roman *Realpolitik*, and, perhaps worse than all these, the
treachery or cowardice of his own familiar friends. Such
things are not borne for the sake of a theological commonplace. Such faith and such endurance are not built upon a
foundation of pious phrases: rather do they stand upon the
rock of a profound and intense religious experience,
the experience of God as Father. The voice from heaven
at the Baptism and the prayer of Jesus in Gethsemane
alike bear witness to this fundamental fact. It is not
a simple matter to grasp what this experience was in its
naked simplicity. It is all too easy to reduce 'God the
Father' to a mere cog in the machinery of dogma or to a
phrase of customary piety. For Jesus 'God the Father' was
neither, but on the contrary a present living reality. This
experience we may comprehend in proportion as we ourselves are made partakers in it, in so far as we receive the
spirit of adoption whereby we cry 'Abba, Father'.

It is by comparison easy to trace the effects of this
tremendous spiritual experience in the life and teaching of
Jesus. Attention has already been drawn to two of them;
the absolute trust and confidence in his Father which Jesus
manifested, and his unquestioning obedience to the
Father's will. From these two spring other characteristics
second only to them in importance.

One of the most striking things about the ministry of our
Lord, and a thing which was as astonishing to his contemporaries as it is to us, is the authority with which he speaks
and the assurance with which he acts. Time and again we
hear that people were amazed, sometimes shocked, at his

sayings and doings. In Mk. i. 22 the reason for the amaze-
ment at his teaching is given: it was because 'he taught
them as one having authority,[1] and not as the scribes'. It
was not merely that his words were novel or unorthodox:
the very manner in which they were said was unusual.
The impression which the utterances of Jesus made on the
people is confirmed by an examination of the sayings themselves. A single phrase, the frequent and emphatic ἀμὴν
λέγω ὑμῖν, 'Verily I say unto you', is enough to set Jesus as
a teacher in a class apart from either prophets or scribes.
When the prophet spoke with authority, it was as the
messenger of God: and the message which he had to deliver
was properly introduced by the formula כה אמר יהוה,
'Thus· saith the Lord'. When the scribe spoke authori-
tatively it was to declare what Scripture or tradition had to
say.[2] When Jesus speaks with authority the formula is
'I say unto you'. It is as difficult to overestimate the
significance of this distinction as it is easy to misunderstand
it. One thing, however, is clear, that the only ultimately
satisfactory explanation of the authority of Jesus is that
which sets the foundation of it in his unique spiritual
experience.

The prophet in ancient Israel found the source of his

---

[1] The theory put forward by H. B. Chajes that ὡς ἐξουσίαν ἔχων in Mk. i.
22 really should be ἐν παραβολῇ (-αῖς) on the supposition that an original
Hebrew כְּמָשָׁל should be emended to בְּמָשָׁל requires the assumption that
parabolic teaching was so strange in the days of Jesus as to cause astonish-
ment when it was used. That this was not the case is shown by Abrahams,
Studies in Pharisaism and the Gospels, 1. 94 ff.

[2] The contrast between the scribal method and that of Jesus is well
brought out by a comparison of a formula found in the early Midrash with a
similar formula used in the Sermon on the Mount. In the *Mekhilta* we find
the words שומע אני, 'I might infer' (lit. I hear), used to introduce a proposed
inference from a biblical text. Where the inference is rejected, the formula of
rejection is תלמוד לומר, 'there is a teaching which says' (lit. to say). In the
Sermon on the Mount we find a somewhat similar formula: ἠκούσατε ὅτι
ἐρρέθη...ἐγὼ δὲ λέγω ὑμῖν. (Cf. Bacher, *Terminologie*, 1. 189 f.; Schechter in
J.Q.R. x. 11.) The difference between Jesus and the Scribes in their methods is
just that which is expressed by ἐγὼ δὲ λέγω ὑμῖν in contrast with תלמוד לומר:
it is one speaking with authority in contrast with others quoting authorities.

authority in his inaugural vision. In that religious experience he discovered himself as the appointed or even
the predestined servant of Jehovah, the accredited
messenger of God to the men and women of his own
generation. His authority was a delegated authority; his
message and his task were prescribed, and only within the
limits of his express commission was he authorised to
speak in the name of the Lord. The scope—and the secret—
of the prophetic authority is perfectly defined by the
prophet Micaiah ben Imlah in the words: 'As the Lord
liveth, what the Lord saith unto me that will I speak'
(I Kings xxii. 14). With Jesus likewise, the source of his
authority is to be sought in the experience at Jordan which
initiates his public activity. But the 'Thou art my Son'
makes him more than a messenger or a servant. The
prophetic commission is relative to a given historical
situation; the filial relation is independent of place, time,
or circumstances. The descent of the Holy Spirit, too,
signifies something permanent. "It is not that Jesus receives an inspired message, but that the spiritual source of
all inspiration takes possession of him, so that when he
speaks it is not that he repeats words given to him but that
the Spirit of his Father speaks in him".[1] These two factors in
the inaugural experience of Jesus explain and justify his
attitude. The complete dependence on the Father carries
with it the astonishing independence of men: and the
conviction of constant possession by the Spirit justifies the
substitution of 'I say unto you' for 'Thus saith the Lord'.

[1] This fact furnishes the explanation of the saying about the unforgivable
sin (Mk. iii. 28–30; Lk. xii. 10 = Mt. xii. 32: Q). The blasphemy which is
really fatal is the blasphemy against the Holy Spirit, that is, the Spirit which
took possession of Jesus at the Baptism. His opponents perceived that
he was indeed possessed by a spirit; but they chose to call the spirit Beelzebub. This is in truth the ultimate blasphemy, far beyond any profane taking
of God's name in vain, beyond intellectual atheism; for it is the flat denial of
all spiritual values whatsoever. In the last resort it makes truth a delusion,
conscience a disease, and reduces man's life to a tale told by an idiot, full of
sound and fury, signifying nothing. It is the worst and the most deadly of all
sins because it is the rejection of God's purpose and the denial of his nature; it
is the betrayal of the cause of humanity—and it is spiritual suicide.

The realisation that the Fatherhood of God was for Jesus a personal religious experience of unparalleled depth and intensity enables us to explain another phenomenon in the Synoptic record, which, otherwise, must remain an enigma: that is, the fact already noticed that Jesus says very little about it, and that only to a chosen few. Rightly understood this reticence is positive evidence of two things: the intense reality and deep sacredness of the experience itself, and the true manhood of Jesus. We are so made that we cannot lightly speak of the things that most profoundly move us: and for every man the Holy of Holies in his life is hedged about with silence. The thoughts that lie too deep for tears do not easily clothe themselves with words: and, if they do, the words are not such as can be shouted from the housetops. Such things as these may be spoken of—or hinted at—only to those who know to take their shoes from off their feet because the place whereon they stand is holy ground. In this matter the Jesus of our earlier records is at one with us: and the wistful words of the modern poet,

> I have spread my dreams under your feet;
> Tread softly, because you tread on my dreams

are but an echo of the sterner maxim in the Sermon on the Mount:

> Give not that which is holy unto the dogs,
> Neither cast your pearls before the swine,
> Lest haply they trample them under their feet,
> And turn and rend you;[1]

which in its turn reminds us of the saying of Plato quoted above: 'To find the maker and father of this universe is a hard task; and when you have found him, *it is impossible to speak of him before all people*'.[2] We can understand the

[1] Mt. vii. 6.

[2] *Timaeus*, 28 c. On this sentence Professor Burnet remarks (*op. cit.* p. 337) that it 'is a sentence of unquestioned authenticity, and fully explains the enigmatic manner in which Plato speaks of the same difficulty to Dionysios (who imagined he had solved it) in the *Second Epistle* (312 e). It also explains

reticence of Jesus just because it answers to something in our own life, something which is wrought into the very texture of our human nature.

These considerations furnish the key to the understanding of the utterance preserved in Q: 'I thank thee, Father, Lord of heaven and earth, that thou hast hidden these things from the wise and prudent, and hast revealed them to babes; yea, Father, for so it was well-pleasing in thy sight. All things are delivered to me by my Father, and no one knows [the Son but the Father, or] the Father but the Son and he to whom the Son wills to reveal (him)'.[1] And

why he never wrote or published the Lecture on the Good, and why in the *Laws*, which was written for publication, he always speaks of God and never of the Good, though the *Laws* must be contemporary with that very lecture'. The deepest problem in the Platonic metaphysics was just the problem which he would not—or could not—throw open to the wrangling of the market-place. It was a matter reserved to those who by stern intellectual discipline had prepared their minds to appreciate the delicacy and gravity of the issues involved: too solemn and serious a thing to be delivered up to the logic-chopping and sophistry and the cheap verbal triumphs of the casual street-corner philosophers.

[1] Mt. xi. 25–27; Lk. x. 21, 22. There are some variations between Matthew and Luke at the end of the saying: Matthew has ἐπιγινώσκει where Luke has γινώσκει; Matthew τὸν υἱόν, τὸν πατέρα and Luke τίς ἐστιν ὁ υἱός, τίς ἐστιν ὁ πατήρ. The former is not a matter of great importance (cf. Armitage Robinson, *Ephesians*, pp. 248–254). Both ἐπιγινώσκειν and γινώσκειν are used in LXX to render עדי: and in the Old Syriac and Peshitta ידע is used in the translation of Mt. xi. 27 and Lk. x. 22. The other difference is not easy of explanation. If 'who is the Son?' is a question of the identity of the Son (= Messiah?), it becomes impossible to give any meaning to 'who is the Father?' The identity of 'the Father' could not be a problem either to Jew or Christian. If, on the other hand, it is a question of the character or nature of the Father or the Son, then the words of Luke come to mean the same thing as those of Matthew.

The text of the passage has been very fully discussed by Harnack (*Sprüche u. Reden Jesu*, pp. 189–216), who concludes that the original form of the saying in Q was: Ἐξομολογοῦμαί σοι, πάτερ, κύριε τοῦ οὐρανοῦ καὶ τῆς γῆς, ὅτι ἔκρυψας ταῦτα ἀπὸ σοφῶν καὶ συνετῶν καὶ ἀπεκάλυψας αὐτὰ νηπίοις· ναί, ὁ πατήρ, ὅτι οὕτως ἐγένετο εὐδοκία ἔμπροσθέν σου. πάντα μοι παρεδόθη ὑπὸ τοῦ πατρός, καὶ οὐδεὶς ἔγνω τὸν πατέρα [or τίς ἐστιν ὁ πατήρ] εἰ μὴ ὁ υἱὸς καὶ ᾧ ἂν ὁ υἱὸς ἀποκαλύψῃ (ib. pp. 205 f.). In this reconstruction the clause 'No one knows the Son but the Father' is rejected as an early interpolation (*ib.* 203 ff.). The clause is also rejected by Wellhausen (*Das Evangelium Matthaei, ad loc.*). The reasons given raise serious doubts as to the authenticity of the clause, though, from the nature of the case, they cannot be absolutely decisive.

the saying, when rightly understood, is additional evidence
for the view here maintained.

Many critics doubt the authenticity of this saying, or
the latter part of it, because of its Johannine flavour.
That it does resemble what we find in John cannot be
denied; but that is no reason for condemning it, unless
we are prepared to lay it down as a canon of criticism
that no saying in the Synoptics which has a parallel in
the Fourth Gospel can be a genuine utterance of Jesus.
Rather the opposite position might well be maintained:
that where matter in the Synoptics resembles matter
in John, there is the possibility either that John is dependent on one or other of the earlier Gospels or that
he has a genuine tradition in common with them. If
we can give a reasonable interpretation of this particular
saying, and one that fits in with what we otherwise
know from our records, there is no point in discarding
it merely because the epithet 'Johannine' may be thrown
at it.

The first question to be determined (or rather guessed) is
the occasion of the saying. In Matthew it is placed very
early in the Marcan framework and long before Peter's
Confession: in Luke it comes much later and after the
Confession. In my opinion the occasion was probably the
Confession itself, which is not likely to have passed without
leaving some trace in Q. Moreover, the note of exultant
thanksgiving which marks the prayer presupposes some
really big response to the ministry of Jesus, some token of
genuine understanding of his mission and himself. Even
without the Lucan words which introduce the prayer we
should gather that it was the spontaneous outpouring of a
great joy: and it would be difficult to find a better occasion
for it than the Confession at Caesarea Philippi. The thanksgiving naturally leads on to the following statement, for it
is the faith and insight of the disciples, above all of Peter,
that make it possible for Jesus to speak more openly to
them concerning the deepest things of his own spiritual

experience. Their understanding invites and wins his fuller confidence.[1]

The saying to the disciples, which follows the prayer of thanksgiving, can now be interpreted as the first step in the revelation which it itself promises. Jesus here begins to speak to his friends of the unique depth and intimacy of the relation between the Father and himself. He claims to know the Father in a way that no one else does: and, obviously, the kind of knowledge here spoken of is not mere theological information but something much wider and deeper, something which involves mind and heart and will to the utmost,[2] so much so that 'communion with God' is a nearer equivalent in English than 'knowledge of God'. This communion with God, which Jesus describes as 'knowing the Father', is thus to be regarded as a two-sided relation including in itself insight into the nature of God who reveals himself as Father to his Son, love towards God which answers to the Father's love experienced by the Son, and complete trust in and obedience to God's will revealed as the loving purpose of the Father for his

[1] In this connection it should be noted that the demand of Jesus for understanding and insight is characteristic of the period before Peter's Confession. After that event he looks for other qualities: loyalty, endurance, self-sacrifice, and the like; and on his own part he speaks to the disciples openly of many things which hitherto have not been mentioned. Cf. Appendix, s. vv. ἀσύνετος, βλέπω, γινώσκω, νοέω (D); οὖς in the expression 'He that hath ears…let him hear' (G); συνίημι (D + G). It looks as if the first period were probationary and the question 'Whom say ye that I am?' a final test to discover who, out of all the mass of people who were acquainted with him, really showed signs of understanding him, of having within themselves that vital something which marks the difference between the follower or adherent and the intimate friend.

[2] What is meant by knowledge of God is to be looked for in the Old Testament rather than in Western ideas of knowledge. The broad distinction is that knowledge of God is there an essential part of religion, whereas our tendency is rather to look upon it as a branch of science and philosophy. The Cartesian division of all truth into Rational Theology, Cosmology, and Psychology still lingers with us. In Hebrew thought דעת אלהים is not theological but religious. It can be put alongside יראת אלהים, 'the fear of God'—which is another name for religion—and classed with חסד and אמת, 'mercy' and 'faithfulness'. Cf. Hos. iv. 1, 6; Is. xi. 2 and Skinner's note; Jer. xxii. 16 (Skinner, *Prophecy and Religion*, pp. 247 f.); etc.

children. In some such way as this we may be content to formulate the experience, so long as we remember that the formulation bears the same relation to the living reality in Jesus as a dried specimen in a *hortus siccus* to the living plant. The experience is one which must in some degree be felt in order to be in any degree understood.

Two things follow as corollaries. First, that he who enjoys this intimate communion with God as Father has everything that is really worth having. This is the true sense of the words πάντα μοι παρεδόθη ὑπὸ τοῦ πατρός μου. The πάντα includes the authority which we find as a matter of fact that Jesus had: it includes a penetrating insight into matters human and divine: and it includes much besides. In Mark the same thing is expressed in the parable of the Vineyard where Jesus calls himself the heir. While we fruitlessly debate whether it was some external (Messianic?) authority or a body of sound doctrine on theology and ethics which Jesus claimed to possess, we miss the real point of the saying, which is that, in virtue of his spiritual experience, he knew himself to possess *all* the gifts which the Father had to bestow.[1]

The other point is raised by the concluding words of the saying, 'No one knows the Father but the Son and he to whom the Son will reveal (him)'. Here Jesus claims not only to stand in a special relation to God, but also to be the means whereby others may be brought into a similar relation. In other words he claims to make the Father real to men in the same sense that the Father is real to him. Through the Son men may come to know the Father, and receive the spirit of adoption whereby we cry 'Abba, Father', assured by the inward witness of the spirit that we are children of God; and if children, then heirs, heirs of God and joint-heirs with Jesus Christ.[2]

---

[1] One may justly compare Ps. lxxiii. 25 in Luther's version: 'Wenn ich nur dich habe, so frage ich nichts nach Himmel und Erde'. On this rendering Kittel (Sellin's *Kommentar*) remarks that 'it is somewhat free, but gives the sense in unsurpassable fashion'.

[2] Rom. viii. 15–17.

We are thus brought to a very simple answer to our
questions. The Father is the supreme reality in the life of
Jesus. His experience of the Father is something so profound and so moving that it will not bear to be spoken
about except to those who have shown themselves to be
fitted to hear. At the same time it shines through his
words and deeds in such wise that those who see him see the
Father. By what he is he makes the Father real to men.
By being the Son he reveals the Father, so that men see the
light of the knowledge of the glory of God in the face of
Jesus Christ. To this one central fact all other things are
subsidiary, so that even the teachings which we have from
Jesus concerning the nature of the Father must yield in
importance to the revelation of the Father in the Son.
Indeed, some of these sayings have their power not because
they present new and original doctrine concerning the
Father, but from the depth and reality of the experience
that lies behind them.

If we now turn to the passages in which Jesus speaks of
the Father, we find that the teaching centres round a few
very simple truths, which are summarised in the Lord's
Prayer. This prayer is in fact a complete statement of what
God's children should desire and ask of their Father in
heaven: and since what we ask of God is the surest indication of the kind of God we believe in, this prayer may
justly be taken as a sketch of what, in the thought of
Jesus, the Father is.

The prayer falls into two main divisions, the first concerned with what may be called world issues, the second
with the affairs of individuals. Both alike are conceived as
being in the hands of the Father: the same God who orders
the course of history with sovereign power also ministers to
the daily needs, material and spiritual, of his individual
children. The sayings which mention the Father may
conveniently be grouped under these heads.

I. *The Father as sovereign arbiter of world history.*

(*a*) The hallowing of his Name. Mt. v. 16 (M): 'So let your light shine before men, that they may see your good works and glorify your Father in heaven'. Cf. Mt. xxiii. 9 (M).

(*b*) The coming of his Kingdom.[1] Mk. viii. 38, 'The Son of Man...when he comes in the glory of his Father'. xiii. 32, 'Only the Father knows the time of the Parousia'. Lk. xii. 32 (Q), 'It is the Father's good pleasure to give you the kingdom'. Lk. xxii. 29 (L), 'I appoint to you, as my Father has appointed to me, a kingdom'.

(*c*) Thy will be done. The best commentary on this petition is the prayer of Jesus in Gethsemane: Mk. xiv. 36, 'Not what I will, but what thou wilt'.

II. *The Father who cares for and ministers to each child.*

(*a*) Daily bread. Lk. xi. 13 = Mt. vii. 11 (Q), 'If ye then being evil know how to give good gifts to your children, how much more will the Father give the Holy Spirit [Mt. good things] to those who ask him'. Lk. xii. 30 = Mt. vi. 32 (Q), 'Your Father knows that ye have need of these things' (food, drink, clothing). Cf. also Mt. xviii. 19 (M).

(*b*) Forgiveness of sins. Mk. xi. 25, 'And when you stand praying, if you have anything against anyone, forgive, that your Father in heaven may forgive you your transgressions'. Mt. vi. 14 f. (M), 'If you forgive men their transgression, your heavenly Father will also forgive you; but if you do not forgive men, neither will your Father forgive your transgressions'. Similarly Mt. xviii. 35 (M).

(*c*) Protection and deliverance. Mt. xviii. 14 (M), 'It is not the will of my Father in heaven that one of these little ones should perish'. Cf. xviii. 10 (M).

There remain a number of cases in the Sermon on the Mount (Mt. vi) where it is emphasised repeatedly that the Father sees in secret, that is, looks to the heart and the motive rather than at the outward act. As Father it is

---

[1] On this petition, however, see below, p. 128 n. 2.

impossible that he should be satisfied with the mere outward observances of piety and righteousness; rather he seeks
that inner affection and devotion of which the outward act
may be a token, but for which it can never be a substitute.

Some of the sayings gathered together here will require
closer consideration at a later stage in other connections.
It will be sufficient at this point to notice that "the Lord's
Prayer is the sum of the teaching of Jesus on the Fatherhood of God" and the significant thing is not so much its
contents as the fact that it is a *prayer*. It reveals God as
concerned with things infinitely great and infinitely little.
Everything from the 'one far-off divine event to which the
whole creation moves' to the daily provision for the least of
his creatures is the object of his care. Everything that
concerns a man from his highest ideals to his humblest
needs may thus be brought in prayer to the Father. The
will of the Father covers the whole life of man: and the
whole man may enter into communion with the Father.
Jesus teaches men about the Father by teaching them to
pray to the Father, to submit their whole life to his loving
care and holy purpose. And this simply brings us back to
what we have already seen to be the essence of the experience of Jesus himself. For him the Father was the
supreme reality in the world and in his own life; and his
teaching would make the Father have the same place and
power in the life of his disciples, that they too may be heirs,
heirs of God and joint-heirs with Jesus Christ.[1]

---

[1] An interesting parallel to the position maintained in this chapter is to
be found in the late Professor W. P. Ker's Clark Lectures (*Form and Style in
Poetry*, pp. 114 ff.). There, after discussing the dependence of Shelley's
Prometheus on the work of Plato, Hume, and Godwin, Professor Ker goes on to
say (p. 117): 'Thus while Godwin's *Political Justice* is a prose prescription for
the future reform of the world, Shelley's *Prometheus* is a poetical revelation of
the world as it really is in the mind of the poet. It is not talk about Ideas; it is
more than allegorical personification. It is reality; active and living beauty
made effectual in articulate speech. It is what it represents—the triumph of
the Spirit over all baseness'. It is just such a distinction as this that we must
draw between the theological doctrine of the Fatherhood of God, whenceso-
ever derived, and 'the Father' as Jesus knew him and spoke of him to his
disciples.

Chapter V

GOD AS KING

THE teaching of Jesus, like much of the prophetic literature of the Old Testament, abounds in metaphor, pictorial expression, and even hyperbole. God clothes the grass of the field, feeds the birds, sends the rain, and causes the sun to rise. Jesus himself is like a physician, a bridegroom, an incendiary. His disciples are fishers of men. The Kingdom is likened to mustard seed, leaven, a valuable pearl, a hidden treasure; it is at hand; people are near it or far from it; one may enter it or be excluded from it. The Gospels are filled with images of this sort, which require interpretation if we are even to begin to comprehend the Gospel. The sayings of Jesus, which refer to the Kingdom of God, are no exception to the general rule. His thoughts concerning the Kingdom clothed themselves in the form of parable, figure of speech, and metaphor: and each man interpreted them as he was able, or as he desired.

Just as every man is apt to find in Jesus his own idealised image, so every man is ready to find in the Kingdom of God his own ideal state. There are two ways of misinterpreting the words of Jesus about the Kingdom. This way, which consists in reading into them our own conceptions of the most desirable social order, is the easier way. The other way, which consists in taking the sayings or some of them *au pied de la lettre*, has also had its followers in every age. The one school thinks largely in terms of natural evolution, the other in terms of supernatural revolution; the one is world-accepting, the other world-renouncing; the one sings:

> Grow old along with me,
> The best is yet to be,

the other

> The world is very evil,
> The times are waxing late.

Two starting places for two views on the Kingdom.

The one school starts from Mt. v–vii conceived as a programme of religious and ethical reform, a set of limiting values to which humanity can approach by ever closer approximations. The other builds upon Mt. xxiv f. understood as the promise of the summary termination of the present world-order and the inauguration of a completely new era. On the one view Jesus of Nazareth is the inspired teacher of new and ultimate ideals of righteousness; on the other he believed himself to be the person whom God had designated to bring the old order to a close and usher in the new. In modern times the one view is represented by the religio-ethical humanitarian school of interpreters of the Gospels; the other by what is called 'thoroughgoing eschatology': and the present position is a kind of theological stalemate. Each side can expose the weakness of its opponents; but neither can make any real progress on its own account.

That these two views are irreconcilable may be admitted. That they exhaust all the possibilities is a matter that may well be questioned. Both cannot be right, but both may be wrong; and in this chapter it will be contended that both are wrong, and that the fundamental misinterpretation lies in supposing that the Kingdom of God is a state of affairs, a social order, anything, indeed, that can be mechanically produced, whether by an evolutionary process on earth or by a divine fiat out of the skies. Whether we think of the New Jerusalem as something to be built in England's green and pleasant land or as descending complete and perfect from heaven, we totally misconceive its nature if we imagine it as a glorified garden suburb, or, in a more refined way, as somewhat akin to the ideal polity of the philosophers. In fact all debate about such questions as whether the Kingdom is present or future: and, if future, when, how, and where it is to appear, are a mere beating of the air until the vital question is first answered—what the Kingdom is.

This holds both of the work of the Christian Church and

of the work of the interpreter of the Gospels. It is not too much to say that Christian people pray 'Thy Kingdom come', and work for 'the extension of the Kingdom' or 'the realisation of the Kingdom on earth', or 'wait for the coming of the Kingdom': and their conceptions of what it is that is to come or be extended or realised are poles asunder. When we turn to the task of interpreting the teaching of Jesus on this all-important matter, the same phenomenon appears: endless discussion of how Jesus expected the Kingdom to come, and when. But these are secondary issues compared with the real question: What did Jesus conceive 'the Kingdom of God' to mean? If that problem were once definitely settled, we could write over many of the others *cadit quaestio*. Our first task therefore is to collect and weigh the evidence furnished by our four sources with the object of discovering, if we can, what meaning Jesus attached to the phrase 'Kingdom of God'. As before, the data will be collected according to source: and the individual sayings will be considered in terms of audience and date.

Mark

i. 15 (G) = Mt. iv. 17 (G):[1]
      The Kingdom of God is at hand.
iv. 11 (D) = Mt. xiii. 11 (D) = Lk. viii. 10 (D):
      To you is given the secret of the Kingdom of God.
iv. 26 (G?):
      The Kingdom of God like a man casting seed.
iv. 30 (G?) = Mt. xiii. 31 (G) [= Lk. xiii. 18 (G)][2]
      The Kingdom of God likened to a grain of mustard seed.

[1] For 'Kingdom of God' in Mark we find in Matthew 'Kingdom of Heaven' (7 times), 'Kingdom of my Father' (once), 'life' (once). For 'the Kingdom of God coming in power' (Mk. ix. 1) Mt. xvi. 28 has 'the Son of Man coming in his Kingdom'. These variants all belong to the class of editorial alterations of Mk, and fall under the symbol RMT. They have no significance except as revealing the idiosyncrasies of the compiler of the First Gospel (cf. above, p. 8) and therefore it is not necessary to take note of them here, where they could only complicate the evidence.
[2] Lk. xiii. 18 belongs to the Q version of this parable. See below under Q. Mt. xiii. 31 f. is a conflation of the Marcan and Q versions. Cf. Streeter, *The Four Gospels*, pp. 246 ff.

ix. 1 (D + G) = Mt. xvi. 28 (D) = Lk. ix. 27 (D + G):
> Some present who shall not taste death until they see the
Kingdom of God coming in power.
ix. 47 (D) = Mt. xviii. 9 (D):
It is better to enter the Kingdom of God with one eye than
to be cast into Gehenna with two.
x. 14 (D) = Mt. xix. 14 (D) = Lk. xviii. 16 (D):
Let the children come to me, do not hinder them, for of
such is the Kingdom of God.
x. 15 (D) = Mt. xviii. 3 (D) = Lk. xviii. 17 (D):
He who does not receive the Kingdom of God like a child
shall not enter therein.
x. 23 (D) = Mt. xix. 23 (D) = Lk. xviii. 24 (D):
How hardly shall the rich enter the Kingdom of God.
x. 24 (D):
How hard it is [for those who trust in riches][1] to enter the
Kingdom of God.
x. 25 (D) = Mt. xix. 24 (D) = Lk. xviii. 25 (D):
It is easier for a camel to go through the eye of a needle
than for a rich man to enter the Kingdom of God.
xii. 34 (P):
Thou art not far from the Kingdom of God.
xiv. 25 (D) = Mt. xxvi. 29 (D) = Lk. xxii. 18 (D):
I will no more drink of the fruit of the vine until that day
when I drink it new in the Kingdom of God.

The most striking feature about these passages is the
division which falls about the time of Peter's Confession.
In the discourse (D + G) which separates the account of
the Confession from that of the Transfiguration we have
what appears to be the last reference to the Kingdom as
something which is coming (Mk. ix. 1). Thereafter Jesus
speaks of entering into the Kingdom, this new mode of
speech first appearing at ix. 47. This fact is obviously one
which demands the most careful consideration.

Further, this new way of speaking about the Kingdom
coincides with the restriction of speech about the Kingdom

---

[1] The words in brackets are rejected by most modern editors and commentators as an interpretative gloss 'inserted to bring the verse into closer
connexion with the context by limiting its generality' (Westcott and Hort,
Notes, p. 26). The expression may come from Prov. xi. 28.

to D audiences. Even Mk. xii. 34 (P) is hardly an exception to this rule; for the conversation between Jesus and
the scribe is exceptionally friendly and entirely free from
polemics. The question of the scribe which opens it is not
meant as a trap, but seems to be quite honestly put in
order to obtain on an important point an opinion which
the questioner believed to be worth having. Jesus answers
accordingly as frankly as he would have spoken to his own
disciples.

There is thus evidence in Mark that in the latter part of
the ministry Jesus began to speak of the Kingdom of God
as something into which men enter. This way of speaking is
employed only when the disciples are the audience, and the
first occurrence of the phrase 'enter into the Kingdom of
God' is in the period which lies between the Transfiguration and the beginning of the journey to Jerusalem.

Q (Streeter's Reconstruction)

LUKE vi. 20 (S):
Blessed are ye poor, for yours is the
Kingdom of God.

MATTHEW v. 3 (S):
Blessed are the poor in spirit, for
theirs is the Kingdom of Heaven.

vi. 46 (S):
Why do you call me Lord, Lord, and
not do what I say?

vii. 21 (S):
Not everyone that says to me Lord,
Lord, shall enter into the Kingdom
of Heaven.

vii. 28 (G):
The least in the Kingdom of God is greater than John the Baptist.

xi. 11 (G):

ix. 60 (G):
Leave the dead to bury their dead;
but go thou and preach the Kingdom of God.

viii. 22 (G):
(Mt omits the latter part.)

ix. 62 (G):
No man putting his hand to the plough and looking back is fit for the
Kingdom of God.

—

x. 9 (D and ultimately G):
The Kingdom of God has drawn
near upon you (ἤγγικεν ἐφ' ὑμᾶς).

x. 7 (D ultimately G):
The Kingdom of Heaven is at hand
(ἤγγικεν).

x. 11 (D ultimately G):
Only know this, that the Kingdom of God is at hand.

Cf. x. 14:

xi. 20 (P):
If I by the finger[1] of God cast out demons then the Kingdom of God has
come upon you.

xii. 28 (P):

[1] See Detached Note A to Chapter III.

xi. 52 (P):

Woe to you...for you have taken away the key of knowledge.

xxiii. 14 (P):

Woe to you...for you close the Kingdom of Heaven against men.

xii. 31 (D):

But seek first his Kingdom.

vi. 33 (S):

But seek first his Kingdom and righteousness.

xii. 32 (D):

Fear not, little flock, for it is your Father's good pleasure to give you the Kingdom.

—

xiii. 18 (G):   Cf. Mt. xiii 31 (G):

The Kingdom of God like a grain of mustard seed.

xiii. 20 (G):   xiii. 33 (G):

The Kingdom of God like leaven.

xiii. 28 (G):   viii. 11f. (G):

Abraham, Isaac, Jacob, and the Prophets in the Kingdom of God. And the sons of the Kingdom sent out into the outer darkness.

xiii. 29 (G):   viii. 11 (G):

People from East and West, North and South come and sit down in the Kingdom of God.

xvi. 16 (P):   xi. 12 (G):

The Law and the Prophets were until John; since then the Kingdom of God is preached as a gospel and everyone presses into it.

From the days of John the Baptist until now the Kingdom of Heaven βιάζεται, καὶ βιασταὶ ἁρπάζουσιν αὐτήν.

xvii. 20 (P):   —

The Kingdom of God cometh not with observation.

xvii. 21 (P):

For lo the Kingdom of God ἐντὸς ὑμῶν ἐστίν.

It will be observed that in several of these examples there is considerable variation between the Matthaean and Lucan versions of the saying. These cases must be considered more in detail before we can attempt to draw any conclusions from the data supplied by Q.

Lk. vi. 46: Mt. vii. 21. The variation between Matthew and Luke is so great that Harnack (*Sprüche u. Reden*, pp. 51 f., 91) leaves it an open question whether the saying belongs to Q or not. If it is to be assigned to Q he prefers the form in Matthew. Against this it may be urged that it is difficult to see how the Lucan form could arise if the Matthaean be the original. Further, the phrase 'My Father in heaven' is characteristic of M,[1] not Q: and the

---

[1] See above, p. 96.

whole notion of entry into the Kingdom as the reward of merit is Matthaean. A more probable view is that the Q form of the saying is preserved in Luke and that the form in Matthew either arises from the conflation of Q and M or is derived from M alone.[1] In either case this saying ceases to belong to the Q list so far as the Kingdom of God is concerned.

Lk. ix. 60: Mt. viii. 22. The words added in Luke are rejected by Harnack (*op. cit.*, p. 13). To his reasons may be added the further consideration that St Luke appears to have a weakness for inserting the 'preaching of the Kingdom of God' in places where it seems appropriate, e.g. Lk. ix. 2, 11. Probably, therefore, this clause should be labelled RL rather than Q.

Lk. ix. 62 is not in Matthew. The question therefore is whether it belongs to Q, in which case we must ask why it is omitted in Matthew; or whether it is a saying from L which St Luke has inserted here because of the appropriateness of the context. Since there is no obvious reason why St Matthew should have omitted it if it stood in Q, the latter alternative seems preferable.[2] In that case the saying will be classed as L.

Lk. x. 11 has no proper parallel in Matthew. Canon Streeter (*Four Gospels*, pp. 190, 254) argues that Lk. x. 3–12 is the Q version of the mission charge, the corresponding passage in Mt. x being a conflation of the Q version with that in Mark. If that be so, we must accept Lk. x. 11 as genuine Q evidence.

Lk. xi. 52: Mt. xxiii. 14. The discourse in Mt. xxiii is a conflation of a speech against Pharisaism from Q with a similar speech from M. The Q speech is represented by Lk. xi. 37–52.[3] In that case the form in Matthew may be regarded as derived from M. What then stood in Q? There

[1] Streeter, *The Four Gospels*, p. 251.
[2] This consideration, for what it is worth, supports the view that St Luke began his career as a gospel-writer by annotating and enriching a copy of Q. See above, pp. 31 n. 2, 69, and cf. Taylor, *Behind the Third Gospel*, p. 16.
[3] *The Four Gospels*, pp. 253 f.

seem to be two possibilities, seeing that it is unlikely that
St Luke would substitute τῆς γνώσεως if τῆς βασιλείας
τοῦ θεοῦ stood in his text of Q. Either the version in
Luke is the Q version of the saying; or perhaps Q had τὴν
κλεῖδα simply, and τῆς γνώσεως is an interpretative addition by St Luke. In either case the form in Matthew should
probably be referred to M.

Lk. xii. 32: no parallel in Mt. For the reasons for regarding this saying as derived from Q see *The Four Gospels*,
p. 284. Here, again, of course, it is possible that we have
to do with an additional saying inserted by St Luke into
his copy of Q, where it seemed to him to go most appro-
priately.

Lk. xvi. 16: Mt. xi. 12. There can be little doubt that
here the form in Matthew is the original. The Lucan
version looks exceedingly like an attempt to clarify an
obscure and difficult saying.

Lk. xvii. 20 f.: no parallel in Mt. This passage may
belong to Q. A plausible reason for its omission from
Matthew may be found in the fact that it lends itself to an
interpretation of the Kingdom of God which would not be
acceptable to the First Evangelist with his stress on the
catastrophic aspect of the apocalyptic hope. (Cf. *The
Four Gospels*, p. 290.)

The result of this discussion is to leave us with the following sayings which may with more or less certainty be
referred to Q. The order is that of Luke. Brackets signify
a certain amount of doubt.

Lk. vi. 20 (S): Blessed are ye poor for yours is the Kingdom of
    God.
vii. 28 (G): The least in the Kingdom of God is greater than
    John the Baptist.
x. 9 (D ultimately G): The Kingdom of God has drawn nigh
    upon you.
x. 11 (D ultimately G): Only know this that the Kingdom of
    God is at hand.
xi. 20 (P): If I by the finger of God cast out demons, then the
    Kingdom of God has come upon you.

xii. 31 (D): Seek first his Kingdom.

[xii. 32 (D): Fear not, little flock, for it is your Father's good pleasure to give you the Kingdom.]

xiii. 18 (G): The Kingdom of God is like a grain of mustard seed.

xiii. 20 (G): The Kingdom of God is like leaven.

xiii. 28 (G): The patriarchs and prophets in the Kingdom of God and the sons of the Kingdom sent forth into the outer darkness.

xiii. 29 (G): People from the ends of the earth come and sit down in the Kingdom of God.

xvi. 16 (P): From the days of John the Baptist, the Kingdom of God βιάζεται, καὶ βιασταὶ ἁρπάζουσιν αὐτήν (text of Mt.).

[xvii. 20 (P): The Kingdom of God cometh not with observation.]

[xvii. 21 (P): The Kingdom of God is among you (ἐντὸς ὑμῶν).]

These passages have this much in common with those in Mark that the sayings which speak of entrance into the Kingdom belong to the latter half of the series. The last announcement that the Kingdom is at hand is at Lk. x. 11. Lk. xi. 20 speaks of it as something now present: with ἔφθασεν ἐφ᾽ ὑμᾶς may be compared Eccl. viii. 14 and Targum; Dan. iv. 21, 25 (Θ) and M.T., where the Aramaic verb is מְטָא; also Tg. Ezek. vii. 2.[1] In the sayings subsequent to xi. 20 the disciples are bidden to seek the Kingdom and are told that the Father will give it to them. In parables the Kingdom is likened to mustard seed and leaven: that is, it is present and growing or working. In a public utterance it is said that patriarchs, prophets and people from the ends of the earth enter into it. We have also the enigmatic saying that the Kingdom is ravished and violent men snatch at it.[2] The last word in Q is that the Kingdom does

---

[1] Cf. Dalman, *Words of Jesus*, p. 107.

[2] I take this obscure saying to be a warning on the part of Jesus against those who imagined that the Kingdom could be established by armed force and political revolution. To anyone who could read the signs of the times it was obvious that fanatical patriotism was a current that was steadily gaining strength and was destined to end in a flood of disasters. The saying that

not come with observable external signs, but is already
present.(1)

The only example in the earlier part of the series, which
might be thought to suggest that the idea of entering the
Kingdom formed part of the teaching of Jesus before, say,
Peter's Confession, is Lk. vii. 28: Mt. xi. 11. A comparison
of the whole passage in Matthew with the parallels in
Luke shows that the discourse in Matthew on John is
composite: Mt. xi. 7–19 = Lk. vii. 24–28; xvi. 16; vii.
31–34. Moreover, Mt. xi. 14 has points of contact with
what is said in Mk. ix. 11 f. The tendency is obviously for
sayings about John to group themselves together: and I am
inclined to think that this process had already begun in Q.
It is therefore possible that this saying belongs to another
and a later context: and I should suggest the time when
the authority of Jesus was questioned by the Jewish
authorities (Mk. xi. 27–33). A comparison of Lk. vii.
28–30 with Mk. xi. 30–33 and Mt. xxi. 28–32 (M) is
instructive. (See Hort, *Judaistic Christianity*, p. 27.)

The evidence from Q does not support the conclusion
drawn from Mark that Jesus speaks only to the disciples of
entering the Kingdom. Lk. xii. 31 (D) is probably to be
understood in this sense; what the disciples are to seek is
entrance to the Kingdom. The saying Lk. xiii. 28 f. is G
according to both Matthew and Luke.

The combined testimony of Mark and Q, therefore,

they who take the sword shall perish by the sword was only too abundantly
fulfilled, first in A.D. 70 and again in the calamitous revolt in the reign of
Hadrian. Cf. *Die Schriften des N.T.* 1. 306.

(1) Taking ἐντὸς ὑμῶν to mean 'among you'. The idea seems to be that the
Kingdom is present in the way that the leaven is in the dough or the seed in
the ground—inconspicuous and largely unnoticed, yet real and potent none
the less. It is probable that we should compare with Lk. xvii. 20 f. the
Pharisaic demand for a sign and the answer of Jesus that no sign would be
given (Lk. xi. 29–32: Mt. xii. 38–42, Q; Mk. viii. 11 f.). Like Jonah to the
Ninevites the Son of Man is the sign to his generation. The Kingdom as a
present reality is a self-authenticating thing, which must be recognised for
what it is. The same is the case—in Q at any rate—when 'the day of the Son
of Man' is in question. It too comes without any sign (Lk. xii. 35–46:
Mt. xxiv. 43–51 (Q); Lk. xvii. 22–30; Mt. xxiv. 26–28, 37–41, Q).

only supports the proposition that in the earlier part of the ministry Jesus speaks of the Kingdom as something that is coming, in the latter part as something into which men enter. Mark alone gives the further point that references to entry into the Kingdom are characteristic of the D sections of the teaching.

M

Mt. v. 10 (S): Blessed are those persecuted for righteousness' sake, for theirs is the Kingdom of Heaven.

v. 19 (S): He who relaxes one of these least commandments and teaches men so, shall be called least in the Kingdom of Heaven.

But he who performs and teaches (them), he shall be called great in the Kingdom of Heaven.

v. 20 (S): Unless your righteousness exceed that of the Scribes and Pharisees ye shall not enter into the Kingdom of Heaven.

vi. 10 (S): Thy Kingdom come.[1] Cf. Lk. xi. 2 (D).

vii. 21 (S): Not every one that saith to me 'Lord, Lord' shall enter into the Kingdom of Heaven but he that doeth the will of my Father in heaven.[2] Cf. Lk. vi. 46.

x. 7 (D ultimately G): Preach saying: The Kingdom of Heaven is at hand.

xiii. 24 (G): The Kingdom of Heaven is like a man sowing good seed in his field.

xiii. 38 (D): The good seed = the sons of the Kingdom.

xiii. 41 (D): The Son of Man will send his angels, and they will gather out of his Kingdom all the scandals and those who do what is unlawful.

xiii. 43 (D): Then the righteous shall shine forth like the sun in the Kingdom of their Father.

xiii. 44 (D?): The Kingdom of Heaven is like a treasure hidden in a field.

xiii. 45 (D?): The Kingdom of Heaven is like a merchant seeking fine pearls.

xiii. 47 (D?): The Kingdom of Heaven is like a net cast into the sea.

[1] Mt. vi. 13: 'For thine is the Kingdom, etc.' is rejected on textual grounds.

[2] The additional words: 'he shall enter into the Kingdom of Heaven' are open to doubt on textual grounds. In any case they add nothing to the sense of the passage and may safely be neglected here.

Mt. xiii. 52 (D): Every scribe disciplined to the Kingdom of
    Heaven is like a householder who brings out of his store
    things new and old.
xvi. 19 (D): I will give thee the keys of the Kingdom of Heaven.
xviii. 4 (D): He who humbles himself like this child, he is the
    greatest in the Kingdom of Heaven.
xviii. 23 (D): The Kingdom of Heaven is likened to a king
    who would make a reckoning with his servants.
xix. 12 (D): There are eunuchs who have made themselves
    such διὰ τὴν βασιλείαν τῶν οὐρανῶν.
xx. 1 (D): The Kingdom of Heaven is like a householder who
    went out very early to hire workers into his vineyard.
xxi. 31 (P): Publicans and harlots precede you into the King-
    dom of God.
xxi. 43 (P): The Kingdom of God shall be taken away from you
    and given to a people producing its fruits.
xxii. 2 (P): The Kingdom of Heaven is likened to a king who
    made a marriage-feast for his son.
xxiii. 14 (P): Woe to you Scribes and Pharisees, hypocrites, for
    you close the Kingdom of Heaven in the face of men; for
    you do not go in yourselves, nor will you let those who
    are entering enter.
xxv. 1 (D): Then the Kingdom of Heaven shall be likened to
    ten maidens.
xxv. 34 (D): Come ye blessed of my Father, inherit the King-
    dom prepared for you from the foundation of the world.

To complete the list we should note Mt. iii. 2, where the
preaching of John the Baptist is summarised in the words:
'Repent, for the Kingdom of Heaven is at hand'; Mt. xiii.
19 and xxiv. 14. These are all to be regarded not as M but
as RMT.

In M as in Mk and Q the preaching of the Kingdom as
something that is approaching is confined to the earlier
part of the ministry. The other conception—that of something into which one enters—is found at all stages in the
ministry according to this source. We must therefore
examine the occurrences which fall before xvi. 19. Three of
these, Mt. v. 19, 20; vii. 21, are in the Sermon on the
Mount, a highly composite discourse as we have already
seen. The only other case which might be thought to

imply an entrance into the Kingdom is Mt. xiii. 43; but this parable seems rather to imply the opposite. The Kingdom is not made up by some people entering and others remaining outside. To begin with everyone seems to be in, good and bad alike, and the final result is obtained by a process of subtraction. The evil-doers are eliminated from the Kingdom and then the righteous shine. This case, therefore, is not on all fours with the others: and, indeed, the parable as a whole, or at any rate its interpretation, is open to considerable suspicion.[1]

If these four cases be disregarded, and we may fairly put them on one side, the remainder of the evidence in M agrees with what we have found in the case of Mk and Q.

L

The sayings concerning the Kingdom which may be assigned to this source are as follows:

Lk. ix. 62 (G): No one putting his hand to the plough and looking back is fit for the Kingdom of God.

xi. 2 (D): Thy Kingdom come.[2]

xxii. 16 (D): I will not eat it [the Passover] until it is fulfilled in the Kingdom of God.

xxii. 29 (D): I grant to you as my Father has granted to me a Kingdom.[3]

xxii. 30 (D): That ye may eat and drink at my table in my Kingdom.

The remaining instances in Luke: iv. 43 (cf. Mk. i. 38); ix. 2 (cf. Mk. vi. 7); ix. 11 (cf. Mk. vi. 34); ix. 60 (cf. Mt. viii. 22); xviii. 29 (cf. Mk. x. 29); xxi. 31 (cf. Mk. xiii. 29) all appear to be editorial additions or alterations by St Luke, and should therefore be classified as RL.

All the genuine L cases are from the latter half of the ministry. Lk. ix. 62; xxii. 29 and 30 suggest entrance to the

[1] Cf. A. H. McNeile, *The Gospel according to St Matthew*, pp. 202 f.

[2] But see *The Four Gospels*, p. 277, where it is argued that the reading found in 162, 700, D (partly), Marcion, Gregory of Nyssa, and Maximus of Turin: 'Thy Holy Spirit come upon us and cleanse us' is what St Luke wrote here.

[3] Cf. *The Four Gospels*, p. 288.

Kingdom. Lk. xi. 2: 'Thy Kingdom come', would form
an exception to the general rule which holds for Mk, Q,
and M, if the text were right; but there is reason to think
that 'Thy Kingdom come' is not what St Luke wrote here,
and that the current reading of almost all MSS is the
result of assimilation to the version in Matthew. The
question however remains: if the place where the prayer
stands in Luke is correct, that is, if the prayer was given to
the disciples in the latter part of the ministry, did it contain the petition 'Thy Kingdom come'? If Canon
Streeter's argument is sound, we have only the testimony
of M for the insertion of the words. Alongside of this we
have to place the fact that St Luke has a weakness for
putting in references to the Kingdom—we have counted
six instances in this Gospel as RL. It is unlikely, therefore,
that he would have omitted the petition had it been known
to him in any reliable tradition. On the other hand 'Thy
Kingdom come' would be a watchword in the circles in
which Matthew was compiled. These considerations seem
to me to render the authenticity of the petition somewhat
doubtful.

    Taking the evidence as a whole, then, it may be asserted
that our four sources are in substantial agreement that
Jesus speaks of the Kingdom as coming in the former part
of his ministry: in the latter part he speaks of people
entering the Kingdom. According to the arrangement of
the story in Mark the turning-point lies somewhere between
the Transfiguration and the beginning of the final journey
to Jerusalem. If this fact stood alone it might perhaps pass
without much notice; but when it is remembered that Jesus
speaks of the Father only in the latter part of the ministry,
and that the important phrase 'Son of Man'[1] also belongs
to this period, we are bound to enquire whether this
change in our Lord's way of speaking of the Kingdom may
not have a deeper significance than appears on the surface.
    The most obvious solution of this problem is that Jesus

    [1] See below, Chapter VII.

MTJ   9

[handwritten note: The inner invisible "kingdom" knows God more as "Father" than king, and as "Son of man".]

[handwritten top margin: came at transfiguration etc. ? is now ? to be entered.]

[handwritten: 144]

held that the Kingdom had come in some real sense during his own ministry. Further we may suppose that the coming of the Kingdom is to be identified with one or other of the outstanding events which mark the turning-point alike in the teaching and in the ministry. The most plausible conjecture will be that which equates the coming of the Kingdom with Peter's Confession: 'Thou art the Messiah'. This great saying was—one can hardly doubt—evoked in the first instance by the cumulative effect of continuous living with Jesus. It was a spontaneous tribute of the disciple to the master, an attempt to make articulate a growing sense of reverence which mingled with the affection and loyalty and admiration that were already present. But it was more than that. It was an acknowledgement of the authority of Jesus in a new way. To the deference due from the disciple to the teacher was added a new thing—the loyalty and devotion of a subject to a king. And no mere earthly potentate, but one divinely anointed. It was in fact the recognition of the Kingdom in the person of Jesus: and with that recognition the Kingdom could be said to have come.

[handwritten left margin: Mt. 16 =]

[handwritten left margin: Student → teacher Subject → King]

We have a similar notion in the Rabbinic literature: and as the matter is one of importance it will be well to cite the relevant passages here. The first is from *Sifre*, §313, on Deut. xxxii. 10 (ed. Friedmann, p. 134 *b*):

Before our father Abraham came into the world, the Holy One, blessed is he, was King, so to speak, only over heaven; as it is said [Gen. xxiv. 7]: 'Jehovah the God of heaven who took me, etc.' But after our father Abraham had come into the world, he made him [God] King over heaven and earth; as it is said [Gen. xxiv. 3], 'I adjure thee by Jehovah the God of heaven and earth'.

[handwritten left margin: Kingdom dated in Abraham & Exodus]

That is, at the time which is spoken of in Gen. xii. 1 the Kingdom was, as it were, effective only in heaven; but with the recognition of it implied in Abraham's words (xxiv. 3), it became effective on earth also.

The same thing is deemed to have happened again at the

Red Sea. The acknowledgement of God's sovereignty, this
time by Israel, is taken to be implied in Ex. xv. 2, 'This is
my God'; and 18, 'Jehovah is King for ever and ever'.
This is the point of the passage in *Sifra* on Lev. xviii. 1 ff.
(ed. Weiss, p. 85 d):

'Speak to the children of Israel and say to them: I am Jehovah
your God. After the manner of the land of Egypt...ye shall
not do'. R. Simeon b. Yohai (c. A.D. 150) said: In another
place (Ex. xx. 2) it says, 'I am Jehovah thy God'. I am
Jehovah and you took my Kingdom upon you in Egypt
(referring to Ex. xv. 2, 18). They said to him: Yes, yes,
[God answered:] If you have taken my Kingdom (מלכותי)
upon you, take also my Commandments: 'Thou shalt have no
other God but me' (Ex. xx. 3). Here (Lev. xviii. 2) it says 'I
am Jehovah your God'. I am he whose Kingdom you took
upon yourselves at Sinai. They said to him: Yes, yes. [God
answered:] If you have taken my Kingdom upon you, take
also my Commandments: 'After the manner of the land of
Egypt...ye shall not do'.

Passages of similar import are Ex. R. 23; *Mekh.* on Ex.
xx. 2; Midr. Ps. xx. § 3; *Pesiḳta*, 16 *b*, etc.[1]

It is evident that the Kingdom is not in these passages
conceived in any geographical or even political sense. It
does not correspond to the empire or the state. It is not a
district over which sway is exercised; neither is it a political
construction. It is not Kingdom as opposed to oligarchy or
democracy. The Kingdom here is a personal relation
between the King and the subject. The claim on God's
part to rule, and the acknowledgement on man's part of
that claim, together constitute the actual Kingdom: and
Peter's Confession may fairly be regarded as just that
acknowledgement that was needed to make the Kingdom
de jure into a Kingdom *de facto*.

Two parables from the *Mekhilta* on Ex. xx. 2 may be
quoted to illustrate this point. The first asks

Why were the Ten Commandments not given at the beginning of the Law? There is a parable: to what is the matter like?

[1] Collected in Strack-Billerbeck, *Komm.* I. 173 ff.

Like one who came into a province. He said to them: I will be
king over you. They said to him: What hast thou done for us
that thou shouldst reign over us? What did he do? He built
them a wall, provided a water-supply for them, made war for
them. He said to them: I will be king over you. They said to
him: Yes, yes. So the Omnipresent[1] brought Israel out of
Egypt, he divided the sea for them, he brought down manna for
them, he caused the spring to flow for them, he brought the
quails to them, he waged war with Amalek for them. He said
to them: I will be King over you. They said to him: Yes, yes.
Rabbi (?) says it was to make known the glory of Israel in that
when they all stood at Mount Sinai to receive the Law, they
were all of them as one heart to receive the Kingdom of
Heaven with joy.[2]   *Kingdom came at Sinai.*

The second parable says:

It is like a human king who came into a province. His
servants said to him: Issue decrees to them. He said to them:
When they have received my kingdom (מלכותי), I will issue
decrees to them; for if they do not receive my kingdom they
will not receive my decrees. So the Omnipresent said to
Israel: I am Jehovah thy God, ye shall not have, etc. I am he
whose Kingdom you received in Egypt. They said to him: It is
so. (God replied): As you received my Kingdom receive my
decrees.[3]

In both these parables the crux of the matter is the
receiving of the Kingdom, the acknowledgement of God as
King. It is obvious that the reception of the Kingdom is
analogous to what we should call allegiance, a personal
loyalty and devotion to the King. But if we carry this
interpretation over into the New Testament passages, it is
obvious that the Kingdom must be conceived as something
through and through spiritual. Just as much as the Fatherhood of God, the Kingdom of God is a personal relation
between God and the individual human being. It differs
in this, that in the Fatherhood the paternal care of God is
in the forefront; in the Kingdom it is the divine authority.

[1] המקום.
[2] *Mekhilta*, ed. Friedmann, p. 66 *b*.
[3] *Ib.* p. 67 *a*.

As Fatherhood desires love
*   " King   " demands obedience*

Further, this conception of the Kingdom as a personal relation enables us to explain certain parables of the Kingdom, notably the Seed growing secretly, the Mustard Seed, and the Leaven, where the emphasis is on the growth of the Kingdom and the extension of its influence. A Kingdom which consists of the King and one subject might fairly be likened to a grain of mustard seed: and the luxuriant growth of the plant until the birds come and build their nests in it suggests an extension of the Kingdom out of all proportion to its humble beginnings.[1] In the two Seed parables the emphasis is on the fact that the Kingdom grows; in the parable of the Leaven it is on the manner of the growth. It is a ferment which gradually penetrates until it affects the whole. That is to say, those who are already of the Kingdom are to the world what leaven is to dough.[2]

[1] The added touch of the birds nesting in the branches of the plant is not without significance. It is reminiscent of Ezek. xvii. 23; xxxi. 6; Dan. iv. 9, 18 (M.T.). Ezek. xvii. 23 is given a Messianic interpretation in the Targum, where the 'goodly cedar' is rendered 'a mighty king' and 'all fowl of every wing' becomes 'all the righteous and all the humble'. In Ezek. xxxi. 6 the Assyrian empire is likened to a tree in which the birds made their nests. The Targum explains this as the subjection of powerful cities by the hosts of Assyria. In the passage from Daniel the tree represents the kingdom of Nebuchadnezzar and the birds subject peoples. These passages alone would justify us in supposing that the reference to the birds in the parable is meant to suggest the extension of the Kingdom even beyond the borders of Israel. Further, in *Eth. Enoch*, xc. 30 there is a reference to the fowls of the air, where it is highly probable that what is meant is the company of repentant Gentiles, who have not participated in the oppression of Israel (Beer, *ad loc.*; Moore, *Judaism*, II. 300). There is, finally, a passage in the Rabbinical literature where the 'birds of heaven' are expressly stated to represent the Gentile nations: Midrash Ps. civ. 13 (ed. Buber, p. 222 a) עליהם עוף השמים ישכון אלו אומות העולם וגו'. We may therefore say that Jesus thought of the Kingdom as increasing by addition until even the Gentile nations should be brought within its scope. Cf. Lk. xiii. 29: Mt. viii. 11 (Q): 'They shall come from East and West and North and South and sit down in the Kingdom of God'.

[2] To this line of thought belong such sayings as 'Ye are the salt of the earth'; 'Ye are the light of the world'; 'So let your light shine before men that they may see your good works *and glorify your Father in heaven*'. Probably we should add Lk. xi. 20: Mt. xii. 28 (Q), 'If I by the finger of God cast out demons, then the Kingdom of God has come upon you'; Lk. xvii. 21 (Q), 'The Kingdom of God is among you'.

[handwritten top margin: → use these parables for Sermon on Church? St... / Church is in the state -- God's instrument to change soc...]

[handwritten left margin: Mot]

[handwritten left margin, vertical: The Church is never the Kingdom, but only its result. "It is the relation of King to individual Subject."]

We are thus brought face to face with what may be called the first manifestation of the Kingdom in the world. Primarily the Kingdom is a personal relation between God as King and the individual as subject. Then it appears in the world as a society, something which might be called the People of God. This society consists of all those who are linked together by the fact of their common allegiance to one King. It is the increase of this society which is pictured in the three parables just considered. The inner compulsion to bring fresh individuals into allegiance to the King constitutes what Jesus likens to the working of leaven in dough, and what in these days we should call the missionary motive. But it cannot be too strongly emphasised that the society is not the Kingdom, but only a manifestation or product of it: and that membership of the society is not entrance into the Kingdom, but only a result of entrance. *[handwritten: Kingdom is always the individual relation]*

This first manifestation of the Kingdom in the world, the 'little flock' which Jesus likens to seed and leaven, is again an agent, an instrument in God's hand, a means towards a yet greater manifestation which lies still in the future. This consummation is variously described. In Mark we are told of a coming of the Son of Man in the glory of his Father with the holy angels (Mk. viii. 38); again, with reminiscences of Dan. vii. 13, of the Son of Man coming on the clouds with great power and glory (xiii. 26). Likewise in Mark xiv. 62, where the imagery is again borrowed from the Old Testament (Dan. vii. 13; Ps. cx. (cix.) 1 ff.), we are shown the picture of the Son of Man seated on the right hand of 'the Power' (i.e. God) and coming with the clouds of heaven. In Q a different terminology is used to describe the same event; it is referred to as 'the day or parousia of the Son of Man'[1] (Lk. xvii.

[1] The question whether παρουσία (Mt.) or ἡμέρα (Lk.) is the authentic text of Q must be left in abeyance at this stage. It is, however, to be remarked that both terms were current in the Early Church; both are found in the earlier Epistles of Paul. For παρουσία cf. I Thess. ii. 19; iii. 13; iv. 15; v. 23; II Thess. ii. 1, 8; I Cor. xv. 23: for ἡμέρα, I Thess. v. 2; II Thess. ii. 2;

24 = Mt. xxiv. 27; Lk. xvii. 26 = Mt. xxiv. 37; Lk. xvii.
30; Mt. xxiv. 39). In M we have, as in Mark, a coming of
the Son of Man in his glory with the angels; and it is
emphasised that the coming is for the final judgement of
the nations (Mt. xxv. 31 f.; cf. the parable of the Wheat and
Tares and its explanation, Mt. xiii. 24-30, 37-43). In L
there is also reference to the coming of the Son of Man
(Lk. xviii. 8; it is also implied in Lk. xxi. 36).

Once these distinctions are made—and they are necessary
distinctions—it becomes clear that the old dispute whether
Jesus conceived the Kingdom as present or future, whether
he pictured it as brought about by a gradual moral and
social evolution or by a catastrophic supernatural act of
God, has arisen out of the confusion of matters in the
Gospel which are really distinct. The Kingdom of God in its
essence is the Reign of God, a personal relation between
God and the individual: and there is no point in asking
whether it is present or future, just as there is no point in
asking whether the Fatherhood of God is present or future.
It is something independent of temporal and spatial
relations. It is a standing claim made by God on the loyalty
and obedience of man. From time to time individuals
admit this claim and accept the sovereignty of God. This is
what is meant by the phrase 'receive the Kingdom of God'
(δέχεσθαι τὴν βασιλείαν τοῦ θεοῦ: cf. Mk. x. 15) which has
its exact parallel in the Rabbinical parables quoted
above[1] (pp. 131 f.).

When the sovereignty of God is thus accepted the
Kingdom becomes a present reality to those who are the

I Cor. i. 8; v. 5; II Cor. i. 14, etc. For discussion of the meaning of the
phrase 'Son of Man' see below, Chapter VII.

[1] Δέχεσθαι τὴν βασ. τ. θ corresponds exactly with לקבל מלכות שמים
(Mekh., ed. Friedmann, 66 b). In this Mekhilta passage it is the Israelites
who accept the sovereignty. So also in Jubilees xii. 19 (tr. R. H. Charles,
p. 94) Abraham says, 'My God, God most High, Thou alone art my God,
and Thee and Thy dominion have I chosen'. In the Mishnah Berakhoth, II. 2
(ed. O. Holtzmann, pp. 48, 49), the individual Israelite is deemed to 'take
upon himself the yoke of the Kingdom of Heaven' when he recites the
Shema' (Deut. vi. 4-9), which is conceived as a confession of faith in the one
true God and a pledge of complete devotion to him.

subjects of the King. In this sense one may speak of the Kingdom—or rather what we have called above the first manifestation of it—as present, and describe it in parables which suggest increase in size and influence.

The final consummation, which is described as the Coming or the Parousia or the Day of the Son of Man is something which, right up to the end of the ministry, is conceived as still in the future.

These three interdependent conceptions of the Kingdom as an eternal fact, as a manifestation in the present life of men, and as a consummation still to come, can be paralleled in Jewish thought before and after the days of Jesus as well as in the early Christian literature. For the idea of the Kingdom as something always subsisting we may compare Ps. cxlv. 13:

> Thy Kingdom is an everlasting Kingdom,
> And thy rule is over every generation;

as also Dan. iii. 33 (E.V. iv. 3); iv. 31 (E.V. iv. 34).[1] The same conception appears in the extra-canonical Jewish literature, e.g. *Psalms of Solomon* xvii. 4: 'The Kingdom of our God is unto everlasting over the heathen in judgement';[2] *Enoch* lxxxiv. 2: 'Thy might, thy Kingdom, and thy greatness, remain to all eternity, and thy rule throughout all generations; all the heavens are thy throne to eternity and the whole earth thy footstool for ever'. The same thing is implied in the common Jewish form of thanksgiving: 'Blessed art thou, O Lord our God, King of the Universe'.[3] In the New Testament we find God

---

[1] For further passages from O.T. cf. Moore, *Judaism*, I. 401 n. 2.
[2] Trans. Ryle and James.
[3] מלך העולם. Cf. also the Jewish hymn *Adon Olam* (Singer, *Authorised Daily Prayer Book*, p. 3):

'He is Lord of the universe, who reigned ere any creature yet was formed.
At the time when all things were made by his desire, then was his name proclaimed King.
And after all things shall have had an end, he alone, the dreaded one, shall reign,
Who was, who is, and who will be in glory'.

Though this hymn is late (it belongs to the Gaonic age) it is nevertheless interesting as stating explicitly what is implicit in earlier Jewish thought.

described as 'the King eternal' (I Tim. i. 17), a title which is repeated in I Clement lxi.[1]

The manifestation of the Kingdom of God on earth in the acceptance of it by individuals is most explicitly stated in the Rabbinical passages quoted above (pp. 130 ff.). It is, however, also frequently implied in passages of the Old Testament, e.g. Is. xliii. 15; xliv. 6; Zeph. iii. 15; Ps. v. 3; lxxxiv. 4, etc. In these and similar passages Israel or the individual Israelite makes the sovereignty of God manifest in the world by acknowledging it and accepting its obligations. It may be claimed that the same is the case where the phrase 'Servant of Jehovah' or its equivalent is used in the second part of Isaiah, especially when it is remembered that 'Servant' in Hebrew has as one of its normal meanings 'subject' of a King.[2]

It may be observed here that this manifestation of the Kingdom in its subjects undergoes a development in the religious history of the Hebrew people similar to that which was noticed above in the discussion of the Fatherhood of God. At first God is King of Israel as a whole, just as he is the Father of the whole nation. Later the tendency is towards the individualising and universalising of this aspect of the Kingdom as also of the Fatherhood. Individual Israelites or Gentiles take upon themselves the yoke of the Kingdom, for example in the recitation of the *Shema'* as a personal profession of faith and devotion. In the New Testament this universalising process reaches its limit in the Pauline doctrine that the Christian community forms the true Israel of God (Gal. vi. 16) in implied contrast to the 'Israel after the flesh' (I Cor. x. 18). Not all Jews belong to this true Israel (Rom. ix. 6); nor does the true Israel exclude Jews (Rom. ii. 28 f.; Gal. iii. 28 f.); all who

---

[1] Lightfoot, *ad loc.*, remarks: 'Here the Eternal King is tacitly contrasted with the temporary kings, the βασιλεὺς τῶν αἰώνων with the βασιλεῖς τοῦ αἰῶνος τούτου (cf. Ign. *Rom.* 6)'.

[2] This may also be the sense in I Thess. i. 9; I Pet. ii. 16; Rev. vii. 3; xxii. 3. The religious use of the term עבד is fully discussed by Robertson Smith, *Rel. Sem.* 1894, pp. 68 f.

are of Christ are the seed of Abraham, the true covenant-
people[1] who worship God in spirit, whether they be of
Jewish or Gentile origin. This community is described by
St Paul as a colony whose mother-country is in heaven.[2]
Its members are described as 'servants of God' or are said
to 'serve God': and in these expressions there may well be
at times a reminiscence of the Old Testament sense of
'servant' as subject of a king.

The final consummation of the Kingdom was looked for
in Old Testament times. As a single example we may
take Zech. xiv. 9:

> And the Lord shall be King over all the earth:
> In that day shall the Lord be one and his name one.

The same hope is expressed in Pss. xcvi–xcix. In the
apocryphal books it appears in such utterances as these
from the *Sibylline Oracles*:

> When Rome shall reign over Egypt...then will the most
> great Kingdom of the immortal King be revealed to men, and
> there will come a holy ruler, to sway the sceptre over all the
> earth, to all the ages of swift-rushing time. (iii. 46–50.)
> Then He will raise up a Kingdom to all eternity over men,
> he who once gave a holy law to the godly, to whom he promised
> to open all the earth and the world, and the gates of the blessed
> and all joys, and an immortal soul, and eternal happiness.
> (iii. 767 ff.)[3]

Again in the *Assumption of Moses* we have the prophecy
(x. 1):

> And then His Kingdom will appear throughout all His creation,
> And then Satan will be no more,
> And sorrow will depart with him.[4]

[1] This I take to be the underlying thought in ἡμεῖς γάρ ἐσμεν ἡ περιτομή
(Phil. iii. 3). Circumcision is the 'Abrahamic covenant'.
[2] Phil. iii. 20 and Dibelius' note (*H.B.N.T.* vol. III. Pt. II. p. 61): 'The
word (πολίτευμα) denotes a colony of settlers in a foreign land, whose
organisation reproduces in miniature the πολιτεία of the home-country and
accordingly is called after it.... If this meaning suits the present passage the
meaning will be: "We have our mother-country (Heimatsreich) in heaven
and are here on earth as a colony of citizens of heaven"'.
[3] Trans. G. F. Moore, *Judaism*, II. 374, 372.
[4] Trans. R. H. Charles.

In the Rabbinical literature we may cite from *Mekhilta* the following passage: R. Eliezer (b. Hyrkanos, c. A.D. 90) said:

When will the name of that one [Amalek = Rome] be destroyed? When idolatry is rooted out with all its votaries, and when the Omnipresent is alone [as object of worship] in the world and his Kingdom shall be for ever and ever; in that hour the Lord will go forth and fight against those heathen.[1]

In the New Testament the thought of the consummation is present, as we have already seen, in the teaching of Jesus. It is also to be found in the Pauline Epistles and other books of the New Testament. St Paul speaks of 'the Day of our Lord Jesus Christ', or 'of our Lord Jesus', or 'of Jesus Christ', or 'of Christ' simply (I Cor. i. 8; v. 5; II Cor. i. 14; Phil. i. 6, 10; ii. 16): of 'the Day of the Lord' in I Thess. v. 2; II Thess. ii. 2. 'The Day of the Lord' is likewise found in II Pet. iii. 10, and 'the Day of God' in II Pet. iii. 12; Rev. xvi. 14. 'The Parousia of Christ' (again the titles vary) is found in I Cor. xv. 23; I Thess. ii. 19; iii. 13; iv. 15; v. 23; II Thess. ii. 1, 8. The Epistle of James has 'the Parousia of the Lord' twice (v. 7 f.): and in II Peter we have 'the Parousia of our Lord Jesus Christ' (i. 16), 'of the Lord and Saviour' (iii. 4), and 'of the Day of God' (iii. 12).

A most striking exposition of the hoped-for consummation of the Kingdom is contained in I Cor. xv. 20–28, particularly *v.* 24 with its picture of the end,[2] when Christ, having subdued every hostile power, hands over the Kingdom to God the Father in order that (*v.* 28) God may

---

[1] *Mekhilta*, ed. Friedmann, f. 56 a. Further Rabbinical passages in Strack-Billerbeck, I. 172–180.

[2] I cannot accept Lietzmann's suggestion that τέλος in *v.* 24 means 'the remainder', the third τάγμα in the resurrection. If St Paul wished to refer to such a class it would have been much simpler to say οἱ λοιποί rather than to make this artificial use of a term which already had a quite definite meaning of its own, and that in his own writings, e.g. I Cor. i. 8. Moreover, it does not seem that St Paul contemplates a resurrection of any but those who are in Christ (cf. R. H. Charles, art. 'Eschatology' in *Enc. Bib.*). Of course the term 'those that are Christ's' is not to be too narrowly construed; it is wide enough to cover, for example, the Old Testament saints.

be all in all. The whole passage is most illuminating for the discrimination between the Kingdom as a present manifestation in the lives of men; the final consummation of the Kingdom at the Parousia; and the Kingdom as the eternal sovereignty of God. The present manifestation is the Kingdom of Christ, who must reign till he has put all enemies under foot (v. 25). The consummation comes when the last enemy, Death, is destroyed at the Parousia and the resurrection of those who are Christ's, and the Kingdom is handed over to God (vv. 23 f.). The eternal sovereignty of God is clearly implied in the statement that it is God who is the ultimate source of all the power and authority by which this triumph is brought about.

We may therefore conclude that, as this threefold way of regarding the Kingdom of God is present in the Hebrew Scriptures which Jesus knew and in the current religious thought of the people among whom he lived, it could hardly have been unknown to him. Further, the fact that it reappears in the earliest documents of Christianity makes it, at the very lowest, possible that he adopted it. When, finally, we find in the Synoptic records clear evidence of this threefold discrimination in the teaching of Jesus, the chain is complete, and we are free to admit the authenticity of all three aspects of the Kingdom in the teaching and can proceed to examine them in more detail.

Before doing this it will be convenient to sum up what conclusions seem to be established by the preceding discussion.

(1) The notions of the Kingdom as a present reality and as a future consummation are not contradictory or mutually exclusive when they are rightly apprehended as corollaries of the eternal sovereignty of God.

(2) In the teaching of Jesus the Kingdom as a present reality is thought of as something that has come into existence during the course of his own ministry.

(3) Jesus speaks of the final consummation of the King-

dom, which lies in the future, as the 'coming of the Son of Man' or as 'the Day' or 'Parousia of the Son of Man'.

(4) The three aspects in which the Kingdom may be regarded are not peculiar to the teaching of Jesus, but are present in the Old Testament, in the Rabbinic teaching, and in the documents of the primitive Christian community.

Ch 5 — Between transfiguration: departure for Jerusalem Jesus begins using new expression: enter Kingdom — instead of "at hand". At Mt. 16 the disciples saw the Kingdom as come in the King. It is relationship — not chronological. allegoric.

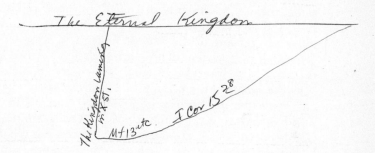

The Eternal Kingdom

The Kingdom elements in O.T.

Mt 13 etc. I Cor 15²⁸

Kingdom is rule of God in individual who chooses to be His subject. It comes in Jesus who will overthrow evil: at last give the Kingdom temporal to God. I Cor 15

The 3 transitions of the Idea 'Kingdom of God' in O.T.
Early: a. territorial   Prophets: a. universal
b. partial   b. Total life - ethic'l, n
c. dependent   c. Sovereign.

The implications of Universal Sovereignty to Prob. of evil. How to
reconcile good God with evil. Apocalypse appealed to masses
recognised both evil & good kingdoms, but the latter would win.
Profoundest was the view of Communion with God as its own reward.

Chapter VI

GOD AS KING: THE ETERNAL SOVEREIGNTY

I. PRE-PROPHETIC AND PROPHETIC IDEAS

THE eternal and absolute sovereignty of God was an integral part of the religious heritage of the people among whom our Lord lived and worked. It was in their sacred Scriptures; it was in their synagogue discourses; it was implied in their daily prayers. In prophetic vision Isaiah had seen the Lord sitting upon a throne high and lifted up.[1] Micaiah ben Imlah saw the Lord sitting on his throne, and all the host of heaven standing by him on his right hand and on his left.[2] The prophetic ministry of Ezekiel was inaugurated by the vision of the throne-chariot of Jehovah.[3] In all these the essential idea is the same, that the sovereignty of God is universal and absolute; and in Ezekiel's vision this absoluteness and universality are pressed to the utmost limit. The Kingship of Jehovah is independent of his special relation to Israel and the fall of Israel leaves his essential sovereignty untouched.[4] 'On the whole the tendency of Ezekiel's vision... is to emphasise the universality of Jehovah's relations to the world of nature and of mankind.... The attributes of God here symbolised are those which express His relation to created existence as a whole—omnipresence, omnipotence, omniscience.'[5] And this vision of God as King, which had been the inspiration of the great prophets, had in the days of Jesus become an article of faith to every pious Jew.[6]

Isa. 6

EZEKIEL

---

[1] Is. vi.   [2] I Kings xxii. 19.   [3] Ezek. i.
[4] Skinner, *The Book of Ezekiel*, p. 35.   [5] *Ibid.* pp. 35 f.
[6] Very significant is the choice of אֲדֹנָי as a substitute for יהוה in the reading of the Old Testament. That this change had taken place by the third century B.C. is shown by the LXX, ὁ κύριος for יהוה. אָדֹן as a *royal* title is very frequent in the O.T., particularly in the historical books: Judges, Samuel and Kings (*B.D.B.* 11 *a*). Moreover, it is to be noted that אֶרֶן and

Jesus taught God's Sovereignty over nature (shown in flowers etc. not
storms) and in men (God had limited Himself) is evil. Man can
choose between kingdom of evil and God. God will win.
conscience in man's evidence that God will win. God makes
exclusive demands upon the individual & provides the power to
fulfil them. It is the kingdom of a Father. We are in this King-
as Sons, not subjects. We belong to the royal far

God as King over a territory & people.

The history of this doctrine of the sovereignty is curiously like that of the doctrine of the Fatherhood of God which was sketched above in Chapter IV. It is probable that the Kingship of God was first thought of as a relation between Jehovah and the nation as a whole. Jehovah was the King of Israel, and Israel was the people of Jehovah: and this Kingship was thought of as something similar to human kingship. The sovereignty of Jehovah was thus a limited thing; but within its limits it was exclusive: 'Thou shalt have no other god before me'. Jehovah has his territory and his people: and on his own ground he will brook no rival, nor will he allow a divided allegiance on the part of his subjects.

But other gods equally have their rights—over their own territory and among their own subjects. When David is driven from the land of Israel he interprets it as being driven into the jurisdiction of other gods than Jehovah. 'Go, serve other gods' does not mean primarily 'go and practise idolatry' but 'go and dwell in a land where Jehovah is not King, where you will be the subject of some other deity'.[1] So also when Naaman the Syrian wishes to worship Jehovah in his native country, he is faced by the practical difficulty that the God of Israel has no standing in Syria. This difficulty is overcome by transporting a quantity of earth from Jehovah's land into the land of Rimmon and thus creating for Jehovah extra-territorial rights within the domain of his Syrian rival.[2]

At this stage of religious development every nation has its own god, and each god is king in his own land and over his own people. Indeed in many cases 'King' is the proper name of the deity. The Semitic word for king occurs, for example, in the names of Melkarth the god of Tyre and of Milcom the supreme god of the Ammonites. Similarly the

עֶבֶד are correlatives. In addressing the king the subject uses the form 'my lord the king' and refers to himself as 'thy servant'.

[1] I Sam. xxvi. 19.
[2] II Kings v. 17 f. Cf. also Num. xxi. 29; II Kings xvii; Ps. cxxxvii. 4; Jonah i. 3.

well-known Moloch, the name of the deity to whom human sacrifices were offered, is merely a distortion of the word *melek*, king.

It thus appears that in the early period of Israelite religious history the sovereignty of Jehovah was regarded as limited in its scope, and this limitation applies both to territory and subjects. But this was not the only way in which limits were set to the rule of Jehovah. Within his own sphere of influence his kingly functions were in practice fairly strictly defined. 'What the Semitic communities asked, and believed themselves to receive, from their god as king lay mainly in three things: help against their enemies, counsel by oracles or soothsayers in matters of national difficulty, and a sentence of justice when a case was too hard for human decision.'[1] Beyond this, the less the divine King interfered in the domestic concerns of his subjects the better for all concerned.

In a third respect the sovereignty of God was conceived as limited by the fact that his people and his land were as essential to him as he was to them. When all gods had their proper spheres of influence the idea of a god, who did not possess a land and a people of his own, seemed to be repugnant to common sense and all decent religious feeling. This conviction of the indispensability of Israel to God set an obvious limit to what God might do with Israel. He might extirpate this or that notorious evildoer; he might punish the people as a whole in various ways, by famine or pestilence or defeat in battle; but that he should willingly consent to the destruction of the nation, that he should surrender his own land to a foreign power, was simply incredible. To do so would be to place *himself* in an impossible position, to disinherit *himself*: and by proceeding to extremities with his people he would do as much harm to himself as to them. Hence it was that prophetic messages of the doom of the nation were received with such angry incredulity.

[1] Robertson Smith, *Religion of the Semites* (1894), p. 64.

The removal of these limitations from the idea of the
sovereignty of God was the work of the great prophets from
the eighth century onwards. If the task of a prophet like
Elijah was to defend the frontiers of Israel against the
incursions of foreign deities, that of Amos and his successors
was to proclaim the supremacy of Jehovah over the whole
world of men and things. He is the sole arbiter of human
destinies: and all the nations, whether they know it or not,
are subject to his will. In this matter the children of Israel
and the children of the Ethiopians are on the same footing
before the Lord: and the same God who brought up Israel
out of Egypt, brought also the Philistines from Caphtor and
the Syrians from Kir (Am. ix. 7). The westward advance
of the hosts of Assyria is by his command (Is. v. 26): and
the widespread empire of Nebuchadnezzar is his gift (Jer.
xxvii. 5–11). At a still later date the rise of the new
Persian Empire under Cyrus is explained as the work of
Jehovah (Is. xli. 1–7; xliv. 24–xlv. 25). Jehovah has
bestowed on Cyrus such titles of honour as 'My Shepherd'
and 'My Anointed' and commissioned him for a career of
conquest even though he remains 'ignorant of the true
God who made his way prosperous'.[1] When the full prophetic message has been proclaimed, Jehovah is no longer
a local god with a limited domain, but one 'that sitteth
upon the circle of the earth, and the inhabitants thereof are
as grasshoppers: that stretcheth out the heavens as a curtain,
and spreadeth them out as a tent to dwell in; that bringeth
the princes to nothing; he maketh the judges of the earth as
vanity' (Is. xl. 22 f.).

Along with this extension of Jehovah's sovereignty
beyond the boundaries of Israel goes a progressive de-
gradation of the gods of other nations. The commandment:
'Thou shalt have no other god before me' gives place
to the statement: 'I am the first and I am the last: and
beside me there is no god' (Is. xliv. 6). The worship of
other gods is no longer merely disloyalty to the God of

[1] Is. xlv. 4 with Skinner's note.

Israel; it is also a sign of the lack of knowledge and understanding. The idolater is not merely wicked: he is also
blind and stupid (Is. xliv. 15 f.). The other gods are not
rival divinities; they are nonentities. In this general
condemnation are involved not only the tribal and national
deities, but also the whole host of nature and fertility gods
and goddesses.[1] The prophet Hosea roundly declares that
it is Jehovah, and not another god, who gives the corn and
wine and oil (Hos. ii. 10); and so the way is prepared for
that assertion of the absolute sovereignty of God over
nature as well as over the nations, which finds its most impressive utterance in the closing chapters of Job (xxxviii-
xli).

A second limitation of the sovereignty of Jehovah, which
is removed by the prophetic teaching, is the restriction of
his functions to such tasks as supporting his people in
battle, giving oracles, and settling difficult points of law or
custom. How simply, not to say crudely, these functions
were conceived in early times is evident from many of the
narratives preserved in the Old Testament. Behind the
story in I Sam. iv lies the notion that if Jehovah would not
voluntarily support Israel against the Philistines, his hand
could be forced by taking the ark into battle. On the same
level is the consulting of the prophets by Ahab and
Jehoshaphat related in I Kings xxii. When Jehoshaphat
says to the King of Israel: 'Enquire, I pray thee, at the
word of the Lord to-day' (v. 5), it is not for the purpose of
learning the rights and wrongs of the case—Ahab has
settled that question himself already—but to find out
whether the proposed expedition will be successful or not.

The religious and moral insight of the great prophets
played havoc with this simple and congenial view of the
functions of Jehovah as King over Israel. Their insistence
that the divine nature must be conceived as absolute

[1] On these cf. Robertson Smith, *Rel. Sem.*, pp. 92–115; Wellhausen, *Prolegomena*[4], pp. 91–97, and *Die kleinen Propheten*[2], p. 100; G. A. Smith, *The Book of the Twelve Prophets*, I. 241–247; Skinner, *Prophecy and Religion*, ch. IV.

holiness and righteousness sapped the very foundations of much of the popular religious belief. "Divine favour could no longer be construed as divine favouritism:" and to be the chosen people of Jehovah was not only a great privilege but also a grave responsibility. 'You only have I known of all the families of the earth', says Jehovah to Israel,' therefore I will punish you for all your iniquities' (Am. iii. 2). The divine King is no longer just a convenient helper in time of need; he is the ever watchful guardian of justice and mercy in the relations of man to man, the swift judge of all wrong and oppression. So all human affairs, all the dealings of men with other men, come under his jurisdiction, and not simply those matters in which men from time to time think fit to invoke his aid.

Further, Kingship of this sort is exercised over other nations besides Israel. The prophecy of Amos opens with a series of oracles directed against the neighbouring peoples to Israel: and the most significant feature about these is that condemnation is passed not only for wrongs done to Israel, but also for wrongs done to other people. Jehovah is portrayed not as the champion of the Chosen People— they also are among the accused—but as the champion of righteousness. The deepening and spiritualising of the conception of Jehovah's sovereignty and the universalising of its scope go hand in hand. As judgement and mercy are more clearly perceived to be of the very essence of the divine nature, so the exercise of these attributes is extended over all mankind. In this connection no passage in the Old Testament is more instructive than the word of the Lord which stands at the end of the book of Jonah (iv. 10 f.): 'Then said the Lord, thou hast had pity on the gourd, for which thou hast not laboured, neither madest it grow; which came up in a night and perished in a night: and should not I spare Nineveh that great city, wherein are more than sixscore thousand persons that cannot discern between their right hand and their left hand; and also much cattle?'

3.

The third limitation of the sovereignty was removed by the prophetic announcement that the relation between Jehovah and Israel was not one of mutual dependence. The notion that any particular nation or territory was essential to God's well-being or prestige was doomed as soon as it was perceived that he was supreme over the whole world and all mankind. Similarly the antique superstition that God in some way needs the oblations of his worshippers had to give way before the discovery, also made by the prophets, that Jehovah's requirements are not ritual but ethical.[1]

Impt. X

By the removal of these limitations of the sovereignty of God, it passed from being a national and limited monarchy recognised by the nation as a unit, to become an aspect of pure monotheism, an ethical and universal reign recognised by the individual. Loyalty to the King of kings is no longer a matter of eschewing foreign cults or of punctual participation in the national ritual; it is rather a personal submission and obedience to the will of Jehovah as revealed through his servants the prophets.

[1] Am. v. 21–25; Hos. vi. 6; Is. i. 10–17; Mic. vi. 6–8; Jer. vi. 19–20; vii. 1–15, 21–23; Is. lxvi. 2–4. In striking contrast to the prophetic way of dealing with the naïve belief that sacrifices and offerings are necessary to the Deity is the satiric treatment of it in the *Birds* of Aristophanes. The picture of the blockade of heaven by Cloud-cuckoo-land, so that the whole supply of sacrificial offerings from earth is cut off and the starving gods are compelled to come to the birds seeking peace at any price, is irresistibly comic, and in another way tragic. It kills the popular religious beliefs by ridicule, but it offers nothing in their place. The invective of the prophets, on the other hand, is accompanied by the showing of a more excellent way. If they root out and pull down, they also build and plant. The rejection of burnt-offerings and meal-offerings is followed in the same breath by a demand for justice and righteousness. The one is a *reductio ad absurdum* of current religious practice: the other is a raising of it to new spiritual levels. Under the acid of Aristophanic satire the old superstitions quietly dissolve and nothing remains; in the white heat of prophetic zeal and insight all the baser elements are burnt away, and only the pure metal of a wholly spiritual religion is left. These things are not without their counterparts in more recent days: and the moral is that real religious reform comes through the really religious. *good*

2. THE DOCTRINE IN POST-EXILIC JUDAISM

This revolution, for it was nothing less, wrought by the prophets, made the conception of the sovereignty of Jehovah a new thing. In the light of the new revelation of God's nature unfolded in the prophetic teaching many of the old traditional beliefs simply wilted and died. But the new truth in its turn raised new problems. When Jehovah was a national God, it was only in times of national distress or disaster that men were set wondering what could be the matter: and, as likely as not, some convenient explanation would be at hand: some taboo had been broken, some ritual observance not correctly carried out.[1] Now with a divine Kingdom wide as the world came the problem of making sense of the whole course of human history. The prophets proclaimed a God whose inmost nature was righteousness and holiness and love; and, forthwith, the hard facts of experience cried out for explanation. The prophets knew this exalted Lord: in visions they had beheld his glory: he had spoken with them; but the great mass of the people, like Job, had heard of him only by the hearing of the ear: and, like Job, their first-hand knowledge was of other things, of pain and evil without and within. The prophets had gone up into the mountain and the God of Israel had been transfigured before their eyes; but it still remained to reconcile that heavenly vision with earthly realities. The question was posed, which has perplexed humanity ever since: how to maintain an honest belief in a sovereign God of perfect

[1] E.g. David's 'sin' in taking a census (II Sam. xxiv) as the explanation of the outbreak of pestilence (Frazer, *Folk-lore in the Old Testament*, II. 555–563); the downfall of Saul's dynasty as the result of Saul's sacrificing a burnt-offering when he should not (I Sam. xiii. 8–14). In general, any misfortune was regarded as the direct result of divine anger—in the stele of Mesha' the all-sufficient explanation of the long affliction of Moab by 'Omri, King of Israel, is that Chemosh was angry with his land—and the only problem remaining was to discover what it was that had provoked God, what steps should be taken to placate him in the present, and how to prevent a like occurrence in the future.

goodness, in face of appalling suffering and apparently triumphant evil in the world.

The task of the Prophets had been to proclaim the existence of one God, the sole ruler over men and things, governing the world in justice, mercy, and love: the heavy task laid upon those who came after them and embraced their doctrine, was to justify the ways of this God to men. The first attempts at a theodicy appear in the prophetic teaching itself,[1] as do the beginnings of Jewish eschatology; but the full development of both comes only at a later date. Indeed the two things commonly go together: for it is one of the easiest solutions of the problem of evil to promise the millennium and the more exact distribution of rewards and punishments at some future date. Moreover it is the popular way out of the difficulty. Mankind is always ready to carry forward a debit balance to next year in the hope that something will turn up: and the writers of apocalypses are always forward to urge the faithful to be patient and wait for the good time that is coming. It was this kind of teaching that helped to keep faith alive in men's hearts during a period when all their experience conspired to quench it. In their day, the apocalypses were in a very real sense 'food for the fed-up'; and before we look down upon them we may well remind ourselves how much they attempted and how much they accomplished.

It is true that the apocalyptic solution was not the only or the only possible answer to the questions raised by the existence of evil and suffering in a world ostensibly ruled by perfect goodness. Such writings as the Book of Job or Psalm lxxiii are a sufficient indication that there were elect souls that had passed beyond the current ideas of their day to find their ultimate satisfaction and peace in direct communion with God, so that the apportioning of kicks and halfpence ceased to trouble them. On the other hand there were those who, like the writer of Ecclesiastes, settled

---

[1] E.g. Is. xxviii. 23–29. Cf. Duhm's notes *ad loc.* in the *Göttinger Handkommentar.*

down to make the best of a bad job. But for the mass of the people the mystical experience of Job and the enlightened stoicism of Ecclesiastes were alike hardly possible. Few could attain that detachment from worldly cares that would enable them to say, either

'If only I have thee, there is nought else in heaven or earth that I desire[1]

or

How the O.T. develops Kingdom of

'Vanity of vanities, all is vanity'.   *Evil — antithesis to*

It was for the majority, for people whose simple faith in God's righteous governance was constantly exposed to the rude shocks of daily experience, that the apocalyptic writings were composed. — *popular appeal of apocalypse lit.*

god is — demons, satan, et.

When once the conviction had taken shape that the personal life and behaviour of the individual were as much the concern of Jehovah as the destinies of the nation, the obvious corollary was that happiness and misery would be apportioned strictly according to moral desert. This is the thesis stoutly maintained, in defiance of all the evidence, by Job's friends. It was the popular belief; and when it broke down, as it must, its place in the affections of the plain man was taken by the apocalyptic hope. We cannot expect to understand or value the apocalyptic literature aright unless it is clearly realised that it is a serious attempt to reconcile a faith in omnipotent goodness with the experience of evil and suffering in the world. In other words the primary interest of the writers of apocalypse is the apologetic: their first endeavour is to frame a philosophy of religion that will cover both the postulates of the prophetic faith and the facts of daily life.

X impt (B)

Their fundamental line of explanation is a qualified dualism: a spiritual kingdom of evil hostile to the beneficent rule of God is, for the time being, *permitted* in the world. This is the bed-rock upon which the whole fabric of apocalyptic teaching is built. The superstructure has two

Temporary ✗ Dualism. of Paul — Eph. etc

[1] Ps. lxxiii. 25 (following Luther's rendering).

Apocalyptic lit. based on philosophy / works. We shall be rewarded for our works, but not now; but in next world. Then all will be balanced.

The answer is: Relationship with God. HE is the reward.

main parts, which are concerned with the present duties and with the future hopes of the religious individual. There are thus three main elements in apocalypse: (i) a central proposition concerning the rule of God in the world; and, as corollaries to that, (ii) a mass of precepts to guide the faithful in the present, exhortations to patience under tribulation and continued loyalty towards God; and (iii) a great variety of predictions concerning the final destiny of the individual and the final consummation of the Kingdom of God. Exclusive emphasis on any one of these aspects—and it is commonly the third which receives more than its proper share—can only result in a distorted view of the teaching as a whole. At the present stage of our enquiry it is the first which we must examine, leaving the detailed consideration of the other two until later.

In the closing centuries of the pre-Christian era arises the notion of an evil spiritual kingdom warring against the Kingdom of God for the mastery over the world and the souls of men. These two opposing forces are conceived as organised on the lines of an oriental state. At the head of each stands a supreme ruler supported by a whole host of subordinates: over against God with his angels stands Satan[1] with his demons. In the development of this doctrine of the kingdom of Satan three leading factors may be detected at work: the influence of old Semitic mythology, the thoroughgoing dualism of the Persian religion, and the results of reflection on certain passages in the Old Testament.

Primitive Semitic superstition peopled the world with a whole host of supernatural beings: and in popular belief

[1] Satan is only one of the names assigned to the Prince of evil in the apocalyptic literature. It is used here because it has become the customary designation. Other names are Mastema (*Jubilees*), Beelzebub (*New Testament*), Beliar (for O.T. Belial) (II Cor. vi. 15; *Jubilees*; *Sibylline Oracles*; *Test. XII Patriarchs*; *Ascens. Isaiah*; cf. Charles on *Asc. Is.* i. 8), Asmodaeus (*Tobit* and in legendary lore about Solomon and his power over the world of demons). On old Jewish demonology cf. the long excursus (No. 21) in Strack-Billerbeck, vol. IV; Blau, *Das altjüdische Zauberwesen*, especially ch. I; E. Meyer, *Ursprung und Anfänge des Christentums*, vol. II, ch. IV.

these continued to exist long after the formulation of a monotheistic faith, which, strictly interpreted, left no room for them. 'In the belief of the heathen Arabs, for example, nature is full of living beings of superhuman kind, the *Jinn* or demons....It appears from several poetical passages of the Old Testament that the northern Semites believed in demons of a precisely similar kind, hairy beings (*sĕʿīrīm*), nocturnal monsters (*līlīth*), which haunted waste and desolate places, in fellowship with jackals and ostriches and other animals that shun the abodes of man.'[1] These beings are dangerous to man in the same way that the wild beasts are dangerous; they are things to be feared and avoided. In the period covered by the apocalypses and the Rabbinical literature this belief in demons continues in full vigour. The evil spirits are as numerous as ever: they are named and their functions described in great detail in apocalyptic and Rabbinical writings.[2] These survivals of early superstition are conceived as spiritual beings, yet having certain resemblances to human beings.[3] They are invisible but can assume visible shapes. They haunt the earth and the air: and are most commonly to be found in places that are ritually impure, such as burial places, or among ruins. They are dangerous at all times; but night is the time of their greatest activity. They are the cause of all kinds of evils and misfortunes to men. They cause diseases of every sort,[4] especially nervous and mental disorders.

[1] Robertson Smith, *Rel. Sem.* pp. 119 f. The whole Lecture (III) contains much information on the primitive belief in demons.

[2] P. Billerbeck in the excursus cited above gives a list of designations for demons comprising: (*a*) שֵׁד, the common Rabbinical name; (*b*) מַזִּיק, injurious demon; (*c*) מְחַבֵּל, destroyer; (*d*) פְּגָעִים, spirits of mischief; (*e*) שְׂעִירִים, goat-like or hairy demons; (*f*) רוּחַ בִּישׁ or רוּחַ רָעָה, evil spirit; (*g*) רוּחַ טוּמְאָה, unclean spirit; (*h*) רוּחַ, spirit.

Of these (*a*) represents the New Testament δαιμόνιον, (*f*) is the equivalent of πνεῦμα πονηρόν, (*g*) of πνεῦμα ἀκάθαρτον.

[3] *Hagiga*, 16 a: 'They eat and drink like the children of men, they are fruitful and multiply like the children of men, and they are mortal like the children of men' (trans. Streane, p. 92).

[4] Strack-Billerbeck, IV. 524.

Demons come from myths

Above all they incite men to sin. In short they performed in the ancient world all the tasks which we should now assign to bacilli, complexes, bad luck, or the less reputable 'isms'.

Satan from Persia

The organisation of this mob of evil spirits into a spiritual kingdom of evil with an arch-fiend at its head would appear to be due in the main to the influence of ideas borrowed from the Persian religion with its fully developed doctrine of the two opposing realms of Ahura-mazda and Ahriman.[1] The clearest evidence of Persian influence on Jewish theology, apart from the general similarity of the two systems, is the use of the name Asmodaeus for the chief of the demons. This name is borrowed directly from the Persian 'Æshma Daeva, the demon of violence and wrath in the later Avesta'.[2]

The third factor in the development of the doctrine of a Satanic kingdom was reflection on certain passages in the Old Testament. The most important of these are Gen. vi. 1–4, which tells of the birth of giants as the result of unnatural unions between the 'Sons of God' and the daughters of men; and the passages where the Satan is mentioned (Zech. iii; Job i, ii; I Chron. xxi. 1).

O.T. used 'demons' to interpret gen 1:4

The midrashic expansion of Gen. vi 1–4, which is preserved more or less completely in *Jubilees* (iv. 15, 22; v. 1–10; vii. 21 f.; x. 1–11), *Ethiopic Enoch* (vi–xvi; xix; lxxxvi), *Slav. Enoch* (xviii), *Test. Reuben* (v), relates that a certain group of angels, the Watchers (cf. Dan. iv. 10, 14, 20; E.V. 13, 17, 23), were sent down from heaven to instruct men in the right way. So far, however, from carrying out this task, they fell through lusting after the daughters of men, with whom they formed illicit unions. Of these unions were born the giants. Now the anger of

14 / 4

---

[1] Meyer, *U.A.C.* II. 58–94, where the religion of Zoroaster is described in detail.

[2] Tobit iii. 8. Ἀσμοδαῖος (א) or Ἀσμόδαυς (B) τὸ πονηρὸν δαιμόνιον. According to Dr H. St J. Thackeray (*Gore's Comm. ad loc.*) the B form is the more primitive. In the Talmud אשמדאי or אשמדיי, e.g. *Pes.* 110 a אשמדאי מלכא דשידי, Asmodaeus king of the demons. (Levy: *N.H.W.B. s.v.*)

God was kindled against the angels who had thus defiled themselves and he commanded that they should be rooted out of all their dominion and bound in the depths of the earth against the day of judgement. Concerning the offspring of the angels it was decreed that they should perish by mutual slaughter. The spirits, which issued from these giants at their death, became the demons. In the lifetime of Noah these evil spirits were already at work corrupting his descendants. Noah therefore prayed to God that they, like their fathers the fallen angels, might be imprisoned. God accordingly gave command to bind them all. Then their chief, Mastema or Satan, came and said (*Jubilees* x. 8–11): '"Lord Creator, let some of them remain before me, and let them hearken to my voice, and do all that I shall say unto them; for if some of them are not left to me, I shall not be able to execute the power of my will on the sons of men; for these are for corruption and leading astray before my judgement, for great is the wickedness of the sons of men". And He said: "Let the tenth part of them remain before him, and let nine parts descend into the place of condemnation".... And we did according to all His words: all the malignant evil ones we bound in the place of condemnation, and a tenth part of them we left that they might be subject before Satan on the earth'.

Satan himself is only mentioned three times in the Old Testament. His first appearance is in Zech. iii which is dated 519 B.C. Here he has the quite respectable office of public prosecutor in the heavenly court. Nor is there here any question of baseless accusation on his part: the 'filthy garments' of Joshua are sufficient proof that Satan had a case to present. In the Prologue to Job (probably fifth century B.C.) he has changed somewhat for the worse. On the most favourable interpretation of his activities he is a kind of detective officer or a common informer: a less kindly judgement would describe him as a combined spy and *agent provocateur*. Yet even here he is still subject to the divine will and limits are set beyond which he may not go.

In I Chron. xxi. 1 (c. 300 B.C.) he has gone yet a step
farther on the easy descent, and is now definitely the enemy
of Israel and the tempter of David. In the later literature
of Judaism, as in the New Testament, he is the avowed
enemy of God and man, the head and front of the whole
kingdom of evil.

This kingdom of evil is the explanation of the troubles
and misfortunes which afflict mankind. The idea of a carefully organised conspiracy of powerful evil beings plotting
his ruin might well strike terror to the heart of the believer;
as a matter of fact, to the really religious it brought something of relief. For the more luridly the iniquity of the
evil kingdom was painted, the more, by contrast, did the
Kingdom of God appear glorious, without spot or blemish.
It was possible to maintain that all the purposes of the
heavenly King were beneficent and good, though some of
them might, for the time being, appear to be thwarted
by hostile powers.

This explanation may fairly be called dualistic, but it is
not a thorough-going dualism. The prophets had done their
work too well for any theory to be admissible that would
impose a real limitation on the one supreme God or set up
any other power as his equal. Though the kingdom of
Satan has great power for all kinds of mischief, it is made
quite clear that this power is not absolute. The God who is
able to bind and imprison nine-tenths of the demons can
lay his hand on the remaining tenth when he will: and the
conviction is always present that in his own good time he
will.

On the other hand, however, if the theory of two opposed
kingdoms is not a perfect dualism, neither is it a perfect
solution of the problem of evil, though it does contain the
germ of what is probably the only solution possible on a
theistic basis. As it stands, it is open to the obvious
objection that it merely pushes the question a few steps
back. One asks: Why does a good God send wars, famines,
pestilences, and the like? The answer that these things are

not directly God's work at all, but the malicious acts of the demons, only serves to raise the further question in one's mind: Why does God have demons in his universe? To this the answer is that God did not make them; they are the progeny of fallen angels. But this again prompts the enquiry: Why did God permit angels to fall? It is clear that this catechism might be continued indefinitely without bringing us any nearer to a satisfactory answer to the original question, since it is the original question that comes up in a different form every time. It is probable, however, that this difficulty would not occur to minds unacquainted with the philosophical objections to a *regressus in indefinitum*.

What is important to notice is that at every stage in this regress the explanation is in terms of the free choice of moral persons. The ills that trouble mankind are due, not to blind mechanical forces, but to the malice of evil spirits: they are willed. The demons themselves are created by the act of spiritual beings who are conceived to have made a deliberate choice between good and evil. In the last resort the whole process is, if not approved, at least permitted by God. If we add to this the evils in the world which arise from the sin of man—and they also are conceived as coming by man's free choice[1]—we have an explanation of the existence and continuance of evil, which is from beginning to end in terms of the free moral action of persons, either human or superhuman. When once the fantastic and mythological trappings of the apocalyptic scheme are removed, there remains the central postulate, which is the foundation of all attempts to find a satisfactory solution for the problem of evil, namely, that it is the price

[1] Cf. *Test. Judah*, ch. xx: 'Know, therefore, my children, that two spirits wait upon man—the spirit of truth and the spirit of deceit. And in the midst is the spirit of the understanding of the mind, *to which it belongeth to turn whithersoever it will*' (trans. R. H. Charles); *Ps. Sol.* ix. 7: 'O God, our works are in our choice, yea, in the power of our own soul: to do either righteousness or iniquity in the works of our hands' (trans. Ryle and James); *Aboth* (ed. Taylor), III. 24: 'Everything is foreseen; and freewill is given' (הרשות נתונה), a saying of R. Akiba.

The Conclusion - of OT idea I evol

Good

that must be paid for freedom." The whole creation groaning and travailing in pain together is a necessary stage in the realisation of the glorious liberty of the children of God[1]

The history of the doctrine of God's sovereignty can thus be very briefly summarised. At the beginning it is national: in the end it is universal. At the beginning it is limited in its scope: in the end there is no limitation from without, and any self-limitation which there may be is only for the time being. That is, the purpose of God is what gives meaning to the world and to the life of man; and this purpose is conceived as wide enough to include the possibility and the actuality of wills hostile to it, without ceasing to be in its entirety the purpose of God. A rule of God, spiritual, world-wide, all-comprehensive: this is the apocalyptic faith, the final result of the travail of religious souls over more than a thousand years.

A simple and illuminating illustration of the way in which the idea of the sovereignty of God developed during this long period is furnished by the history of the word 'enemy' as applied to the enemies of God. In the early literature of the Old Testament the political enemies of Israel are *eo ipso* the enemies of God. Thus for example the ancient song of Deborah, after recounting the discomfiture of the Canaanites and the death of Sisera, ends with the wish:

So let all thine enemies perish, O Lord.[2]

The principle is laid down explicitly in Ex. xxiii. 20–22 (E):

Behold, I send an angel before thee, to keep thee by the way, and to bring thee into the place which I have prepared. Take ye heed of him, and hearken unto his voice; provoke him not: for he will not pardon your transgressions, for my name is in him. But if thou shalt indeed hearken unto his voice, and do

[1] Rom. viii. 21 f. It may be added that in St Paul's opinion it was worth it: 'I reckon that the sufferings of this present time are not worthy to be compared with the glory that shall be revealed in us' (viii. 18).
[2] Judg. v. 31: cf. Num. x. 35 (JE); I Sam. xxx. 26 (Amalekites).

all that I speak; then I will be an enemy unto thine enemies, and an adversary unto thine adversaries.

The following verse (RJE) explains this as meaning:

Mine angel shall go before thee, and bring thee in unto the Amorite, and the Hittite, and the Perizzite, and the Canaanite, the Hivite, and the Jebusite: and I will cut them off.

This political and nationalist view of the enemies of Jehovah continues up to the days of the great prophets, and survives in the Book of Nahum, which is nothing but a seventh-century echo of the song of Deborah.[1]

By the prophets enmity towards God is interpreted in moral and spiritual ways. The enemies of Jehovah are marked out not by outward signs like race or language or nationality, but by moral qualities. The 'enemies' of Is. i. 24 are the same persons as the 'transgressors and sinners' in i. 28. This stage of the development is most clearly marked in the Psalms, where 'God's enemies' and 'evildoers' or some equivalent expression frequently stand in synonymous parallelism. Thus,

Ps. xxxvii. 20: The wicked shall perish,
  And the enemies of the Lord shall be as the fat of lambs.
lxviii. 2 f.: Let God arise, let his enemies be scattered:
  Let them also that hate him flee before him.
  As smoke is driven away, so drive them away.
  As wax melteth before the fire, so let the wicked perish at
    the presence of God.
lxviii. 22. But God shall wound the head of his enemies
  And the hairy scalp of such an one as goeth on still in his
    trespasses.[2]

[1] Cf. T. H. Robinson, *Prophecy and the Prophets*, pp. 113 f.
[2] Cf. also Ps. lxxxix. 23; xcii. 10; xcvii; Ps. cxxxix. 19–22 is specially interesting in this connection. Here the enemies of God are identified with the 'wicked', 'the bloody men', and those who speak wickedly against him and take his name in vain. The psalmist goes on to say that he hates them and counts them as his own enemies, thus exactly reversing the order of things in the old days. Then the political enemies of Israel were automatically the enemies of Jehovah; now the rebels against Jehovah's moral laws are his enemies and consequently the enemies of all who serve and follow him.

In the apocalyptic literature, as we have already seen, it is the spiritual kingdom of evil which is the real enemy of God: and, in a derived sense, men who transfer to the evil kingdom that allegiance and service which properly should be devoted to God. This is also the view of the matter taken in the New Testament, in St Matthew's parable of the Wheat and Tares for example; and most explicitly in St Paul's statement that 'we wrestle not against flesh and blood, but against the principalities, against the powers, against the rulers of the darkness of this world, against the spiritual hosts of wickedness in the heavenly places'.[1]

Thus we find, when we trace out the history of the idea, that it has passed through three easily recognisable stages: and at each stage the development has been in the direction of deepening and spiritualising its content and of individualising its application: from political to moral and from moral to spiritual; from the nation to the human individual and thence to all self-conscious beings. The first stage recognises no moral distinctions: a whole people can be included in a common condemnation and put under the ban. The second stage makes individual behaviour the test; but it is at the best only a rough and ready criterion for immediate practical purposes. It would operate to exclude the publican and the harlot from the Kingdom of God. The final stage makes the only criterion the disposition of the individual will—for or against God: and the inevitable corollary is that the final application of the test can be in God's hands alone, for only he can search the heart.[2]

3. THE TEACHING OF JESUS

When we turn to the teaching of Jesus we find that what he says about the sovereignty of God is remarkable not so much for novelty as for the intensity with which the sovereignty is felt as a dominant factor in his life. What we have already seen in the case of the Fatherhood of God is

[1] Eph vi. 12; cf. also Lk. x. 19 (L).
[2] Cf. Appendix III, s.v. ἁμαρτωλός.

equally true of the sovereignty. It is not a mere article in a creed, but a present reality in the life of Jesus. The Kingdom in this wide sense is not a topic for theological discussion; it is rather "the sphere in which he lives and moves and has his being." His preaching of the Kingdom is not just the pointing of his hearers to some happy state in the future, when the will of God will be perfectly realised; it is primarily the living of a life of complete loyalty to God and unquestioning obedience to his will here and now. The core of all that Jesus teaches about the Kingdom is the immediate apprehension and acceptance of God as King in his own life. From this central experience all the rest of the teaching on the Kingdom naturally follows. 'Thy Kingdom come' may be paraphrased 'Thy will be done on earth as it is in heaven'. The former petition may be no more than man's request to God; but the latter, if it be sincerely meant, becomes a claim of God upon him who prays. It must be construed first of all 'Thy will be done by me': and, from the beginning of the ministry to its end, this is what the Kingdom means for Jesus. The kingdoms of the world with all their glory are not to be weighed against the loyalty that is due to God: 'Thou shalt worship the Lord thy God and him only shalt thou serve'. So the ministry begins. As it draws towards its close the same voice is heard in the garden: 'Not what I will but what thou wilt'. The best that the world can offer and the worst that it can threaten are alike powerless to divert him from this one allegiance.

In the light of this unique devotion and loyalty to the heavenly King all the words of Jesus concerning the heavenly Kingdom are to be read and interpreted. "The essence of his preaching of the Kingdom is in the words 'Thy will be done': all the rest is commentary."

But the application of this principle is to beings with wills of their own. From the Old Testament Jesus takes over the conviction that God's will is done in the natural world: and in so doing he gives it a characteristic turn of his own. The Old Testament writers tend to seek the manifestation of God's sovereignty over nature in the large and impressive:

> The heavens declare the glory of God;
> And the firmament showeth his handywork.[1]

The most violent and awe-inspiring convulsions of nature are tokens of his presence: he is not in them, but they herald his approach.

> And behold the Lord passed by, and a great and strong wind rent the mountains, and brake in pieces the rocks before the Lord; but the Lord was not in the wind: and after the wind an earthquake; but the Lord was not in the earthquake: and after the earthquake a fire; but the Lord was not in the fire: and after the fire a still small voice.[2]

A recent writer sums up the Hebrew view of nature by saying that 'it is the stern side of nature that comes under observation as a rule' and that 'nature is merely a mirror of God's strength, majesty and power'.[3] It need not be maintained that this way of regarding nature is exclusively Hebrew, or that it is the only way in which nature is contemplated in Hebrew literature.[4] It is, however, characteristic. If we ask ourselves how the Old Testament writers portray the sovereignty of God over the natural world, it is the picture of Jehovah riding upon the storm-wind and the earth trembling at his approach that rises to our minds.

With the teaching of Jesus it is otherwise. He finds the tokens of God's rule over nature not in the occasional and stupendous manifestations of power, but in the common-place things of the field and the hedgerow which any man might pass by without a thought. The wild flowers in the field and the daily provision for the birds take the place of earthquake and storm. Not even a sparrow can fall to the

---

[1] Ps. xix. 2.
[2] I Kings xix. 11 f. Cf. Pss. xviii. 7–16; xxix; civ; cxiv; Hab. iii; Job xxxviii–xli; etc.
[3] P. C. Sands, *Literary Genius of the O.T.*, p. 76.
[4] I. Abrahams, *The Glory of God*, ch. 1.

ground without God. Account is kept of the hairs of a disciple's head. In another connection it is implied that a truer token of God's rule is to be seen in the fact that we can forecast to-morrow's weather from this evening's sky than in a miraculous turning of the sun to darkness or the moon to blood. The sovereignty of God in the natural world is construed by Jesus in terms of beauty and order and a providential care over all his creatures.

We must not take this as an anticipation of the Argument from Design. It is something much simpler and much deeper. There is no idea here of an elaborate adaptation of means to ends by which the glowing colours of the wild flowers should attract the insects in search of honey to fertilise the seed, thus producing food for the birds and ensuring a fresh crop in the following year, when the same process will be repeated. We are not asked to argue from the intricacy of the machinery to the ingenuity of its inventor. The whole emphasis is on the personal relation of the Creator to his creatures. God clothes the lilies of the field and God feeds the birds, one might almost say, because God is fond of beautiful flowers and fond of birds. As Jesus sees it, the material universe reveals chiefly the love of God. The picture of God making clothes for the flowers and preparing meals for the sparrows is the picture of a God who is Lord of Creation by being the servant in love of all his creatures. The statement: 'He that would be chief among you must be the servant of all', has its application even in the heavenly places. There, indeed, it has its deepest meaning and its perfect realisation.[1]

The key to all this lies in the simple fact that the heavenly Father and the heavenly King are one and the same person: and the Kingship and the Fatherhood are one and the same thing looked at from different points of view. The Kingdom of God is, in the highest and purest sense, a

---

[1] Cf. Philo, *De opif. mundi*, 61: 'God exerts his providence for the benefit of the world. For it follows of necessity that the Creator must always care for that which he has created, just as parents do for their children'.

paternal government. God is most truly King because he is most truly Father. And, on man's side, the yoke of the Kingdom becomes easy and its burden light, just in proportion as it is realised that it is the badge, not of servitude, but of service, and service of such a kind that the King who is our Father gives far more of it than he receives.

There is one further implication. When Jesus says of the lilies of the field that Solomon in all his glory was not arrayed like one of them, it is not merely the distinction between the beauty of nature and the products of human artistry that is in question. Rather the point of the saying seems to be that the flower has a glory of its own not by any efforts of its own, but simply by being what God meant it to be, no more and no less. The ambitions and the pride of a Solomon may and do run counter to God's will, so that the more he becomes what he desires to be, the less he resembles what God meant him to be. He is clothed indeed with a glory of sorts, but it is a glory that comes short of the divine glory revealed in the wild flowers. In the natural world God's will is done because there is no other will competing with his. In the world of self-conscious beings the case is different. Pitting their wills against God's they can fall below the level of the beasts of the field or inanimate things. That is the risk of freedom. On the other hand, they have the capacity of bringing their wills into subjection to God's will: and so of rising to a higher glory. Man's destiny is not to be so much clay in the hand of the potter; but to be a loyal subject of the divine King, a loving son of the divine Father. If the glory of Solomon falls below that of the lilies of the field, the light of the knowledge of the glory of God in the face of Jesus Christ is something immeasurably far above anything in the natural world.

It is in the world of self-conscious beings that the discrepancy between what is and what ought to be appears. It is obvious that in human life the will of God is not done

on earth as it is in heaven; that, in the full sense, the
Kingdom has not come. The explanation given in the
Gospels of the problem of evil does not differ in the main
from that offered in the apocalyptic literature. Over
against the Kingdom of God stands the kingdom of Satan.
Demons cause all kinds of ills to men. From Mark iii.
23–27 and the corresponding Q passage (Lk. xi. 17–23)[1] it
is clear that Jesus conceived the demons as organised into
an evil kingdom hostile to the Kingdom of God. The issue
of the conflict is not in doubt. God by merely lifting a
finger can check the power of the enemy (Lk. xi. 20: Q):
and that fact is an earnest of the complete subjugation of
all the powers of evil in God's good time.

Between these two warring kingdoms stands man: and
to one or other of them he must give his allegiance. No
man can serve two masters. According as a man chooses
God or Satan, so he chooses for himself life or destruction.
Here again it is the absoluteness of the sovereignty that
appears. It cannot be indefinitely evaded. This is the conclusion to be drawn from such parables as the Vineyard
(Mk), the Great Feast (Q), and the Pounds as recorded in
Luke. For man the supremely important choice is whether
he will accept the rule of God or be miserably destroyed
fighting a useless and hopeless battle against it. In comparison with this all other matters are trifles. No sacrifice is
too great to make in order to have a part in the Kingdom.

[1] The parallel passage Mt. xii. 25–30 appears to be a conflation of Marcan
with Q material.

Any theory that these sayings are 'accommodated' to the level of knowledge of the audience addressed is to be rejected. Those who believe in the
existence of a personal Devil and evil spirits will find no difficulty, but rather
support, in these texts for their belief. Those who cannot entertain such
beliefs should, if they are candid, admit that the most probable explanation
of the sayings is that the real humanity of Jesus necessarily involved limitation of his knowledge of matters of fact: that to be a genuine human life the
life of Jesus must be lived under the same conditions as other people's.
There does not seem to be any other view which can be plausibly maintained.
This case is on all fours with the question of the Davidic authorship of Ps.
cx, assumed by Jesus (Mk. xii. 35–37) and nowadays regarded by O.T.
scholars as extremely unlikely. (Cf. C. H. Turner ad loc., Gore's Commentary,
N.T., p. 100.)

It is better to enter the Kingdom maimed than to be cast whole into the unquenchable fire (Mk. ix. 43–48). Life itself is not too high a price to pay for entrance into the Kingdom (Mk. viii. 34–38). Friendships and family ties are to be sacrificed if need be (Mk. x. 29 f.; Lk. xiv. 26 f., Q, 28–33, L). Nothing that the world can offer is to be compared for a moment with the claims of the Kingdom of God. On the other hand, nothing that the world can threaten is to be allowed to scare one away from allegiance to the Kingdom. 'Fear not those who destroy the body, and after that are unable to do anything further; fear him who has power after killing to cast into Gehenna. Yea, I tell you, fear *him*' (Lk. xii. 4 f.: Mt. x. 28: Q). And it is God who has this awful power.

These passages, which are among the most emphatic in the teaching of Jesus, are all directed to one end: to impress upon men the fact that in life there is one choice whose urgency and importance outweigh every other consideration, the choice, namely, of the rule under which they are to live. The final destiny of man lies in the disposition of his own will—for or against God.

For our immediate purpose the importance of this fact lies in its implications. There are two claimants for man's allegiance: God and Satan.[1] God and Satan are the heads of two warring kingdoms. But in this war it is not a case of balancing chances and casting in one's lot with the probable victor. As Jesus presents the case there are no chances. The issue of the conflict is not in doubt. The Kingdom of God must and will triumph: and the choice which is offered to man is a choice between a Kingdom that is destined for victory and one that is doomed to destruction. It is true that things as they are do not appear to support this contention. The kingdom of Satan makes large promises and threats. There are times when the servants of God seem to be engaged in a losing battle. But for Jesus

---

[1] Or God and mammon, or God and self. They all come to much the same thing in the end.

the final result is already assured: the sovereignty of God is absolute. The absolute sovereignty of God is thus not a dogma accepted on the authority of tradition nor the conclusion of a philosophical enquiry; it is a postulate of religious faith. This faith is founded upon an ethical demand and confirmed in experience. There is a demand made in man's life at its best by his own conscience that righteousness should triumph there. And whenever the better self does in fact score a victory over the meaner and baser elements in our nature, that victory is seen as a step forward towards our true destiny. This personal experience can be regarded as a reflection of the cosmic drama. The small but persistent voice within echoes the inexorable demands of the heavenly King: its eternal demand that righteousness should rule our lives becomes the faith that righteousness must rule the world. And our personal victories over evil in our own lives take on a new perspective as elements in a greater triumph which is being won on a world-wide battle front. The awe and wonder inspired by the contemplation of the moral law within become adoration of a God who is the beginning and the end of it, the origin of its demands, and the goal of our efforts to fulfil them. We work out our salvation; but it is God who works in us.

This revelation of the sovereignty of God, partial and fragmentary in our own lives, we find in its fullness in the life that is recorded in the Gospels. It is a point of the highest importance that both in theory and in practice Jesus reduces the whole of morality to a single principle. 'And one of the scribes came...and...asked him, What commandment is the first of all? Jesus answered, The first is, Hear, O Israel; The Lord our God, the Lord is one: and thou shalt love the Lord thy God with all thy heart, and with all thy soul, and with all thy mind, and with all thy strength' (Mk. xii. 28 ff. R.V.). Complete devotion to God, in other words recognition and acceptance of his absolute sovereignty, is the foundation of all good living.[1] It is significant that the Scribe who approves this answer to his question is told: 'Thou art not far from the Kingdom of God'.

The principle here laid down by Jesus in learned debate is the principle which governs his life. At the beginning of his ministry the Tempter offers him the world—for a consideration. His answer is: 'Thou shalt worship the Lord thy God, and him only shalt thou serve' (Mt. iv. 10 = Lk. iv. 8: Q). At the end his prayer is: 'Not what I will, but what thou wilt'. This unquestioning obedience to God's will flows from the conviction that God's will is something that may not be questioned.

But God as the absolute King does not only make exclusive demands upon men; he is also the source of the power necessary to meet those demands. Wherever, in the life of the individual, or in the world, the forces of evil are checked, there the sovereignty of God is manifested. 'If I by the finger of God cast out devils, then is the Kingdom of God come upon you' (Lk. xi. 20: Mt. xii. 28: Q). Such happenings as these are straws to show which way the wind blows. They are a sign, not that the kingdom of Satan is split by internal dissension but that a greater power is at work in the world. 'No one can enter into the house of the strong man (i.e. Satan), and spoil his goods, except he first bind the strong man; and then he will spoil his house' (Mk. iii. 27; parallel in Lk. xi. 21 f.: Q). Against the might of the Kingdom of God all the forces of evil are powerless.

This consciousness of being the vehicle of an irresistible power runs through all the teaching of Jesus: and it is something which he seeks to impart to his disciples. They are to know that they are not sent to warfare at their own charges. Rather they should understand that behind their efforts is the power of God. So they will be, as Jesus himself is, free from all anxiety and all fear. For himself he can say: 'All things are delivered unto me of my Father'

---

[1] For the relation of this principle to 'the second' commandment and to the 'Golden Rule' see below, Chapter IX.

(Lk. x. 22 = Mt. xi. 27: Q): and on every page of the Gospels we may find evidence of the authority, the sureness of touch, and the calm courage, that spring from this knowledge. To his disciples he says: 'Fear not, little flock, for it is your Father's good pleasure to give you the Kingdom' (Lk. xii. 32: Q?); and again: 'I appoint unto you a Kingdom, even as my Father appointed unto me, that ye may eat and drink at my table in my Kingdom, and ye shall sit on thrones judging the twelve tribes of Israel' (Lk. xxii. 29 f.: L?). If we are right in attributing the former of these two passages to Q, it follows in that document on sayings which stress the dangers which face the disciples. They seem a pitifully small force to attack the great hosts of evil; but they are not to be afraid, for the last word is with God. The second statement stands in St Luke's account of the Last Supper and follows closely upon the announcement by Jesus of the impending betrayal. The confidence that rings through these words does not come from any outward signs that the cause is prospering, but from a faith in the absolute sovereignty of God.

Very similar to these sayings is the exhortation to the disciples which has been preserved in two, possibly three, of our sources: Mk. xiii. 11; Lk. xii. 11 f. (Q); and Lk. xxi. 14 f. (?L).[1] The three versions of the saying are as follows:

Mk (xiii. 11)	Q (Lk. xii. 11 f.)	?L (Lk. xxi. 14 f.)
And when they lead you to judgement and deliver you up,	And when they bring you before the synagogues, and the rulers, and the authorities,	
be not anxious beforehand what ye shall speak but whatsoever shall be given you in that hour, that speak ye: for it is not ye that speak but the Holy Ghost.	be not anxious how or what ye shall answer or what ye shall say:	Settle it therefore in your hearts not to meditate how to answer:
	for the Holy Spirit shall teach you in that very hour what ye ought to say.	for I will give you a mouth and wisdom,
		which all your adversaries shall not be able to withstand or to gainsay.

[1] Cf. V. Taylor, *Behind the Third Gospel*, pp. 104–109.

Even in the matter of making their defence before
worldly tribunals the disciples are to feel that they have all
the resources of the eternal Kingdom behind them. This
knowledge is to free them from anxiety. Moreover, the
defence which will be given to them will be unanswerable.

There is much more of the same kind in the Gospels.
The disciples are not to fear poverty. God will provide for
their needs. They are to be rid of all fear and all anxiety.
Why? Because they are servants of the Kingdom of God
and behind them is the supreme power in the universe.
They do not fight in their own strength, nor do they live on
their own resources. They have all the strength and all the
resources of the eternal Kingdom to draw upon.

We may sum up the whole matter by saying that, as it
appears in the life and teaching of Jesus, the sovereignty of
God is essentially the working out, to a predetermined
and inevitable end, of God's holy purpose. This purpose
embraces in its scope both the natural world and the world
of self-conscious beings. Its motive is love, its means
service, and its end a state of things where the will of God
is done on earth as in heaven. The sovereignty of God over
nature is demonstrated not by the trampling march of
supernatural power in some great cataclysm, but by his
constant care over all his creatures, even the humblest. It
is manifested in human life, not by legions of angels
sweeping forward to crush the forces of evil, but by the
realisation in those who accept its rule of a strange power
to overcome evil with good. This power is recognised, by
all who experience it, as the strongest thing in the world,
and as something which must finally prevail. In other
words, the throne of the universe is founded upon a
Father's love. This is probably the clue to 'the mystery of
the Kingdom'.

1. Simple belief that God is king of His people, those who obey Him. But with the prophets obedience is defined personally & vigorously, & only a minority are so inclined. It was believed they were special to God & would be protected etc. The nation is no longer the Kingdom, but the Remnant is.
2. Those who have not bowed to Baal anticipate the Remnant (Elijah)
3. Isaiah I uses the remnant idea prominently. He names his son accordingly etc. His disciples are an attempt to bring the remnant together. Isaiah individualized the remnant – as the persons who obey God. You were not in remnant by accident of birth, but by choice. The judgment & doom announced by Amos would destroy the nation, but the remnant would survive it, altho not escape it
4. Josiah – 621 BC – attempted by legislation to reform the nation so as to realize the ancient ideal: The Nation = the Remnant, but he failed.
5. Hence Jeremiah emphasis: Law is inward, individual, & is forgiveness, not a matter of birth, but character: disposition.

Chapter VII
GOD AS KING: THE KINGDOM IN THE WORLD

I. ISRAEL

– The idea itself goes back at least to 750 B.C.

"THE kingship of God has its manifestation on earth in the existence of a people whose King he is." The conception that Jehovah is the King of Israel can be traced very far back in the history of Hebrew religion. We have already seen that in Rabbinic thought the kingship of God was accepted by Israel at the Red Sea or at Sinai (above, pp. 130 f.). But this thought is older than Rabbinical Judaism: it meets us in the so-called 'Blessing of Moses' (Deut. xxxiii), a poem, not by Moses indeed, but certainly of early date.[1]

> And he (Jehovah) became king in Jeshurun
> When the heads of the people were assembled
> All together the tribes of Israel.[2]

It is here stated that 'Jehovah assumed, as it were, the sovereignty over Israel, when the tribes with their leaders were gathered about Him, on the "day of the Assembly" at Sinai'.[3]

In Ex. xix. 5 f. (J) the promise is made by Jehovah:

> Now therefore, if ye will obey my voice indeed, and keep my covenant, then ye shall be a peculiar treasure unto me from

---

[1] Three different dates are suggested: (a) the period of the Judges (Kleinert, Sellin); (b) shortly after the division of the kingdom, in the reign of Jeroboam I (Dillmann, Westphal, Driver); (c) the reign of Jeroboam II (Graf, Kuenen, Reuss, Stade, Cornill, D. C. Simpson, G. F. Moore, and others). Some scholars would separate vv. 2–5, 26–29 from the Blessings proper and assign them to a later date. So Bertholet (*K.H.C.*), who regards these verses as a separate psalm later than the Deuteronomic age: and von Gall (*Wellhausen-Festschrift*, p. 150), who puts them down as post-exilic. On the other hand, Sellin (*Einl.*[3] p. 26) finds in vv. 5, 28, 29 indications which support the age of the Judges as the date for the whole chapter.

[2] Deut. xxxiii. 5; trans. Driver, *Deuteronomy* (*I.C.C.*), p. 390.

[3] Driver, *op. cit.*, p. 394.

6. Isaiah II: 'Servant songs' – where the Remnant are the Exiles who are not spared suffering, but fulfil their mission thru it – not the saved, but the saving remnant. He does not use legislation as Josiah, but exhortation. Israel has no future as a political kingdom. That has already been given to Cyrus. Her future is as a spiritual kingdom with a mission to world to demonstrate the Sovereignty of God by their existence. All Israel will someday be restored. Here the Kingdom is on earth in a people wholly devoted to Jehovah as King & used by Him to extend His Kingdom throughout the world, not by force of arms but by spiritual power. This is the prototype of Evangelical Xianity & taken up by Church. – A similar our view was propounded by Ezekiel – & taken up by Judaism. Here in the most bifurcated

among all peoples: for all the earth is mine: and ye shall be unto me a kingdom of priests, and an holy nation.

'The verses, in style and thought, approximate to Deuteronomy, and may have been expanded by the compiler of JE'.[1] In that case they may be dated in the early part of the seventh century B.C.

The oracles of Balaam (Num. xxiii f.) also present the conception of God as King over Israel:

Jehovah their God is with them and the shout of a King among them.[2]

The date of these oracles is disputed. Von Gall argued for the post-exilic period. More recently Sellin and Burkitt decide for a much earlier date before the division of the kingdom. Burkitt[3] regards the oracles of Balaam as 'the longest and most characteristic monument of the earliest Israelite prophecy, after it became articulate'.

It will be noted that all these passages affirm the kingship of Jehovah over Israel without qualification: and that in every case scholars are divided as to their date. Ultimately the question is whether they reflect a belief which goes back to the period before the establishment of the monarchy or whether they are the reading into the past of ideas which first became prominent at the time of the decline and fall of the Hebrew kingdoms.

Now it is well known that in I Samuel we have two parallel accounts of the appointment of Saul as king over Israel. The older and historically more valuable account is preserved in ix. 1—x. 16; xi; xiii. 1–7 a, 15 b–23; xiv. In this version of the story Samuel anoints Saul as 'prince' (נגיד) over Israel at the direct command of Jehovah (ix. 15 ff.; x. 1). This appointment by Jehovah has its sequel when, after Saul's victory over the Ammonites, he is publicly recognised by the people as king (xi. 15). The

---

[1] Driver, *ad loc.* (*Camb. Bible*), cf. Introd., p. xi.

[2] Num. xxiii. 21 (Burkitt, 'The Prophets of Israel', in *Gore's Commentary*, p. 421).

[3] *Op. cit.*, p. 420.

The Two acct's of Saul's anointing to Kingship

7. Ezekiel sees kingdom on earth in Palestine, restored nation as His subjects; Jerusalem capital -- the admiration & envy of the world, Jews hereafter luxury; enemies ruthlessly crushed. Here the restored nation is the remnant -- non missionary -- Hating the world!

8. After Exile, Hebrews followed Ezekiel; tried to rebuild. (Ezra, Neh. Haggai Zech) excluded the Samaritans. But once more legislation failed, as under Josiah.

9. Within Israel is Israel - those who personally decided to make God King - "Hasidim" who do it by keeping the Law. They fight only for religious freedom, not power. The "law lovers" are now the remnant. But not only law, but birth is Pharisee. Both by blood & choice.

second account is contained in viii; x. 17–24; xii; x. 25–
27 a. Here the circumstances are reversed. It is not
Jehovah who makes the first move in the matter, but the
people. They are dissatisfied, rightly, with the conduct of
Samuel's sons in the office of the judgeship and the elders
come to him at Ramah saying: 'You are now old, and
your sons do not walk in your ways; we would therefore
have you now to set us up a king to judge us, like all other
nations' (viii. 4 f.). Saul is chosen by lot and becomes
king with the consent, but certainly not with the approval,
of Jehovah. What is implied throughout this account, and
explicitly stated in xii. 12 is that Jehovah is sole King over
Israel and that Israel's demand for a human king is
inconsistent with exclusive loyalty to Jehovah, and is
indeed a rejection of him (viii. 7; x. 19).

To the same way of thinking as this second account
belongs the story related in Judg. viii. 22 f.:

> And the men of Israel said unto Gideon, Rule over us, both
> thou and thy son, and thy son's son, for thou hast saved us out
> of the hand of Midian. And Gideon said unto them, *I* will not
> rule over you, neither shall my son rule over you; Jehovah shall
> rule over you.

Concerning the date of this passage from Judges and the
second account in Samuel scholars have differed widely.
Wellhausen and Stade[1] maintained that I Sam. vii. f.;
xii; were a product of the Deuteronomic school; but the
tendency of more recent investigation is to put these
chapters back to an earlier date. Budde pointed out that
the passages in Samuel have noticeable affinities with the
Hexateuch source E, and made it probable that they are a
pre-Deuteronomic work.[2] Following upon this Burney
argues that the passage in Judges together with I Sam.
viii. 6 f.; x. 19; xii. 17; all clearly exhibit the hand of E²,
where E² represents the later prophetic school of historians
working in the Northern Kingdom shortly after the time of

[1] A. v. Gall, *op. cit.*, p. 150.
[2] Driver, *L.O.T.*⁹, p. 177.

Hosea and largely under the influence of his prophetic teaching.[1] More recently Sellin carries the second narrative in Samuel still farther back to the period before Hosea, suggesting a date about 800 B.C.[2] At the same time he would regard such verses as Gen. xxxvii. 8; Ex. xix. 6; Num. xxiii. 21; Deut. xxxiii. 5; as characteristic of E and marks of the strong theocratic tendency of that document.[3]

Whether or not we accept Sellin's conclusions, it would appear that a strong case is made out for the existence of the idea that Jehovah is the only true King over Israel as early as the latter half of the eighth century B.C. if not earlier.

If then the idea of Jehovah's kingship is not a theological compensation for the political disasters which swept away the earthly rulers of Israel, we must ask how it came into existence. To this question the most plausible answer is that it grew up along with the earthly kingdom. There is good reason to believe that the Hebrews found *Melek* as well as *Ba'al* already used as a divine name or title by the Canaanites[4] and thence borrowed the word as a title for Jehovah. When the kingdom became a well-established institution under David and Solomon, the conception of Jehovah's kingship would gain in clearness and definiteness.[5] So in the earlier account of Saul's appointment Jehovah nominates him practically as viceroy. Later,

---

[1] Burney, *The Book of Judges*, pp. xli–l, 183 f., 235 on Judg. viii. 23: 'The conception of Theocracy here put forward belongs to the later eighth century stage of prophetic thought'. The passages in Hosea which seem to regard the appointment of a king as a defection from Jehovah are viii. 4, 10 (as emended: Burney, p. 184); x. 3; xiii. 10 f.

[2] Sellin, *Einleitung*[3], p. 77.

[3] *Ibid.*, p. 47.

[4] S. A. Cook in *Cambridge Ancient History*, II. 350. H. Zimmern, *K.A.T.*[3], pp. 469 ff.

[5] Theological conceptions often reflect the social conditions of the time. In the account of the organisation of Olympus given in the *Iliad* Zeus is the first-born son of Kronos; in Hesiod he is the youngest. 'Thus Homer adopts the system of primogeniture, while Hesiod is all for the opposite and probably earlier custom of *Jüngsten-recht*' (Lang, art. 'Mythology' in *Enc. Brit.* (11th ed.), XIX., p. 140 b).

when the deficiencies of the monarchy became apparent—
perhaps in the anarchical conditions which prevailed in
Northern Israel after the death of Jeroboam II—it became
natural to regard the calamities which had befallen as the
result of the usurpation by man of an office which rightly
belonged only to Jehovah.

2. THE REMNANT

Originally the relation between Jehovah and Israel is
simply conceived. Israel is his people or his inheritance:
and what is required from them is exclusive loyalty to him
and obedience to his will as revealed in *torah* and prophecy.
On Jehovah's part it is understood that he will make
Israel the special object of his favour and secure them in
possession of their land. So long as the requirements of
Jehovah are not made too exacting, this doctrine works
well: so long as the standard is not pitched too high, the
majority of the people can attain to it. Again, so long as
the national politics march prosperously, it is easy to
believe that Jehovah is carrying out his part of the com-
pact and that therefore all is well. It was the prophets who
came proclaiming woe unto those who were at ease in
Zion, secure in their comfortable faith. In the days of
Elijah it began to be proclaimed that the popular notion of
what constituted loyalty to Jehovah was not good enough.
Into the midst of the blatant prosperity of the reign of
Jeroboam II came Amos with his announcement of
imminent political calamity.

These two factors work together. As the standard of
loyalty and obedience is raised, the number of people who
may be expected to attain to it decreases. It ceases to be
an ideal for the nation and becomes an ideal for an elect
few within the nation. So the doctrine of the Remnant
emerges. Similarly as it becomes clear that it is the destiny
of Israel to be overrun by the armies of the alien, the conclusion follows that any deliverance which there may be
will only be for a part of the people, and the further con-

clusion is easily drawn that it is the righteous remnant who will be saved.

Thus in the theophany at Horeb (I Kings xix) Elijah is enjoined to anoint Hazael as king of Syria, Jehu as king of Israel, and Elisha as prophet in succession to himself. The prediction follows:

And it shall come to pass, that him that escapeth from the sword of Hazael shall Jehu slay: and him that escapeth from the sword of Jehu shall Elisha slay. Yet will I leave me seven thousand in Israel, all the knees which have not bowed unto Baal, and every mouth which hath not kissed him (xix. 17 f.).

Here 'seven thousand is a round number for the faithful minority who will be spared in the judgement. It is an anticipation of the later prophetic doctrine of the Remnant, the pious kernel, the Israel within Israel, to whom belongs the promise of the future'.[1]

This doctrine of the Remnant is one of the dominant thoughts of Isaiah.[2] It is symbolised in the name which is borne by his son Shear-jashub—a remnant shall turn (sc. to God and be saved). It appears frequently in the prophecies attributed to him. And it became a maxim for his practical work as a religious leader in Israel. His gathering together of a band of disciples to whom his teaching was committed (Is. viii. 16–18) may fairly be regarded as an attempt to 'consolidate the Remnant'. This last feature is of great importance in its bearing on the conception of the Kingdom of God unfolded in the Gospels. For in Isaiah's teaching the doctrine of the Remnant is, in the main, an eschatological idea. The Remnant is what is left when the judgement is overpast. But if the interpretation here adopted of Is. viii. 16 ff. be correct, it is clear that there is a sense in which the Remnant might be a present reality in Israel, 'the nucleus of the future people of God'.[3]

In prophecies later than Isaiah's the doctrine reappears

[1] Skinner, *Century Bible, ad loc.*
[2] On the doctrine of the Remnant in Isaiah cf. Skinner, *Camb. Bible, Isaiah*, i., pp. lxii–lxiv.
[3] *Ibid.*, p. lxiv.

in Zephaniah (ii. 3–9; iii. 13), Joel (iii. 5), Micah (iv. 4–7), Amos (ix. 8–10, on the assumption that this is part of a later addition to Amos), and Malachi.[1]

But it would be a mistake to suppose that the influence of the doctrine of the Remnant was confined to those writers who make use of the word 'remnant'. On the contrary, it may be said that the central idea of the doctrine was destined to be fruitful in all the later development of Hebrew religion. "In the doctrine of the Remnant a decisive step is taken towards the individualising of religion;" and this religious individualism modifies in one essential matter the idea of a people of God. Amos had announced that Jehovah's exclusive recognition of Israel meant exemplary punishment for all Israel's transgressions (Am. iii. 2). Isaiah saw that the nation as a political entity was doomed. The Remnant which was to survive the judgement would take the place formerly held by the nation as a whole. But there is this significant difference between the old dispensation and the new. Membership in the nation came by accident of birth; in the Remnant it is a matter of deliberate choice by the individual. If our interpretation of Is. viii. 16 ff. is correct, the vitally important thing is no longer to be a son of Abraham, but to be a disciple of Isaiah with all that that implies.[2]

The promulgation of the Deuteronomic law book in the reign of Josiah (621 B.C.) may justly be regarded as a serious attempt to bring the people of Judah as a whole under the obligations and privileges of the Remnant. 'The conceptions and aims of Deuteronomy are thoroughly prophetic. It seeks to realise the hoped-for Kingdom of God as promised by the prophets. Israel is to become a holy people, governed by the will of God.'[3] But it attempts to do this by external means: and this is the secret of its failure. It was not possible to accomplish by a public

[1] Cf. Driver, *Minor Prophets* (*Century Bible*), p. 295.
[2] This is the doctrine which is taken up and proclaimed by John the Baptist (Mt. iii. 7–10 = Lk. iii. 7–9: Q).
[3] Cornill, *The Prophets of Israel* (E.T.), p. 83.

nr Clarkenag etc.

administrative act something which required the private choice of the individual. The people could not be made into a Remnant, in Isaiah's sense, by the fiat of Josiah. The history of Israel is full of attempts to turn the prophetic message into 'practical politics'. Church history likewise. The attempts mostly miscarry. The life-giving spirit evaporates in the process and only the dead letter of the law remains.

The failure of the covenant entered into in 621 may well have inspired Jeremiah with the 'idea of the new covenant (Jer. xxxi. 31–34) of which the positive features are three: (1) *Inwardness*: "I will put My law in their inward part", (2) *Individualism*: "All shall know Me", (3) *Forgiveness of sins*: "Their sins I will remember no more"'.[1] Here it is emphasised again that membership of the true people of God will be a matter of disposition and character rather than birth. *cf John Baptist*

The idea of the Remnant reappears in a new form in the Servant Songs incorporated into Deutero-Isaiah (xlii. 1–4; xlix. 1–6; l. 4–9; lii. 13–liii. 12). The view taken here is that these passages are the work of an earlier writer, and that the author of Is. xl–lv worked them into his own prophecies. On this hypothesis the relation of the Servant Songs to the rest of Deutero-Isaiah is somewhat similar to that between the Remnant passages in Isaiah proper and the Deuteronomic legislation. The word 'Servant' occurs in Is. xli. 8; xlii. 19; xliii. 10; xliv. 1 f., 21; xlv. 4; xlviii. 20; and in these cases the reference is clearly to the historic nation of Israel represented by the community of the exiles. On the other hand the identity of the person depicted in the Servant Songs has been hotly disputed ever since they were isolated by Duhm in 1875. The controversy centres round the question whether the Servant is an individual or a group: and many theories have been put forward, none, it must be confessed, free from difficulties. To the present writer it seems that the most probable inter-

[1] Skinner, *Prophecy and Religion*, p. 329.

pretation is that which finds in the Servant the picture of
the ideal Israel. This ideal Israel is not, however, a purely
imaginative creation; but something developed out of the
Remnant as conceived, and in some degree actualised, by
Isaiah. *The Remnant was not protected — so suffering became Redemptive*

The spiritual kernel of the nation had not enjoyed any
miraculous deliverance from the calamities which over-
whelmed the Judean kingdom. Rather they had suffered
more acutely than the rest of the people. The life of such a
man as the prophet Jeremiah is a sufficient demonstration
of this: and there must have been others like-minded who
suffered in the same way, though not perhaps in the same
degree. The old doctrine of the Remnant, passed through
the fire of their affliction, emerges in a new form and with
a new content. The difference may be stated simply in this
way, that whereas the Remnant was to be a *saved* few, the
Servant of Jehovah is to be a *saving* few. The brand plucked
from the burning is to become a light to lighten the
Gentiles. *Seen the true remnant were not protected from suffering, they saw that their suffering had a purifying purpose for the nation.*

We may surmise that this conception of the Remnant in
its new form was taken up by the author of Deutero-
Isaiah and used by him as an ideal to set before the people
of Israel as a whole. For him the whole community which
has survived the Exile is to be the Servant of Jehovah, and
to realise in itself the ideal represented in the Songs. The
method by which he seeks to bring this about is not
legislation, as in the Deuteronomic reform, but exhortation.
The time of judgement and punishment for Israel is over:
and the prophet is sent to call the people to a new task,
a world mission. They are to be restored to existence as
a nation, not to be a great political power—the political
power is already entrusted to Cyrus—but to be a spiritual
force in the world, to demonstrate by their very existence
the universal sovereignty of Jehovah.

The status of the restored Israel, as pictured in Deutero-
Isaiah, is sufficiently indicated by the choice of the name
'Servant of Jehovah' as the name of the community as a

whole. It has been pointed out above (p. 142 n. 6) that the word עֶבֶד, Servant, was regularly used in the days of the Hebrew kingdom to mark the difference in rank between king and subject.[1] Even the highest officers of state are the king's servants; and the rule is that in addressing the monarch the subject uses the words 'my lord, the king' and refers to himself as 'thy servant'. It is therefore arguable that this is the sense in which the word 'servant' is to be understood in the name 'Servant of Jehovah': that what is chiefly stressed is the relation of the restored Israel as subject to Jehovah as its heavenly King. This is borne out by the evidence furnished by the proper name Malchijah (= Jehovah is my King). This name was probably first coined in the seventh century, and it occurs frequently after the Exile.[2] It appears also in the Aramaic documents of the Jewish colony at Elephantine.[3] This means that the theocratic idea was gaining ground among the people generally from the seventh century onwards.

If this interpretation of the Servant passages is correct, it will follow that what is pictured in the Servant Songs and pressed upon the exiled Israel by the writer of Is. xl–lv is the idea of a Kingdom of God on earth in the sense of a people wholly devoted to Jehovah as their King and used by him as an agent for the extension of his Kingdom throughout the world. They are to conquer the world, not by force of arms, but by spiritual power; not to establish an earthly empire after the manner of Assyria and Babylon but to bring men under the sway of Jehovah; not to compel the unwilling submission of vassal states to themselves, but to attract individual men and women to voluntary acceptance of Israel's King as their King.

With this ideal for Israel we may contrast the expectations of the other great prophet of the Exile, Ezekiel. He also pictures a restored Israel as the people of God, and a

[1] Cf. R. H. Kennett, *The Servant of the Lord*, pp. 6 ff.
[2] Cf. G. B. Gray, *Studies in Hebrew Proper Names*, pp. 119 f.
[3] Cowley, *Aramaic Papyri of the Fifth Century B.C.*, Index, s.v. מלכיה.

restored Palestine as the personal demesne of Jehovah.
The new Jerusalem is to be the seat of Jehovah and the
capital of his Kingdom.   From his throne in the new
Temple he will rule his own people, showering benefits
upon them, and ruthlessly crushing every hostile nation
that dares threaten their peace and prosperity.   It is
obvious that here the notion of the Remnant has taken a
form different from that which meets us in the Servant
passages in Deutero-Isaiah. The restored Israel, purified   *in Ezekiel*
by the fiery affliction of the Exile, is the Remnant which   *ledsewent care.*
turns to enjoy salvation, whatever may be the fate of the   *non - missionary*
rest of the world.

We have, then, in these two prophecies of the Exile two
explicit formulations of the Remnant doctrine, both
destined to have a tremendous influence on the subsequent
development of religion. That of Ezekiel may be said to be   *most*
the prototype of strict Judaism; that of Deutero-Isaiah
the prototype of Evangelical Christianity. The Remnant   *xxx*
doctrine bifurcates at this point: and in all later religious
teaching, where it is present, it takes the form either of a
saved Remnant or a *saving* Remnant: and the religion
becomes accordingly either Pharisaic, in the proper sense
of that much-abused word, or Apostolic.[1]

The history of Hebrew religion after the Exile is the
story of how, despite some protests, the conception of
Jehovah's people as an exclusive body developed and
penetrated the whole life of the community.[2] Utterances
such as Jonah; Zech. ix. 1–10; Is. lvi. 1–8; and the Book of
Ruth were unavailing to stem the tide of particularism.
The dominant ideal is that of the Holy People settled in the
Holy Land with Jehovah their King as the glory in the
midst of Jerusalem and as a wall of fire round about.[3]
Even when it is said[4] that 'many nations shall join them-
selves to the Lord in that day, and shall be to me a people',

---

[1] See below, pp. 186 ff., and Detached Note C at end of this chapter.
[2] Cf. L. E. Browne, *Early Judaism*, especially Chapter XII.
[3] Zech. ii. 9 (E.V. ii. 5).
[4] Zech. ii. 15 (E.V. ii. 11).

what is in the mind of the writer is not the result of any
missionary activity; but rather that the restored and
glorified Israel will be the admiration and envy of the
whole world so that the better elements at least of the
Gentiles will hasten to attach themselves to it and share in
its privileges.

After the return from the Exile strenuous efforts were
made to bring this ideal community into existence. The
prophetic work of Haggai and Zechariah, the administrative and legalistic activities of Ezra and Nehemiah are
all directed to this main end. Elements of the population
deemed to be unworthy were eliminated. Samaritan
advances were rejected. If the interpretation of Is. lxiii. 7–
lxiv. 11 suggested by L. E. Browne[1] is correct, this
passage represents the Samaritan protest against this
rejection. In that case the words of lxiii. 19 are very
significant: 'We have become "from everlasting Thou
hast not ruled over them: Thy name was not named upon
them"'.[2] Rejection from the community of Israel is
equivalent to being outlawed from the Kingdom of God on
earth. The new community, growing up around Jerusalem
after the Exile, is the Kingdom of God in its present
manifestation.

No more than the Deuteronomic reforms did the policy
of Ezra and Nehemiah secure what it was designed to
secure: once more it proved impossible to legislate the
ideal community into existence. The yoke of the Kingdom
could not be imposed where it was not freely accepted:
and if it were freely accepted by all, there would be no
occasion to impose it. In the troubles which followed the
partition of the Empire of Alexander the Great it speedily
appeared that not all Israel after the flesh was truly
Israel. Yet, as in former days, there remained those who
maintained their loyalty to Jehovah in the face of all that
the Seleucid monarchs could offer or threaten. Once more
there was a faithful Remnant, an Israel within Israel.

<hr/>

[1] *Early Judaism*, pp. 70–86.   [2] *Ibid.*, p. 84.

This spiritual kernel of the nation proclaims its allegiance in many of the Psalms:

Ps. v. 3: Hearken unto the voice of my cry, my King and my God.

xliv. 5: Thou art my King, O God.

lxxxiv. 4: O Lord of hosts, my King and my God.

cxlv. 1: I will extol thee, my God, O King.

There has been the same controversy regarding the 'I' of the Psalms as in the case of the 'servant of Jehovah', whether, namely, the term is to be interpreted individually or collectively. As in the case of the Servant, the view here taken is that the 'I' is the Remnant in Israel, the community within the community. The voice of the group as a whole is the same as the voice of the individual member because the content of the song is the one thing which binds them together.[1] Consequently what is said in the first person singular may be said in the first person plural:

Ps. lxxxix. 19: The Holy One of Israel is our King.

This confession of faith and loyalty may be heard in many other Psalms.[2] It is one of the characteristic notes of the Psalter. The faithful community that speaks in such terms to God is described in the Psalms as 'the Pious' or 'the Saints' (*Ḥăsîdîm*), 'the Righteous' (*Ṣaddîḳîm*), or 'the Upright' (*Yěšārîm*): and it is possible to gather from the history of the Jewish people during the last centuries before Christ who and what manner of men they were.

They appear again in the Book of Daniel as 'the Saints'[3] (*Ḳaddîšîn*) and here it is clear that the character that goes with the name 'Saint' is character of the type represented in Daniel himself and the three youths, Shadrach, Meshach, and Abed-nego. Once more in the so-called Psalms of Solomon we meet with an Israel within Israel: 'the Righteous', 'the Saints', 'Saints of God', 'Saints of the

[1] Cf. H. Roy, *Die Volksgemeinde und die Gemeinde der Frommen im Psalter*, p. 11.

[2] E.g. x. 16; xlvii f.; lxviii. 25; lxxiv. 12; xcv; xcviii. 6; xcix. 1; cxlix. 2.

[3] Dan. vii. 18, 21, 22, 25, 27.

Lord'.[1] These are the true Israel, 'the flock of the Lord' as distinct from those who dwell with the saints in hypocrisy.[2] The confession of faith of this godly Remnant is in the same terms as that of their counterpart in the canonical Psalter:

Blessed be the glory of the Lord, for he is our King. (v. 22.)

O Lord, thou art our King henceforth and even for evermore, for in thee, O God, our soul exulteth. (xvii. 1.)

The Lord, he is our King from henceforth and even for evermore. (xvii. 51.)

Now we know who are the speakers in the Psalms of Solomon. They are the Pharisees, the spiritual descendants of the Asidaeans[3] (Hăsîdîm) who, in the days of the Maccabean revolt, showed themselves most zealous for the observance of the Law, preferring to die rather than take up arms, even in self-defence, on the Sabbath. When the Asidaeans did join the forces of Judas Maccabaeus, they fought solely for the Law and the right to observe it. So soon as this object was achieved they withdrew from the campaign, having no interest in or approval of the wars for political freedom. This temper is inherited by the early Pharisees. They, likewise, are entirely out of sympathy with the ambitions and pretensions of the Hasmonean dynasty. Their chief, almost their only, concern is with the observance of the Law and the practice of their religion. Their political creed is patience and resignation, even in the face of foreign invasion.

It is not difficult to see how men of this stamp could declare that God was their King. According to Robertson Smith's definition of the old Semitic idea of the divine kingship quoted above (p. 144) it involved three things:

---

[1] The word ὅσιος 'saint' is regularly used as a translation of חסיד in the LXX version of the canonical Psalms. It may therefore be inferred that it represented the same Hebrew in the Psalms of Solomon. Cf. Ryle and James *ad* Ps. Sol. iii. 10.

[2] Compare Ryle and James, *The Psalms of Solomon*, Introd., p. li.

[3] I Macc. ii. 42; vii. 13; II Macc. xiv. 6. Schürer, *G.J.V.*[4] I. 203; II. 472 f. Moore, *Judaism*, I. 59 f.

help against their enemies, counsel by oracles or sooth-sayers in matters of national difficulty, and a sentence of justice when a case was too hard for human decision. The two last were already given in the Law and the Prophets, the former definitely closed as a canonical collection, the latter also virtually a closed collection, the voice of prophecy having ceased for the time being.[1] All that Israel needed to know for guidance in faith and morals was already contained in the Law. That was God's fulfilment of two-thirds of what was expected from him. That he would also perform the first part of the kingly task and deliver his people from all their enemies was a matter of faith: and the business of the faithful was to wait with patience on his good pleasure.

At this stage, therefore, recognition of the sovereignty of God means unreserved obedience to his will as revealed in the Law. The Kingdom of God is manifested on earth—in part at any rate—by the fact that there exists a community of people who are *his* people, who own him as their King and show their loyalty by their obedience to his commands. Their final vindication against all who are alien from the commonwealth of God, the heathen empires abroad and the apostates at home, is something which lies still in the future, but which is nevertheless certain to come, since it is in God's hands, and in his own good time he will surely bring it to pass.

This faithful community ought to include the whole of Israel; but Israel as a whole comes short of the standard set up for membership of it. Thoroughgoing observance of the written Law and the oral tradition, which gathered round the sacred text, was a task for which not many would have the inclination: and even where the inclination was present the nature of men's occupations often made it exceedingly difficult, if not impossible, to carry on their

[1] The problem what to do with the stones of the altar defiled by Antiochus Epiphanes was left unsolved until a faithful prophet should arise. The inference is that the phenomenon of prophecy had ceased but that the hope remained that it might be revived in the future.

*The
Law Lovers*

7.

Pharisee

business and at the same time maintain a scrupulous regard for all the precepts and prohibitions. The result is that the Remnant appears in a new form and under a new name. It is now the community of those whose delight is in the Law of Jehovah, who meditate on it day and night, and make it the norm by which their lives are ordered: and it bears the name 'Pharisee' (Aram. *Pĕrîšā*, Heb. *Pārûš*).

Concerning the meaning of this name there can be little doubt that it means simply 'separated'. The question then arises: What is the point of the name? To this question various answers have been given.[1] Two of these, differing but not incompatible, may be noticed here. That proposed independently by Professor M. I. Hussey[2] and Professor Ed. Meyer[3] seeks the origin of the name in the events of 163 B.C. when the Asidaeans, who had fought under Judas Maccabaeus until the religious liberty of the nation was assured, declined to follow him in further campaigns for political ends and withdrew from the alliance with him. On this interpretation the Asidaeans got the name 'Pharisees' with the sense 'seceders'. The other interpretation, which is put forward by Professor G. F. Moore,[4] is an answer to the question: What did the Pharisees themselves take their name to mean?[5] He observes that 'in the Tannaite Midrash *parûsh* is frequently associated with *kadôsh*, "holy"'. From the passages which he quotes he infers that 'separateness in these contexts is synonymous with holiness;...the ideal of holiness for Israelites is the ideal of separateness, and it is easy to see how those who made it their end to fulfil this ideal might take its name

---

[1] Summarised in Moore, *Judaism*, I. 60 ff.

[2] *Journal of Biblical Literature*, XXXIX. 66–69, cited by Moore, *op. cit.*, p. 62 n. 1.

[3] *Ursprung u. Anfänge des Christentums*, II. 283 f.

[4] *Op. cit.*, p. 61.

[5] Professor Moore starts from the supposition 'that it may have been a name originally assumed by them'; but this is not essential to his interpretation. The name might be given in one sense and accepted by them in another. Christians use 'friend of publicans and sinners' as an honourable title of Jesus; but it was not so meant by those who conferred it upon him.

Pĕrūshīm as a less presuming title than *Ḳĕdōshīm*'. As has been said already, these two interpretations are not necessarily incompatible. It may well be the case that the name Pharisee was first conferred in derision upon the Asidaeans by those who were annoyed by their secession from what was deemed to be the national cause. Once given the name would stick, and at a later period it may have been consciously accepted by the party and given a new interpretation suitable to their own ideals. A similar development may be observed in the name Christian, which was apparently given in the first instance as a nickname and later adopted by the followers of Christ as an honourable title.[1]

For our present purpose one of Dr Moore's passages may be quoted in full, as it has a direct bearing on the idea of the Kingdom as manifested in the lives of its subjects on earth. The *Mekhilta*, commenting on Ex. xix. 6: 'Ye shall be unto me a kingdom of priests and an holy nation', says: '"Holy"—holy, hallowed, separated from the peoples of the world and their detestable things'.[2] Here the word-is used to explain what is meant by a holy nation: and it is perhaps not without significance that the interpretation should appear in connection with one of the earliest passages which we can quote for the existence of the belief that Jehovah's kingship is to be manifested in the people of Israel.

It is to be noted that while the Pharisees, like all previous embodiments of the Remnant, did not form more than a fraction of the whole nation, yet the Pharisaic ideal was one which was put forward as the ideal for the people as a whole. This also is entirely in line with previous formulations of the Remnant idea. There were never wanting those who would try, by one means or another, to make the Remnant co-extensive with the entire nation. In the apocalyptic literature in general it is expected that

---

[1] Cf. A. Carr, *Horae Biblicae*, pp. 47 ff.
[2] *Mekhilta*, ed. Friedmann, f. 63 *a*.

Israel, perhaps purged of its more unworthy members and
increased by conversions from the better part of the
Gentiles, will be the Remnant that will turn to God and
survive the last convulsions of the existing state of things.
This belief is stated most definitely in *Jubilees* xv. 31 f.:

> For there are many nations and many peoples, and all are
> His, and over all hath He placed spirits in authority to lead them
> astray from Him. But over Israel He did not appoint any angel
> or spirit, for He alone is their ruler, and He will preserve them
> and require them at the hand of His angels and His spirits, and
> at the hand of all His powers in order that He may preserve
> them and bless them, and that they may be His and He may be
> theirs from henceforth for ever.[1]

Dr H. J. Wicks says that the only writer in all the
apocalyptic and apocryphal literature between 200 B.C.
and A.D. 100 who entirely despaired of the future of Israel
in this world and the next is the author of x. 6–xii. 4
in the *Apocalypse of Baruch*:[2] and this writer, according
to Dr Charles, is probably a Sadducean priest writing just
after the fall of the Temple in A.D. 70.[3] For a Sadducee
this event might well mean the extinction of all hope, as it
was the end of everything for which his party stood. For
the Pharisees, however, who, whatever faults may be
alleged against them, did certainly look to the things that
are unseen and eternal rather than the things that are
seen and temporal, the destruction of the Temple, while it
was a great blow and a matter for regret and sorrow, yet
did not touch the chief matters about which they cared.
Least of all did it have any real bearing upon the ultimate
destiny of the true Israel. Such things had happened
before and Israel had survived: and Israel could still
survive as God's own people; for it possessed something
greater than the Temple—the Law as the charter of its
existence.

---

[1] Translated R. H. Charles.
[2] *Doctrine of God*, p. 254.
[3] *Apocalypse of Baruch*, pp. lxiii f., 14 ff.

3. THE CHURCH

Deferring for the moment the examination of material contained in the Gospels, we may conclude this summary survey by considering the last formulation of the Remnant doctrine as it appears in the primitive Church. The matter has been so well put by Canon Streeter[1] that one can hardly do better than quote his words:

The first Christians did not regard themselves as a new society, but as the ancient 'People of God', that is, as that portion of the Church of the Patriarchs and Prophets which had not, by rejecting the Messiah, forfeited its birthright and cut itself off from the 'promises of Israel'. Many of the prophets had proclaimed that only a 'remnant' of Israel after the flesh would repent and be saved; others had foretold that in the Messianic age Gentiles also would be brought to share the religious privileges of Israel. The Christian position was that, by recognising Jesus as Messiah, they and they alone understood the prophets aright. The number of Jews who had rejected the Messiah was larger than might have been expected, so also was the number of Gentiles who had accepted Him; but that did not in any way alter the fundamental position that only the community of those who did accept Him could claim to be the 'Israel of God'.

According to St Paul the period through which the Church is passing is one in which the Kingdom of God in the fullest sense is gradually being realised. Christ reigns and must reign till all enemies are subdued. Then he will hand over the Kingdom perfect to God the Father.[2] The true Israel or people of God are those who, under Christ's rule, are engaged in the warfare for the consummation of the Kingdom. In one respect they differ from the Zealots of Judaism, who were always ready to take up arms for the liberation of Israel from the dominance of the kingdoms of the world, in this, namely, that their warfare is not against men but against hostile spirit forces of one sort or another. And as their warfare is spiritual, so

---

[1] *The Primitive Church*, pp. 47 f.
[2] I Cor. xv. 20–28. See above, pp. 139 f.

the weapons with which it is waged are spiritual: truth, righteousness, the preparation of the gospel of peace, faith, salvation, the word of God.[1] In this aspect the Church is, so to speak, the army of the Kingdom of God, engaged in the task of conquering every hostile power and winning the world for Christ and ultimately for God.

In this way of looking at it the Church is, as it were, the *militia Christi*; but there is also what may be called the civil aspect in contrast to the military, and this finds expression in Phil. iii. 17–iv. 1, more particularly in iii. 20. Here the πολίτευμα of Christians is said to be in Heaven: and if the interpretation of πολίτευμα proposed by Dibelius[2] is, as I believe, correct, the sense of the passage is that the Christian community on earth is a colony whose constitution reproduces in miniature the constitution of the Kingdom in heaven. The figure which St Paul here uses is borrowed from the political practice of Greece and Rome rather than from Hebrew or Jewish custom, for obvious reasons. An illustration must be more familiar than the thing illustrated. But what is conveyed under the figure is at bottom the old Hebrew and Jewish idea that God has his Kingdom on earth in the existence of his chosen people who accept him as their King. The true Israel or the Israel of God, the army of Christ, and the colony of heaven are just different ways of describing one and the same thing, a thing whose origin lies far back in the history of Israel.

If, then, we are correct in our tracing of the idea of God's kingship manifested on earth in a people faithful to him in all circumstances as an element in the true religion of Israel from an early date, and as something which was taken up as an essential part of the Christian Gospel, we may ask the question: What are the fundamental character-

[1] Eph. vi. 10–20. Cf. Rom. xiii. 12; II Cor. x. 3–6; I. Thess. v. 8 ff. Further passages from N.T. and early Christian literature in Harnack, *Militia Christi*, pp. 93 ff. Cf. Dibelius, 'Das Bild von der Waffenrüstung des Frommen' in *H.B.N.T.* III. ii. 122 f.

[2] *H.B.N.T. ad* Phil. iii. 20 (quoted above, p. 138 n. 2).

istics of the doctrine? Having ascertained these, we may
enquire whether they are present in the recorded utterances of Jesus.

4. FUNDAMENTAL PRINCIPLES

The former question admits of a fairly simple answer.
The essential elements in the doctrine of a divine Kingdom
manifested in human life emerge most clearly when it is
remembered that the relation implied in the idea is two-
sided. The Kingdom is a relation between God as King
and man as subject, and the relation is maintained by the
contributions of both parties to it. What God offers as
King is:

(a) _Protection_. He is the true rock and fortress, the sure
defence of his people. The denunciations of foreign
alliances which we find so often in the prophetic writings,
the frequent declarations in the Psalms, and, in the days of
the Maccabees, the refusal of the Asidaeans to engage in
warfare for political ends, are all evidence of the firmness
with which this belief was held. It was easily held in times
of prosperity: and even when things went utterly wrong it
remained an article of faith among the faithful. God's
deliverance might be deferred because of sin, or for some
other reason, but it was none the less sure: and elect souls
would always possess themselves in patience and wait for
the time when God would again intervene with a strong
hand and an outstretched arm to deliver his people as he
had delivered them in the days of Moses.

(b) _Guidance_. It is part of the faith of prophecy and
apocalyptic that all the issues of world history are in the
hands of God, and with them, of course, the tasks and
destinies of his own people. He alone knows the end from
the beginning and he alone, therefore, can indicate with
infallible certainty what should be the policy of his people.
To provide this guidance or leadership God admits
certain men into his confidence and reveals to them
enough of his secret purposes to make it perfectly clear

what his people ought to do at every crisis in their history.[1] This conviction on the part of the prophets is what justified their political activities. They could dare to pit their advice against the policies of kings and nobles just because they felt themselves to have a surer, because God-given, knowledge of what must come to pass.

(c) *A way of life*. God combines the functions of legislator and judge for his people. He is both the giver of the Law and its vindicator. For Judaism, as it existed at the beginning of the Christian era—and Judaism means Pharisaic Judaism—the possession of the Law was the crowning demonstration of the kingship of God over Israel. Deliverance from enemies might tarry, the voice of prophecy might be silent, but the Law remained as a proof that there was a King over Israel. To recite the *Shema'*—the quintessence of the Law and in a sense symbolic of the whole—was equivalent to taking upon oneself the yoke of the Kingdom of God: and, similarly, to accept the yoke of the Law was to be delivered from the yoke of royalty (i.e. of earthly kingdoms) and the yoke of worldly cares.[2]

God is thus King in a very large and absolute sense. He is conceived as exercising in person the various functions which, in a modern state, are assigned to the military forces of the Crown, the Cabinet Ministers, the Legislature, and the Courts of Law. And from his decisions there is no appeal, against his power none can stand. And it is to be noted that these are things that do not lie entirely in the

---

[1] This is the claim of the earliest writing prophet: 'The Lord God doeth nothing, except he have revealed his secret counsel (סוֹד) to his servants the prophets' (Am. iii. 7). It is implied in many earlier narratives, for example the vision of Micaiah b. Imlah (I Kings xxii): and it is reaffirmed or implied in many later prophetic utterances, for example Jer. xxiii. 18, 22. It is also the basis of all apocalyptic writings that their supposed authors are admitted to the counsels of God and have the divine purpose revealed to them. This purpose they then record in a kind of secret code, to which, of course, only the elect possess the key.

[2] *Aboth*, iii. 8 (ed. Taylor) in the name of R. Neḥoniah b. Haḳḳanah, a *Tanna* of the first generation and teacher of R. Ishmael.

future. They are functions exercised in the present, as they have been in the past, and will be in the future. God has wrought deliverance before and he will do it again. One day he will do it so thoroughly that it will never need to be repeated. He has given guidance in the past in the affairs of his people: and he will do it again as need arises. He has given the Law once for all as the standing symbol and organ of his government. Finally in every age he has his subjects, who willingly and gladly acknowledge his sovereignty, place themselves under his protection and guidance, and order their lives according to his laws. This is the Kingdom in its present reality.

On man's side there is a contribution to be made. What God requires from the subjects of his Kingdom may be summarised as follows:

(a) *Loyalty,* complete and absolute, to the King. In the earliest times this loyalty was doubtless largely a matter of course. It was only with the complication of life and the growth of civilisation that other claimants to the loyalty of the Israelite appeared, and the necessity of making a definite choice arose. It is worth noticing that this call to choose between Jehovah and other claimants comes at about the same time as the idea of the faithful Remnant, that is, in the days of Elijah. The prophet's call to Israel: 'Choose this day whom ye will serve'—Jehovah or Baal— belongs to the same time as the revelation to the prophet that there are seven thousand left in Israel who have not bowed the knee to Baal. At this stage the choice is between Jehovah and other gods. At a later stage it is a choice between Jehovah, as the God of all righteousness, and the Prince of evil. In whatever form the alternative is displayed, the claim of God is absolute. There can be no half-way house and no divided allegiance: and only those who accept God as King without any reservations are members of his Kingdom.

(b) *Trust is* the consequence of the conviction of God's protection and guidance. The demand for it is manifested

early in the history of Israel, and perhaps, most impres-
sively in the prophecies of Isaiah at the time of the Syro-
Ephraimite alliance against Judah (Is. vii. 1–17; cf. viii.
9 f.). Exhortations to trust in Jehovah are frequent in the
Psalms. The ground of such counsels as these,

> Trust in the Lord and do good (xxxvii. 3);
> Commit thy way unto the Lord:
> Trust also in him, and he shall bring it to pass (v. 5);
> Rest in the Lord, and wait patiently for him (v. 7),

is the conviction that

> The Lord loveth judgement,
> And forsaketh not his saints;
> They are preserved for ever:
> But the seed of the wicked shall be cut off (v. 28).

The writer of the Epistle to the Hebrews found in this
quality the secret of all that was most splendid in the
history of Israel, as well as the spring of all true religion.
For him the Hebrew Roll of Honour is filled with the
names of those who had trusted God to the uttermost.

(c) *Obedience* to the revealed will of God is the corre-
lative on man's part to God's activity as guide and legislator to his people. The moral and religious demands of
God are conveyed to the nation by means of *torah* and
prophecy: and it is constantly emphasised in the Old
Testament that these ethical and spiritual requirements
should take first place.

> Thus saith the Lord of Hosts, the God of Israel: Add your
> burnt-offerings unto your sacrifices and eat ye flesh. For I
> spake not unto your fathers, nor commanded them in the day
> that I brought them out of the land of Egypt concerning burnt-
> offerings or sacrifices: but this thing I commanded them,
> saying, Hearken unto my voice, and I will be your God, and
> ye shall be my people: and walk ye in all the way that I
> command you, that it may be well with you.[1]

[1] Jer. vii. 21–23. 'Nicht Opfer will Gott, sondern Gehorsam: sagt
Jeremia der Prophet des Gehorsams, der im eigensten Leben den Gehorsam
bis zum Tode bewiesen hat. Das einzige gottgefällige "Opfer" ist das Opfer
des Willens' (Volz, *Der Prophet Jeremia, ad loc.*, p. 101).

There is no need to multiply examples. The Old Testament, especially the post-exilic books, is full of affirmations of the blessedness of the man whose delight is in the Law of the Lord: and that this is not mere pious aspiration is sufficiently demonstrated by one shining example from the days of the persecutions under Antiochus Epiphanes:

At that time many who sought righteousness and judgement went away into the wilderness to dwell there, they and their children, and their wives and their cattle; for their lot grew ever harder to bear. And it was told to the king's officers and to the troops that were in Jerusalem in the city of David that men who had transgressed the edict of the king had gone away into the hiding-places in the wilderness. And many went in pursuit of them, and when they found them, they set themselves in array against them and offered battle on the Sabbath day. And they said to them: Enough! come out and act according to the king's command and you shall live. But they said: We will not come forth nor act according to the king's command, to profane the Sabbath day.

Immediately the king's troops advanced to the assault. But the Jews made no response; they did not even fling a stone at them, nor barricade the caves, saying: Let us all die in our integrity; heaven and earth are our witness that you destroy us without just cause.

So the troops closed in battle with them on the Sabbath. And they died, they, and their wives, and their children, and their cattle, about a thousand persons.[1]

On this passage no comment is necessary save this, that the obedience contemplated and here exemplified is 'obedience unto death', the kind of obedience that is due from subject to king.

The Kingdom of God on earth may thus be defined as a community whose faith envisages God as their King in the sense that he and he alone is their protector, guide and legislator: and whose rule of life is summed up in complete loyalty, trust, and obedience towards their King.

[1] I Macc. ii. 29–38. For another example of the same spirit cf. Dan. iii, especially *vv.* 14–18.

We now turn to the question whether such a conception
is to be found in the teaching of Jesus.

5. THE TEACHING OF JESUS

The investigation of the materials supplied by the
Synoptic Gospels is complicated by the fact that there are
three different questions to be considered. In the pre-
Christian period, as we have seen, the Kingdom on earth is
a simple relation between God as King and men as his
subjects. In the Gospels it is not so simple. We have to
reckon with the fact of Jesus: and the problem of the
Kingdom resolves itself into: (a) the relation of Jesus as
subject to God as King; (b) the relation of the followers of
Jesus as subjects to God as King; (c) the relation of the
followers of Jesus to Jesus as Messiah. The first of these has
already been touched upon above;[1] but the relevant points
may be repeated in the present context.

(a) It is to be noted first of all that the whole of the
ministry is dominated by the conceptions which we have
seen to be fundamental in the idea of the Kingdom on
earth. The experience of the Baptism is followed by the
Temptation: and in these we are granted an insight into
the deepest and strongest convictions of Jesus. As the
record stands it shows us Jesus set between two opposing
realms, the divine and the satanic. Thus at the very outset
a vital choice has to be made. It is true that the temptations can be and have been interpreted in many ways.
From a purely ethical point of view they may be regarded
as appeals to three fundamental lusts in human nature—
the physical appetites, the thirst for admiration and the
esteem of our fellows, and the desire for power. But their
context shows that this line of explanation is not sufficient.
The real significance of the temptations lies in their
bearing upon the vocation of Jesus. They are designed to
undermine the relation between Jesus and God, to impair
his obedience, trust, or loyalty. That it is loyalty to God that

[1] Ch. VI. § 3.

is aimed at in the offer of the kingdoms of the world, and trust in God in the invitation to leap down from the pinnacle of the Temple is sufficiently obvious. That obedience to God is being attacked in the challenge to turn stones into bread is not, at first sight, so clear; but it becomes clear when the reply of Jesus is read in its original context.[1] There it appears that 'every word that proceedeth out of the mouth of God' is the same thing as 'all the commandments of the Lord' and that the way of life is in obedience to the will of God. The point of our Lord's answer can be put perfectly in the words: 'My meat is to do the will of him that sent me'.[2]

The Baptism and the Temptation are thus intimately related. If the one may be regarded as the announcement of God's choice and appointment of Jesus as Messiah, the other may equally be regarded as our Lord's deliberate choice of God as the sole object of his loyalty, trust and obedience, that is, as his King. In all his work the Father is to be the paramount chief and the paramount interest: everything that he does is to be done for God, with God, and under God. He is to be in the most complete sense the Servant of the Lord, the perfect subject of a perfect King.

It is not the way of Jesus to talk very much about this relation between God and himself; but there are hints here and there in his words which shed some light on what is the spiritual background of all his practical activities. We may note Mt. xii. 28 = Lk. xi. 20 (Q) where he implies that the power which he exercises is not his own but derived from God. In Mk. iii. 31–35 he finds his true kinsmen among those who do God's will. In Mk. x. 40 and xiii. 32 he is careful to explain that there are things which God keeps in his own hands, matters, therefore, which must be left in God's hands, while his servants content themselves with doing his will. Again there is great significance in the references to service as an ideal for the disciples and as a

---

[1] Deut. viii.   [2] John iv. 34.

guiding motive in his own life.[1] What is implied in all these sayings is that service of man is service of God, that the practical application of 'Thou shalt love the Lord thy God with all thy heart' is 'Thou shalt love thy neighbour as thyself'.

The prayer of Jesus in Gethsemane reveals the same loyalty, trust, and obedience, that we find in the Temptation story. They shine out in the midst of disappointment and disillusionment as clearly as they did at the beginning of the ministry.

The conclusion is that the foundation of all our Lord's teaching about the Kingdom, all his efforts to bring men into the Kingdom, and all the claims that he makes upon men, is his complete and whole-hearted acceptance of the yoke of the Kingdom in his own person. What he offers to men is not an academic doctrine but something which he has tried and proved in his own experience. He comes to men, not with an invitation to a conference on religion and ethics, but with a summons to follow him. Follow me, take my yoke upon you and learn of me, drink my cup, be baptised with my baptism: these are the lines of his approach to men.

(b) We should now expect that what Jesus has to say in his preaching of the Kingdom will be directed towards producing in them those qualities of loyalty, trust, and obedience which he himself manifests towards God. And this is the case. The great issue of life is represented as the choice between God and some other ruler of one's life. 'No man can serve two masters: Ye cannot serve God and mammon.'[2] The first essential of discipleship is to say 'No' to self, that is, to every private and personal interest that might interfere with one's complete devotion to the Kingdom.[3] True wisdom consists in assigning proper

[1] Mk. ix. 35; x. 43-45; Mt. xxv. 44 f.; Lk. xii. 37; xvii. 8; xxii. 26 f. All hese sayings are D.

[2] Mt. vi. 24 = Lk. xvi. 13 (Q).

[3] Mk. viii. 34 ff.; Lk. xiv. 26 f. (Q). Cf. Mt. x. 37 f.

values to human interests: therefore seek first the Kingdom of God.(1) The fatal thing is to be unable to discern between the Kingdom of God and the kingdom of evil; and the wickedest slander is to represent the subjects of God as tools of Beelzebub.[2] Again, once the Kingdom is discerned, it appears as something which must be obtained at whatever cost.[3] It is better to enter the Kingdom maimed than to be cast hale and hearty into Gehenna.[4]

The basic thought which underlies all these diverse modes of expression is that there are two ways, one leading to life and the other to destruction. The way of life is the way of the Kingdom and the acceptance of its yoke, the deliberate choice of God as King, and steadfast loyalty to him in all circumstances.

The second element in the conception of man's right attitude to God as King is trust: and this is inculcated most strongly in the teaching. Jesus urges upon his hearers, and especially upon his followers, that the whole destiny of the world and of the individual is in the hands of God: and that, therefore, anxiety is to be avoided. Anxiety about worldly things stifles and chokes the word that is sown in men's hearts.[5] Worry about the next meal or the next suit of clothes is worthy only of the heathen Gentiles. Those who seek the Kingdom may rest assured that the King is able to provide for all their needs.[6] When the disciples are brought up for trial they are not to worry about the terms of their defence. They will be instructed by the Holy Spirit.[7] In the storm on the lake Jesus reproaches the disciples not merely for cowardice, but also for lack of trust.[8] They are to fear nobody save God: and him they are to learn to trust.[9]

[1] Mt. vi. 33 = Lk. xii. 31 (Q).
[2] Mk. iii. 28 f.; Lk. xii. 10 ‖ Mt. xii. 32 a (Q).
[3] Mt. xiii. 44 ff., parables of Treasure and Pearl (M).
[4] Mk. ix. 43–48.   [5] Mk. iv. 19.
[6] Mt. vi. 25–33 = Lk. xii. 22–31 (Q).
[7] Mk. xiii. 11; Mt. x. 19 f. = Lk. xii. 11 f. (Q).
[8] Mk. iv. 40.   [9] Mt. x. 26–33 = Lk. xii. 2–9 (Q).

The third element, obedience, is equally prominent. The
prayer which Jesus taught his disciples contains, in one
version of it,[1] the petition 'Thy will be done on earth as it is
in heaven': and here the primary reference must be to the
life of him who prays, if the prayer is to be at all sincere.
The mark of kinship to Jesus is the doing of God's will.[2]
This obedience is conceived in the deepest and most far-
reaching way as a complete subordination of the human
will to God's will. The motto for any son of the Kingdom,
as for Jesus himself, is: 'Not what I will but what thou wilt'.
What is required is something which goes beyond the
prescriptions of *torah* and tradition: 'Unless your righteousness exceed the righteousness of the Scribes and Pharisees
ye shall not enter into the Kingdom of Heaven'.[3] 'When
you shall perform all things that are commanded you, say:
We are unprofitable servants, we have done (only) what
we were bound to do.'[4] It is clear from these passages and
many others of similar import, that Jesus set up a standard
of obedience to God every whit as rigorous as the most
rigorous exposition of the Law. It is a mistake to suppose
that Jesus, in this matter, is nearer to the school of
Hillel than to the school of Shammai. The exact contrary
is the case. In the one clear instance when Jesus gave
an opinion on one of the points in dispute between
the two schools, his decision is for an interpretation of
the Law stricter even than that of Shammai. This, however, is merely by the way. What Jesus is concerned
about is not the decision of particular legal problems, but
the disposition of man's will towards God: and here he
demands the complete subjection of the whole man to
God's will.[6]

---

[1] Mt. vi. 10 (M).   [2] Mk. iii. 35.
[3] Mt. v. 20 (M).   [4] Lk. xvii. 10 (L).
[5] On the question of divorce. The Jewish views on the matter in the first
century A.D. are admirably summarised by Abrahams, *Studies in Pharisaism
and the Gospels*, 1. 66 ff. I assume that it is as certain as anything can be in
N.T. criticism that the qualifications παρεκτὸς λόγου πορνείας and μὴ ἐπὶ
πορνείᾳ (Mt. v. 32; xix. 9) are not part of the genuine teaching of Jesus on
this point.
[6] On this question see the further discussion below, Chapter IX.

(c) In all that has so far been sketched of our Lord's teaching about the Kingdom on earth there is nothing which might not have been uttered by an enlightened Rabbi of a liberal turn of mind, and very little to which the most orthodox could take exception. In the matter of the relation of men to himself, however, Jesus introduces a new factor into religion, and into the idea of the Kingdom. This requires fuller treatment and may therefore be made the subject of a separate section.

6. THE PLACE OF JESUS IN THE KINGDOM ON EARTH

The decisive point is Peter's declaration: 'Thou art the Christ'. From this point onwards the life and teaching both move in a new direction. We have to notice a number of striking features in the teaching.

(a) A regular feature of the speech of Jesus before this point is the demand for insight and understanding on the part of his hearers. This is now replaced by a demand for loyalty and endurance on the part of his followers.

(b) The disciples are admitted much more fully than before into the confidence of Jesus. That this is the case we have seen in connection with the doctrine of the Father-hood of God.[1]

(c) The title 'Son of Man' belongs exclusively to the period after Peter's Confession.

(d) As we have already noticed, the 'coming' of the Kingdom is replaced by 'entrance' into the Kingdom.[2]

(e) There is a subtle yet unmistakable change of tone in the utterances of Jesus. He becomes, if possible, more authoritative, more dogmatic in his speech than before.

(f) To the period after Peter's Confession belongs the enunciation of the three great paradoxes of the Kingdom:

He who would save his life shall lose it, and he who loses his life shall save it.

The last shall be first, and the first last.

He who would be chief in the community must be the servant of all.

[1] Above, Chapter IV.   [2] Above, Chapter V.

On each of these points something must now be said.

(a) The following words and phrases are peculiar to the period before Peter's Confession: ἀσύνετος, βλέπω and γινώσκω in those cases where the words signify seeing below the surface of things, having insight or the like, καλύπτω, κρυπτός (?), μυστήριον, νοέω. All these are discussed in Appendix I. They belong to the D sections of the teaching.

The expression: 'He that hath ears...let him hear', which belongs to the G sections. See Appendix II, s.v. οὖς. συνίημι. See Appendix IV.

The inference to be drawn from these data is that in the former part of the ministry Jesus is constantly asking for one thing especially, namely, religious and moral insight. His complaint is that men cannot read the signs of the times, that figures so diverse and, in their separate ways, so significant as John the Baptist and himself are dismissed with an abusive epithet—'madman' or 'libertine'. In his public teaching he is constantly faced by the inability or unwillingness of people to understand himself and his message. What his audience, and especially the religious leaders, wanted was a clear-cut statement of his position and his claims, supported by definite proof, a sign from heaven or the like. Instead they are offered little stories or texts from the Old Testament with the injunction to 'think it over'. Jesus brought to a people saddled with a great mass of authoritative decisions on a thousand different points of religion and morals the challenge to decide for themselves on a number of perfectly simple and vital issues. But the perception of the real issues must be the work of the individual himself: and the decision must be his own spontaneous act. This is the *raison d'être* of parabolic teaching, as we have already argued. Its object is to awaken insight and understanding, to bring men to think for themselves and decide for themselves on the issues that concern their true blessedness.

Why then does this demand of our Lord's cease after Peter's Confession? It is difficult to resist the obvious *[handwritten top margin: 'M Pt': Each person in his thinking on Jesus respectfully, is wither B.C. in records where Jesus is great teacher, prophet, enunciator of wisdom: a way of life.(Sermon of Mt., ex.) or A.C. where Christ is God, the revelation, the Mediator &, Savior. Only can we come to the latter by insight not only into the Kingdom, but the Person of Xst..?]*

[handwritten right margin: & that by "learning of Him" Mt 11]

conclusion that it is because the response for which Jesus
was seeking had come in Peter's recognition of him as the
Messiah, a recognition all the more impressive because
there was no real ground for it beyond what Peter had
learned about Jesus by being with him and listening to his *[X]*
words. Signs such as the authorities expected and required had been definitely refused by Jesus himself. No *[ou Mt 16]*
voice from heaven had publicly declared 'This is the
Messiah'. Jesus himself had made no claim to the title.
His answer to the messengers from John the Baptist had
been: 'Tell John what you hear and see', with the implica- *[John Baptist]*
tion that John must draw his own conclusions from the
data. From the same data Peter drew his conclusion, and
was immediately ordered to say nothing about it in
public. The same injunction is laid upon the other disciples.[1]
Why? It may seem presumptuous to dispose in a single
sentence of a problem to which whole volumes have been
devoted; but if there is anything in the arguments which
have just been advanced the answer to the question must
be the perfectly simple one that the Messiahship of Jesus
was something which each man must discover for himself *[XXX]*
by his own insight and understanding.[2] *[good "D"]*

Once this fateful decision has been reached by Peter and *[Then they are]*
his fellow-disciples, the demands of Jesus change. Accord- *[ready for the]*
ing to the Marcan account the pregnant phrase 'for my *[Revelation]*
sake' (ἕνεκεν ἐμοῦ) now first makes its appearance:[3] and *[reserved for]*
[left margin: a.] *[right margin: the "Remnant" only.]*

[handwritten: 'For the R. only']

[1] Mk. viii. 30.

[2] This is the point of the saying in Mt. xvi. 17 (M): 'Blessed art thou,
Simon bar Jonah, for flesh and blood hath not revealed it unto thee, but my
Father in heaven' and also, if our placing of it is correct, of the Q saying,
Mt. xi. 25 f. = Lk. x. 21, 'I thank thee, Father...that thou hast hid these
things from the wise and prudent and hast revealed them unto babes'. The
recognition of the Messiahship depends, not on the acceptance of any
human testimony or authority, but on the working of a divinely illuminated
understanding.

[3] Mk. viii. 35; x. 29; xiii. 9. There are also two instances from Q: Mt. v.
11 ‖ Lk. vi. 22; and Mt. x. 39. The latter of these appears to be the Q parallel
to Mk. viii. 35, in which case it should be reckoned as an utterance subsequent
to Peter's Confession. The former is from Matthew's Sermon on the Mount
with a parallel in Luke's Sermon on the Plain. The phrase 'in my name' also
belongs to the period after Peter's Confession.

the things that must be borne 'for my sake' are the loss of property, friends, relatives, personal liberty, and even life itself.

Many other passages state this claim more particularly. Acknowledgement and denial of Jesus will each receive their just recompense in the future.[1] That the reward of faithful service is great is emphasised in the parables of the Talents and the Labourers in the Vineyard. On the other hand Jesus is at pains to show that the conditions are severe and that men must count the cost before they throw in their lot with him.[2] Those who wish to have a share in the future glory must also share the present humiliations and sufferings.[3] Unfaithfulness to Christ is a shameful thing: and of the man who betrays him it is said that it were better for that man if he had not been born.[4]

It is plain that after Peter's Confession Jesus makes the claim for a loyalty to himself which elsewhere is reserved for God. Loyalty to Jesus is identified with loyalty to the Kingdom. This point is one which must constantly be borne in mind in any attempt to state our Lord's conception of his Messiahship.

(b) To him that hath shall be given. The reward of insight is admission to fuller confidence. So in the days that follow Peter's Confession we find that Jesus speaks more freely to his immediate followers than before. Mark tells us that regarding his approaching sufferings he spoke to the disciples frankly:[5] and we need not suppose that such frankness was shown in his treatment of this subject alone. The evidence is all the other way. We find Jesus speaking openly of things that go to the very heart of his own religious experience: the Fatherhood of God as the only foundation for a living faith, the 'Son of Man' as the true Messianic ideal, entrance into the Kingdom as the true

[1] Mk. viii. 38; Mt. x. 32 f. = Lk. xii. 8 f. (Q).
[2] Parables of the Building of a Tower and Setting out on a Campaign, Lk. xiv. 28–33 (L).
[3] Mk. x. 35–40.   [4] Mk. xiv. 21.
[5] Mk. viii. 32: καὶ παρρησίᾳ τὸν λόγον ἐλάλει.

goal for all man's strivings. Such things as these are the
burden of our Lord's discourses to his disciples in the
second period of the ministry. So much is this the case
that it might almost be laid down as a canon for the interpretation of the teaching that those passages which fall
after Peter's Confession and are addressed to the disciples
should be regarded as the key to all the rest.

(c) The complex and difficult problems raised by the
phrase 'Son of Man' will require fuller discussion at a later
stage (§ 7). The evidence is all but conclusive that the
phrase is not used by Jesus in its special sense until after
Peter's Confession, and then only in sayings addressed to
the disciples.

(d) We have already seen that after Peter's Confession
Jesus speaks of entrance into the Kingdom rather than of
the coming of the Kingdom. What is significant for the
place of Jesus in the Kingdom is the general resemblance
between the conditions of entrance which he lays down and
the conditions of discipleship. The demands which God,
according to Jesus, makes on a would-be citizen of his
Kingdom and those which Jesus makes on a would-be
disciple are practically identical. The essential qualifications can be set side by side:

Entrance into the Kingdom.	Discipleship.
A childlike spirit (Mk. x. 15).[1]	
Readiness to sacrifice (a) material goods (Mk. x. 23; cf. Lk. xii. 29 ff.: Q), (b) physical well-being (Mk. ix. 47), (c) family ties (Lk. ix. 61 f.: L).	Complete self-sacrifice (Mk. viii. 34; Lk. xiv. 28–33: L) involving family ties (Mt. x. 37; Lk. xiv. 26: Q) and even life itself (Mk. viii. 35; Mt. x. 39: Lk. xvii. 33: Q).
Absolute obedience to God's will (Mt. v. 20; vii. 21: M).	Obedience to Jesus (Mk. viii. 34; Mt. x. 38; Lk. xiv. 27: Q).
	Persevering loyalty to Jesus in all circumstances (Mk. viii. 38; Mt. x. 32 f.: Lk. xii. 8 f.: Q).

[1] In this connexion it is worth noticing that Jesus addresses his disciples as
'children' (τέκνα: Mk. x. 24). Further a comparison of Mk. ix. 37 with
Mt. x. 40 suggests that this mode of address was not uncommon. In the
Marcan context, which appears to be the original, it is clear that 'children'
is meant to be taken literally. Once the saying is removed from its narrative
setting the 'children' of Mk. ix. 37 become the disciples in Mt. x. 40 (cf. also

The inference to be drawn from this comparison would seem to be that, in the mind of Jesus, to become a genuine disciple of his and to enter into the Kingdom of God amounted to much the same thing. If we now make the further comparison between the theoretical requirements for entrance into the Kingdom or discipleship of Jesus on the one hand and the actual lot of Jesus himself on the other, the command 'Follow me' takes on a new significance. It begins to appear that an essential part of the Messianic office as Jesus conceived it was not to bring the Kingdom of God to men but to bring men to the Kingdom of God. This is clearly realised by the author of the Epistle to the Hebrews when he calls Jesus 'the pioneer and perfecter of Faith'.[1] He leads the way into the Kingdom and the call to his disciples is a call to follow in his footsteps, drink his cup, and be baptised with his baptism.

It is at this point that we definitely part company with the eschatological interpretation of the Gospel. It is true that Jesus goes up to Jerusalem with the knowledge that he is going to his death. What is not supported by our evidence is the notion that he thought his death would force the coming of the Kingdom. He does not set out to compel God to prepare the banquet, but to compel men to come in to a banquet that is already spread. The journey to Jerusalem is not an attempt to take the Kingdom of God by storm, but a final attack on the kingdom of Satan. The aim is to deliver men, even at the cost of his life, out of the thraldom of sin into the service of their true King. The moral of the parable of the Vineyard is that the obligations of the Kingdom are present obligations: that of the parable

Lk. x. 16; Jn. xiii. 20). This change would take place the more easily if 'children' was the regular word which Jesus used in speaking to his disciples. The vocative παιδία occurs in Jn. xxi. 5 and in I Jn. ii. 14, 18; τέκνα (or τεκνία) in Gal. iv. 19; τέκνον in I Tim. i. 18; II Tim. ii. 1. It may well be that the writers of the epistles were following a custom established in the first instance by Jesus himself. Cf. the Rabbinical use of בני, e.g. Tos. *Nega im*, viii. 2, translated S.B. 1. 527 f.

[1] Heb. xii. 2. Cf. the notes of Davidson, Westcott, Windisch (*H.B.N.T.*), and Hollmann (*S.N.T.*), *ad loc.*

of the Great Feast is that the blessings of the Kingdom are present blessings; but men will neither enjoy the one nor face up to the other. To the end of the ministry the appeal of Jesus is to men: and his complaint is not that the coming of the Kingdom is delayed, but that men will not hear the call to enter into a Kingdom that is already present.[1]

(e) In the earliest stages of the ministry the authority with which Jesus spoke astonished his hearers. After Peter's Confession we find that this trait becomes, if anything, more pronounced. An indication of this is furnished by the use of the word 'Amen' by Jesus, a highly characteristic mode of speech for which there is no real parallel elsewhere. The manner in which it is used to introduce a saying, 'Verily I say unto you...' is similar to the use of the introductory formula, 'Thus saith the Lord...' in Old Testament prophecy.[2] Now the remarkable thing is that the vast majority of the instances, where Jesus makes use of this characteristic way of emphasising what he is about to say, occur after Peter's Confession. Of thirteen cases in Mark only two are recorded before that event. With our other sources it is more difficult to be certain; but for Q it is a probable estimate that eight out of ten cases fall after Peter's Confession: and for M the figures are four[3] before and four or five after. L presents only two cases, one at the beginning (Lk. iv. 24) and the other at the end (xxiii. 43) of the ministry. The result for the four sources together is thus nine cases before Peter's Confession and twenty-four or twenty-five after, and of the nine early cases three are in St Matthew's Sermon on the Mount, and may belong anywhere.

If we look only at the evidence of Mark, we find that nine out of the thirteen instances recorded in the Gospel are placed in the period after the journey to Jerusalem has

[1] Lk. xiii. 34 f. = Mt. xxiii. 37 ff. (Q).
[2] See above, pp. 105 ff.
[3] It should be noted that three of these four cases are in the composite Sermon on the Mount.

begun. And it must be said that this fact fits in well with
the picture drawn in Mk. x. 32—a solitary figure with his
face set towards Jerusalem and a handful of perplexed and
frightened disciples straggling behind. In this last period
there is a terrible certainty about everything that Jesus
does and says. We are in the presence of one for whom duty
and destiny have become one and the same thing. At
every point he is the 'Yea' to God's promises and demands
and therefore there is no changeableness or uncertainty
about him.[1]

We may ask what it is that gives this added certainty.
How is it that in the second part of the ministry there is
only one possible way, and that the road to Jerusalem and
the Cross? How is it that, once this journey has begun,
Jesus speaks with such dogmatic assurance? The answer to
these questions lies close at hand. "At Caesarea Philippi
Peter acclaimed Jesus as the Messiah and Jesus took him at
his word." The Messiah *de jure* becomes also the Messiah *de
facto*[2] and therewith the whole of his future course becomes
clear to him, however obscure it may sometimes appear to
us. He goes up to Jerusalem as Messiah—though the
Messiahship is known only to himself and his little band of
followers—to claim his Kingdom, which is the Kingdom of
God. To call men to enter the Kingdom, to break their
allegiance to the kingdoms of the world, to bring them to
their one true loyalty and their only true peace, all this lies
behind the resolve to go up to Jerusalem. As Messiah he
must lead a revolt and raise an insurrection, not a nationalist rising against Rome, but a religious rebellion against
everything that is inconsistent with a complete devotion to
the heavenly King, whose representative on earth he is.
He must attack all the institutions which hinder men from
entering the Kingdom: and he does so. The Messianic
entry into Jerusalem does not stand alone. It is of a piece
with the denunciation of Pharisaism and the cleansing of

---

[1] Cf. the testimony of Paul, II Cor. i. 15–20.
[2] Cf. above, pp. 129 ff.

the Temple. He flings down his challenge to the civil power, to the priesthood, and to the party of the Scribes and Pharisees: and he does it with the sure knowledge that he will be rejected by the elders and the priests and the scribes and be handed over to the Gentile power for death.

The eschatological theory is, therefore, undoubtedly right in the assertion that Jesus went up to Jerusalem to die and not merely on a teaching mission. But the going up and dying are not to be conceived as an attempt to precipitate the final catastrophe and force the Kingdom to come. They are rather to be regarded as the first and decisive battle in the campaign of the Kingdom of the Messiah against the whole kingdom of evil. In that battle Jesus will fight in the front rank and, if need be, alone. He is a leader who leads. And his utterances in this closing phase of his earthly ministry are marked by the precision and peremptoriness that belong to operation orders in a military campaign.

as against Schweitzer

(*f*) In the light of these considerations we may see light on the paradoxes of the Gospel. Their application is in the first instance to Jesus himself and then to his followers. It is Jesus himself who will save his life by losing it; he is the chief who is servant of all. The contrast which he draws is between the world-empires, where self-assertion is the passport to power, and the Messianic Kingdom, where self-sacrifice and service are the only tests of greatness. The King in this Messianic Kingdom is not above the law, but is himself the first exponent of it. The principle that he who would be greatest must be servant of all is embodied in the Son of Man who comes not to be served but to serve; and he who saves his life by losing it is first of all the Son of Man who gives his life as a ransom for many. He is highly exalted and is given a name that is above every name *because* he humbled himself and became obedient even to the death of the Cross.

These different pieces of evidence all point in the same direction. Any one of them taken alone might be held to signify very little; but the cumulative effect of them is to mark out Peter's Confession as the watershed of the Gospel history. Indeed it is not too much to say that Peter's inspired declaration at Caesarea Philippi has changed the whole course of the world's history. At all events it is the dividing line between two sharply contrasted, yet complementary, periods in our Lord's activity. The keynote of the former period is set by the parable of the Sower, that of the latter by the parable of the Vineyard and the Wicked Husbandmen. There is one sense in which we may justly speak of a 'Galilean springtide' if we understand it as a time in which Jesus was sowing the word of the Kingdom. The seed grows secretly and presently the full corn is seen in the ear and the time of harvest is come. That point is marked by Peter's Confession. Henceforward it is a case of seeking for the fruit of all the sowing: and the second period of the ministry is a period of harvest and ingathering of men for the Kingdom.

Or we may put the matter in terms of the doctrine of the Remnant. Then the second part of the ministry can be regarded as the consolidation of the Remnant, Jesus himself being its founder and leader. It must, of course, be understood that it is a saving Remnant that is to be formed.

Or again the difference may be expressed in terms of the Kingdom of God. Here the first period is one of announcement: 'The Kingdom of God is at hand'. The second period is marked by the recognition of the Kingdom by Peter who perceives in Jesus the promised Messiah. Henceforward the call to men is to come in.

Once more, we may consider the figure of Jesus himself. In the first period he appears as the teacher who speaks with authority. In many ways he resembles the prophets of old. Indeed there were some who had seen him and who thought of him simply as a prophet. Once he has been recognised by Peter as the Messiah he becomes more exigent. He makes the largest possible demands on the loyalty, trust, and obedience of his followers. And he does

Jesus -- the Leader. Example. We follow in His steps all the way thru death ; resurrection ; we are in the eternal Kingdom.

THE KINGDOM IN THE WORLD 211

this without in any way lording it over them. He is master of them all because he is most fully the servant of God: and he is the servant of them all because he is their master in the Kingdom. The picture of the Messiah which Jesus presents to us in his own person is that of one who is in the last degree exacting without being in the least degree arrogant, and who, at the same time, is servant to all without being menial to any. These things can only be explained in one way, namely, that in Jesus every interest is subordinated to the interest of the Kingdom. He may make the largest demands because his demands are God's: he is asking nothing for himself. He can give the humblest service to his followers, and still be their master, because his service is given freely without seeking for anything in return.

The fact with which we have to reckon at all times is that in the teaching of Jesus his conception of God determines everything, including the conceptions of the Kingdom and the Messiah. The Kingdom *is* where God's will is done on earth as it is in heaven. But what is God's will but the expression of God's nature? The Messiah is the person who realises the Kingdom by utter obedience to God's will, by voluntary identification of his will with God's. The Kingdom on earth manifests itself as the society of all those who follow the Messiah and take upon themselves the yoke which he bears. In this sense the Messiah is the firstborn of many brethren and the founder (or pioneer) and perfecter of faith. It is this conception of Messiahship for which Jesus used the enigmatic term 'the Son of Man': and to the consideration of this term we must now turn.

7. THE SON OF MAN

The problems raised by the use of this phrase are among the most complex and difficult in New Testament study. They embrace questions both of philology and exegesis: and definite generally accepted conclusions are still very few in comparison with the vast amount of labour and learning expended on the various problems which have arisen.

212   GOD AS KING

We have, however, one piece of firm ground on which to build. It may now be regarded as extremely probable, if not absolutely certain, that ὁ υἱὸς τοῦ ἀνθρώπου in the Gospels is nothing but a slavish rendering of an original Aramaic *bar nāshā* (בַּר נְשָׁא or בַּר אֱנָשָׁא) and that the idiomatic translation of *bar nāshā* would be not ὁ υἱὸς τοῦ ἀνθρώπου but simply ὁ ἄνθρωπος, 'the man'.

A second fact, which may help to solve our problem, is that the word 'man' was taken up into the esoteric vocabulary of the apocalyptic literature and used, not in its literal sense but as a symbol for something else. This adoption of the word took place at least as early as the second century B.C. in the Book of Daniel. There[1] we find the expression 'one like to a son of man', that is 'a human figure': and this phrase is not to be understood literally, but as an ideogram, if one may so describe it, meaning 'the people of the saints of the Most High'. The same kind of thing occurs in the *Similitudes of Enoch*[2] and in *IV Esdras*[3] when the ideogram is usually read as 'the Messiah'.

Now whether *bar nāshā* in an utterance of Jesus was to be taken in the simple literal sense or as a symbol for something else could not possibly be determined from the mere word itself. It could only be determined either by the way in which the word was said or by the context, or both: and it is obvious that there is here ample room for misunderstanding and misinterpretation. A disciple hearing the word *bar nāshā* on the lips of Jesus might take it up in the wrong way. The translator of an Aramaic record of the teaching of Jesus might misunderstand the word in any given case. The evangelist compiling his Gospel from sources oral or written might equally make mistakes. In the end, when we come to our Gospels as they stand, we find that there is an established convention that when the evangelist, or one of the authorities on whom he relies,

[1] Dan. vii. 13.   [2] *Enoch* xxxvii–lxxi.
[3] *IV Esdras* xiii.

thinks that *bar nāshā* is meant by Jesus in the plain sense, it
is rendered by ὁ ἄνθρωπος: and when it appears to have an
apocalyptic reference it is rendered by ὁ υἱὸς τοῦ ἀνθρώπου.
Since, however, the evangelists or their authorities may
quite conceivably be mistaken in their interpretation, it
becomes necessary to examine for ourselves all the cases in
which ὁ ἄνθρωπος or ὁ υἱὸς τοῦ ἀνθρώπου is used.

The occurrences of the latter phrase in the Synoptic
Gospels are as follows:

Mt. viii. 20; ix. 6; x. 23; xi. 19; xii. 8, 32, 40; xiii. 37, 41;
xvi. 13, 27, 28; xvii. 9, 12, 22; xviii. 11; xix. 28; xx. 18, 28;
xxiv. 27, 30 (*bis*), 37, 39, 44; xxv. 31; xxvi. 2, 24 (*bis*), 45, 64.
Mk. ii. 10, 28; viii. 31, 38; ix. 9, 12, 31; x. 33, 45; xiii. 26;
xiv. 21 (*bis*), 41, 62.
Lk. v. 24; vi. 5, 22; vii. 34; ix. 22, 26, 44, 56, 58; xi. 30; xii.
8, 10, 40; xvii. 22, 24, 26, 30; xviii. 8, 31; xix. 10; xxi. 27, 36;
xxii. 22, 48, 69; xxiv. 7.

Of these Mt. xviii. 11 and Lk. ix. 56 are generally
rejected on textual grounds. Lk. xxiv. 7 stands in a class by
itself.

The next step is to eliminate all those cases which can
safely be put down to editorial revision of the sources.
Here the obvious starting-point is the material taken up
by the other evangelists from Mark. In this way Mt. xvi.
13, 28 and xxvi. 2 are rejected as editorial modifications of
what is given in Mark.

We can now set out the remaining passages according to
the source in which they are found and the audience to
which they are addressed. We begin with Mark.

Mk. ii. 10 (P): The Son of Man has power on earth to forgive
sins.
ii. 28 (P): The Son of Man is lord of the Sabbath.

(Peter's Confession.)

viii. 31 (D): The Son of Man must suffer many things and be
rejected.
viii. 38 (D + G): The Son of Man coming in the glory of his
Father with the holy angels.

ix. 9 (D): The Son of Man rises from the dead.

ix. 12 (D): The Son of Man suffers many things and is set at nought.

ix. 31 (D): The Son of Man is betrayed, killed, and rises again.

x. 33 (D): The Son of Man is betrayed, suffers, is killed, and rises again.

x. 45 (D): The Son of Man came not to be served but to serve, and to give his life a ransom for many.

xiii. 26 (D): They shall see the Son of Man coming on the clouds with great power and glory. (Dan. vii. 13 f.)

xiv. 21 (D): The Son of Man departs (this life) as it is written concerning him.

xiv. 21 (D): Woe to the man by whom the Son of Man is betrayed.

xiv. 41 (D): The Son of Man is betrayed into the hands of sinners.

xiv. 62 (P): Ye shall see the Son of Man sitting on the right hand of the Almighty and coming with the clouds of heaven. (Ps. cx. 1; Dan. vii. 13.)

Here we have fourteen cases of which only two fall before Peter's Confession. Again all are D with four exceptions— ii. 10, 28; viii. 38; xiv. 62. Of these ii. 10 and 28 will be dealt with presently; viii. 38 is in a passage where the conditions of discipleship are being laid down; xiv. 62 is in the reply to the High Priest at the trial, that is, it is spoken at a time when the knowledge of the Messianic claims of Jesus is already public property. Moreover, it is a quotation from the Old Testament.

The two sayings Mk. ii. 10, 28, belong to the class of which it can most plausibly be said that the term 'Son of Man' in them represents a misunderstanding of an original Aramaic *bar nāshā*. The question has been discussed again and again: and the only result of the discussion is to make it clearer that 'man' and not 'son of man' is the proper rendering of *bar nāshā* in these two passages.[1] They may, therefore, be left out of account in the further discussion here.

[1] A recent and excellent discussion is in *The Beginnings of Christianity*, 1. 378 f.

The result is that we have in Mark twelve cases of the use of the phrase 'Son of Man', to which, so far, no objection need be taken. All of these are later than Peter's Confession: and all of them are D with the two exceptions— viii. 38 and xiv. 62—already dealt with.

Q

(Streeter's reconstruction. The order followed is that of Luke.)

Lk. vi. 22:	**Mt. v. 11:**
Persecution 'for the sake of the Son of Man'.	Persecution 'for my sake'.
vii. 34 (G):	**xi. 19:**
The Son of Man came eating and drinking.	The same.

(Peter's Confession.) here

ix. 58 (G):	**viii. 20:**
The Son of Man has no place to lay his head.	The same.
xi. 30 (G):	**xii. 40 (P):**
The Son of Man shall be a sign to this generation.	The Son of Man in the heart of the earth three days and nights.
xii. 8 (D):	**x. 32 (D):**
The Son of Man will acknowledge those who confess him.	I will acknowledge those who confess me.
xii. 10 (D):	**xii. 32 (P):**
Speech against the Son of Man will be forgiven.	The same.
xii. 40 (D):	**xxiv. 44 (D):**
The Son of Man comes when not expected.	The same.
xvii. 22 (D):	No parallel.
Ye shall desire to see one of the days of the Son of Man.	
xvii. 24 (D):	**xxiv. 27 (D):**
The Son of Man comes like lightning.	The same.
xvii. 26 (D):	**xxiv. 37 (D):**
The days of the Son of Man like the days of Noah.	The same.
xvii. 30 (D):	No parallel.
It shall be the same (as the destruction of Sodom) in the day that the Son of Man is revealed.	

In two of these cases (Lk. vi. 22 and xii. 8) the use of 'Son of Man' in the Lucan version of the saying is not supported by Matthew. With regard to the first, a comparison of Mk. x. 29 with Lk. xviii. 29 shows that the Marcan ἕνεκεν ἐμοῦ καὶ ἕνεκεν τοῦ εὐαγγελίου has been altered in Luke to εἵνεκεν τῆς βασιλείας τοῦ θεοῦ. It is possible, therefore, that in this case also we have to do with editorial revision and that the form in Mt. v. 11 is the more original. On the other hand, Lk. xii. 8 stands nearer to the Marcan version of the same saying (Mk. viii. 38); and Mt. x. 32 shows traces of editorial revision, notably in the phrase 'before my Father in heaven'.[1] The balance of probability here is in favour of the Lucan version being more original than that in Matthew.

But in the sayings which remain there are some in which 'Son of Man' is probably due to misunderstanding. The plainest case is Lk. xii. 10 = Mt. xii. 32. Here we have the Q version of a saying which is also preserved in Mk. iii. 28 f. (P).[2] In Matthew the Q form of the saying is inserted into the Marcan context, thus producing the usual conflate account. In Luke the saying is dissociated from the account of the Beelzebub controversy and appears in a different context. The question arises which of the two

---

[1] On the secondary nature of this phrase see p. 96, above.

[2] That Mk. iii. 28 f. and Lk. xii. 10 = Mt. xii. 32 are different versions of the same saying is clear from the fact that the essential elements are common to both. ἀφίημι and ὁ υἱὸς τοῦ ἀνθρώπου appear in the Greek text. βλασφημεῖν εἰς and εἰπεῖν λόγον κατά may be taken back to a common source in Aramaic. εἰπεῖν λόγον would be a literal rendering of אֲמַר שָׁלָה (so read by Hitzig, Bevan, Marti, and Torrey), which in Dan. iii. 29 is translated by βλασφημεῖν (LXX) and εἰπεῖν βλασφημίαν (Theodotion). We may compare Job ii. 9 where בָּרֵךְ 'bless', euphemistically used for 'curse', is rendered in the Greek version by εἰπόν τι ῥῆμα εἰς κύριον. Is it possible that in the words of Jesus here there is an actual quotation of the Aramaic of Dan. iii. 29? If the argument in Detached Note A to Chapter III above is sound, we may hesitate before answering this question in the negative. It may well be that the allusion, if it be an allusion, is intended to bring to the mind of the Pharisees the sharp contrast between Nebuchadnezzar's attitude and their own. In the Daniel story the heart of the king is softened by the miracle of which he is a witness; here the cure of the demoniac only serves to harden the hearts of the Pharisees.

versions of the saying is correct: and this question must be answered in favour of Mark.[1] Thus Lk. xii. 10 = Mt. xii. 32 is eliminated from our list as a case in which 'Son of Man' means simply 'man'.

Lk. vii. 34 = Mt. xi. 19 presents a somewhat different problem. The context makes it perfectly clear that in this case 'Son of Man' is a mere periphrasis for the first personal pronoun. We could substitute 'I' for 'the Son of Man' and the saying would not lose any of its point. It is equally clear that if *bar nāshā* stood in the original Aramaic form of the saying, it must have been meant in its special sense. The general meaning 'man' is certainly inadmissible here. There seem to be three possibilities: either (i) the phrase here is due to a redactor, e.g. the compiler or translator of Q; or (ii) Jesus used *bar nāshā* in the special sense; or (iii) he used some expression which could at the same time mean 'I' and be capable of giving rise to the Greek text here. Against the first and second of these it may be objected that there is no very obvious reason why 'Son of Man' should either have been used by Jesus or interpolated by a compiler of his sayings in this particular case. If it is an interpolation, the interpolation has been done in a very haphazard manner. Why, for example, should 'Son of Man' be substituted for 'I' here and not for 'me' in Lk. vii. 23 = Mt. xi. 6, where it would stand far more plausibly? Again, why should Jesus use the apocalyptic counter *bar nāshā* when it is obvious that it is his personal character that is being contrasted with that of John the Baptist? There remains the third alternative.

In the Galilean vernacular the expression *hāhū' gabrā* (ההוא גברא) 'that man', 'a certain man' is used as a substitute for 'I' in certain cases.[2] The idiomatic rendering of the expression would be ἐγώ; a literal translation would be ὁ ἄνθρωπος ἐκεῖνος (οὗτος) or ἄνθρωπός τις. Now the

---

[1] So Wellhausen, *Das Evangelium Matthaei*, 62 f.; Foakes Jackson and Lake, *Beginnings of Christianity*, 1. 380.

[2] Dalman, *Gramm.*, p. 108; *Words of Jesus*, pp. 249 f.

same effect could be produced by the use of the indeter-
minate form *bar nāsh* instead of *bar nāshā*. *Bar nāsh* means
simply 'a man': and in the context before us it could be
used as a substitute for 'I' in the same way that the *hāhû'*
gabrā is used in Rabbinic writings of Palestinian origin. If
this be granted, it is possible to see how ὁ υἱὸς τοῦ ἀνθρώπου
has got into our Greek text. It is a misunderstanding of
bar nāsh[1] which would have been more correctly translated
by ἄνθρωπός τις, 'a certain man' (i.e. Jesus himself). In
English the passage should probably be rendered:

There came John (the Baptist) neither eating nor drinking...,
There came one (*sc.* myself) eating and drinking...,

in which case it ceases to concern us for the purposes of the
present enquiry.

In Lk. ix. 58 = Mt. viii. 20 the simple meaning 'man' is
ruled out, since men in general have somewhere to lay
their heads: the homeless man is the exception. In this
case, therefore, the choice lies between original *bar nāsh*
in the same sense as in the case just discussed—'I have no
place to lay my head'—and an original *bar nāshā* used as an
apocalyptic symbol. The latter seems the more probable
here. The terms of the offer by the would-be follower make
it clear that he realised that Jesus had no fixed abode: and
he would not need to be told what he already knows. This
passage will therefore be retained in the list of cases where
bar nāshā has a special connotation. It is to be remarked
that in Luke's order it falls after Peter's Confession and is
the record of a conversation between Jesus and a man who
desired to become a disciple.[2]

Lk. xi. 30 and Mt. xii. 40 are two widely divergent

---

[1] Cf. the discussion of this passage by Wellhausen, *Skizzen*, VI. 205 f.

[2] More than this we cannot say. As usual Matthew and Luke, while
agreeing closely as to the words spoken on either side, give entirely different
accounts of the circumstances. According to Matthew, the conversation
took place when Jesus was on the point of embarking on board ship, and the
interlocutor is a scribe. According to Luke, Jesus and his disciples are on a
journey by road, and we are not told anything about the person who makes
the offer. It is clear that the Q sayings have no narrative context of their
own.

verses in a passage in which Matthew and Luke are other-wise in close agreement. Both cannot well be from Q. It is possible that both are interpolations, and this hypothesis has in its favour the fact that in the Marcan account (Mk. viii. 11 f.) the refusal of a sign is blunt and unqualified. Against this is the consideration that it is curious that St Matthew and St Luke should independently have made interpolations at precisely the same point. Further, it appears from Q (Lk. xii. 54 ff.) that Jesus had more to say on the subject of signs than is recorded in Mark. It is, therefore, not necessary to conclude that both Mt. xii. 40 and Lk. xi. 30 are interpolations here. It is also clear that Mt. xii. 40 ought to be rejected as contradictory of what has preceded. For what is offered in *v.* 40 is just what is asked for in *v.* 38 and refused in *v.* 39. Moreover, the Ninevites repented at the *preaching* of Jonah, not because they were aware of his miraculous deliverance from the sea: and all that Jesus claims is that, if Jonah could by his preaching evoke a response from the heathen Ninevites, a greater than Jonah has the right to expect no less from the Chosen People. We therefore regard Lk. xi. 30 as the original in this case. It expresses correctly what we find elsewhere to be the attitude of Jesus, an attitude which can be expressed in modern terms by saying that religious truth is self-authenticating and requires no external prop or authority. His position is this: 'The prophets have told you, John the Baptist told you, I tell you: and unless you wilfully shut your eyes and harden your hearts, you must see that our witness is true'.

The question remains: In what sense is 'Son of Man' in Lk. xi. 30 to be understood? The choice would appear to lie between 'a man' (*bar nāsh*) as in Lk. vii. 34, and *bar nāshā* in the special sense. A decision is not easy; but, on the whole, the balance of probability inclines to the former alternative. Jesus himself and all that he represents, his teaching, his life—all this is the sign and the only sign that shall be given.

The remaining passages (Lk. xii. 40; xvii. 24, 26 with parallels in Matthew; and Lk. xvii. 22, 30 in Luke only) are all, with the possible exception of Lk. xvii. 22, concerned with the Parousia. They are all subsequent to Peter's Confession and all addressed to the disciples. It is obvious that in these cases *bar nāshā* is used in its special sense as an apocalyptic symbol. To these we may add Lk. ix. 58 and xii. 8. The result is seven passages from Q relevant to the present enquiry. Six of them are D and later than Peter's Confession: and one (ix. 58) is also later than Peter's Confession and spoken to one who desired to be a disciple.

M

The passages peculiar to this source are:

Mt. x. 23 (D): Ye shall not have finished with the cities of Israel till the Son of Man come.

xiii. 37 (D): He who sows the good seed is the Son of Man.

xiii. 41 (D): The Son of Man will send out his angels and they will gather out of his Kingdom all the stumbling-blocks and doers of lawlessness.

(Peter's Confession.)

xix. 28 (D): When the Son of Man shall sit on the throne of his glory ye also shall sit on twelve thrones.[1]

xxiv. 30 (D): Then the sign of the Son of Man shall appear in heaven.

xxv. 31 (D): When the Son of Man comes in his glory and all the angels with him.[2]

It is to be noted that all these passages belong to the D class. Three of them are placed after Peter's Confession: and these all relate to the Parousia. The phrase Son of Man is obviously used in its special sense in these three

[1] Reasons for assigning Mt. xix. 28 to M rather than Q: Streeter, *Four Gospels*, p. 288.

[2] Besides these six passages there are also the following peculiar to Matthew: xvi. 13, 28; xxvi. 2, which are merely editorial expansions of the corresponding texts in Mark; Mt. xxiv. 39, which is probably editorial also, though it may belong to Q. It makes no difference to the present discussion whether it is Q or editorial since it is only a repetition of Mt. xxiv. 37 (Q).

cases. The three which St Matthew places before Peter's Confession now call for closer examination.

Mt. x. 23 follows on a passage which appears to have been lifted bodily from Mk. xiii. The passage in question, Mt. x. 17–22, is in very close verbal agreement with Mk. xiii. 9–13.[1] Again Mt. x. 23 a, 'When they persecute you in one city flee to another', with its suggestion of violent opposition to the preaching of the Twelve is totally unsupported by anything in the other accounts of the sending forth of the Twelve or the Seventy. It is suggested both by Mk and Q that they may not get a hearing for their message; but that is all. Further, we may gather from the Q account of the charge (Lk. x. 2 = Mt. ix. 37 f.) that the reason why time was not to be wasted on the unresponsive was that the number of missionaries was very small in comparison with the ground to be covered. Neither does the solemn leave-taking prescribed both in Mk and Q for those occasions when the Apostles are rejected (Mk. vi. 11; Lk. x. 10 f.) agree with the picture of the Apostles being harried from one place to another, which meets us in Mt. x. 23 a.[2] We cannot rely on v. 23 a as trustworthy evidence of what Jesus said in his charge to the Apostles. It presupposes circumstances of which there is no trace in the other accounts of the charge: and it may quite well represent the ideas of the Early Church rather than the words of Jesus himself.[3]

The second half of the verse is just as much open to suspicion as the first. It can hardly be reconciled with Mk. xiii. 10. Again it has close affinity with Mt. xvi. 28: 'There are some of those standing here who shall not taste death

[1] There are very slight traces of what may be conflation with Q in v. 19; cf. Lk. xii. 11 f., μεριμνήσητε and πῶς ἢ τί.

[2] It should be noted that in the speech against Pharisaism in Q (Lk. xi. 37–xii. 1) the simple διώξουσιν of Luke (xi. 49) becomes διώξετε ἀπὸ πόλεως εἰς πόλιν (Mt. xxiii. 34).

[3] Cf. Streeter, *The Primitive Church*, pp. 34 ff. It is just possible that behind Mt. x. 23 a there is a simpler form which said no more than 'When you are rejected in one place go to another', and that this has been reinterpreted and modified in the light of Mt. x. 17–22.

till they see the Son of Man coming in his Kingdom'. But a comparison of Mt. xvi. 28 with Mk. ix. 1 shows that 'Son of Man' is an editorial insertion. It may be the same in Mt. x. 23 *b*.

The verse as a whole does not inspire confidence. There may lie behind it a genuine utterance of Jesus. Indeed, Mt. x. 5–8, 23–25 may belong to an original M account of the mission charge. But if that is so, it appears that the original wording has been modified by the beliefs and experience of the primitive Jewish Christian Church. The evidence of Mt. x. 23 is therefore to be regarded with grave suspicion: and we cannot build anything on it with confidence.

Mt. xiii. 37 and 41 are also open to serious suspicion. Both the parable and its interpretation present a conception which is foreign to the rest of the teaching of Jesus about the Kingdom on earth, and has affinities rather with the saying of John the Baptist concerning wheat and chaff. They also identify the Kingdom with the Church; and the Church is already a *corpus permixtum*. That is, they presuppose a state of affairs which had not yet developed at the time when this parable is supposed to be spoken, though it had begun when the Gospel was compiled. The interpretation is thoroughly Rabbinic in style: it is, in fact, a *Midrash* on the parable. Further, the parable itself stands in Matthew exactly in the place where Mark's parable of the Seed growing secretly, which is not in Matthew, ought to stand, and it has a good many points in common with that Marcan parable.[1] It looks as if the parable of the Wheat and Tares in Matthew is a free adaptation of the Marcan parable, or else a conflation of it with other matter, designed to meet the circumstances of a time when the Church contained members who, in the view of the writer of this parable, were unworthy of their

---

[1] These are ἡ βασιλεία (τοῦ θεοῦ Mk: τῶν οὐρανῶν Mt; the usual change), ἄνθρωπος, ἐπὶ τῆς γῆς Mk: ἐν τῷ ἀγρῷ αὐτοῦ Mt (cf. Mk. iv. 31 and Mt. xiii. 31), καθεύδειν, βλαστᾶν, χόρτος, καρπός, θερισμός.

place and false to its true ideals as he conceived them. From xiii. 41 we may infer that these ideals were those which St Paul is fighting against in the Epistle to the Galatians.[1]

We are forced to the conclusion that both the parable and its interpretation are secondary, a working up at a later date of the Marcan parable of the Seed growing secretly. We cannot, therefore, safely take Mt. xiii. 37 and 41 into account in the present enquiry.

Mt. xix. 28 is a passage of which another version occurs in L (Lk. xxii. 28–30). It will have to be considered when the evidence from the four sources is put together.

Mt. xxiv. 30 may be part of the M tradition concerning the Parousia and the Last Things or it may be merely a Matthaean expansion of Mk. xiii. 26. The former view is perhaps the more probable. It would seem that there was a certain amount of M material bearing upon the Parousia and the Final Judgement.[2]

The passages from M relevant to our present purposes will thus be: Mt. xix. 28; xxiv. 30; xxv. 31; all of which are D and all in the second half of the ministry.

L

The texts from this source containing the phrase 'Son of Man' are:

Lk. xviii. 8 *b* (D): When the Son of Man comes will he find faith on the earth?

xix. 10 (G): The Son of Man is come to seek and to save the lost.

---

[1] With τοὺς ποιοῦντας τὴν ἀνομίαν cf. Mt. xxiii. 2 f.; v. 18 f. These passages are, like our parable, concerned with one thing—the strong upholding of the Jewish Law, written and oral, as an integral part of the Gospel. And, doubtless, the writer of this parable, if he were looking for tares to uproot, could have found them in plenty in such a Church as the Corinthian, where freedom from the Law had been interpreted by some as freedom from all restraint whatsoever.

[2] Mt. xxiv. 10–12 may be the M version of what is given by Mk. xiii. 21–23 and by Q (Lk. xvii. 23 f. = Mt. xxiv. 26 f.). Mt. xxv. 1–13 (M) has obviously to do with the Parousia and Mt. xxv. 31–46 is certainly the M account of the Last Judgement.

xxi. 36 (D): Watch...that ye may be able to stand before the Son of Man.

xxii. 48 (D): Judas, dost thou betray the Son of Man with a kiss?

xxii. 69 (P): From now shall the Son of Man be seated on the right hand of the power of God.

These five passages are all placed after Peter's Confession: and three of the five are in D contexts.

The connexion of Lk. xviii. 8 *b* with the immediately preceding parable of the Unjust Judge and the Importunate Widow is not at all clear. The parable itself is a companion piece to the parable given in Lk. xi. 5–8 (L) where a man obtains what he needs by persistent asking. The underlying thought in both cases is: Ask and ye shall receive. In the present case the thing that is to be asked for is that God will vindicate his elect, in other words that righteousness may triumph over evil. If, then, the saying about the Son of Man finding faith is in place here, the faith referred to can hardly be other than faith that God will do this: and, since the coming of the Son of Man may be taken to be synonymous with God's vindication of the elect, the saying may mean: 'When the Son of Man comes, will he find anyone expecting his coming?' If that be the correct interpretation, the 'Son of Man' here represents *bar nāshā* in its technical sense, and the reference is to the Parousia.

The alternative is to suppose that 'Son of Man' is used in the same way as in Lk. vii. 34 = Mt. xi. 19 (Q), and regard the saying as referring to the present. The sense will then be: this parable shows what ought to be the attitude of men, but when a man (*sc.* Jesus) comes in search of this faith does he find it? People, on the whole, neither believe that God can do this thing nor do they desire that he should.[1] Lk. xix. 10 is a saying with no place to lay its

---

[1] The nearest verbal parallel to the saying is Lk. vii. 9 = Mt. viii. 10 (Q) 'I have not found such faith, no, not in Israel'. We may compare also the parable of the Great Feast in Lk. xiv. 16–24. There the point of the parable is

head. It is expelled from Mt. xviii. 11 and Lk. ix. 56 by the editors on textual grounds: and, though it is firmly fixed here so far as manuscript evidence goes, there are those who would maintain that it is superfluous, on the ground that the story of Zacchaeus is finished at *v.* 9. That may be the case. It is quite possible that it was a saying without any context, which, because it was so obviously genuine, had to be fitted in somewhere. It belongs to the same line of thought as Mk. x. 45.

Lk. xxi. 36 and xxii. 69 obviously refer to the Parousia.

Lk. xxii. 48 belongs to the L account of the arrest of Jesus. The parallel account in Mark does not give this remark of our Lord. It may be none the less authentic on that account. If Mk. xiv. 21 and 41 are genuine utterances of Jesus, Lk. xxii. 48, which belongs to the same way of thinking, may be genuine also.

If we now attempt to co-ordinate this evidence, we find that most of the sayings fall into two well-defined classes. One of these contains the sayings which refer to the Parousia, the other those which refer to the Passion. These may be exhibited in tabular form to show the extent to which our four sources cover the same ground.

I. Sayings referring to the Parousia:

Mark	Q (Luke's order)	M	L
viii. 38	Lk. xii. 8	—	—
xiii. 26	xii. 40 xvii. 24 xvii. 26 xvii. 30	Mt. xxiv. 30 xxv. 31	Lk. xxi 36
xiv. 62	—	—	xxii. 69
—	—	xix. 28	

that it is a reply to the conventional piety of the saying: 'Blessed is he that shall eat bread in the Kingdom of God'. The parable says: 'You say that, but you don't really mean it: you merely pretend to desire the Kingdom of God'. In view of these considerations I am inclined, though with great hesitation, to prefer the second alternative.

II. Sayings referring to the Passion:

Mark	Q	M	L
viii. 31	—	—	—
ix. 9	—	—	—
ix. 12	—	—	—
ix. 31	—	—	—
x. 33	—	—	—
x. 45	—	—	—
xiv. 21	—	—	—
xiv. 41	—	—	xⁱ·ii. 48
—	—	—	xxii. 69
—	—	—	[xxiv. 7]

III. Passages not included in I or II are: Lk. ix 58 (Q); xix. 10 (L); and xvii. 22 (? Q or L).

It is only necessary to compare Tables I and II to perceive that, whereas the connection of the Son of Man with the Parousia is attested by all four sources, Mark is the principal and almost the only witness for connecting the Son of Man with the Passion. The texts in Table I will be discussed in the next chapter. For the present we confine our attention to those which deal with the rôle of the Son of Man in the existing order of things.

We have to recognise that in regard to the connection of the Son of Man with the Passion our witnesses are divided: Mark and L against Q and M. In Mark the sufferings and death and resurrection of the Son of Man are a prominent and integral feature of the story in the second part of the ministry. The evidence is equally clear, though not so overwhelming, that this conception was also embodied in Proto-Luke.[1] In Q and M, on the other hand, there is no

[1] The relevant passages are Lk. xvii. 25; xxii. 48, 69; xxiv. 7. These all belong to L except xvii. 25, which, according to Streeter's reconstruction, would be assigned to Q. It should, however, be noted that this passage has no parallel in Matthew. In this respect it does not stand alone. There are two other passages embedded in blocks of Q matter—Lk. xii. 49 f. and xiii. 31–33—both implying the Passion and again both without a parallel in Matthew. Both fit neatly into their contexts: and it would seem that in these two cases we have to do with L matter inserted into the most appropriate

case where it can be maintained with any confidence that
the idea of the Passion is connected with the Son of Man.
In the case of Q this is not altogether surprising; for we
have already seen good reasons for believing that Q contained no Passion narrative.[1] Again, in M it may be that an
intense interest in the Parousia has tended to throw into the
background the thought of the Passion, the latter being
regarded as merely the prelude to the former.[2] We cannot,
therefore, build much on the silence of Q and M: and we
are entitled to seek an explanation of the matter supplied
by Mk and L.

It will be convenient to state at once the theory which
will be maintained in the following pages. It is that 'Son
of Man' in the Gospels is the final term in a series of conceptions, all of which are found in the Old Testament.
These are: the Remnant (Isaiah), the Servant of Jehovah
(II Isaiah), the 'I' of the Psalms, and the Son of Man
(Daniel). It has been argued above that it is the idea of the
Remnant which is the essential feature about each of
these: and it is now suggested that Son of Man in the
Gospels is another embodiment of the Remnant idea. In
other words, the Son of Man is, like the Servant of Jehovah,
an ideal figure and stands for the manifestation of the Kingdom of God on earth in a people wholly devoted to their
heavenly King. How, then, does it come about that in the
Gospels the term 'Son of Man' is so often and so obviously
a designation of Jesus himself? The answer to this question
is that the restriction of the denotation of the term is the
outcome of the prophetic ministry of Jesus. His mission is
to create the Son of Man, the Kingdom of the saints of the
Most High, to realise in Israel the ideal contained in the
term. This task is attempted in two ways: first by public

place in Q. The same may be true of xvii. 25 unless it is merely an editorial
gloss. These cases are further evidence in favour of the theory that the nucleus
of Proto-Luke is not the collection L, but an annotated copy of Q.

[1] See above, Chapter II.
[2] Cf. Mt. xxvi. 64. The ἀπ' ἄρτι is significant as showing the point of view
of the First Evangelist, which largely reflects that of his special source

altho the opportunity to be Messiah is open to the people, the corporate group, only He can fulfil?

appeal to the people through the medium of parable and sermon and by the mission of the disciples: then, when this appeal produced no adequate response, by the consolidation of his own band of followers. Finally, when it becomes apparent that not even the disciples are ready to rise to the demands of the ideal, he stands alone, embodying in his own person the perfect human response to the regal claims of God.

It may be objected to this interpretation of 'Son of Man' that it does not square with what is given in the *Similitudes of Enoch* and *IV Ezra*. There the name appears to represent a personal Messiah: and it may be argued that this should govern the exegesis of those passages where 'Son of Man' is used in the Gospels. The answer to this objection is two-sided.

First, it is not so clear as it once appeared to be that 'Son of Man' in *Enoch* must be construed as the title of an individual Messiah. It is only one of several names used. Besides 'Son of Man' we find 'the Righteous one', 'the Elect one', and 'the Anointed one'. Moreover, we find that beside 'the Elect one' and 'the Righteous one' there are frequent references to 'the (my) Righteous ones' and 'the (my) Elect ones' in the plural. It is at least arguable that the singular term in these cases is the name for the body made up by the individuals included in the plural term. The faithful Remnant may be personified as the Elect one and the Righteous one or regarded as the community of the Elect and the Righteous. Even the title 'the Anointed one' need not be construed of a personal Messiah. There are cases in the Old Testament where it is most probably to be regarded as a title of Israel, either the whole people or the spiritual kernel of the nation.[1] If we

[1] Hab. iii. 13, where 'thine anointed' stands in synonymous parallelism to 'thy people'; Ps. lxxxix. 39, 52 ('Wir haben demnach hier eine ganz eigenartige *Umbiegung der messianischen Idee* vom persönlichen Herrscher aus Davids Stamm auf die Gesamtheit des Volkes.... *Israel muss jetzt den Messias ersetzen, ja ihn darstellen*'—Kittel, *Die Psalmen*, p. 297). Perhaps also Pss. xxviii. 8; lxxxiv. 10. It is a possible interpretation of Is. lv. 3–5 that the promises made to David are to be inherited by the people.

may rightly interpret 'the Elect one', 'the Righteous one' and 'the Anointed one' in this sense, as representing the elect nation, it is natural to take 'Son of Man' in the same sense: and it may be pointed out that this would allow the reconciliation of Chapters lxx and lxxi with the rest of this part of *Enoch*. 'As the text stands now two views are taken of the Elect one. According to one (Enoch xlviii. 6) he was "chosen and hidden before him (God) before the creation of the world and for evermore". According to the other, Enoch himself is "that son of man" (Enoch lxxi. 14)'.[1] Obviously, a historical person cannot become the pre-existent heavenly Messiah, if that Messiah is himself already a person. But if the Son of Man in *Enoch* is, as in Daniel, a figure representing the Kingdom of the Saints of the Most High, then it is possible to take *Enoch* lxx f. as the story of the patriarch's entry into the Kingdom as its first member.[2]

But, secondly, even if the Son of Man in *Enoch* stands for a personal Messiah, and if this is the sense which the term bore in the apocalyptic teaching current in the days of Jesus, we are not therefore bound to assume that this is the sense in which he used it. There is no obvious reason why one who was always ready to appeal from the Pharisaic oral tradition to the sense of Scripture should have accepted uncritically the apocalyptic tradition. When Jesus quotes he quotes from Daniel, not from *Enoch*: and it is in Daniel that the figure of the Son of Man is explicitly said to represent the people of the Saints of the Most High.

In any case, the interpretation of the phrase 'Son of Man' which is put forward in these pages must stand or fall as it furnishes or fails to furnish a satisfying explanation of the Son of Man passages *in the Gospels*. As we have seen, these

[1] Foakes Jackson and Lake, *The Beginnings of Christianity*, 1. 370 f.
[2] This interpretation is supported by what is said in lxxi. 16 f. Enoch and those who follow in his footsteps are to form an indissoluble society. The question of the meaning of 'Son of Man' in *Enoch* xxxvii–lxxi has recently been discussed by Messel, *Der Menschensohn in den Bilderreden des Henoch* (Giessen, 1922), to which, unfortunately, I have not access.

passages mostly refer either to the immediate suffering or
to the coming vindication of the Son of Man. We shall deal
here with the former class.

The sayings of Jesus concerning the suffering of the Son
of Man correspond so closely with what is recorded in the
Gospels concerning his own Passion that it was the most
natural thing in the world to regard them simply as prediction of the Passion. And so, in a sense, they are. But to
take them as mere prediction is not enough. These sayings
are the enunciation of a general principle, of which the
actual suffering of Jesus is the supreme example. This
principle has its roots far back in the history of Hebrew
prophecy. It is a product of the struggle of the prophetic
spirit with the problem of suffering, and, in particular, the
problem created by the sufferings of the righteous.

The problem is posed by Habakkuk[1] who asks how God
can tolerate the oppression of the righteous by the wicked.
To this question the prophet can find no answer save the
assurance that 'the righteous shall live by his faithfulness'.[2]
A great step forward is taken in the Servant Songs in
Deutero-Isaiah. The conviction has here been reached
that the sufferings of the righteous Servant of Jehovah—
the ideal Remnant—are part of God's plan, necessary
steps towards a consummation in the light of which they
shall seem worth while: and that they have a redemptive
power for others.

It has been urged above that the Exile marks a turning-
point in the development of the doctrine of the Remnant.
From the time when the Servant Songs were composed
onwards, there are two ideals of the Remnant. The one
ideal, that of a Remnant that saves by self-sacrifice and
suffering, is embodied in the Servant of Jehovah and in the
figure of the Son of Man in the teaching of Jesus. The
other ideal, that of a saved Remnant, is embodied in

[1] Hab. i. 12 ff.
[2] Hab. ii. 4. Doubtless the faithfulness here spoken of is fidelity to Jehovah
in all circumstances. Cf. T. H. Robinson, *Prophecy and the Prophets*, p. 118.

Ezekiel's vision of the restored Israel and finds its issue in Pharisaism. It was a true instinct that found in Jesus the fulfilment of Isaiah liii, for the 'Son of Man' is the lineal descendant of the 'Servant of Jehovah' and Jesus by being the 'Son of Man' realises the ideals contained in the picture of the Lord's Servant.

But the striking correspondence between the predicted fate of the Son of Man and the actual fate of Jesus may easily blind us to another correspondence, equally striking, between the 'Son of Man' predictions and the demands made by Jesus on his disciples. Again and again it is impressed upon them that discipleship is synonymous with sacrifice and suffering and the cross itself. This at once suggests that what was in the mind of Jesus was that he and his followers *together* should share that destiny which he describes as the Passion of the Son of Man: that he and they *together* should be the Son of Man, the Remnant that saves by service and self-sacrifice, the organ of God's redemptive purpose in the world.

In our records one at least of the disciples—Peter—is represented as offering to go with Jesus even to death; and his enthusiasm carries the others with him.[1] It is to be noted that Jesus does not reject this offer. He knew that the resolution of his followers would break down when the crisis came; but there is not a hint that he would not have allowed them to go to the cross with him, had their courage not failed. The evidence is all the other way: and it is surely significant that the first announcement of the fate of the Son of Man is followed by the saying: 'Whosoever wishes to follow after me, let him deny himself, and take up his cross and follow me',[2] and the third announcement by the question to James and John: 'Are you able to drink the cup that I drink, or to be baptized with the baptism with which I am baptized?'[3] Whether the ortho-

[1] Mk. xiv. 26–31; Lk. xxii. 31–33 (L).
[2] Mk. viii. 34 and parallels. Cf. Lk. xiv. 27; Mt. x. 38 (Q).
[3] Mk. x. 32–40.

dox theories of the Atonement would have been differently framed if Jesus had been crucified between James and John, instead of between two thieves, is a question into which we cannot well enter here. It is sufficient to note that the historical fact appears to be that when Jesus speaks of the sufferings of the Son of Man he means something in which he and his followers should share. That he did in fact suffer alone was due to the failure of his disciples to rise to the claims of the idea of the Son of Man.

This interpretation of the 'Son of Man' sayings which refer to the Passion is supported by what we find in the Pauline Epistles. The Apostle does not hesitate to speak of his own sufferings as supplying what is lacking in the sufferings of Christ.[1] Again he speaks of the sufferings of Christ as overflowing into the life of the believer;[2] or he tells us that participation in Christ's sufferings is part of his own highest ambition;[3] or he calls the scars of persecution in his own body the marks of Jesus.[4] In what St Paul has to say in these passages we may read *his* response to the demands of Jesus on his disciples. They are so many ways of saying that he is drinking Christ's cup and being baptized with his baptism.

Further, Paul tells us in the passage cited from Colossians that his sufferings are for the sake of the body of Christ, that is, the Church.[5] Elsewhere he speaks of Christians being granted the privilege of suffering for Christ.[6] Again, Christ loved the Church and gave himself for it.[7] We have

[1] Col. i. 24. This verse has always presented difficulties to the theologian. The difficulties are stated by Lightfoot in his Commentary. It may, however, be questioned whether the rather subtle distinction between Christ's sufferings as *satisfactoriae* and as *aedificatoriae*, by which he seeks to overcome the difficulty, was either present to Paul's mind or likely to have suggested itself to his Colossian readers.

[2] II Cor. i. 5.

[3] κοινωνίαν παθημάτων αὐτοῦ, Phil. iii. 10. Cf. Rom. viii. 17.

[4] Gal. vi. 17.

[5] Col. i. 24, ὑπὲρ τοῦ σώματος αὐτοῦ. Cf. II Cor. i. 6, ὑπὲρ τῆς ὑμῶν παρακλήσεως καὶ σωτηρίας.

[6] Phil. i. 29, τὸ ὑπὲρ αὐτοῦ πάσχειν.

[7] Eph. v. 25, ὑπὲρ αὐτῆς.

here different aspects of what is in reality one thing: for Christ, the Apostles and all the believers together form one body of which Christ is the head and all the others are members. Whatever happens to one part of the organism affects the whole. 'If one member suffers, all the members suffer with it; if one member is glorified, all the members rejoice with it.'[1] There is thus a sense in which Paul can speak of the sufferings of any Christian as the sufferings of the whole body of Christ. The whole body suffers in the sufferings of each individual. There is a further point. These corporate sufferings tend towards a glorious consummation. To share the sufferings of Christ has as its result the sharing in his glory.[2] We have thus, as an integral part of the Apostle's thought, the conception of the Church as a living organism reproducing and continuing in its own life the sufferings and the exaltation of its Head.

Now it has often been pointed out that the term 'Son of Man' does not appear in the Pauline writings: and the question arises why a conception which played so large a part in the teaching of Jesus should have disappeared so soon from the preaching of his followers. Professors Kirsopp Lake and Foakes Jackson have suggested that the reason why it does not appear in the Pauline corpus may be that Paul 'was too good a Grecian to translate *Bar-nāshā* by so impossible a phrase as ὁ υἱὸς τοῦ ἀνθρώπου, and rendered it idiomatically by ὁ ἄνθρωπος'.[3]

The passages which are relevant here are I Cor. xv. 45–49 and Eph. ii. 13–18. In the former of these it seems certain that the second man who is from heaven is the Son of Man of Dan. vii. 13. In all probability Paul is here thinking of Jesus as the head of the new humanity in contrast to Adam as the head of the old. In the second passage the sense is different. Jesus is the creator or founder of 'one new man', that is a new humanity. He has united

---

[1] I Cor. xii. 26.
[2] Rom. viii. 17; II Cor. iv. 10 f.; xiii. 4.
[3] *Beginnings of Christianity*, I. 380. So also J. Weiss *ad* I Cor. xv. 47.

Jew and Gentile 'in one body'. This is the body of Christ which suffers and is to be glorified, the body of which Christ is the head.

If this interpretation is correct, we have in the Pauline teaching the same conception of the Son of Man as in the teaching of Jesus, with just that difference of orientation which arises from the historic facts of the death of Jesus and the resurrection. In the interval between the teaching career of the Master and the preaching mission of his Apostle the Son of Man idea has been incarnated in the person of Jesus. The Son of Man is no longer a mere religious ideal: it has been realised to the full in Jesus, the head of the new humanity: and men are now called to become 'the man' by union with him. As we study the life of Jesus we seem to see him become the Son of Man, realise the Son of Man ideal, by a process of elimination; when we turn to the teaching of Paul, we find the same idea being carried to further and fuller realisation by a process of inclusion. The road to the cross is a road of ever-increasing loneliness: and at the end of it Jesus is absolutely alone. From that point onwards, if we read Paul aright, there is an ever-increasing fellowship of the sufferings of Christ. The prophecy of Jesus is fulfilled: 'The cup that I drink ye shall drink: and with the baptism that I am baptized withal shall ye be baptized'. This word could not be fulfilled in his lifetime; it is fulfilled after and through his death and resurrection.

8. CONCLUSIONS

The result of this discussion may be summarised as follows. The Kingdom of God is manifested on earth and in the present in the existence of human subjects who own God as their King, who look to him for protection, guidance, and a rule of life, who offer to him their absolute loyalty, complete trust, and willing obedience. That is the ideal. Wherever it is to any extent realised, there we have the Remnant. In the history of Israel the ideal takes various forms and appears under various names; but the underlying principles remain the same. The ideal is represented in the figures of the Remnant, the Servant of Jehovah, and the Son of Man. Likewise in the history of Israel we find from time to time attempts to bring this ideal to realisation in the life of the nation or a part of the nation.

Over against the Kingdom of God stands the kingdom of Satan: and between the two kingdoms there is war.

Our reading of the Synoptic sources is that in the life of Jesus the ideal set forth in the highest reaches of Israelite religion is fully realised, and the conflict between the Kingdom of God and the kingdom of Satan brought to a decisive issue.

Jesus proclaims the Kingdom of God, he states the demands it makes, he declares the glories it promises. He calls men to receive it, to enter into it. He sets out to create in Israel that Son of Man. But not many can be found to go with him any part of the way, and none to follow him to the end. The last part of the way he travels alone: and at the cross he alone is the Son of Man, the incarnation of the Kingdom of God on earth. The Son of Man is rejected and slain.

That ought to be the end of the story; but it is not. The sufferings and death of Jesus are the birth-pangs of the Son of Man. The cross proves to be the key that opens the Kingdom of God to men. The death of Jesus accomplishes what his teaching could not. Within a few years we find Paul living, suffering, and rejoicing in Christ. By dying Jesus has brought the Son of Man into existence, given to that dream-figure a body, a local habitation, and a name. It is the Church, his own body, of which he is the head.

The warfare against the forces of evil continues—the Church is the Kingdom at war—but the decisive battle has been fought and won at the cross, and the time must come when Christ shall subdue all enemies and hand over the Kingdom to God.

If this line of interpretation is correct, we have one continuing ideal which we can trace from its beginnings in early Hebrew religion through all the strivings and aspirations of prophets, psalmists, and apocalyptists to the teaching of Jesus and Paul. We can see its fragmentary and incomplete realisation in the better part of the Chosen People, and its perfect expression in the life and death of our Lord. We can see that expression reproduced and reincarnated in the life of the Church wherever its members are in living union with their living head. Whether we begin with the religion of the Old Testament and work our way forward through prophecy and apocalyptic, or whether we start from the fact of the Early Church and try to trace it to its beginnings, the idea of the faithful Remnant is the Ariadne thread that leads us to the centre of the labyrinth. There we find the Crucified, who took upon himself the form of a servant and became obedient unto death: and we understand why every knee must bow and every tongue confess that Jesus Christ is Lord, to the glory of God the Father.

Place of Jesus: To Remnant He is King — to whom they offer loyalty, trust obedience for His protection, guidance: way of life. Thus He leads them thru death & resurrection into Fullness. He is Example — we Follow Him to Kingdom. He is our Guide, Infallible Captain: He will lead us to the Kingdom apart from Him we're bound to miss it. We will with Him suffer, die, reign; be glorified. Before Mt 16 He was an example: in the succession. After Confession He is the God appointed Joshua — the only leader into the Kingdom

Son of Man — corporate: personal meaning; only He truly was " " " however. Two Classes of uses: Passion: Parousia Here are His followers are incorporated. "In Xst" in Paul.

DETACHED NOTE C

The terms 'Disciple' and 'Apostle'

The word 'disciple' ($\mu\alpha\theta\eta\tau\acute{\eta}s$) is very common in the Synoptic Gospels in narrative. It is, however, curiously rare in utterances of Jesus himself. The only examples—out of more than 150—in the three Gospels are:

(a) Mk. xiv. 14. Jesus enquires for a place where he may eat the Passover with his disciples (parallels in Mt. xxvi. 18; Lk. xxii. 11).

(b) Q; Lk. vi. 40; Mt. x. 24 f.

The disciple is not above his teacher.... (Mt.; Lk.)

It is enough for the disciple that he become like his teacher. (Mt.)

But when perfectly trained he will be like his teacher. (Lk.)

(c) Q; Lk. xiv. 26 f. (Mt. x. 37 f.)

Lk. If anyone comes to me and does not hate his father and his mother and children and wife and brothers and sisters, and even his own life, he cannot be my disciple. Whoever does not carry his cross and come after me cannot be my disciple.

Mt. He who loves father or mother more than me is not worthy of me, and he who loves son or daughter more than me is not worthy of me, and he who does not take his cross and follow after me is not worthy of me.

(d) Lk. xiv. 33 (L).

Thus, therefore, everyone of you who does not bid farewell to all his possessions cannot be my disciple.

(e) Mt. x. 42 (cf. Mk. ix. 41).

And whoever gives one of these little ones only a cup of cold water in the name of a disciple, verily I say unto you, he shall not lose his reward.

Here 'in the name of a disciple' appears to be substituted for the Marcan 'in the name that ye are Christ's', i.e. *qua* followers of the Messiah.

The passages with which we shall be concerned in this note are (b) and (c).

The most striking variation between the two versions of the saying in (c) is

$$o\mathring{v}\kappa \ \check{\epsilon}\sigma\tau\iota\nu \ \mu o\upsilon \ \check{\alpha}\xi\iota os \ \text{(Mt.)},$$
$$o\mathring{v} \ \delta\acute{\upsilon}\nu\alpha\tau\alpha\iota \ \epsilon\mathring{\iota}\nu\alpha\acute{\iota} \ \mu o\upsilon \ \mu\alpha\theta\eta\tau\acute{\eta}s \ \text{(Lk.)},$$

and we look in the first instance for a possible Aramaic original which might give rise to the variants. The word μαθητής is generally taken to represent an original Aramaic תַּלְמִידָא: and in the Syriac versions the word is regularly rendered by ܬܠܡܝܕܐ.

The Hebrew equivalent תלמיד is regularly used of the disciples of the Rabbis (e.g. *Aboth* ii. 10, ed. Taylor: 'Rabban Jochanan b. Zakkai had five disciples [תלמידים]'). But it does not appear how μου ἄξιος could have arisen out of a misunderstanding or corruption of תלמידי.

If, however, we begin with μου ἄξιος, a possibility which seems worth examination emerges. These words may be rendered into Aramaic by שָׁוֵי לִי.[1]

The Eastern Aramaic dialects have a word שׁוּלְיָא[2] which occurs in the Babylonian Talmud and in Mandaic. In b. *Pesahim* 108 *a* we find שׁוּלְיָא דְנַגְרֵי, 'carpenter's apprentice'; in b. *B.Q.* 32 *b*, שׁוּלְיָא דְנַפְּחֵי, 'blacksmith's apprentice'; in b. *Šabb.* 96 *b* we have a reference to weaver's apprentices, the same word being used. In Mandaic we find the same word used in the *Qolasta* (II, l. 10).[3] The passage runs:

ועתהיב לאשואליא אוקוריא רבא אכואת אבאהאתא

'The disciple is bound to hold his master in equal honour with his parents'.

'My disciple' could therefore be in Aramaic שׁוּלִי. If, then, we may retranslate οὐκ ἔστιν μου ἄξιος by

לית הוא שוי לי

it becomes at once possible to take it as a corruption or misreading of לית הוא שולִיי, 'he is no disciple of mine', which in the Lucan version has been expanded to give our present Greek text. The suspicion arises that Jesus did not use the common word תַּלְמִידָא to describe his intimate followers, but the unusual word שׁוּלְיָא.

---

[1] Cf. Wisd. iii. 5, where εὗρεν αὐτοὺς ἀξίους ἑαυτοῦ is rendered in the Syriac version (ed. de Lagarde) by ܘܐܫܟܚ ܐܢܘܢ ܕܫܘܝܢ ܠܗ.

[2] So written and pointed by Dalman, *Wörterbuch*[2], 417 *a*.

[3] Ed. Lidzbarski, *Mandäische Liturgien*, p. 6.

We now turn to the other passage from Q. This runs:
'The disciple is not above his master....
It is sufficient for the disciple that he be like his master'. (Mt.)
'But when perfectly trained he will be like his master.' (Lk.)
The version of the saying in Matthew is rendered thus into
Aramaic by Dalman:[1]

לית תלמידא לעיל מן רביה....
מסת לתלמידא דיהי כרביה

I venture to suggest the following:

לית שוליא רב [2]מן רביה
מסת לשוליא דיהי שוי לרביה

If this retranslation gives the saying in anything like its
original form, we have a double play on the words רבא and

שוליא. This playing upon words is a not uncommon feature in
Old Testament prophecy:[3] and it need, therefore, cause us no
surprise to find it in the teaching of Jesus.

Supposing that our argument, up to this stage, is sound, the
question arises: Why שוליא rather than תלמידא as our Lord's
designation of his disciples?

It is tempting to see in the choice of the word a definite
opposition to the whole scribal system. The *talmid* of the
Rabbinical schools is primarily a student. His chief business
was to master the contents of the written Law and the oral
Tradition. The finished products of the Rabbinical schools
were learned biblical scholars and sound and competent
lawyers. The life of a *talmid* as *talmid* was made up of study of the
sacred writings, attendance on lectures, and discussion of
difficult passages or cases. Discipleship as Jesus conceived it
was not a theoretical discipline of this sort, but a practical task
to which men were called to give themselves and all their
energies. Their work was not study but practice. Fishermen
were to become fishers of men, peasants were to be labourers in

---

[1] *Jesus-Jeschua*, p. 207.

[2] Dalman's לעיל מן is a literal rendering of the Greek text. The Syriac
versions have, however, ܡܢ ܪܒܗ or ܡܢ ܪܒܗ. The two parallel sayings
in the Gospel of John (xiii. 16; xv. 20) both have μείζων in place of ὑπέρ:
and there can be no doubt that that is the meaning here.

[3] As also in the Ḳoran. Cf. Nöldeke-Schwally, *Geschichte des Qorāns*,[2] I.
42 f.

God's vineyard or God's harvest field. And Jesus was their Master not so much as a teacher of right doctrine, but rather as the master-craftsman whom they were to follow and imitate. Discipleship was not matriculation in a ‘Rabbinical College but apprenticeship to the work of the Kingdom.

It may be added that there is something appropriate in the choice of ‘apprentices’ rather than ‘students’ as the name for the disciples of Jesus, when we remember that the Master himself was brought up as a village carpenter and the majority of his disciples were workers with their hands.

The Greek word μαθητής would be a correct rendering of שוליא. There are cases in the Papyri when it undoubtedly has the meaning of ‘apprentice’ (Moulton-Milligan, *Vocabulary*, s.v.).

The word ἀπόστολος presents a somewhat different problem. It occurs but rarely in the Gospels and is common in Acts and the Pauline Epistles, whereas μαθητής, which is common in the Gospels and Acts, is not found at all in the remaining books of the New Testament. It is not proposed in the present note to attempt to follow up all the discussion concerning the use of the term in the primitive Church, but rather, on the assumption that Jesus actually used the name as a designation of certain of his followers,[1] to enquire what he meant to convey by the choice of it.

The cases where the word occurs in the Synoptic Gospels are:

(*a*) Mk. iii. 14: ‘And he appointed twelve (whom he called Apostles)’.

The bracketed words are now commonly rejected on textual grounds as an insertion from Lk. vi. 13.

(*b*) Mk. vi. 30 = Lk. ix. 10: The Apostles return to Jesus and report to him all that they have done and taught.

(*c*) Mt. x. 2: The names of the twelve Apostles are these (followed by the list).

(*d*) Lk. vi. 13: Jesus summons his disciples and from them selects twelve whom he calls Apostles.

The passage Lk. vi. 12–16 is parallel to Mk. iii. 13–19 and independent of it. Presumably it belongs to Luke's special source L.

(*e*) Lk. xi. 49; cf. Mt. xxiii. 34: Here Jesus speaks of the sending of prophets and apostles (Lk), or prophets, sages, and

[1] This assumption is questioned by some critics (e.g. Wellhausen), as it seems to me, on insufficient grounds.

scribes (Mt), and of the evil treatment they receive. Whether Luke's or Matthew's version of the saying is the more original must remain doubtful.

(*f*) Lk. xvii. 5. The Apostles said to the Lord: Increase our faith.

This introduces a saying of Jesus of which a parallel version occurs in Mt. xvii. 20. Lk. xvii. 6 is probably from Q, but xvii. 5 may be only St Luke's narrative setting of the Q saying.

(*g*) Lk. xxii. 14 (Jesus and the Apostles sit down to the Last Supper) is probably from L, parallel to but independent of Mk. xiv. 17.

(*h*) Lk. xxiv. 10. The women announce the Resurrection to the Apostles (L).

Of these (*b*), (*c*) and (*d*) appear to be the important passages for our present purpose. We note that they all occur in connection with the Mission of the Twelve. In Mk. iii. 14 we are told that Jesus 'appointed twelve, that they might be with him, and that he might send them out (ἀποστέλλῃ) to preach and to have authority to cast out demons'. There are here two objects in view: the creation of a circle of intimate companions, and the establishment of a missionary body. The choice of the name 'Apostle' is obviously connected with the latter aim.

These two objects of the appointment of the Twelve allow the word 'Apostle' to bear two senses in the Early Church. On the one hand it can refer to the college of the Twelve: on the other it may have the significance of 'missionary'. The history of the use of the term in the Church is the history of the supersession of the latter meaning by the former.[1] In process of time the 'Apostles' came to enjoy the same sort of status and regard in the mind of the Church as was accorded in Islam to the 'Companions' ('Aṣḥāb) of Mohammed.[2] The primary sense of the word is the ruling sense with St Paul. While he allows a special dignity to the Twelve, he holds fast to the idea that an Apostle is primarily a missionary.[3] In so doing we believe that he represents the mind of Jesus on the matter.

In this connection the passage in Gal. ii. 11 ff. is very instructive. There we are told that Peter ate with the Gentile Christians at Antioch until certain emissaries came down from

[1] Harnack, *Mission*[3], i. 314.
[2] Cf. Muir, *The Life of Mohammad* (ed. Weir), pp. xxx f.
[3] Harnack, *op. cit.*, i. 311, 'Paulus hält den weiteren Apostelbegriff fest, aber die zwölf Jünger sind ihm der Urstock des Apostolats'.

Jerusalem. Thereupon, moved by fear of the Jewish Christians, he withdrew and separated himself. The words which Paul uses are ὑπέστελλεν καὶ ἀφώριζεν ἑαυτόν. In ἀφώριζεν ἑαυτόν we can recognise a reference to the etymological sense of the word Pharisee. *Perîšā* = separated: ἀφώριζεν ἑαυτόν = he separated himself = he played the Pharisee.[1] In ὑπέστελλεν there is quite possibly a deliberate play on the word ἀπόστολος.[2] The literal meaning is 'he withdrew', with the suggestion, conveyed by the choice of this verb, that he 'turned his apostleship up-side down'. This means that at the back of Paul's mind is the idea that Pharisaism and what may be called Apostolicity are two fundamentally opposed notions. In this it may well be that he also represents the mind of Jesus.

If our account in the preceding chapter of what Jesus conceived the Kingdom of God on earth to be is correct, it may quite well be the case that Jesus deliberately chose the name Apostle (שְׁלִיחָא) as the exact contrary of Pharisee (פְּרִישָׁא). He speaks of himself as coming to call not the righteous but sinners. He is called the friend of publicans and sinners. The ideal which he sets before himself and before his disciples·is that they should be the saving Remnant of Deutero-Isaiah rather than the saved Remnant of Ezekiel. They are to be the preservative (the salt of the earth) rather than the preserved. The motto of Pharisaism is 'Ye shall be holy as I am holy': and the holiness required is construed as separateness from every-thing that defiles.[3] The idea contained in the word 'Apostle' is that of the beneficent activity which overcomes evil by redeeming the sinners from the thraldom of the kingdom of Satan into the service and freedom of the Kingdom of God. Its motto might accordingly be: 'Be ye therefore merciful, as your Father in heaven is merciful'.

From this point of view the fact that the narrower conception of Apostleship prevailed so soon in the Church, and that 'Apostle' became a title of rank and privilege, the dignity attaching to a close corporation—like the title 'Companion' in Islam—can only be regarded as a calamity and the complete reversal of the original intention of Jesus. It is part of the irony

---

[1] For ἀφώριζεν ἑαυτόν the Peshitta has ܪܫܐ.

[2] For similar plays upon words cf. Phil. iii. 2 f. κατατομή: περιτομή; II Thess. iii. 11, ἐργαζομένους: περιεργαζομένους; Rom. xii. 3, ὑπερφρονεῖν: φρονεῖν: σωφρονεῖν.

[3] See above, p. 187.

of the case that Paul, who held most strongly to the wider interpretation and the literal meaning of the term, should have his reward in being added by the Church to the Apostolic College before its doors were finally closed to the servants of Jesus Christ and the Kingdom of his Father.

The interpretations of 'Disciple' and 'Apostle' here proposed fit in, it is claimed, with one another and with the conclusions reached in the preceding chapter. Taken together, they furnish evidence—if any be needed—of the fundamental opposition between the teaching of Jesus and the idea of Pharisaism. It is often suggested that the criticism which Jesus directed against the Pharisaic system was concerned with the abuses of it and the hypocrisy of some of its professed adherents. But, while the criticisms of Jesus are often applied to points of detail, they are founded upon a vital difference of principle—a difference which can in germ be traced back to the days of the Exile. The difference is put by Jesus as plainly as it can be in the contrasted portraits of the Father and the Elder Brother in the parable of the Prodigal Son. It is the Father who is to be imitated by the Apostles: and the true Apostle is he who can say with Jesus:

The Spirit of the Lord is upon me, because he hath anointed me to preach good tidings to the poor:

He hath sent me[1] to proclaim release to the captives,
And recovering of sight to the blind,
To set at liberty them that are bruised,
To proclaim the acceptable year of the Lord.

[1] ἀπέσταλκέ με.

Chapter VIII

GOD AS KING: THE FINAL CONSUMMATION

1. ESCHATOLOGY IN GENERAL

[margin handwritten: p 185]

[margin handwritten, top: but religion is not only a future escape from life's realities — it is an escape in them, yes; but more, not an escape — but the redemption of the whole situation. Hardship is made holy!]

[margin handwritten left: good quote "]

WHENEVER a living faith in a righteous, holy and loving God is brought up hard against the facts of human experience, some sort of eschatology must emerge if men are not to deny either their faith or their experience." It may be said, moreover, that the character of a religion is determined by its eschatology, by the way in which it overcomes the opposition between what is and what ought to be. There is thus great justice in Biedermann's advice that one should begin the reading of any book on dogmatics at the end, because in its eschatology the innermost character of the system comes out most clearly.[1] In principle there are three possible resolutions of the contradiction between what is and what ought to be.

[margin handwritten: The kind of esch. that emerges determines the quality of the religion.]

[margin handwritten: good.]

It may be said that what is determines what shall be, and that 'ought to be' is a mere dream incapable of fulfilment. *[handwritten: What happens to an eschatology — without God. There is no 'ought to be' — only what is, is.]* *[handwritten: no purpose.]*

That Man is the product of causes which had no prevision of the end they were achieving; that his origin, his growth, his hopes and fears, his loves and beliefs, are but the outcome of accidental collocations of atoms; that no fire, no heroism, no intensity of thought and feeling, can preserve an individual life beyond the grave; that all the labours of the ages, all the devotion, all the inspiration, all the noonday brightness of human genius, are destined to extinction in the vast death of the solar system, and that the whole temple of Man's achievement must inevitably be buried beneath the débris of a universe in ruins—all these things, if not quite beyond dispute, are yet so nearly certain, that no philosophy which rejects them can hope to stand. Only within the scaffolding of these truths, only on

[margin handwritten: use.]

[1] Th. Haering, *The Christian Faith: A System of Dogmatics* (E.T.), II. 831.

[handwritten bottom: Here there is no morality (justice or mercy), no supernatu[re]. In this eschatology the end is only the outcome of the causes. Is this not the view that Judaism ended up with? Where is G[od]]

what is — what ought to be is not only tension between actual & ideal but is an eschatological question. What ought to be, shall become thru what is because God is present at work. Russell would say what will be, will be thru what is. We say "ought".

THE FINAL CONSUMMATION   245

stay with the sinking ship, i.e.

the firm foundation of unyielding despair, can the soul's habitation henceforth be safely built.[1]

Or it may be said—and this is the New Testament doctrine—that what is is a necessary stage in the realisation of what ought to be; that the sufferings of this present time are the birth-pangs of a new and better age, a warfare whose inevitable end will be the subjection of every hostile power that God may be all in all. Whether this consummation comes soon or late, by a catastrophic act of God or by a slow process of evolution, is a matter of detail. The essence of the matter is that what ought to be shall be.

2.

Theism

Or, finally, it may be argued that the contradiction between what is and what ought to be is essentially illusory, a false distinction arising from the finite nature of human knowledge. 'To perfect knowledge, or in reality, there is no "good" or "bad", no "perfection" or "imperfection". Everything is what it is as a necessary consequence of the "order of the universe" or the "laws of nature".[2]

these are values — imposed by mind of man but are not inherent in nature itself. There is no difference.
3 we see wrong.
pantheism

Of these three, only the second and third admit of a religious interpretation. The first is thoroughgoing naturalism, and even if, as in the form given to it by Epicurus, it allows the existence of gods, these are conceived as entirely apart from the world and supremely indifferent to what goes on in it. The second view is theistic. The third is pantheistic. It is clear that it is only the second, or theistic view that can admit an eschatology. For in thoroughgoing naturalism there is no room for a future hope, and in thoroughgoing pantheism there is no occasion for it. In the one case our hopes are doomed to disappointment; in the other, did we but know it, they are already more than

they can't affect the natural process.

X

[1] B. Russell, *Mysticism and Logic*, pp. 47 f.
[2] H. H. Joachim, *A Study of the Ethics of Spinoza*, p. 3. Cf. Spinoza, *Ethics*, Preface to Book IV; *Short Treatise on God, Man and his Well-being* (tr. Wolf), pt. I. ch. VI, 'Good and evil or sin, these are only modes of thought, and by no means things, or any thing that has reality.... For all things and works which are in nature are perfect'. 'All things are necessarily what they are, and in Nature there is no good and no evil' (*ib.*, pt. II. ch. IV).

Cannot all 3 be right. 1. Yes, what shall be is determined by what is. But God is the unknown quantity & the history of causes' effects — moving history toward what 'ought' to be. (3) Therefore, if we could see as God can see — the 'evil' of experience is really thru redemption, good. So to Paul in Rom 8⁸ — Christ does not only redeem man but history itself, causes, circumstances. It has impersonal effects as well as personal.

realised. Accordingly we find that a developed eschatology accompanies a theistic faith, and that the principal
sources for beliefs of this character are the monotheistic
religions: Zoroastrianism, Judaism, Christianity and
Islam.

Once the intimate connection between a theistic faith
and a future hope is realised, it can be laid down that the
faith will largely determine the hope. Both in form and
context eschatology will be modified by the nature of the
God believed in. The Golden Age that is to come is, both
in its nature and in the manner of its appearing, the
realisation of the divine purpose: so that the petition 'Thy
Kingdom come' can forthwith be translated into 'Thy will
be done on earth as it is in heaven'. But this in its turn
presupposes belief in a God who has a will of his own: that
is, a God who is thought of primarily in terms of moral
personality.

The student of Jewish eschatology finds himself confronted by a bewildering maze. Many of the documents
are composite; most of them appear to have been freely
interpolated, rearranged, and edited,[1] and even when
literary criticism has done its perfect work and all the
components are analysed out, there still remains the difficult task of comprehending the meaning of the texts. The
writers of the apocalypses present us with rewritings of
past history, descriptions of the circumstances of their own
times, and forecasts of the future, clothed in symbolic
language not always easy to be understood. Moreover, the
different writings do not agree among themselves in their
predictions of the future. Some promise a Messiah, others
see the future Golden Age introduced by the act of God
himself. In some the Final Judgement precedes an eternal
Messianic Kingdom; in others it follows a temporary
Messianic Kingdom. Sometimes the Golden Age is to be
realised on earth, at other times the earth is conceived as no

---

[1] E.g. *The Apocalypse of Baruch*, Dr R. H. Charles's analysis in the introduction to his edition of the text, pp. liii–lxv.

fit place for it. There are resurrections of the righteous only: and there are general resurrections.

Nor are the difficulties eased by researches in the sphere of Comparative Religion. It does not help our comprehension of the apocalypses when we learn that this idea or that term is ultimately borrowed from Babylonian mythology or from the theology of Zarathustra, any more than it helps our understanding of a Beethoven Symphony when we hear that the theme of this or that movement is borrowed from an old folk-song. The significant thing is not whence the composer has got his material, but what he has done with it. And in the apocalypses what we require to understand is what the writer does with his materials, what kind of hope for the future emerges from his speculations as a whole.[1]

Hence we are driven back on our two fundamental propositions:

(1) *Eschatology arises from the clash of what is with what ought to be, if faith in a God of righteousness is to be maintained.*

(2) *The nature of the future hope is determined through and through, both as to its content and as to the manner of its realisation, by the nature of the God who is believed in.*[2]

These two propositions can be illustrated from the history of Hebrew and Jewish religion. Here the first beginnings of an eschatology can be seen to come into existence along with the ethical monotheism of the prophets. In Amos[3] we meet for the first time with a term which runs through all subsequent eschatology— 'the Day of the Lord' (יום יהוה). It is there introduced

---

[1] Cf. Wellhausen, 'Zur apokalyptischen Literatur' (*Skizzen und Vorarbeiten*, Heft 6, pp. 233 ff.).

[2] Strictly speaking, Gunkel's well-known axiom of the correspondence of *Urzeit* and *Endzeit* is a logical corollary to this proposition. The two epochs correspond because the purpose of God, which runs through and determines the whole process, is one and homogeneous throughout. The end answers to the beginning because all things are in the hands of God who sees the end from the beginning.

[3] Am. v. 18–20.

in a way which makes it evident that it is already familiar
to those whom the prophet addresses. But it is merely
introduced in order that its significance may be radically
transformed. It is evident that for the people of Israel the
Day of the Lord is not his day but theirs, the day of their
triumph and their prosperity. The Day of the Lord is
Israel's trump card. Amos announces that, on the contrary,
it will be in truth Jehovah's Day, the day of the revelation
and complete vindication of his character as a God of
absolute righteousness. It will, therefore, be a day of
judgement on all evildoers, Israel included.

The contradiction between what is and what ought to
be is now clearly manifest in the utter discrepancy between
the demand of Jehovah for national righteousness and the
actual unrighteousness of all the nations, above all of Israel.
It is symbolised in the figure of the plumbline and the
leaning wall. How is the contradiction to be resolved? For
Amos, with his conception of the nature of Jehovah, only
one solution is possible. Jehovah will judge the nations
and punish their iniquities: and upon Israel, the most
favoured nation, the severest judgement will fall.

At this stage the prophetic vision is concerned with the
nation as a whole, and the eschatology is also national.
The burden of the prophecies of Amos is what God is
about to do to Israel and the neighbouring peoples. The
eschatology of the individual does not come in until a
much later stage.

As the prophetic conception of Jehovah gains in depth
and fullness, so the expectation of what he will do develops.
In the genuine prophecies of Isaiah, for example, we find,
along with the idea of the Day of the Lord, the idea of the
Remnant, of the Messianic King, and of Zion as the
inviolable seat of Jehovah's sovereignty. As in Amos, so in
Isaiah the Day of the Lord is a day of judgement. But,
unlike Amos, Isaiah sees beyond the judgement to a
better day. The zeal of the Lord will not be exhausted by
the destruction of all that is contrary to his righteous

a new nation, 12

purposes: he will go on to establish his own Kingdom in the world. He will save for himself a true people—the Remnant; he will govern them by a chosen ruler filled with his own spirit—the Messiah; he will appoint to them a permanent centre—Zion.[1] This consummation, when it comes to pass, will be the vindication at once of Jehovah's righteousness and of the loyalty of those who are true to Jehovah in the present; and the obvious course for the individual is to fit himself by repentance and new faithfulness to be a partaker in the good time that is to come when the judgement is overpast.

This means that the prophetic eschatology is already on the way to become individual rather than national: for a man becomes one of the Remnant—the true Israel—by his act of repentance and his life of faithfulness to Jehovah and obedience to the word of the Lord.

During the prophetic activity of Jeremiah the Day of the Lord dawned for Judah: and, as had been prophesied, it was darkness and not light. The nation received at the Lord's hand double for all her sins. Consequently we find in the later prophecies of Jeremiah an eschatology mainly occupied with the restoration. Out of the ruins of the kingdom that has passed away God will produce a new Israel governed by a genuine Scion[2] of the house of David, and united to Jehovah by a New Covenant. In the idea of a New Covenant written upon the hearts of men the individualising and spiritualising process is carried yet a stage further. The nation is no longer the unit of religion though it is still the sphere of religion.[3]

But with the emergence of the individual as the religious unit comes the problem of his destiny. What can be made of the fate of the man who is obedient to the heavenly vision now, but does not survive to share in the consummation; who endures the sufferings of this present time

[1] Cf. Skinner, *Isaiah*, i. pp. lx–lxx.
[2] צמח צדיק (Jer. xxiii. 5).
[3] Skinner, *Prophecy and Religion*, p. 309.

without living to behold the glory that is to be revealed?
The question is raised by Habakkuk.

> Art thou not from of old,
> O Yahweh, my holy God,
> Too pure of eyes to see ill,
> Nor on trouble canst thou gaze?
> Why then silently gaze upon traitors,
> When the wicked engulfeth the righteous?[1]

Here again we have the conflict between what is and what
ought to be. The lot of those who are faithful should be
something better than suffering and oppression: they ought
not to descend to the grey half-lights of Sheol without
tasting the joys of the coming Golden Age. That such
things should happen is felt to be inconsistent with the
nature of God.

Ultimately this contradiction is resolved along two lines:
first, it is taught in the Servant Songs that the sufferings of
the righteous are not due to divine negligence, but rather
that they are in some way included in the purpose of God:
that suffering borne for the sake of the Kingdom actually
is one of the most potent means—perhaps the most potent—
towards its realisation. And, secondly, the hope emerges
that those who die, not having received the promises, will
be raised from the dead when the time comes. This
second line of explanation comes much later and is only
fully developed in the apocalypses.

In the eschatology of Ezekiel we find the chief stress
laid on the ideal of the restoration of Israel and the establishment of a purified land of Israel as the permanent
dwelling-place of Jehovah. The idea of a Messianic King
is very much in the background, for Jerusalem will bear
the new name יהוה־שמה, 'Jehovah is there'. In the
picture of the Holy Land laid out like a Dutch garden and
the rebuilt Jerusalem with its Temple all perfectly sym-
metrical, we have the foreshadowings of the New Jerusalem
which appears in the later apocalypses. And again it is

[1] Hab. i. 12 a, 13, trans. T. H. Robinson, *Prophecy and the Prophets*, p. 116.

clear to everyone who studies the prophecy that the whole
picture of the future is dominated by Ezekiel's conception
of Jehovah.

The situation which confronts the author of Deutero- *Isaiah II*
Isaiah is again a contradiction between faith and fact.
Jehovah is for faith the God of the whole world and, in a
special sense, of Israel. Yet it appears that the facts of
history contradict both articles of faith. For the Gentile
nations with their idolatrous worship have the upper hand:
and Israel has been destroyed as an independent nation.
The last word appears to be with Bel and Nebo. The
answer of the prophet is that the real supremacy of
Jehovah is demonstrable in what Jehovah has done and is
about to do. The disasters of Israel and the triumph of
Israel's foes were of God's appointment. They were his
punishment for Israel's sin. And even as formerly he raised
up a heathen power to punish Israel, so now he is raising
another to restore her to her land. Cyrus is the anointed
of Jehovah and his power rests on Jehovah's will. More
than that, God is calling Israel to a new task and endowing
her with new powers for the conversion of the Gentiles.
These two things work together. Jehovah is making the *cf Paul in Rom 11*
Gentiles powerful for the restoration of Israel, and Israel *in a spiritualized*
mighty in spirit for the redemption of the Gentiles, to the *sense.*
end that the salvation of God may be known to the ends of
the earth.

Again, the conception of God determines the hope of the
future. Jehovah is the one true God who manifests himself in righteousness and saving power. Consequently the
consummation that he will bring to pass is one in which all
false gods are put down and he alone is recognised and
worshipped. He will be vindicated before the world by his
restoration of Israel and by the salvation that will come
from him, through Israel, to all nations. The polemic in
Deutero-Isaiah is not against flesh and blood, but against
the spiritual powers of evil in false gods and all the mischief that follows from their worship. This stands in sharp

contrast to the prophecies of Ezekiel, where oracle after oracle is directed against foreign nations.[1] Ezekiel's God is primarily the God of Israel using his universal powers for the exclusive benefit of Israel. The God of Deutero-Isaiah is the God of the whole world, who uses Israel for the working out of his universal purposes. And the conceptions of the future in the two prophecies differ accordingly.

Such were the pictures held before the eyes of the exiles on the eve of the return from Babylon. That of Ezekiel appears—naturally—to have had the wider popular appeal. But the realities of the situation to which the exiles came back did not correspond to the expectations that had been aroused. The land fit for heroes to live in turned out to be a land where only heroes could live. The old contradiction arose in a new form. The purpose of God had been announced by the voice of prophecy: and the purpose still awaited realisation. To the rest of faith's perplexities was added the problem of unfulfilled prophecy. It was the more puzzling because not all prophecies had remained unfulfilled. The predictions of doom and disaster had come true to the letter. It was only the promises of the good time coming that tarried.

Some explanation had to be found: and one was found in the failure of the people to rebuild the Temple.

Ye looked for much, and, lo, it came to little: and when ye brought it home, I did blow upon it. Why? saith the Lord of hosts. Because of mine house that lieth waste, while ye run every man to his own house.[2]

The promise is conditional. Once the work of the Temple is seriously taken in hand the good things that have been promised will begin to appear.[3]

But even with the second Temple completed the expected consummation did not come. The power of the heathen empires was not broken. This or that empire

---

[1] Cf. Driver, *Introd.* (9th ed.), pp. 286 f.
[2] Hag. i. 9.   [3] Zech. viii. 9-13.

might collapse; but its place was taken by another. The Persian Empire gave place, not to the Kingdom of God or of his Anointed but to the Empire of Alexander the Great. After his death Ptolemies and Seleucids fought over the division of the spoils: and Palestine, from its geographical position, became inevitably a perpetual battlefield.

The Maccabean rising did indeed raise hopes which seemed about to be fulfilled in the person of John Hyrcanus;[1] but they were not fulfilled. It was no divine Kingdom, but one of the earth earthy, over which Alexander Jannaeus presided. The Hasmonean dynasty modelled itself not on the ideals of Jewish piety, but on the Ptolemies and the Seleucids. The disillusionment and disgust of the better part of the people find utterance in the so-called *Psalms of Solomon*.[2] The splendid dreams of the prophets of the Exile were apparently farther than ever from realisation.

The writers of the apocalypses had to frame their message to explain why God had implemented only his promises of evil; why the hopes of the nation were continually deferred; why generation after generation of the faithful went down to the grave without seeing the promised salvation. To reconcile the closing chapters of Ezekiel with the actualities of life in Palestine in the days of Antiochus Epiphanes or Alexander Jannaeus or Herod the Great or Pontius Pilate was the task of the apocalyptic writers. They had perforce to go beyond the standpoint of the pre-exilic prophets, and to construct a philosophy of history.

The great difference between prophecy and apocalypse is that in prophecy the destiny of Israel is a private matter between Jehovah and the nation. The destiny of Israel is determined by the behaviour of Israel: and of that behaviour Jehovah is the final judge. The rise and fall of

---

[1] *Test. Levi*, xviii. 2 ff.; *Test. Judah*, xxiv. 1 f. Cf. R. H. Charles, *Between the Old and New Testaments*, pp. 82 ff.

[2] *Ps. Sol*. xvii. 5–10, 21–24, with the notes of Ryle and James.

other nations are not relevant to this moral issue between Israel and Israel's God. God may use Assyria or Babylon to punish Israel, or Persia for Israel's restoration; but he uses them in much the same way as he uses earthquake or famine or pestilence. He has no permanent relations with, or interest in, the other nations such as he has for Israel. In the drama of history, as the prophets read it, there are only two actors, Jehovah and Israel. The other nations are supers. They make their appearances on the stage, but the play is not concerned with them.

In apocalyptic it is not so simple. The destinies of Israel are part of a larger scheme which embraces the destinies of all nations: and not merely of nations but of a host of other things besides. The stage for the apocalyptic drama is wider than Palestine. It includes the earth and heaven and hell too. Hosts of angels and legions of devils have their parts as well as the nations of the world. The drama takes the form of war between the kingdoms of light and darkness, of God and Satan. And the fortunes of Israel are bound up with the progress and issue of that conflict.

To Israel before the Exile, viewing with well-founded apprehension the inexorable advance of the Assyrian or Babylonian world-power, prophecy could say: These things are the punishment for your sins. To Israel after the Exile, condemned to be the battle-ground of new empires at war with one another, apocalyptic says: These things must be, but the end is not yet. While the prophetic call is for repentance in face of approaching judgement, the apocalyptic message is an exhortation to be faithful and patient under the present trials in view of the approaching vindication of God's people.

The central and essential element in Jewish eschatology is thus the idea of the two kingdoms, the false kingdom and the true, the Kingdom of God and the kingdom of Satan. Israel is the manifestation on earth of the one; the world-empires are successive manifestations of the other.

For the time being the Satanic kingdom, in one or other of its incarnations, has the upper hand on earth, though it has already been defeated and cast down from heaven. But it is only for a time: and when the time is up God will intervene, either in person or through his representative the Messiah, to break for ever the hostile power and to establish his own eternal Kingdom of truth and righteousness. In that day his people will be vindicated and enter into that prosperity and happiness now denied to them. Concerning the details of this consummation there is a great deal of difference between the various apocalypses. There are different accounts of how and when it is to come to pass; but there is fundamental agreement as to what it is that is to be looked for.

The question when the Messianic Kingdom was to be established was essentially the question when the series of manifestations of the Satanic power would come to an end. It was complicated by the fact that in the Book of Jeremiah a definite period of time had been set. In seventy years, according to this prophecy (Jer. xxv. 11; xxix. 10), Israel was to be restored and the Messianic Kingdom established (xxiii. 5 f.). The Babylonian Empire passed away and the Persian took its place. The Persian Empire, in its turn, gave way to the Macedonian: and still the promise was not fulfilled. Consequently in the Book of Daniel the seventy years of Jeremiah are interpreted as seventy weeks of years (490 years) and the consummation is thus thrown once more into the immediate future. The Macedonian domination was succeeded not by the Messianic Kingdom, but by the Roman Empire, and so the calculations of Daniel had to be revised by the writers of *II Baruch* (xxxvi–xl) and *IV Esdras* (x. 60–xii. 35) in order to include this new fact in the plan of world-history. What is common to all these statements and restatements is the conviction that the present dispensation is drawing to a close and that the tyranny under which the elect are at the moment suffering is the last effort of the kingdom of Satan. The good time is close at hand and the next kingdom will be the fully realised Kingdom of God.

The prophets had expected the Kingdom to be established in the land of Israel with its centre in Jerusalem. This expectation is shared by the earlier apocalypses. As time went on, however, men began to despair of the kind of consummation they looked for being realised on earth. By the end of the second century B.C. the conviction arose that 'the eternal Messianic Kingdom can attain its consummation only in the world to come, into which the righteous should enter through the gate of resurrection'.[1]

A more important question than the time or place of the final consummation is that of its scope: Who will enjoy the benefits which God will then bestow upon men? Here there are differing views to record; but the general tendency of the apocalyptic writers is to exclude the Gentiles or the greater part of them from the good time that is coming. The most catholic spirit is shown by Ben Sira and the author of the *Testaments of the XII Patriarchs*, both before the end of the second century B.C. The narrowest and meanest views are held by the authors of *Jubilees, II Maccabees, Enoch* xci–civ, the *Assumption of Moses*, and the *Salathiel Apocalypse* in *IV Esdras*. Where the whole Gentile world is not marked down for destruction, it is very often the case that only a few of the Gentiles will be converted and so escape the lot of their more numerous brethren. And it must be added that, as a rule, the salvation of any Gentile at the final consummation is to be regarded as an uncovenanted mercy.

In this the apocalyptic literature as a whole, apart from such notable and noble exceptions as *Ecclesiasticus* and the *Testaments*, shows its affiliation to be to Ezekiel rather than to Deutero-Isaiah. The Gentiles are 'by nature children of wrath...alienated from the commonwealth of Israel, and strangers from the covenants of the promise, having no hope and without God in the

[1] R. H. Charles, *Between the Old and New Testaments*, p. 71.

world'.[1] The difference of status between Israel and the
Gentiles can be put quite simply in this way, that when the
perfect Kingdom is being considered the question with
regard to Israelites is: Who, if any, will be excluded?
while with regard to the Gentiles it is: Who, if any, will
be admitted?'

These questions continued to be discussed in the Rabbinical schools. There is a record of a debate between
R. Eliezer b. Hyrcanus and R. Joshua b. Hananiah on the
text: 'The wicked shall return to Sheol, all the Gentiles
who forget God' (Ps. ix. 18). The former, taking the relative
clause as a descriptive statement in apposition to 'all the
Gentiles', maintains that no Gentile has a portion in the
world to come. The latter, taking the relative clause as
limiting the term 'all the Gentiles', draws the conclusion
that only those Gentiles who forget God will be excluded.
The opinion of R. Joshua prevailed in orthodox Judaism:
and the orthodox doctrine is enshrined in the sentence of
Maimonides:[2] 'The pious of the nations of the world have
a portion in the world to come', as the orthodox hope is in
the *Alenu* prayer[3] with its petition:

We therefore hope in thee, O Lord our God, that we may
speedily behold the glory of thy might, when thou wilt remove
the abominations from the earth, and the idols will be utterly
cut off, when the world will be perfected under the Kingdom of
the Almighty, and all the children of flesh will call upon thy
name, when thou wilt turn unto thyself all the wicked of the
earth. Let all the inhabitants of the world perceive and know
that unto thee every knee must bow, every tongue must swear.
Before thee, O Lord our God, let them bow and fall; and unto
thy glorious name let them give honour; let them all accept the
yoke of thy Kingdom and do thou reign over them speedily, and
for ever and ever. For the Kingdom is thine, and to all

[1] Eph. ii. 3, 12. Paul is here stating the position of Gentiles from the point
of view of his own pre-Christian Judaism.

[2] Maimonides, *Comm. on the Mishnah, Sanh.* x. 2; חסידי אומות העולם
יש להם חלק לעולם הבא:

[3] *Authorised Daily Prayer Book* (ed. Singer), pp. 76 f. Abrahams, *Companion*, pp. lxxxvi ff.

eternity thou wilt reign in glory; as it is written in thy Law, the
Lord shall reign for ever and ever. And it is said, And the
Lord shall be King over all the earth: in that day shall the
Lord be One, and his name One.

In all these developments one factor remains constant:
the special position of Israel or of the better part of Israel.
Even in the *Alenu* prayer the broad universalist petition
just quoted is preceded by a statement of the peculiar
privileges of the Chosen People. The good time coming is
first and foremost a good time for the faithful Israelites.
Such Gentiles as may be admitted to share in it, share in it
as proselytes to Israel. That such a plan of salvation lays
its author open to the charge of partiality is a real difficulty:
and it was felt and the attempt made to meet it.[1] And
undoubtedly there was a real inconsistency in the singling
out of one nation by a God of perfect righteousness and
universal dominion for a position of special privilege. The
fact is, as we can see clearly enough now, that as usual
the whole doctrine is governed by the conception of God:
and in this case the inconsistency arises from the fact that
there are two ideas of God determining the form which the
apocalyptic expectations should take. There is, on the
one side, the prophetic idea of God as the righteous
sovereign of the whole world: and there is, on the other, the
older notion of God as the national God of Israel to the
exclusion of all other nations. It is the presence of these
two ideas that makes the difficulty, a difficulty which is
always present from Ezekiel to *IV Esdras* and never overcome.

One way in which this fatal inconsistency could have
been avoided would have been by giving the leading place
in the development of Jewish eschatology to the ideas of
Deutero-Isaiah rather than to those of Ezekiel: to have
made the peculiar privilege of Israel to consist in being a
light to lighten the Gentiles rather than a brand plucked

[1] E.g. by the writer of *The Book of Jubilees*. Cf. H. J. Wicks, *The Doctrine of
God in the Jewish Apocryphal and Apocalyptic Literature*, pp. 147–151.

separated

from the burning: to have looked upon Israel as the saving
Remnant rather than merely the saved Remnant. But this
did not take place. The development of the future hope in
Jewish circles was throughout dominated by the ideals set
forth in the concluding chapters of Ezekiel: and it is only
when we come to the Gospels that we find a radical
reformation of eschatology by the introduction of the
ideal of the Servant of Jehovah into the framework of the
divine plan of salvation. In the teaching of Jesus *the*
eschatological figure is that of the Son of Man. This
conception, we have already seen reason to believe, is
essentially the Remnant. It is, moreover, the Remnant
both as the present manifestation of the Kingdom of God
on earth, and the Remnant as it shall be when the final
consummation takes place. As a present manifestation of
the Kingdom, the Remnant or Son of Man plays the part
of the Servant of Jehovah. In the final consummation the
Remnant is gloriously vindicated as foretold in the Book of
Daniel.[1] And the one is the necessary prelude to the other.

In considering the eschatological element in the teaching
of Jesus we have, therefore, to bear in mind a special
principle in addition to the two fundamental principles[2]
which govern eschatology in general. This special principle
is that *the final consummation is not a compensation for the
sufferings of the faithful in the present, but the result of them.* The
Remnant is committed to a present rôle of service and
sacrifice, not as something to be endured until better times

[1] The interpretation of the 'Son of Man' in the Gospels adopted here
has close affinities with that proposed by Dr Charles. There is, however, this
important difference, that whereas he regards 'Son of Man' in the Gospels as
arising from the union of the Servant in Deutero-Isaiah with the 'Son of Man'
in Enoch, our view is that it is the union of the Servant idea with the idea of
the 'Son of Man' as presented in Daniel. That is, on our view the 'Son of
Man' in the teaching of Jesus is the Remnant; on Dr Charles's view it
stands for the pre-existent supernatural Messiah. If, however, it should turn
out to be the case that 'Son of Man' in Enoch is to be understood in much the
same sense as in Daniel, then there would be no essential difference between
the two views. In any case, the epoch-making thing is the introduction into
the eschatological scheme of ideals taken from Deutero-Isaiah rather than
from Ezekiel.
[2] See above, p. 247.

come, but as something to be embraced in order that
better times may come." The differentia of the Christian
eschatology is that the work of faith and the labour of
love are added to the patience of hope." The Kingdom as
the Suffering Servant is an 'interim' state only in the sense
that the seed growing secretly is an interim state towards
the full corn in the ear, or the leaven in the dough to the
finished loaf. The final consummation is not to be a
violent reversal of the present, but the fulfilment of it. It is
the same Son of Man that is rejected and killed and that
comes with the clouds of heaven with great power and
glory: and the two states are linked as antecedent and
consequent.

We may therefore approach the actual sayings of Jesus
about the final consummation with three guiding principles
in mind:

(a) The consummation is the resolution of the contradiction between what is and what ought to be.

(b) It is determined both in what it is and in the manner
of its appearing by what is held to be the nature of God.

(c) It is continuous with the present manifestation of the
Kingdom in a Remnant and is the fruition of the service
and sacrifice of the Remnant.

2. THE ESCHATOLOGICAL TEACHING OF JESUS

It is usual to begin an account of the eschatological
teaching of Jesus with the thirteenth chapter of Mark. The
chief objection to making this passage the starting-point of
our investigation is that it is highly improbable that it was
ever delivered by Jesus in the form in which we have it.
Many modern scholars are of the opinion that this 'Little
Apocalypse' was already in circulation as a separate
document at the time when St Mark wrote his Gospel. It is
quite possible that this was the case, though definite proof
is lacking.

The Early Church was certainly obsessed by the idea of
the imminent return of the Lord; and there would be

nothing surprising in the existence of a document pur-
porting to give the authentic words of Jesus on a matter
which was of vital interest to his followers. In compiling
such a document the writer would naturally incorporate
such sayings of Jesus as he supposed to refer to the coming
manifestation of the Kingdom in power. Any or all of these
sayings might well be genuine utterances of the Lord, but
by the way in which they were put together a new total
effect would be created, which might be quite different
from anything which Jesus meant to say. This, as a matter
of fact, is what appears to have happened in Mk. xiii.

The vital point is that the picture of the times of the
end given in the Little Apocalypse does not square with the
account given by our other sources, notably Q, or with the
statements of Paul. As we have it in Mk. xiii there is a
series of predicted events—the destruction of the Temple,
wars, earthquakes, famines, a storm of persecution, great
tribulation in Judaea, the rise of bogus Messiahs and
false prophets, supernatural appearances in the sky, and
finally, as the culmination of all this, the coming of the
Son of Man, and the ingathering of the elect from all parts
of the world. As an appendix is added the parable of the
Fig Tree, followed by sayings indicating that the time of the
Parousia is unknown to all but God himself and that the
disciples must therefore be on the alert lest they be taken
unawares when it happens.

Now the Q account of the Day of the Son of Man is
totally different. When we turn to Lk. xvii. 22–37 we find a
picture of mankind going about their ordinary business,
occupied with the daily routine of merchandise and
matchmaking, eating and drinking. The masons are on
the scaffolding; the farmer is at work in his fields; the
women are grinding meal. And suddenly the Day is
upon them.

Of similar import are the sayings preserved in L (Lk.
xxi. 34–36) and the Pauline doctrine in the early epistle to
the Thessalonians (I Thess. v. 1–10).

These two pictures are irreconcilable. Our authorities are divided: Q, L, and Paul against the Little Apocalypse. Moreover, the Marcan account is divided against itself. For the concluding sayings (Mk. xiii. 32–37) agree with Q, L, and Paul against what has gone before.[1]

Beside the fact that the Marcan Apocalypse as a whole contradicts what we are elsewhere told about the Parousia, has to be set the other fact that we find in the details of the Apocalypse sayings that agree with what is given in our other sources. Thus the statement that the disciples will be persecuted can be paralleled from Q (Lk. xii. 11 f.). Mk. xiii. 12 is parallel in thought to Lk. xii. 51 ff. = Mt. x. 34 ff. (Q). The prophecy concerning false Messiahs and false prophets (Mk. xiii. 21 f.) appears also in Q (Lk. xvii. 23 = Mt. xxiv. 26). The ingathering of the elect from the four winds is in the same line of thought as the statement (Lk. xiii. 29 = Mt. viii. 11: Q) 'They shall come from East and West and North and South, and sit down in the Kingdom of God'. The prophecy of terrible calamities that are to come upon Judaea and its people (Mk. xiii. 14–20) has echoes in Lk. xiii. 34 f. = Mt. xxiii. 37 ff. (Q); and Lk. xix. 41–44 (L); xxiii. 27–31 (L). The conclusion to be drawn is that Mk. xiii is a compilation containing genuine utterances of Jesus, but that the way in which the sayings have been arranged is such as to give a wrong impression of his eschatological teaching.

---

[1] It may be that vv. 32–37 represent the original answer of Jesus to the question put to him in v. 4. This would make a perfectly good connection and bring Mark into agreement with our other authorities. It would also fix the limits of the Little Apocalypse. This document would extend from xiii. 5 to xiii. 31. It is to be observed that the opening words ὁ δὲ Ἰησοῦς ἤρξατο λέγειν αὐτοῖς suggest the beginning of an address rather than the answer to a question; and when Mark has elsewhere ἤρξατο διδάσκειν (iv. 1; vi. 2, 34; viii. 31), λαλεῖν (xii. 1), or λέγειν (x. 32), it is never in answer to a question. The Marcan formula to introduce the answer to a question is ὁ δὲ ἀποκριθεὶς εἶπεν αὐτοῖς (x. 3) or ὁ δὲ ἀποκριθεὶς αὐτῷ λέγει (xv. 2). The introductory formula is corrected in Mt. xxiv. 4 to καὶ ἀποκριθεὶς ὁ Ἰησοῦς εἶπεν αὐτοῖς. It may also be added that Mk. xiii. 31 forms a fitting close to the Little Apocalypse; and that if we go past v. 31, v. 32 comes in as a complete anticlimax.

This chapter, therefore, cannot safely be used as a starting-point in an enquiry concerning what our Lord had to say about the consummation of the Kingdom. A better line of approach may perhaps be to take first the sayings concerning the Son of Man which have reference to the Parousia. These are tabulated above (p. 225).

The first of these is preserved in Mk and Q (Mk. viii. 38; Lk. xii. 8 f.; Mt. x. 32 f.):

Mk	Q (Luke)
	Everyone who acknowledges me before men
	The Son of Man will acknowledge him before the angels of God.
Whoever shall be ashamed of me and my words	But he who denies me
in this adulterous and sinful generation	before men
The Son of Man will be ashamed of him	Will be denied
When he comes in the glory of his Father with the holy angels.	before the angels of God.[1]

The Q version of the saying is the more complete. It also preserves best the poetical form and strict parallelism. The diction is simple and direct. It is therefore probable that we have here the more primitive form of the saying.[2] However this may be, both versions tell substantially the same story: that the lot of the individual on the Great Day depends strictly on his attitude to Jesus in the intervening period. In both documents the saying occurs in a context predicting trials and sufferings for the disciples: and it is clear that what is in question is the reward of loyalty and the judgement on apostasy.

A second group of sayings describes the Parousia. The

---

[1] The chief variations in Mt. x. 32 f. are secondary. The substitution of 'I' for 'the Son of Man' is dogmatic interpretation. 'My Father in heaven', which takes the place of 'the angels of God', is a favourite phrase with the First Evangelist (see above, p. 37). It is possible that 'will be denied' in Luke is an abbreviation for 'the Son of Man will deny him'.

[2] It may be added that the Q expression ὁμολογεῖν ἐν is an Aramaism, being a word-for-word rendering of the Aramaic בְּ אוֹדִי. To this part of the saying there is no parallel in Mk; but the idiom of Q suggests closeness to the original words of Jesus. Cf. Burkitt, *Earliest Sources* (1922), pp. 23 f.

account in Mark (xiii. 26 f.) is given in language partly borrowed from Daniel (vii. 13 f.):

2.

> They shall see the 'Son of Man coming with the clouds'[1] with great 'power and glory'. And then he will send out his angels and 'gather up' the elect 'from the four winds', from the extremity of the earth to the 'extremity of heaven'.[2]

In Q the principal feature of the Parousia is its unexpectedness. This is explicitly stated as the lesson to be drawn from the parable of the Robbed Householder (Lk. xii. 39 f. = Mt. xxiv. 43 f.), and it is enforced by comparisons with lightning, the Deluge, and the destruction of Sodom (Lk. xvii. 23–30; Mt. xxiv. 26–28, 37–39). There may also be a reference to the gathering of the elect in the statement:

> There shall be two men in one bed (Mt, 'in the field'): one will be taken, the other left.
>
> There shall be two women grinding together: one will be taken, the other left. (Lk. xvii. 34 f. = Mt. xxiv. 40 f.)

Peculiar to Matthew is the half-verse (xxiv. 30 *a*):

> And then the sign of the Son of Man shall appear in the sky and all the tribes of the earth shall mourn.[3]

And there is also the long description of the Last Judgement (Mt. xxv. 31–46: M):

> When the Son of Man comes in his glory accompanied by all the angels, then he will sit upon his glorious throne. And all the nations will be gathered before him, and he will separate them one from another as a shepherd separates sheep from goats, and he will set the sheep on his right hand and the goats on his left. Then the King will say to those on his right: 'Come, ye blessed of my Father, inherit the Kingdom prepared for you from the foundation of the world. For I was hungry and you

---

[1] ἐν νεφέλαις. Cf. Dalman, *Words of Jesus*, p. 242; and Mk. xiv. 62 where μετά replaces ἐν. This use of ἐν may be an extension of that which appears in such phrases as ἐν μαχαίρῃ (Pap. Tebt. 1. 16). The clouds of heaven are a symbol for that power of God by which 'the Kingdom of the Saints will be ushered in' (cf. Bevan, *Short Commentary on the Book of Daniel*, p. 119). We might paraphrase by saying that the 'Son of Man' comes armed with that divine power for which 'the clouds of heaven' is a symbolic expression.

[2] Cf. Zech. ii. 10 (E.V. ii. 6); Deut. xxx. 4.

[3] Cf. Zech. xii. 10–14. There the mourning is confined to the clans of Israel.

fed me. I was athirst and you gave me drink....' Then the
just will answer him saying: 'Lord, when did we see thee
starving and nourish thee, or thirsty and give thee drink...?'
And the King will answer and say to them: 'Verily I say unto
you, inasmuch as you did it to one of these least brethren of
mine you did it to me'. Then he will say to those on his left:
'Depart from me, ye cursed, into the everlasting fire prepared for
the devil and his angels. For I was hungry and you did not feed
me...'. Then they too will answer saying: 'Lord, when...?'
Then he will answer them saying: 'Verily I say unto you,
inasmuch as you did it not to one of these least ones, you did it
not to me'. And these shall go into everlasting punishment,
but the just into everlasting life.

There are three figures to be distinguished in this
passage: the Son of Man, the King, and the Father. The
Father is clearly God, and it is remarkable that the judgement is not carried out by him, but by the King. The King,
we must suppose, is Christ. Is 'the King', then, merely a
synonym for 'the Son of Man'? In view of what follows
we may well doubt it. For it appears that the King
addresses both the righteous and the wicked as spokesman
for a body which comprises himself and his brethren. The
brethren must be human beings, seeing that they have been
in a position to receive human kindnesses from the
righteous or to be denied them by the wicked. And they
are distinct from both parties. The only possible conclusion
would seem to be that they are included in the concept
'Son of Man'. The Son of Man will then be the Danielic
Kingdom of the Saints, of which Jesus is the head: and the
Parousia is the elevation of this body to supreme power
over all the nations of the world. The Parousia is followed
by the Judgement, in which the fate of the nations is
determined by their attitude to the Kingdom of the Saints
and its members.

There is another passage to be taken into consideration,
this time from the source L. It is given in Lk. xxi. 34–36.
Like the Q sayings, it emphasises the suddenness and
unexpectedness of the Day and the necessity of strict self-

control, watchfulness, and prayer if the disciples are 'to be able to escape the things that are going to happen and to stand before the Son of Man'. With this we may compare the sayings in Mk. xiii. 33–37; Lk. xii. 35–46: Mt. xxiv. 43–51 (Q); and the parable of the Talents.

In the trial before the High Priest (Mk. xiv. 62; Lk. xxii. 69: L) a fresh quotation from the Old Testament is amalgamated with the quotation from Daniel. According to Mark, Jesus says: 'You shall see the Son of Man "seated at the right hand" of the Power[1] and "coming with the clouds of heaven"'. The Lucan (L) version of the saying is 'From now on the Son of Man shall be "seated at the right hand" of the power of God'. The reference is to Ps. cx. 1:

An oracle of Jehovah for my lord: Sit thou at my right hand Until I make thine enemies a footstool for thy feet.[2]

[1] 'The Power' means simply God. Cf. Dalman, *Words of Jesus*, pp. 200 ff. The word δύναμις here represents the Hebrew גבורה and Aramaic גבורתא. A fuller collection than Dalman's of examples of its use in Rabbinic sources is given in Strack-Billerbeck, i. pp. 1006 f.

[2] This quotation appears again in a polemical passage (Mk. xii. 35–37) which has been much discussed without any very satisfactory conclusion being reached. There can be no question that in Jewish (Pharisaic) circles it was held that the Messiah would be a descendant of David (*Ps. Sol.* xvii. 23): and it was certainly believed in the Early Church that Jesus was in fact so descended. The reason for these beliefs is doubtless to be found in O.T. prophecies (e.g. II Sam. vii. 12; Jer. xxx. 9; Ezek. xxxiv. 23; etc.). The question which Jesus puts to the Pharisees is: How can the Davidic descent of the Messiah be reconciled with the fact that David in this Psalm calls him 'My Lord'? This question has its point on condition that the title to the Messianic office lies in the claimant's ability to trace his descent from David. In other words, if it is a condition of being Messiah that the Messiah should be able to show a pedigree going back to David, then David can rightly say to him: 'You owe your position to me'. And that means in effect: 'You are only the latest—and most powerful—member of a dynasty, of which I am still the head'. That being so, David cannot fitly call the Messiah 'My Lord'.

What Jesus appears to be maintaining here is that, where the title to Messiahship is concerned, the question of Davidic or non-Davidic descent is irrelevant. In doing this he is carrying a stage farther the argument of John the Baptist: 'Think not to say: "We have Abraham as our father", for I tell you that God is able of these stones to raise up children to Abraham'.

The title to Messiahship depends on other things than physical descent. So far as we can gather from the Gospels it depends on two things. (a) There must be a call from God himself. This seems to be the significance of the

In order to grasp the significance of this saying it is necessary to place it in its historical setting. It comes from the lips of Jesus at the moment when he is completely alone, deserted by all his followers and faced by a body of men obviously determined on his death and only concerned as to how it can most easily be compassed. He and the cause he represents are alike helpless unless there be help with God. The reply of Jesus to the High Priest's question is at once a confession of trust in God and a defiance of worldly power. By killing him the members of the priestly caste hope to crush the movement which he has begun. They will speedily be undeceived. They can kill the body, but after that they have no more that they can do. And he by losing his life will save it.

At this stage in the life of Jesus we have in fact reached the point at which the Son of Man becomes an individual person, not by a process of speculation, but by the logic of facts; not in apocalyptic theory, but in life. 'Son of Man' in the teaching of Jesus is a symbol for the Remnant in the purest and noblest form in which it could be conceived. His claim to the Messiahship is a claim to be the head of

vision at the Baptism. (6) The Messiah must be the incarnation of the Kingdom. That is, he must express and fulfil in his own person the ideals of the Kingdom. The principle which Jesus lays down is that the head of the Kingdom of the Saints must be the servant *par excellence*. And his claim to be the head is thrown into the form 'I am among you as one that serveth'. In these two respects the Messiahship is sharply distinguished from the kingships of the world. There the foundations of kingly authority are dynastic descent and the possession of compulsive power. Jesus will not found his title upon either. From all that we can learn of the mind of Jesus it seems certain that he would have regarded the kingdom of David and Solomon as just one more of the kingdoms of the world: and it is not credible that he would have lifted a finger to restore its vanished glories or to claim its throne for himself. 'The coming kingdom of our father David' meant nothing to him; the Kingdom of God meant everything. And the two kingdoms had nothing in common.

The argument thus appears to mean: David would not call the head of a restored Davidic kingdom 'My Lord' any more than he would have so accosted Solomon. But if the kingdom which David saw by inspiration was the true Kingdom of God, he could indeed call the head of that Kingdom 'My Lord'. For that Kingdom is of a higher order than his: and its head has nobility of a kind that does not rest on pedigree or power. He is greater than David or Solomon: and he is greater in his own way, not theirs.

the Remnant in virtue of fulfilling those ideals. And now, standing alone against the world, he *is* the Remnant. He is the Son of Man because he alone is equal to the claims of the Son of Man ideal. Son of Man and Messiah have been united in one person, his person. And in his person they are at the mercy of world powers. But God will still have the last word, and he will vindicate the Son of Man. In the meanwhile the Son of Man-Messiah occupies the place of supreme honour, second only to God himself.[1] His work and himself are henceforth safe in God's care.

There remains one saying which is preserved in Matthew (xix. 28). In the form in which it there appears it is probably to be assigned to M.[2] It runs:

And Jesus said unto them, Verily I say unto you, that ye which have followed me, in the regeneration when the Son of Man shall sit on the throne of his glory, ye also shall sit upon twelve thrones, judging the twelve tribes of Israel.[3]

Here the disciples are promised places of honour at the future consummation. The saying fits in well enough with the picture of the end as it is given in M (Mt. xxv. 31–46) if the interpretation proposed for that passage (p. 265) is correct.

What conclusions can we draw from these data? It is clear that:

---

[1] Cf. Kittel, *Die Psalmen*, p. 356. The citation from Ps. cx. 1 coupled with Ps. viii. 5–7 reappears in the eschatological passage I Cor. xv. 25–28. Paul makes one important change. He makes Christ the subject of $\theta\tilde{\eta}$ in xv. 25 rather than God, who is subject of $\theta\tilde{\omega}$ in the psalm. The rôle of the risen Christ is the active one of subduing the forces of evil rather than the passive one of waiting for God to do it for him. But it is clear from the following statements of Paul that he conceives the power by which this is done to be the power of God. The Christ 'puts down' these forces because God has 'subjected' them to him. He is God's agent, armed with God's powers to effect God's purposes. This restatement was inevitable for Paul with his experience of the continuing power of Christ in his own life and in the life of the Church.

[2] Streeter, *The Four Gospels*, p. 288. There is a partial parallel in L (Lk. xxii. 28–30).

[3] This also has its echo in Paul: Rom. viii. 17, 'Heirs of God, and joint-heirs with Christ; if so be that we suffer with him, in order that we may be glorified with him'.

(a) The consummation is to be something which will take the world by surprise. This is the testimony of Mark (xiii. 32–37), Q (Lk. xii. 39 f.; xvii. 23–30), and L (Lk. xxi. 34–36). That being so, it follows that it is not to be thought of as a peaceful reformation of the existing order, but as a drastic revolution by which a new order of things is introduced. The Kingdom of God in its final manifestation does not emerge by some evolutionary process out of the kingdoms of the world; it displaces them. There is no question, therefore, of a restoration of the Davidic kingdom, for it also is only one of the kingdoms of the world.[1]

(b) This final manifestation appears first as a judgement at which the principal criterion will be the attitude taken up by men to Jesus himself. This is attested both by Mark and Q. He who acknowledges Jesus will be acknowledged by the Son of Man; he who denies Jesus will be denied by the Son of Man. The primary reference of this saying would appear to be to those who are, in some sense, already committed to discipleship of Jesus. They are to be judged in the future by their loyalty to him in the present. That is to say, if our contention is right that 'Son of Man' stands for the Remnant, the true Israel of which Jesus is the head, then faithfulness to Jesus in the present carries with it the assurance of a place at his side in the day of the Son of Man, in the day when the Remnant shall be vindicated. The 'Son of Man' in the present is a name for Jesus plus any who take up the cross and follow him: the 'Son of Man' coming in glory and power is the same, Jesus and all who have faithfully followed him, Christ plus those that are Christ's, who suffer with him and are glorified with him.[2]

[1] See above, p. 266 n. 2.
[2] Rom. viii. 17; I Cor. xv. 23; I Thess. iv. 14: 'Them that are fallen asleep in Jesus will God bring with him [Jesus]'. The ground of the Pauline statement here is that the Christians belong to Jesus, are members of his body (Rom. xiv. 8; I Cor. vi. 14 f.). (Cf. W. Lueken on I Thess. iv. 14; S.N.T. 3rd ed. 1917.) Many things become clear if we may make the equation: 'Son of Man' in the Gospels = 'the man from heaven' = Christ the first-fruits plus those that are Christ's = Christ the first-born plus many brethren = Christ the head plus the members of his body, in the Pauline Epistles.

But all this is only preliminary to the Judgement proper,[1] which is carried out by the Son of Man. Here all mankind are on trial. The criterion remains the same: each individual is judged by his treatment of Jesus. In the application of it a new principle is enunciated: 'Inasmuch as ye did it to one of these least brethren of mine, ye did it to me'. Here the brethren referred to cannot be those on the left hand or on the right. They must be those for whom the King is spokesman, those who, along with him, make up the 'Son of Man'. The 'Son of Man' is a corporate body and the rest of mankind are judged by their treatment of that body in the days of their power and its weakness. This much is clear from the account in Mt. xxv.[2] Whether or not the whole passage be accepted in every detail as authentic teaching of Jesus, we at least have confirmation from other sources for two points. For the Judgement as carried out by the corporate body we have the saying to the Twelve preserved independently by M and L[3]: 'Ye shall sit on twelve thrones judging the twelve tribes of Israel'. And, again, for the principle of 'Inasmuch' we may quote Mark (ix. 41): 'Whoever gives you a cup of water in the name that ye are Christ's, verily I say unto you that he shall not lose his reward'; and Luke (x. 16 Q?: cf. Mt. x. 40): 'He who hears you hears me, and he who rejects you rejects me, and he who rejects me rejects him that sent me'.

This last saying forms a connecting link with another utterance concerning the Last Judgement:

The Queen of the South shall rise in the Judgement with the men of this generation and condemn them; for she came from the ends of the earth to hear the wisdom of Solomon, and,

---

[1] Mt. xxv. 31–46 (M).

[2] If this interpretation of Mt. xxv. 31–46 is correct we have a threefold division at the Judgement: 'Son of Man', those on the right hand, and those on the left. Curiously enough the early eschatology of Mohammed also has a threefold division of mankind at the Judgement: *sābiqūn*, those of the right hand, and those of the left hand. Cf. *Koran*, Sura lvi; Nöldeke-Schwally, *Geschichte des Qorāns*, I. 43, 106.

[3] Mt. xix. 28; Lk. xxii. 30.

behold, a greater than Solomon is here. The men of Nineveh shall rise in the Judgement with this generation and condemn it; for they repented at the preaching of Jonah, and, behold, a greater than Jonah is here.[1]

Taking all these sayings together, the general principle emerges that every generation will be judged by its response to such manifestation of the sovereignty of God as was available in its day. In the days of the Queen of Sheba it was the wisdom with which Solomon was endowed by God.[2] To the generation of the Ninevites to whom Jonah preached, it was the imperious call to repentance and amendment of life. To the generation that saw the ministry of Jesus, it was that ministry in word and deed as he carried it out in his own life and as he meant it to be carried out in the life of the society of which he was the head. The whole matter can best be understood when it is viewed in the light of the conception of an age-long conflict between the Kingdom of God and the kingdom of evil. In that conflict the Judgement marks the final act, the complete subjection of all the powers of evil. And the judgement on the individual is determined by his attitude in the conflict. The question is really: Which side was he on? The disposition of a man's will determines his destiny.

It may be observed here that in the Judgement, as Jesus pictures it for us, the scales are heavily loaded on the side of mercy. The saying that even a cup of cold water given to a disciple will be rewarded shows Jesus as eager to find the slightest indication that a man is 'for him'. The gift of a cup of cold water is just about the absolute minimum; but even the minimum counts, if it be given from the right

---

[1] Mt. xii. 41 f. = Lk. xi. 31 f. (Q).

[2] It is noteworthy that Jesus says nothing whatever about the other features of Solomon's greatness—his wealth, the splendour of his court, his magnificent buildings—though, according to the Old Testament account, these also threw the Queen into ecstasies. Judging from what Jesus says elsewhere about the glories of Solomon this omission would seem to be deliberate.

motive.[1] A gift, even the smallest, in the name of Jesus is essentially a gift for the advancement of his cause, the cause of God and God's righteousness, in the world: and such a gift is presumptive evidence that the heart of the giver is in the right place, that he is 'not against us' but 'for us'.

The Judgement is thus (i) universal in its scope. It embraces all peoples and all generations. And (ii) the criterion is strictly ethical and religious in character. Each individual is judged on his merits: and his merits are determined by the disposition of his will towards the Kingdom of God as it is manifested in his day and generation.

Now if these two propositions are taken seriously, it will follow that Israel will not enjoy any special privilege as compared with the rest of mankind in the Day of Judgement. There will be no room for a most favoured nation. And this is precisely what we find to be the case in the teaching of Jesus. He shows no pro-Israelite bias: and in this his eschatological sayings differ remarkably from the Jewish apocalypses. In these there is a natural and understandable expectation that Israel will, on the whole, emerge from the Judgement unscathed. Leaving out of account the exceptionally wicked in Israel and the exceptionally righteous among the Gentiles, the impression one gets from the Jewish apocalypses is that the average Israelite stands a much better chance than the average Gentile of attaining to a share in the bliss that lies beyond the last convulsions of the present age. In the eschatology of Jesus it is not so. Besides the passage quoted above (p. 270) from Q, where Gentiles from Nineveh and the Queen of Sheba are represented as coming through the Judgement better than the contemporaries of Jesus, there is another Q[2] passage where the issue of the Judgement is declared to be more favourable to Tyre and Sidon than to the towns of Galilee. Again in Mt. viii. 11 f. = Lk.

---

[1] Cf. the story of the Widow's Mite.
[2] Mt. xi. 21–23 = Lk. x. 13–15.

xiii. 28 f. (Q) we have a picture of men coming from the ends of the earth to sit down with the patriarchs and prophets in the Kingdom of God, and the 'Sons of the Kingdom'[1] cast into outer darkness. A similar picture is presented by the parable of the Vineyard in Mark and by the parable of the Great Feast.

We may compare these utterances with typical statements from the Jewish apocalyptic literature:

The best part of mankind, the people of Israel. (*Eth. Enoch* xx. 5.)

I beheld till a great sword was given to the sheep (Israel) and the sheep proceeded against all the beasts of the field (Gentiles) to kill them, and all the beasts and the birds of heaven fled before them. (*Eth. Enoch* xc. 19.)

I (God) shall give to thy (Jacob's) seed all the earth which is under heaven, and they will judge all the nations according to their desires, and after that they will get possession of the whole earth and inherit it for ever. (*Jub.* xxxii. 19.)

No longer shall Jerusalem endure desolation,
Nor Israel be led captive,
For the Lord shall be in the midst of it. (*Test. XII Patr., Dan.* v. 13.)

Thou didst choose the seed of Abraham before all the nations,
And didst set thy name upon us, O Lord; and thou wilt abide
    among us for ever. (*Ps. Sol.* ix. 17 f.)

He (God) never withdraweth his mercy from us (Israel), but though he chasteneth with calamity, yet doth he not forsake his own people. (*II Macc.* vi. 16.)

Then thou, O Israel, wilt be happy,
And thou wilt mount upon the neck[s and wings] of the eagle,
And (the days of thy mourning) will be ended.
And God will exalt thee,
And he will cause thee to approach to the heaven of the stars,
And he will establish thy habitation among them.
And thou wilt look from on high and wilt see thy enemies in
    Ge(henna),
And thou wilt recognise them and rejoice,

---

[1] Mt. viii. 12. Luke has simply 'you'.

And thou wilt give thanks and confess thy Creator.[1] (*Ass. Mos.* x. 8–10.)

The contrast between the two sets of utterances is as sharp as it could well be. Yet we are not entitled to say that the severity with which Jesus speaks is due either to a lack of affection for his own people or to an inadequate sense of the wrongs which Israel had suffered at the hands of the Gentile powers. He who wept over Jerusalem and said: 'Jerusalem, Jerusalem...how often would I have gathered thy children together as a hen gathers her chickens under her wings—and ye would not', cannot be accused of indifference or coldness towards his fellow-countrymen. And when we remember that the earthly life of Jesus was spent entirely in a country occupied by an alien army, and that his public ministry fell within the procuratorship of Pilate, a governor who earned from the Jews the epithets 'inflexible, merciless and obstinate', we can hardly suppose that he was either ignorant of or indifferent to the evils which necessarily arise when one nation is entirely in the power of another with totally different customs, ideals, and beliefs. The fact is that the sayings of Jesus on the fate of Jews and Gentiles in the Judgement are unaffected by bias one way or the other. Their character is determined by the fundamental principle that in the Judgement the question of race will be irrelevant, and every man will stand or fall by his own attitude to the claims of God and God's Kingdom so far as they are known to him.

(c) The Parousia with its accompanying Judgement marks the close of the present era, the destruction of everything that is hostile to the Kingdom of God, the final victory of the Kingdom of God over all the forces of evil. And here we may note another striking difference between the teaching of Jesus and the popular apocalyptic expectations. In the latter the consummation of the Kingdom of God is looked for in a great conflict in which the hostile

[1] The translation here given is that of Dr Charles (ed. 1897), pp. 42 f.

world-powers will be overthrown and destroyed either by the Chosen People,[1] or by the Messiah,[2] or by angelic powers,[3] or by God himself.[4] The teaching of Jesus ignores all this and goes back to the scene portrayed in Daniel (vii. 9–14). The end of the present era is not a great battle but a great trial. The victory which is marked by the Parousia is not obtained by force either of earthly arms or of supernatural weapons. It is in the strictest and most literal sense a moral victory. There are not wanting indications that in the apocalyptic literature, especially the later books,[6] the idea of a general Judgement came in along with that of a final battle, the Great Assize beside Armageddon; but in general it may be said that when the idea of a universal Judgement appears in Jewish apocalyptic, it is as an accompaniment to the idea of the defeat of the world-powers. The final victory ushers in the Messianic Kingdom, and after the period set for the Messianic Kingdom comes the Judgement. In the apocalyptic teaching of Jesus the idea of the Final Judgement has completely displaced that of the great assault and defeat of the world-powers. This is another way of saying that Jewish national expectations have no place in his plan of the future and that his thought moves entirely in the sphere of ethical and religious considerations. The Parousia and the Judgement are essentially and exclusively the victory of good over evil and the elimination of the latter from the world.

---

[1] *Eth. Enoch* xc. 19; xci. 12.

[2] Ps. ii; Is. xi. 4; *Ps. Sol.* xvii. 23–27; *Orac. Sib.* iii. 652 ff.; *Apoc. Baruch* xxxix. 7–xl. 2; lxx. 9; lxxii. 2–6; *Eth. Enoch* xlvi. 4–6; lii. 4–9; *IV Ezra* xiii. In this last passage the destruction of the massed enemies is not accomplished with earthly weapons but by supernatural power. The idea of the destruction of the world-powers by fire goes back to Ezekiel (xxxix. 6).

[3] Dan. xii. 1 (Michael); *Ass. Mos.* x. 2 (the Angel = Michael).

[4] Zech. xiv. 3–5; *Ass. Mos.* x. 7; *Test. XII Patr., Asher* vii.

The contrary impression is derived from the Little Apocalypse, which, as we have already shown, is not to be relied on. The peculiar character of the account there given of the Last Things arises from the fact that the Little Apocalypse is a composite work.

[6] *Enoch* xc. 20–27; *IV Esdras* vii. 26–44. Cf. Moore, *Judaism*, II. 338 ff.

4. (d) Parousia and Judgement mark the division between the present age and the age to come. They usher in what is described as 'the Kingdom of God' or as 'life'. These two terms appear to be used interchangeably. Thus in Mk. ix. 43, 45 Jesus speaks cf 'entering into life' and in *v.* 47 of 'entering into the Kingdom of God'. In Mk. x. 17 Jesus is asked: 'What shall I do that I may inherit eternal life?' and on the rejection of his counsel he remarks, 'How hardly shall they that have riches enter into the Kingdom of God'. These two names we may regard as names for the same thing looked at from two different points of view. 'The Kingdom of God' describes the state of things after the Judgement as seen from the divine point of view. It is God's sovereignty consummated by the annihilation of everything hostile to it. It is a universe cleansed from all evil. From the point of view of man's hopes and aspirations existence under these conditions may well be called life, for it is 'the sum-total of all that constitutes life in its fullest sense,—the true life'.[1]

Concerning the conditions of this life after the Judgement Jesus is reticent;[2] but there are passages in his teaching which indicate in a general way how he conceives it. In the reply to the question put by the Sadducees concerning the Resurrection he states that the life of man after the Resurrection will be similar to that of the angels.[3] Elsewhere the life of the perfected Kingdom is likened to a feast or, more particularly, a wedding feast. This figure, which belongs also to the Jewish picture of the future, is

[1] E. Haupt, *Die eschatologischen Aussagen Jesu*, p. 85, quoted in Dalman, *Words* (E.T.), p. 162.

[2] A similar reticence on the part of the earlier Rabbis is noted. Cf. S.B. IV. 1131.

[3] Mk. xii. 25. The parallel passage in Luke (xx. 34–36) is to the same effect, but appears to be independent of Mk. Cf. Taylor, *Behind the Third Gospel*, pp. 99 f.

[4] Mk. xiv. 25; Lk. xiii. 29 = Mt. viii. 11; Lk. vi. 21 (Mt. v. 6); Lk. xii. 37 (Q); Mt. xxv. 1–13 (M); the Parable of the Great Feast, Mt. xxii. 1–14 (M) and Lk. xiv. 16–24 (L); Lk. xxii. 30 (L).

[5] For the feast as a type of the joys of the righteous in Jewish belief see Dalman, *Words* (E.T.), pp. 110 ff., and, in greater detail, S.B. IV. 1144–1165.

doubtless meant to express the abundant joy and satisfaction which will be the portion of those who are found
worthy at the Judgement. Further, there are sayings which
indicate that the life beyond the Judgement will be a
sphere of enlarged responsibilities and opportunities.[1]
Jesus, in fact, does no more than show what will be the
quality of the life in the consummated Kingdom of God. It
is spiritual; it is full of joy but not merely passive enjoyment;
for it is also a more intense activity than is possible in the
present world. For the rest it is:

Things which eye hath not seen nor ear heard,
Which entered not into the heart of man,
Whatsoever things God hath prepared for them that love him.[2]

(e) A more difficult question, and one which has given
rise to much controversy, is that of the time of the Parousia.
The evidence furnished by the Synoptic records leads to a
simple conclusion. We have first of all the statement,
abundantly attested, that the Parousia will come suddenly
and without warning.[3] Then we have the definite declaration (Mk. xiii. 32):

Concerning that day and that hour no one knows, not even
the angels in heaven, nor even the Son, but only the Father.

On the other hand we have a series of sayings in Mark
which certainly appear to set a time limit within which the
Parousia is to take place. These are:

Jewish opinion was divided on the question whether the feast should be
placed in the Messianic age or in the world to come, which follows the
Messianic age.
[1] *E.g.* Lk. xii. 42–46 = Mt. xxiv. 45–51 (Q), especially Lk. xii. 44 = Mt.
xxiv. 47. The Lucan parable of the Pounds (Lk. xix. 12–27: ? Q or L),
especially *vv.* 17 and 19.
[2] I Cor. ii. 9. That this passage is based on Is. lxiv. 3 as understood by the
Rabbis is made highly probable by Strack-Billerbeck, *ad loc.* It is a commonplace of Jewish and Early Christian belief that the conditions of life in the
world to come are unknown to man: and in Rabbinical circles Is. lxiv. 3 is
the proof-text for this belief. In Early Christian writings the Pauline text or
some form of it appears in I Clem. xxxiv. 8; II Clem. xi, xiv; *Mart. Polyc.*
ii; Ps.-Clem. *Ep. ad Virg.* i. 9; *Const. Apost.* vii. 32; Irenaeus V. xxxvi (ed.
Harvey, II. 429).
[3] See above, p. 269.

(1) Verily I say unto you that there are some of those standing here who shall not taste death till they see the Kingdom of God coming in power. (ix. 1.)

(2) Then [after the troubles in Judaea] they shall see the Son of Man coming on the clouds with great power and glory. (xiii. 26.)

(3) Ye [the Sanhedrin] shall see the Son of Man seated on the right hand of the Almighty[1] and coming with the clouds of heaven. (xiv. 62.)

The natural interpretation of (1) and (3) is that the events described as 'the coming of the Kingdom of God in power' or 'the session of the Son of Man' or 'the coming of the Son of Man with the clouds of heaven' will take place within the lifetime of the persons addressed. The same thing is implied, if not expressly stated, in the exhortations to the disciples to be watchful and ready because the Son of Man comes when least expected (Lk. xii. 40; Mt. xxiv. 42: Q; Mk. xiii. 33; Lk. xxi. 34–36: L). There would be no point in telling men to be on the alert for something which might not happen until centuries after they had died. If then, we take all these indications in their simple and natural interpretation, we are left with the conclusion that Jesus expected the Parousia to take place during the lifetime of some at least of his contemporaries, the exact time being a secret known only to God. That this was also the expectation of the primitive Church is not open to doubt.[2]

As it happened, the Parousia did not come during the lifetime of that generation: and, consequently, the Church had to readjust its ideas in order to avoid the necessity of saddling Jesus with an unfulfilled prophecy. This was done in various ways. The Fourth Gospel, regarding the Parousia as essentially equivalent to the Judgement, takes the latter as something which lies not in the future but in the present. The Parousia is conceived, one might almost say, *sub specie aeternitatis*.

[1] τῆς δυνάμεως.
[2] I Thess. iv. 15–v. 3; I Cor. xv. 51 f.; Phil. iv. 5; I Cor. xvi. 22.

For God sent not the Son into the world to judge the world; but that the world should be saved through him. He that believeth on him is not judged; he that believeth not *hath been judged already*, because he hath not believed on the name of the only-begotten Son of God. *And this is the judgement, that the light is come into the world* and men loved the darkness rather than the light; for their works were evil.[1]

When we come to later times we can see the way in which the difficulty of the non-appearance of the Parousia was met by considering the exegesis of such a text as Mk. ix. 1. Briefly there are three methods.

The first is to explain 'the coming of the Kingdom of God in power' as not the Parousia, but some other event which had actually happened within the lifetime of the contemporaries of Jesus. Thus Theodotus,[2] followed by other patristic interpreters, regards the prophecy as fulfilled when the three intimate disciples were present at the Transfiguration about a week later.[3] Another explanation makes the coming of the Kingdom equivalent to the Fall of Jerusalem in A.D. 70. This line is taken by many post-Reformation expositors.[4] Or again it may be argued that the prophecy was fulfilled in 'the coming of the Spirit and the power manifested in that triumphant march of the Gospel through the Empire which was already assured before the death of at least some of the original apostolate'.[5]

The second method consists in assigning a mystical sense to the expression 'taste death'.[6] In Origen's *Commentary on John* (viii. 51 f.) a careful distinction is drawn between 'tasting death' and 'seeing death'. Origen argues

[1] Jn. iii. 17–19. Cf. W. Heitmüller in *S.N.T.*³ IV. 20.

[2] Clem. Alex. *Excerpta ex Theodoto*, § 4; Origen, *Comm. in Mt.* xii. 31, cited by Swete, *ad loc.*

[3] While this explanation might account for Mk. ix. 1 it fails to cover Mk. xiv. 62.

[4] E.g. Wetstein, *Nov. Test. Graecum* (ed. 1751), I. 434: 'Intelligo adventum Christi ad excidium Hierosolymorum, qui imaginem quandam judicii ultimi, de quo commate praecedenti sermo est, gerebat'.

[5] Swete, *Comm. on Mark, ad loc.* A similar view is taken by Headlam, *Life and teaching of Jesus Christ*, pp. 260 f. Swete does not exclude a 'secondary reference' to the Transfiguration.

[6] Origen, *op. cit.* Cf. *Comm. in Joann.* xx. 43 f. (ed. Brooke, II. 103–106).

that as there are diversities of physical sensation so there
are diversities of spiritual apprehension. Thus the Lord
considered as 'the living bread that cometh down from
heaven' is capable of being tasted and of nourishing
the soul, considered as wisdom he can be seen and admired.
Now as the Lord is capable of being tasted or seen, so his
enemy Death is likewise capable of being tasted or seen.
'To taste death' is the opposite of 'tasting the Lord': and
it can be defined in this fashion: 'He who utters what is
contrary to the words of eternal life, tastes death, and not
only tastes it but is sated with it as with food'.

It is not necessary to pursue the argument further.
Once this interpretation of 'tasting death' is established,
exegesis need be troubled no longer about the bodily
death of the Apostles.

The third method consists in a combination of the other
two. It is used by Jerome,[1] who interprets the text first
allegorically after the manner of Origen (*secundum sub-
limiorem sensum*), and then historically. As to the first, the
death spoken of by Jesus must be the death caused by sin:
and 'to taste death' signifies a greater subjection to the
power of sin than 'to see death'. To be tempted and to
resist temptation is to see death but not to taste it. To be
tempted and to allow the mind to dwell with pleasure on
the temptation is to taste death. A further stage is to
proceed to the actual commission of the sinful act. This is
to feed on death, to be sated with death. Now the Apostles,
as such, did not even taste death in this sense. So far the
'sublimer meaning'. Now we turn to the historical sense.
The reference, according to Jerome, is to the Transfiguration. In seeing Christ transfigured the Apostles saw him as
he would be when he should reign: and thus the prophecy
was fulfilled within a few days of its utterance.

There are objections to all these interpretations. As
against the allegorising of Origen and Jerome it is to be
said that 'to taste death' means simply to die in the

---

[1] *Tractatus in Marci Evangelium: Anecdota Maredsolana*, III. ii. 346–353.

ordinary way.[1] Therefore, whatever Jesus meant by 'the coming of the Kingdom in power' it was something which he expected to take place before the physical decease of some of his disciples. But once a time limit is set—say before A.D. 100—the exegesis of 'the coming of the Kingdom in power' becomes a matter not so much of enquiring what the words meant for Jesus, as of finding some event in the first century to which they can be suitably applied. And it is more than a little embarrassing to the conscientious interpreter to realise that, whatever else 'the coming of the Kingdom in power' may be, it must primarily be an event in the first century. The ungodly might easily find occasion to mock in the fact that, while orthodox commentators have differed widely about the nature of 'the coming of the Kingdom in power'—Transfiguration, Fall of Jerusalem, Pentecost, successful missionary activity—they are unanimous about the time—all in the first century.

In detail it can be argued against the Transfiguration as the fulfilment of this prophecy that it does not account for the similar saying in Mk. xiv. 62. The High Priest and his party certainly did not see the Transfiguration. For the Fall of Jerusalem as a fulfilment of the prophecy there is simply nothing to be said. The ruthless suppression by a great military empire of an insane rebellion in an outlying part of its territory has as much—or as little—to do with the coming of the Kingdom of God in power as the suppression of the Indian Mutiny.

Against the identification of the coming of the Kingdom with the outpouring of the Spirit and the astonishing progress of Christianity in the first century is to be set the fact that the people who lived through these great events did not make the identification. Paul, who was at the very head of the triumphant march of the Gospel through the Empire, still looks for some greater thing. According to the account in the Acts of the Apostles, Peter found in the

[1] S.B. ad Mt. xvi. 28.

descent of the Spirit the fulfilment, not of Mk. ix. 1, but of
Joel iii. 1 ff. (E.V. ii. 28 ff.).

The fact is that, in order to maintain any of these interpretations, we have to suppose a wholesale misunderstanding of our Lord's words in the earliest days of the
Church, and that a misunderstanding which arises from
taking his words in their plain natural sense. It is on every
count more satisfactory to suppose that it is the patristic
and modern commentators who have done the misinterpreting; and that these arbitrary explanations of 'the
coming of the Kingdom in power' would never have
arisen if the prophecy had been couched in a form
which allowed its postponement into the indefinite
future.

The conclusion thus appears to be that Jesus expected
the consummation of the Kingdom to take place at some
time in the immediate future, and that this expectation was
not realised. The question how far this conclusion must
affect Christology is one which properly belongs to
systematic theology or apologetics; but it may be touched
upon here. Put bluntly the question is: Was Jesus infallible? Must every statement of his be accepted as
'Gospel truth'? At other points this issue is already raised
in a less acute form. It is clear from our records that Jesus
accepted the current theory which ascribed various
physical and mental disorders to demon-possession.
Modern science has rejected the demons in favour of other
agents—complexes, obsessions, bacteria and the like. Again,
it appears from the argument which Jesus bases on the
opening words of the 110th Psalm that he believed it to
have been written by David. Modern literary criticism of
the Old Testament takes a different view. Again, Jesus
treats the story of Jonah preaching to the Ninevites as
sober history. Old Testament scholars treat the book of
Jonah as a *midrash* on II Kings xiv. 25. Now in speaking of
possession by demons, or in regarding David as the author
of the Psalter, or in taking the narrative in Jonah as

history, Jesus was simply living his life under the conditions of his day and generation.

On the other hand, the evidence is overwhelming that Jesus was able to bring relief to many who were 'possessed by demons'. We may not agree with the diagnosis, but we have no good reason to doubt the cure. And again, while modern students of the Old Testament may not accept the opinions on matters of literary criticism or Hebrew history current in the days of Jesus and accepted by him, yet they would be of one mind in declaring that in the power of penetrating to the very heart of the Old Testament and of extracting from it the living and authentic word of God he stands alone.

The unfulfilled prediction of the early Parousia may well be a similar case to these. The date of the Parousia is a question which is easily separable from the more important question of the nature of the Parousia. And it is quite possible that Jesus should have been mistaken about the former without being wrong in his account of the latter. The date belongs to history; and if Jesus was limited by the ideas of his times in the matter of past history, it is conceivable that he should be similarly limited in the matter of future history. Some colour is lent to this hypothesis by the fact that current ideas on the date of the Final Consummation tended to place it in the immediate future.[1] Apocalyptic writers generally assume that they are living in the last days and that the coming deliverance is on the threshold. In other words the belief in the nearness of the Day of the Lord is not one of the unique features in the eschatology of Jesus but a belief which, like the belief in demons or the Davidic authorship of the Psalter, was the common property of his generation.

From a theological point of view it may be argued, therefore, that the important question is not whether Jesus was correct in his dating of the Parousia, but whether he was right in his description of its nature; or rather, whether

[1] See above, pp. 255 f.

the picture which he gives is one which present-day theology is prepared to accept and embody in its teachings. That question is one which lies outside the scope of the present work. Our business is to discover what Jesus taught rather than to determine whether his teaching is likely to be palatable to present-day theology. It may, however, be remarked in passing that St Paul's statement that if the Christian hope has no reference beyond the present life then Christians are of all men the most pitiable,[1] is one that will bear a great deal of pondering.

There is one thing which must be said before we leave this subject. The eschatology of Jesus in its essential features is of a piece with the rest of his teaching. The ideas of a Judgement, of the elimination of evil from the world, and of a blessed immortality for those who are loyal to God in this life—these ideas are necessary corollaries to the central idea of the Kingdom. If the outline of the teaching set forth in the preceding chapters is even approximately correct, the premises are established from which the eschatological conclusions inevitably follow. The whole religion of Jesus centres round the twin conceptions of the heavenly Father and the heavenly King. If there is no final victory of good over evil, the Kingdom of God becomes an empty dream. If there is no inheritance for the saints in light, the Fatherhood of God is a vain delusion. 'If children, then heirs' implies logically 'if not heirs, then not children'. Whether the Final Consummation comes soon or late, suddenly or gradually, it is bound to come if the name 'Kingdom of God' corresponds to anything real: and unless the Spirit of adoption whereby we cry, 'Abba, Father' is a lying spirit, the faithful in the present age must have a share in its glory when it comes."

[1] I Cor. xv. 19.

Experience and faith force an eschatology. The nature of the God you believe in determines the kind of esch. — 3 possible eschatologies, 2 o/w are secular.

O.T. variety of views: Amos 'day of Lord', Isaiah I to mercy, Jer. individualizing; Ezekiel, nationalism; Isaiah II — Suffering Remnant.

Apocalypses — take their start with Ezekiel; stopped by facts force the 'Day' into future. Nationalistic again; conflict of good & evil,

Jesus: Son of Man is the Remnant — in Him & Dubious little Apocalypse. On Mt. 25 — ethical, universal, sent by God, Christ as Messiah Son of M. when? Jesus made a mistake here

Chapter IX

RELIGION AND MORALS

1. THE 'ETHICS OF JESUS'

THE main strength of Jesus lay in his ethical teaching. If we omitted the miracles and a few mystical sayings which tend to deify the Son of Man, and preserved only the moral precepts and parables, the Gospels would count as one of the most wonderful collections of ethical teaching in the world.[1]

This is the verdict of a distinguished Jewish scholar. The same writer also says that

Jesus is, for the Jewish nation, *a great teacher of morality and an artist in parable*.... In his ethical code there is a sublimity, distinctiveness and originality in form unparalleled in any other Hebrew ethical code.... If ever the day should come and this ethical code be stripped of its wrappings of miracle and mysticism, the Book of the Ethics of Jesus will be one of the choicest treasures in the literature of Israel for all time.[2]

These words doubtless reflect the opinion and the aspirations of many outside the Jewish fold. Many who are disgusted by ecclesiasticism, unmoved by ritual, and incredulous of dogma would gladly drop everything except the 'Ethics of the Sermon on the Mount'.

It is therefore the more necessary to lay down at the outset that the 'Ethics of Jesus', in the sense in which Dr Klausner speaks of them and many others think of them, do not exist and never have existed. Nor will such a book ever exist save by the process of tearing some of the moral aphorisms of Jesus out of their true context and fitting them into another and probably alien context. As we shall see in the sequel the moral teaching of Jesus is part and parcel of his religion and is not separable from it

[1] J. Klausner, *Jesus of Nazareth*, p. 381.
[2] *Op. cit.*, p. 414.

except by violence. The notion that we can wander at will through the teaching of Jesus as through a garden, plucking here and there an ethical flower to weave a chaplet for the adornment of our own philosophy of life, is an idea that is doomed to disappointment, for the nature of plucked flowers is to wither. The ethical maxims of Jesus, abstracted from the religion out of which they grow, become mere counsels of perfection which we may indeed respectfully admire, but which have no immediate reference to the affairs of our ordinary life.[1]

To divorce the moral teaching of Jesus from his teaching as a whole is thus to make it practically useless: it is also to make it theoretically unintelligible. For all the moral precepts of Jesus, in the last resort, flow from a single principle which is not itself moral but religious; and the understanding of any part of the ethical teaching demands a grasp of the whole religious context in which it has its place. In other words, the ideal picture of human life which Jesus draws in what he has to say about morals, is a picture of life in the Kingdom of God on earth, life as it may be lived by men who acknowledge one supreme loyalty, in whose hearts one supreme passion burns; and it is only as we hear the call to that loyalty and feel that passion that the moral teaching of Jesus grows luminous.

To say that in the teaching of Jesus morality is inseparably bound up with religion is simply to say that he stands in the direct line of succession to all the prophets and psalmists and sages of Israel. The idea of ethics as an independent discipline, which might be studied for its own sake independently of other disciplines, simply did not present itself to the Hebrew mind. We cannot divide the study of the prophetic literature into prophetic theology and

[1] This fact is recognised by Klausner. 'It is no ethical code for the nations and the social order of to-day' (p. 414). He does not, however, appear to perceive the contradiction involved in an ethical code being 'one of the most wonderful in the world' and at the same time without any message of practical value to the men and women who have to live in the world to-day.

prophetic ethics without making an artificial separation of
things which are in their inmost nature one.[1]

An interesting parallel to this may be found in a very
different sphere. The Golden Age of Greek philosophy
knows nothing of ethics as an independent discipline. The
connection there is not indeed with Greek religion, for
'by the time of Plato the traditional religion of the Greek
states was, if taken at its face value, a bankrupt concern'.[2]
The place which in Hebrew prophecy is occupied by
religion is taken in Greek philosophy by the idea of the
city-state. Thus it comes about that in the *Republic* the
answer to the question: What is justice? has to be sought by
enquiring what is the constitution of an ideal city. And
again, we find Aristotle apologising for appearing to
separate ethics from politics.[3]

It is quite wrong to say the Ethics studies the Good for Man
from the point of view of the individual, while the Politics deals
with the realisation of that good by the agency of the state. The
subject of both works is equally 'Politics', and there is not a
single word in either of them or anywhere else which could be
interpreted as setting up any such science as ἠθική in distinction
to πολιτική...The Ethics asks the question 'How is the Good
for Man realised?' and the answer it gives is that legislation is
the means of producing character, and that upon character
depends the possibility of that activity which constitutes
Happiness or the Good for Man. The Politics takes up the

---

[1] The mere use of the terms theology and ethics is apt to be misleading
when we apply them to the Old and New Testaments. For example, the
word theology can be literally translated by the Hebrew דעת אלהים but
there is a whole world of difference in meaning between the two terms. To
the modern mind theology is a department of knowledge, an orderly account
of what may be known about the Deity. To the Hebrew mind דעת אלהים is
the Rule of Faith and the Rule of Life—the whole Covenant of God—
written on the hearts of God's people (Jer. xxxi. 31–34). It is the true piety
(Hos. vi. 6). It goes along with mercy and truth (Hos. iv. 1). It is not the
occupation of a handful of scholars but a necessity of life for all. Without it
the people perish (Hos. iv. 6). The Hebrew term thus includes both faith and
morals—and more besides; but it is not what we mean by theology or
ethics or both together.

[2] Gilbert Murray, *Four Stages of Greek Religion*, p. 107.

[3] *Eth. Nic.* 1094 b.

inquiry at this point and discusses everything connected with legislation and the constitution of the state. The whole forms one πραγματεία or μέθοδος, and there is no word anywhere of ἠθική as a separate branch of study.[1]

This is to say that, while for the Hebrew prophet the achievement of man's highest good is inseparably bound up with true religion, for the great philosophers of Greece it is inseparably bound up with citizenship in an ideal city.[2] Both alike find man's highest good as something realisable only in a social order—the people of God or the ideal city. The point at which they differ is in their approach to the question: What is man's true life? Where the Greek philosopher counsels man: 'Know thyself', the Hebrew prophet, speaking in the name of Jehovah, says: 'Seek me that ye may live',[3] or 'Man shall not live by bread alone: but by every (word) that proceedeth out of the mouth of God shall man live'.[4]

Hence it comes about that the Hebrew Rule of Faith and Rule of Life are together embodied in the *torah,* which we usually render by the English word 'Law' though it is something very different from what we mean by law. *Torah* is properly the revealed will of God: a corpus of divine instructions to man. In three important respects it differs from what we call law.

(a) Its scope is far wider. It does not merely include what we take in under the heads of Civil, Criminal, and Canon Law. It covers also what we should put into doctrinal statements, prayer-book rubrics, text-books on public health and sanitation, and treatises on morality. In short it deals with the whole life of the Israelite from the cradle to the grave.

[1] Burnet, *The Ethics of Aristotle,* Introd. § 15. Cf. the whole section, §§ 13–19.
[2] It may be remarked in passing that much of the moral chaos of the present day would seem to be due to the attempt to maintain an ethical code which is a hotch-potch of Platonic, Aristotelian, Christian, and other less valuable maxims in a social order, which, whatever else it may be, is neither the ideal city of Plato and Aristotle nor the Christian 'City of God'.
[3] Am. v. 4, 6, with Driver's notes (*Camb. Bible, ad loc.*).
[4] Deut. viii. 3.

(b) The manner of its promulgation is different. Being a
God-given code it is oracular rather than statutory. It is
transmitted through the medium of God's representatives,
the priests or the prophets. The congregation of Israel is
not called in to ratify the decrees but only to accept them.

(c) It follows from the way in which the *torah* comes into
operation that its provisions are in their nature irreform-
able and incapable of repeal. The written codes embodied
in the Pentateuch might be added to—they themselves are
the product of a long process of development by successive
additions—but they could not be subtracted from. Not a
jot or a tittle could pass away from them. Thus it comes
about that in the Rabbinical schools, matters, such as the
Temple ritual, which had no longer any but an anti-
quarian interest were treated with the same serious
deliberation as matters of permanent religious and ethical
importance. They were all in the same divine corpus and
therefore it was not for man to say that one was worthy of
study and another not. Again, when the laws concerning
the Sabbath or the periodical remission of debts produced
inconveniences, which threatened to dislocate entirely
the social and economic life of the people, the remedy was
sought not by way of repealing the ordinances in question
but by way of legal fictions, the 'Erub¹ and the Prosbul.² In
this way the letter of the Law might be preserved while its
operation in practice was greatly softened, if not entirely
nullified.

These things are best understood when they are viewed
against the background supplied by the idea of the Kingdom of God. The Law in Jewish eyes was nothing less than
the revealed will of God as Israel's King. The Law is
perfect and unchangeable to all eternity because it is the

¹ *Mishnah*: '*Erubin.*
² *Mishnah*: *Shebi'ith* x. 3 ff. The *Prosbul* (פרוזבול) is ascribed to Hillel
(fl. c. 20 B.C.). The origin of the '*Erub* appears to be unknown. Talmudic
legend carries it back to Abraham (*Gen. R.* 49; b. *Yoma* 28 b) or Solomon
(b. '*Erubin* 21 b). The Mishnah, however, cites no authorities earlier than the
Schools of Hillel and Shammai.

work of the perfect and unchangeable Lawgiver. It is the proof that there is a King over Israel; as it is the charter of Israel's existence as God's people. The obedience of Israel to the Law is the chief mark of their loyalty to their heavenly King.[1]

The moral requirements embodied in the Law may therefore be regarded under three aspects.

(a) They are prescribed by God. By far the commonest description of the Law in the Old Testament is 'the Law of Jehovah' or 'the Law of Jehovah our God' or the like. The moral precepts are the revelation of the character of God and of the character which he demands in man. All is summed up in the words: 'Ye shall be holy as I am holy'.

(b) They are revealed through God's servants. So in the Old Testament we find frequent references to 'the Law of Moses', Moses being in Hebrew and Jewish eyes the typical agent of the divine revelations. In the work of making known the will of God, priests, prophets, and sages all have their part. In the days of Jesus the written *torah* was, and had been for long, a fixed corpus enjoying canonical dignity; but alongside the written Law was a great mass of oral traditions, many of them of great antiquity,[2] as well as a continually growing body of rules deduced by the Rabbis from the sacred text itself. And a properly authenticated oral tradition, or a deduction from the written Law properly arrived at, enjoyed an authority equal to that of the Pentateuch itself.[3] Rules for the exegesis of the written Law (*the Seven Middoth*) were in existence at least as early as the time of Hillel, that is, before the close of the first century B.C.

---

[1] See above, Chapter VII, § 4.

[2] Along with the written Law Moses was believed to have received other oral instructions which were handed down through the authorities listed in the Mishnah (*Aboth*, 1). Hence the phrase הלכה למשה מסיני became the technical term for any authoritative tradition whose origin was lost in the mists of antiquity (Strack, *Einleitung in Talmud u. Midras*, 5th ed., p. 7).

[3] Strack, *Einleitung*, p. 5; S.B. 1. 741–747, 909 f.; Schürer, *G.J.V.* 11. 381–384, 391–400.

(*c*) They are laid upon God's people as an unconditional obligation, as a distinctive mark whereby they are separated from all other people, and as a means whereby they may attain to their true blessedness.[1]

These things are fundamental to the Hebrew and Jewish view of moral obligation; and they are fundamental to the teaching of Jesus in general and to that part of it which we call ethical in particular. The moral demands which he makes are conceived throughout as proceeding from God through himself to the community of his disciples.

(*a*) The divine origin of the teaching is involved in the fact that the life of Jesus is one of unreserved obedience to God's will and that his teaching is the echo of his life. The maxim which governs his own conduct is: 'Thy will be done'; and the moral demands which he makes are those which he himself obeys, that is, they are what he himself sees to be the will of God. When Jesus says: 'Heaven and earth shall pass away; but my words shall not pass away', he is claiming for his teaching the same status and validity which is elsewhere claimed for the canonical Scriptures.[2] When he says, 'Behold my mother and my brethren; whoever does the will of God, the same is my brother and my sister and my mother',[3] he is referring to those who give ear to his own teaching and respond to its ethical and religious demands.

(*b*) The sense of being the agent of God's revelation of his will is the secret of the authority with which Jesus speaks. His 'I say unto you' is to be paralleled by the 'Thus saith the Lord' of the great prophets.[4] This authority was noticed by the people who heard him speak and the tone of his teaching struck them as being very different from that of the scribes. Here we have to do with a difference of method in dealing with moral problems. The scribal method of definitions of terms and deduction from

---

[1] Deut. xxviii.
[2] Mk. xiii. 31. Cf. Lk. xvi. 17; Mt. v. 18 (Q).
[3] Mk. iii. 34 f. Cf. Lk. vi. 46 (Q); Mt. vii. 21 (?M or Q).
[4] See above, pp. 207 f.

already established rules and decisions could not but compare unfavourably with Jesus' way of piercing by prophetic insight to the heart of any moral problem. In his method of dealing with moral questions as in his manner of delivering his decisions Jesus is akin to the prophets. A single example will make this clear. The question is that of the grounds of divorce.

Mal. ii. 13–16

And this again ye do: ye cover the altar of the Lord with tears, with weeping, and with sighing, insomuch that he regardeth not the offering any more, neither receiveth it with good will at your hand. Yet ye say, Wherefore? Because the Lord hath been witness between thee and the wife of thy youth, against whom thou hast dealt treacherously, though she is thy companion and the wife of thy covenant.... Let none deal treacherously against the wife of his youth. For I hate putting away, saith the Lord, the God of Israel....

Deut. xxiv. 1 f.

When a man taketh a wife, and marrieth her, then it shall be, if she find no favour in his eyes, because he hath found some unseemly thing[1] in her, that he shall write her a bill of divorcement and give it in her hand, and send her out of his house. And when she is departed out of his house she may go and be another man's wife.

Mk. x. 2–9[2]

And there came unto him Pharisees, and asked him a test question.[4] Is it lawful for a man to put away his wife? And he answered and said to them: What did Moses command you? And they said: Moses permitted to write a bill of divorcement, and to put her away. But Jesus said to them: For your hardness of

Mishnah Gittin IX 10[3]

The school of Shammai (first cent. A.D.) say: A man shall not put away his wife unless he have found in her something shameful;[5] for it is said (Deut. xxiv. 1) 'Because he hath found some unseemly thing in her'. The school of Hillel say: Even if she lets his food burn; for it is said (Deut. xxiv. 1): 'Because he hath

---

[1] עֶרְוַת דָּבָר.

[2] Cf. Lk. xvi. 18; Mt. v. 32.

[3] See S.B. i. 313 ff.

[4] πειράζοντες αὐτόν. (The verb is the same that is used in I Kings x. 1 to describe the questioning of Solomon by the Queen of Sheba.) On the whole incident cf. Burkitt, *Gospel History and its Transmission*, pp. 98 ff.

[5] דבר ערוה obtained by transposing the words of Deut. xxiv. 1 (ערות דבר), thus obtaining a sense like that of λόγος πορνείας (Mt. v. 32). The phrase in Mt. v. 32, which is almost certainly not part of the genuine teaching of Jesus, may perhaps have been derived from the exegesis of Deut. xxiv. 1 which was adopted by the school of Shammai. Cf. Abrahams, *Studies in Pharisaism and the Gospels*, i. 71.

heart he wrote you this commandment. But from the beginning of the creation, 'Male and female made he them' (Gen. i. 27). 'For this cause shall a man leave his father and mother, and the twain shall become one flesh' (Gen. ii. 24). So that they are no more twain but one flesh. What therefore God hath joined together let not man put asunder.

found some unseemly thing in her'. R. Akiba (martyred c. A.D. 135) says: Even if he finds another woman more beautiful than her, for it is said (Deut. xxiv. 1): 'It shall be if she find no favour in his eyes'.

It is clear that we have here two contrasted methods of approach to the question. The Rabbinical discussion is occupied entirely with the definition of the terms of the written law. Everything turns on the construction of such phrases as 'unseemly thing' and 'find favour'. The school of Shammai would restrict the meaning of 'unseemly thing' to acts of unchastity. The school of Hillel would give the term a wider connotation so as to cover any failure on the part of the wife in her domestic duties. The dictum of R. Akiba based on another part of the same text goes farther still. The method of Jesus, on the other hand, is analogous to that of the prophet Malachi. He brushes aside not merely the question of the meaning of Deut. xxiv. 1, but also the sacred text itself. The permission to divorce is a mere concession made by Moses. Jesus will make no concession. The real question is what was God's intention when he instituted marriage. In the eyes of Jesus it is a life-union whose claims are superior even to those of parents.[1] Malachi gives out bluntly the statement that God hates divorce. That is the negative side. Jesus gives the positive will of God in relation to marriage.

As the expositor of God's will Jesus thus occupies a position in the new community of his followers analogous to that held by Moses in Israel; and his way of life as shown by his example and his precepts becomes the norm for Christians. Hence Paul can speak of the Law of

[1] We can gather how highly Jesus estimated the claims of marriage on the husband and wife from the high standard of honour which he regarded as due to parents. The claims of marriage are higher still.

Christ[1] just as the Old Testament speaks of the Law of Moses.

(c) While the moral demands of Jesus, conceived as the requirements of God, are of universal application and validity, their primary application is to the community of those who accept the teaching as a whole, that is, of those who 'enter into the Kingdom of God' embracing its privileges and responsibilities, and attaching themselves as disciples to Jesus. Together they form a community—the Kingdom of God—which stands in contrast to the kingdoms of the world: and the contrast lies just in the difference of moral standard and behaviour. 'You know that thus and thus they behave among the Gentiles; but *it is not so among you.*'[2] To accept the moral standard of Jesus is to be not far from the Kingdom of God.[3] And, on the other hand the things which Jesus condemns as contrary to his way of life are not described as shameful or disgraceful but as hindrances to a man's entering the Kingdom.[4]

---

[1] Gal. vi. 2. The expression is by no means common. It occurs again in Barn. ii. 6; Ign. *ad Magn.* ii. For further references cf. J. Weiss, *ad* I Cor. ix. 21.

[2] Mk. x. 42–44. The Old Testament parallel to οὐχ οὕτως δέ ἐστιν ἐν ὑμῖν is to be found in II Sam. xiii. 12, 'It is not so done in Israel', for which the Lucianic MSS of the LXX have οὐκ ἔστιν οὕτως ἐν τῷ Ἰσραήλ. Cf. Gen. xx. 9; xxix. 26; xxxiv. 7. Just as the Chosen People had a moral standard by reference to which one might summarily reject certain acts as 'simply not done', so the followers of Jesus are to have a kind of unwritten law in the light of which certain acts will not even be entertained as possible.

On Mk. x. 42 ff. see Detached Note D at the end of this chapter.

[3] Mk. xii. 28–34.

[4] E.g. sins occasioned by the physical appetites or the natural tempers and inclinations of men: Mk. ix. 43–48. Entrance into the Kingdom in these verses is no doubt thought of as entrance into a state of future blessedness, but the sharing of that future bliss is conditional upon entrance into the Kingdom in the present. The things which exclude people from the joys to come do so by preventing them from entering the Kingdom in its present manifestation. This comes out clearly in the case of the rich young ruler (Mk. x. 17–31) who asks 'What must I do to inherit eternal life'—in the future. The final answer of Jesus is a command to sacrifice all, and join the company of disciples—in the present. When this demand is rejected the comment of Jesus is to the effect that wealth is a powerful hindrance to entering the Kingdom, where the reference is both to the present service and the future reward.

Similarly in the Pauline Epistles. The list of vices in Gal. v. 19 ff, leads up

The moral standard set up by Jesus is therefore to be conceived as given to the New Israel—the community of his followers—as the old Law was given to the Chosen People, to be the charter of their existence as a people of God.[H] Entrance into the Kingdom or discipleship—they come to much the same thing[1]—involves acceptance of the way of life which Jesus teaches and exemplifies.

In the result the moral teaching of Jesus appears not as an independent ethic—either 'interim' or any other sort—but as an integral part of his conception of the Kingdom of God. It is the way of the Kingdom, the way in which God's will may be done on earth as it is done in heaven, the way in which the subjects of the Heavenly King may show their loyalty to him through their obedience to his will.

2. JESUS AND THE JEWISH LAW.

The frequent conflicts between Jesus and the Scribes and Pharisees are really conflicts between the prophetic spirit and the legal, between two ways of approaching the problem of conduct. The broad distinction between these two attitudes is that the prophetic is concerned primarily with persons, the legal with acts.

The prophetic ideal is that right actions should be the spontaneous expression of a right disposition in man, the good fruit that grows on the good tree. Consequently the first essential is the radical transformation of the human heart; and, therefore, the prophetic call is at bottom a call to repentance, that is, to a complete change of a man's disposition towards God and his neighbour. Once this change is effected the man can be trusted to do the right thing, one might almost say, instinctively. All that he requires for his guidance is some simple rule like: 'Do justly and love mercy and walk humbly with thy God'.

to the statement that 'those who do such things shall not inherit the Kingdom of God'. Cf. I Cor. vi. 9 f.; Eph. v. 3 ff.

[1] See above, pp. 205 ff.

of two approaches
to child training too.

The legal method rests on the proposition that character is, in the long run, determined by conduct: and that if only a correct standard of conduct can be set up and enforced, men will be habituated to virtue. By the doing of good acts the character of the doer becomes good. The first essential therefore is an authoritative code of morals declaring what is the right course of conduct in any given circumstances: and as circumstances may vary indefinitely the tendency is for the code to become more and more complicated, until the determination of what is to be done, or not to be done, becomes the business of experts. The foundation of the Jewish code is the body of 613 precepts contained in the Pentateuch, together with a number of oral traditions of unknown antiquity believed to have been given to Moses at the same time as the written Law. The business of the lawyers was to construe these precepts, to define their terms, and to apply them to cases as might be necessary from time to time. For example the Law forbade the doing of work on the Sabbath. That seemed simple enough. But opinions might differ about the meaning of the term 'doing work'. The obvious way out of the difficulty, and the way which the Rabbis took, was to append a schedule to the statute in question specifying clearly and definitely what actions fell under the description 'work'. This schedule, containing a list of 39 sorts of work, is preserved in the Mishnah.[1] As time went on this list was still further elaborated, each of the 39 classes of action being further defined and subdivided.[2]

It is easy to dismiss all this learned activity with the contemptuous epithet 'pettifogging', just as it is easy to forget that an exactly similar process is going on continually in the law courts of any civilised country, and that matter and methods not so very unlike the Rabbinic may be found in Christian text-books of moral theology. It is, in fact, much easier to denounce the scribal system

---

[1] *Shabb.* VII. 2; cf. S.B. I. 615 ff.
[2] Details in S.B. *loc. cit.*

than to do without it: and so long as we entrust our
business to our lawyer and our chartered accountant, and
our conscience to our father-confessor, any criticisms we
may pass upon Jewish legalism will be perilously like the
rebukes which Satan administers to Sin.

It is therefore the more necessary to keep before our
minds what is the fundamental difference between Jesus
and the Jewish lawyers, and the key to all the differences
between them. It is that Jesus is primarily concerned with
the individual as a soul to be saved or lost. He sees men
standing at the cross-roads; and the concern of all concerns is whether they will take the way of life or the way of
destruction, whether they will give their whole allegiance
to God or not. In other words the programme of Jesus—if
one may so call it—is not in the first instance a plan of
social reform, but a call for a religious revival. The Law,
on the other hand, is not primarily concerned with the
individual, but with the community as a whole. Even
when the Rabbis are dealing with the case of a particular
person, the principles upon which they act and the conclusions to which they come are such as are applicable
throughout the society. Any changes which can be brought
about by legal means are changes in the Law and not
changes in the human heart. It may well be the case that
judicious legal and social reforms may have as their
result an improvement in the general standard of behaviour
in the community, just as a genuine religious conversion
will have results in the life of the person who experiences it.
But these results, though outwardly similar, are not the
same thing. A single example may suffice to make this
clear.

The law takes elaborate precautions, by means of oath,
cross-examination, and severe punishment of the crime of
perjury, to ensure that witnesses shall tell the truth. These
measures may be effective[1] and a witness may tell the truth,

[1] Recent judicial declarations would, however, suggest that they are not
nearly so effective as might be thought.

because he is impressed by the solemn nature of his oath, or because he is unable to deceive a skilful cross-examiner, or because he fears the punishment visited upon a perjured witness. The law starts with the assumption that the witness may have strong motives for lying, and proceeds to furnish stronger motives for telling the truth. With this we have to contrast what Jesus says on the subject of oaths and truth-telling:

> But I say unto you: swear not at all; neither by heaven, for it is the throne of God; nor by earth, for it is the footstool of his feet; nor by Jerusalem, for it is the city of the Great King. Neither shalt thou swear by thy head, for thou canst not make one hair white or black. But let your word be yea, yea, nay, nay. Anything beyond this is (the result) of the evil (in the world).[1]

This is far more than a mere demand for the abolition of oaths in the law courts or elsewhere. What Jesus envisages here is a state of affairs in which oaths, cross-examinations, and punishments for perjury are alike unnecessary, because a man's word is enough: because, in other words, he can be trusted to tell the truth. And he can be so trusted because he has been changed in himself, with the result that truthfulness has become more precious in his eyes than any seeming advantage that might be gained by falsehood.

We may set the man whom Jesus has in his mind's eye beside the man whom the law contemplates. To identical questions they may give identical answers, true answers in the sense that their statements conform to the facts. But there the resemblance ends. In regard to what takes place in their minds between the hearing of the question and the utterance of the reply, there may be, and probably will be, the widest difference. And this difference is the significant thing. The results are similar; but in the one case the speaking of the truth is the resultant of conflicting motives;

[1] Mt. v. 34-37 (M). Probably we should read as in Jas. v. 12: 'Let your "Yea" be yea, and your "Nay" be nay'.

in the other it is the spontaneous act of a transformed personality.

"The moral demands of Jesus presuppose a changed nature and disposition in man: they imply a previous con-version. The kind of goodness that Jesus expects is the fruit of a religious transformation, the shining of a light that has been kindled in the heart. It follows that, of all the ob-jections that can be urged against the moral teaching of Jesus, the objection that it is impracticable 'because you can't change human nature' is the most inept. Jesus was not so foolish as to imagine that moral demands such as his could be fulfilled without some radical change in men's dispositions, nor was he so devoid of faith in God and man as to despair of the possibility of such a change.

The fact that Jesus is chiefly concerned with the heart of man as the spring of conduct rather than with the Law as the regulative force in society is brought out quite clearly in the argument with the Scribes and Pharisees and sub-sequent discussion with the disciples, recorded in Mk. vii. 1–23. The question of eating without a preliminary washing of the hands is raised by the Scribes and Pharisees. This attack is met by Jesus with a counter-attack on the whole oral tradition[1] followed by the statement that it is not the things that come from outside, but the things that spring up within that defile a man. These things are described generally as 'evil thoughts' (οἱ διαλογισμοὶ οἱ κακοί). Evil conduct springs from an unregenerate heart just as evil fruit grows on a corrupt tree. And what holds of evil holds similarly of good. Both sides of the matter are expressed in the saying preserved in Q (Lk. vi. 45 = Mt. xii. 35):

The good man out of the good treasury of his heart produces
        good:
And the evil man out of evil produces evil;
For out of the fulness of the heart the mouth speaks.

    To anyone who held such a view as firmly as Jesus held it

On Mk. vii. 6–13 see further Detached Note E at end of this chapter.

the multiplication of rules of conduct, and even the observance of them, could only appear as the cleansing of the outside of the dish and the platter. And when, as happened often enough in Judaism—and often enough in the Church also—a punctilious regard for the *minutiae* of ritual and behaviour usurped the place that should be taken by the fruits of the spirit, mercy and faithfulness, there was only one name for that—hypocrisy.

The opposition between Jesus and the Scribes and Pharisees is thus a fundamental difference of principle. It is the opposition of two conceptions of virtue. For Jesus good living is the spontaneous activity of a transformed character; for the Scribes and Pharisees it is obedience to a discipline imposed from without. The Scribes and Pharisees rightly perceived that these two ideals were incompatible and that if the ideal of Jesus prevailed, it meant, not a reform of the Law, but the substitution of something else for it. They therefore opposed the new teaching with all their might, just as at a later date they opposed the Pauline restatement of it.[1] For Pharisaism the question whether the ideal of Jesus should win the allegiance of the people was a matter of life and death. The Scribes and Pharisees perceived, as Paul did later, that Christ would be the end of the Law. They saw that the teaching of Jesus meant revolution not reform in Judaism: and any measure, however drastic, that would avert such a calamity was justified in their eyes. Whatever may be thought of the priestly caste or the Roman governor, it can at least be said for the Scribes and Pharisees that, in their opposition to Jesus, and in whatever part they had in compassing his death, they at any rate were conscientious and acted in what they believed to be the highest interests of the Jewish people and the Jewish faith.

Once this basic difference between Jesus and the ex-

---

[1] For an exposition of the moral teaching of St Paul, which brings out its essential similarity to that of Jesus as sketched above, cf. C. Anderson Scott, *Christianity according to St Paul*, pp. 197–207.

ponents of the Jewish Law is grasped, the corollary
follows that it is a mistake to regard the ethical teaching of
Jesus as a 'New Law' in the sense of a reformed and
simplified exposition of the Old, or as a code of rules to
take the place of the code of Moses and his successors.
What Jesus offers in his ethical teaching is not a set of
rules of conduct, but a number of illustrations of the way in
which a transformed character will express itself in conduct. This distinction is clearly brought out in the discussion between Jesus and 'a certain lawyer' recorded in Lk. x.
25–37. The question of the interpretation of the commandment 'Thou shalt love thy neighbour as thyself' arises. The
lawyer desires a definition of 'neighbour'. Jesus replies
with the parable of the Good Samaritan: and by the time
the parable is finished, he has brought the matter round
from a discussion of the meaning of 'neighbour' to a
concrete example of 'neighbourliness'. The lawyer's
question is never answered. In place of a rule of conduct to
obey he is given a type of character to imitate. This is
typical of the method of Jesus in dealing with moral
questions. He refuses to legislate, because he is concerned
with the springs of conduct rather than with the outward
acts.

It is further to be observed that just as he declines to be
drawn into the academic discussion of legal terms, so in
practice he refuses to decide concrete cases. When he is
approached by one of the parties in a dispute about an
inheritance, he refuses to arbitrate. He does not, however,
stop there. He goes on to call everyone concerned to a
different way of approaching the question. He makes it
plain that were it not for the vice of covetousness, there
would be no dispute and, therefore, no need for an
arbitrator.[1]

Throughout it is clear that for Jesus all legal questions,
all questions of behaviour, all questions about the relations
of man to man, are questions of character, questions

---

[1] Lk. xii. 13–21 (L), 22–34 (Q).

Hence Xch: State separation is not a Chr. idea.

affecting, not merely the life and property, but the souls of the persons concerned; and therefore they are at bottom religious questions in the strictest sense, questions concerning the relation of the individual soul to God and to God's Kingdom and righteousness. The result is that whereas the Law becomes increasingly more elaborate and complicated by the continual promulgation of new decisions, so that in every new case that arises it is necessary for experts to review all the previous rulings which may have a bearing upon it; in the method of Jesus every case is brought back to be dealt with by the individual concerned in the light of one or two perfectly simple principles of a religious nature. Moral questions, that is all questions concerning man's life, are taken out of the jurisdiction of all other parties, including even Jesus himself, and brought before the bar of the conscience of the responsible person. He must decide for himself: and he must decide in the light of simple principles which any man can apply for himself if he accepts them. To these principles we now turn.

3. THE GROUND-PRINCIPLES OF THE MORAL TEACHING OF JESUS.

It has already been suggested that the moral standard set up by Jesus is a standard of example rather than precept. That standard is given in part by the parabolic teaching in such figures, for example, as that of the Good Samaritan; and in part by the life of Jesus himself. It is, however, possible to discover what are the governing principles lying behind these examples: and we have evidence in our records that Jesus had these principles clearly before his own mind. They are elicited in a discussion with one of the Scribes which has come down to us in two slightly different versions.[1] The Marcan account is to this effect.

Jesus is engaged in dispute with various parties, and the

---

[1] Mk. xii. 28–34; Lk. x. 25–28 (L).

aptness of his replies attracts the attention and admiration of one of the Scribes, who, apparently desiring to have the opinion of so wise a teacher on an interesting question, asks him: 'Which commandment is the first of all?' Jesus answers: 'The first is: Hear O Israel, the Lord our God is one Lord, and thou shalt love the Lord thy God with all thy heart and with all thy soul and with all thy mind and with all thy strength.[1] The second is this: Thou shalt love thy neighbour as thyself.[2] There is not another commandment greater than these'. The scribe receives this reply with enthusiasm: 'Well said, Master, you say truly that (God) is one and that there is not another beside him. And to love him with all the heart and with all the understanding and with all the strength, and to love one's neighbour as oneself, is more than all the burnt-offerings and sacrifices'. Jesus, in turn, appreciates the spirit shown in the scribe's response and closes the conversation with the remark: 'Thou art not far from the Kingdom of God'.

The question put by the Scribe was, we know, one that was raised from time to time in the Rabbinical schools, and one to which various answers were given by different authorities.[3] But it was as Haggadah, material for edification, that the question was raised and answered. The answers did not rank as legal decisions; they were not binding, as rules of faith or conduct. This or that Rabbi might give it as his opinion that a particular commandment was the most important of all but his opinion did not abate in the least degree the importance of every other commandment,[4] nor did it release him or anyone else from

---

[1] Deut. vi. 4 f.
[2] Lev. xix. 18.
[3] Details in S.B. 1. 900–908 especially p. 904 note *i*.
[4] A man's private opinion about the importance of any given commandment is not a criterion of the importance attached to it in heaven. Hence the saying of R. Judah ha Nasi: 'Be attentive to a light precept as to a grave, for thou knowest not the assigned reward of precepts' (*Aboth*, II. 1, ed. Taylor). This notwithstanding that the same authority declares that the commandment concerning the keeping of the Sabbath outweighs every other commandment (p. *Berachoth* 1, 3°, 14, cited S.B. 1. 905).

the absolute obligation to obey every other commandment[1]. The importance assigned to this or that commandment was entirely relative. It might mean logical priority, that all other commandments might be deduced from the selected one, or it might merely mean that the Rabbi concerned set great store by this commandment and took particular pleasure in obeying it.

With Jesus it is different. The priority which he assigns to the two great commandments is absolute. It is not that they are the general principle (כלל) from which all other precepts may be deduced; nor is it that they are commandments with a strong personal appeal to himself. They are the result neither of logical analysis of the *torah* nor of a process of selection by personal preference. They are commandments which actually take precedence of every other. For Jesus these two stand in a class by themselves. There is no other commandment that can come before them to claim man's obedience. They enjoy priority, not logical or relative, but absolute.[2]

The difference may be illustrated by a comparison. There is a well-known story which relates how a Gentile came to Hillel offering to become a proselyte on condition that Hillel should teach him the whole Law while he stood on

[1] This absolute obligation was relaxed in times of severe persecution when if a Jew were faced with the alternative 'transgress or be killed' he might transgress any commandment except those which forbid idolatry, the uncovering of nakedness, and the shedding of blood (b. *Sanhedrin* 74 a. Cf. the careful discussion by J. W. Hunkin in *J.T.S.* xxvii. 272–283).

[2] It is worth noting that this assertion of the absolute priority of the two great commandments has been softened down to an assertion of merely logical priority in Matthew. 'There is not another commandment greater than these' gives place to 'On these two commandments hangs the whole law, and the prophets'. By this change the whole mass of *torah* and tradition which has just been shown out at the front door is quietly brought in again at the back. This is just another indication that where the Law is in question Matthew is simply not to be trusted. How, for example, is it possible to reconcile Mt. v. 18 f. with our Lord's own treatment of the Mosaic law of divorce? He does not hesitate to brush aside the prescription of Deut. xxiv. 1 as a mere concession to human imperfection. The two statements Mt. v. 18 f. and Mk. x. 5–9 are incompatible; and it is not difficult to determine which of the two genuinely represents the mind of Jesus.

one foot. Hillel accepted his offer and said: 'What is
hateful to thee do not to anyone else; this is the whole Law
and the rest is commentary; go and study'.[1] In the Lucan
account (x. 25–28) of the discussion of Jesus with the
lawyer we are told that when the lawyer gave the two great
commandments as the teaching of the Law, Jesus answered:
'Thou hast answered right: this do, and thou shalt live'.
For Hillel the commentary is every whit as essential as the
Golden Rule. For Jesus the two commandments are in
themselves sufficient, without any supplement whatever, as
a complete guide to anyone who wishes to live.

It is important to notice that these two great commandments are as little 'legal' as it is possible for them to be.
They do not prescribe or forbid any particular action. They
apply entirely to the disposition which man is to have
towards God and his neighbour. Consequently they are not
enforceable. If they are to be fulfilled at all, it must be by
the willing obedience of man. A man can be compelled to
abstain from work on the Sabbath; but he cannot be
compelled to love God with all his heart. In other words,
if the secret of good life lies in these two precepts, it lies in a
change of heart, an inward transformation (μετάνοια), the
corollary to which is an outward reformation of behaviour. For Judaism good conduct is a part of religion;
for Jesus it is a product of religion.

The relation of the great commandments to one another
is a perfectly simple one. The first presupposes that man
has discovered God as his Father. The vision of the Lord
sitting upon his throne high and lifted up may inspire awe
and terror; the heavenly King may demand loyalty and
obedience; only the Father who cares for his children can
be loved in the way that is thought of here.

But the discovery of God as Father carries along with it
the discovery of neighbours as brethren. The experience of
God's love brings with it the knowledge that that love is for
all men. In the light of God's love to himself a man sees

_____
[1] b. *Shabb.* 31 a.

other men, as it were, through God's eyes: and to see them
in this way is to love them. The kind of love that is meant
here is not to be watered down to a mere general benevo-
lence. 'If I bestow all my goods to feed the poor...but
have not love, it profiteth me nothing'.[1] Nor is the commandment to be evaded by saying that we cannot control
our likes and dislikes. 'If a man say, I love God and hateth
his brother, he is a liar'.[2] The love of neighbours is something which overrides likes and dislikes. It is something
more than acts of kindness, for it is the root from which
they spring. It is a new relation towards men, created by a
new relation to God.

Jesus himself is the standing example of this attitude
towards God and man, which he demands from his
followers. It is no accident that he is called 'the friend of
publicans and sinners'—the lover of the unlovely and the
unlovable. His own ideal of divine love, which is the
pattern for human love, is portrayed for us in the father of
the prodigal and the elder brother: and we must remember
that neither the selfish libertine who went abroad nor the
cantankerous prig who stayed at home is an amiable type
of character. Nevertheless the father goes out to meet
them both: and as the father is, so must men be who
aspire to be his children.[3]

It might be objected that these two precepts are too
vague and indefinite to afford any practical guidance to
men in their behaviour to one another. It might be said
that the best of men with the highest motives and the best
intentions are still liable to make mistakes: and that even
those who love one another may wrong one another
through ignorance or faulty judgement or from some
other cause that might not have been effective, if there had
been some clear rule of conduct as a guide.

This objection is met by the provision of the precept
which is commonly known as the Golden Rule. Treat men

[1] I Cor. xiii. 3.   [2] I John iv. 20.
[3] Lk. vi. 27–36 (Q).

as you would wish them to treat you.[1] A good deal of ink
has been expended in discussing whether the Rule stated
thus in positive form is superior or not to the negative
form given by Hillel.[2] The discussion loses some, if not
most, of its interest when we remember that it is not a
fundamental principle of the moral teaching of Jesus, but
only a rule of thumb for the guidance of those who are
already presumed to have the root of the matter in them.
The relation between the two great commandments and
the Golden Rule is analogous to that between the two
great principles of Kant's moral theory. To the great
commandments corresponds Kant's famous declaration:
'Nothing in the whole world, or even outside of the world
can possibly be regarded as good without limitation
except a *good will*'.[3] To the Golden Rule corresponds what
Kant calls the 'Supreme Law of pure practical Reason':
'Act so that the maxims of your will may be in perfect
harmony with a universal system of laws'.[4] For Kant the
good will is the source and spring of morality: the Law of
practical Reason is a guide for action.

A similar distinction may be observed in early Judaism.
R. Jochanan ben Zakkai had five distinguished pupils.
'He said to them, Go and see which is the good way that a
man should cleave to. Rabbi Li'ezer said, A good eye;
R. Jehoshua' said, A good friend; and R. Jose said, A
good neighbour; and R. Shime'on said, He that foresees
what is to be; R. La'zar said, A good heart. He said to
them, I approve the words of Ele'azar ben 'Arak rather
than your words for his words include your words.'[5] The
difference between the ethic of Jesus and that of Judaism is
again simply this, that with Jesus the fact that the good
heart is fundamental is accepted and carried to its logical

[1] Lk. vi. 31; Mt. vii. 12 (Q). The Matthaean version of the Rule has the
characteristic Matthaean gloss: 'For this is the Law and the Prophets'.
[2] For instance in G. Friedlander's *The Jewish Sources of the Sermon on the
Mount*, Chapter XVII. For Hillel's form of the Rule see above, p. 305.
[3] *The Metaphysic of Ethics*, Sect. I.
[4] *The Critique of Practical Reason*, First Part, Bk. I. Ch. i. § 7.
[5] *Aboth*, II. 12 (ed. Taylor; p. 35).

conclusion while in Judaism the whole apparatus of Law and Tradition is still maintained beside the moral principle which renders it obsolete. The profound truth set forth by Ele'azar and endorsed by Jochanan b. Zakkai is treasured up as Haggadah, but the Halakhah goes on as before and maintains its supreme place as the norm of life.

4. SIN AND FORGIVENESS

The Westminster Assembly of Divines, in their Shorter Catechism, defined sin as 'any want of conformity to or transgression of the Law of God'. This definition is too narrow to cover the different ways in which Jesus regards sin. Moreover, if there is anything in the previous discussion, sin is not primarily a matter of omissions and commissions, but a condition of the soul, analogous to disease in the body. This analogy is implied in the saying: 'They that are whole have no need of a physician, but they that are sick: I came not to call the righteous, but sinners'[1]: and something similar lies behind the sayings concerning trees and fruit, the good and the evil man producing good and evil respectively out of the treasury of the heart, and the teaching about what defiles a man. Just as bodily pain, sickness, high temperature, and the like are not the disease itself, but only the signs or symptoms of it, so the follies and crimes of men are the signs and symptoms of the morbid condition of men's souls. This is the fundamental point and the explanation why, in the ministry of Jesus, so much stress is laid on repentance (μετάνοια, change of character) rather than on reformation of behaviour.[2] The attempt by rules and regulations to mend the manners of mankind is to treat symptoms instead of disease.

It is this inward wrongness which works mischievously both in the sphere of religion and in the sphere of morals: defiling a man, that is, rendering him unfit for communion with God; and giving rise to those outward acts which bring shame and disgrace upon himself and harm to his fellows.

[1] Mk. ii. 17. [2] Above, pp. 297 ff.

The way to cure this is not to treat the symptoms, but to study them and to discover the nature of the underlying cause in the heart. There is ample evidence that Jesus did consider the ways in which the infection of sin affects human life: and it is clear that he was led by these considerations to diagnose the central evil as something which we can express in one word—self-love. This self-love is the condition of the soul in which self and its desires occupy the place which should by right be taken by God and neighbour. From this single root spring all the follies and vices of mankind: self-assertion (ὑπερηφανία), self-seeking (πλεονεξίαι), self-indulgence of all kinds (πορνεῖαι, μοιχεῖαι, ἀσέλγεια), to name only a few from the list in Mk. vii. 21 f.

It comes to this, that if the essence of the law of life is: 'Thou shalt love God, and thou shalt love thy neighbour as thyself', the essence of the law of sin and death is: 'Thou shalt love thyself'—and these two are contrary.

Hence it is that the first step towards a new and better life is to deny oneself (ἀπαρνησάσθω ἑαυτόν)[1], that is, to transfer the love, which is concentrated on self, to its proper objects—God and neighbour. It is not simply an ascetic discipline that is contemplated here—Jesus was no ascetic—but a complete change and redirection of man's interest and care. Love is to be no longer a centripetal but a centrifugal force. This is the change of heart that is described as repentance (μετάνοια): and it is obviously something that goes far deeper than mere regret, however sincere, for particular acts of wrong-doing.

So long as this drastic change remains uneffected, the relation between man and God and between man and his neighbour is wrong, and in practice the evil consequences of this wrong relation may range from the omission to do good to the deliberate commission of evil. As between man

[1] Mk. viii. 34; Lk. xiv. 26 f.; Mt. x. 37 f. (Q); Lk. xvii. 33 (Q). The hard saying about 'hating' one's relatives is to be understood in the light of the fact that what passes for 'love' of relatives is often only a subtle form of self-love.

and man the bad results are sufficiently obvious. As between man and God they are described by Jesus in a number of important parables.

(a) The 'sinner' is hopelessly in debt. The insolvent debtor is the subject of two parables (Mt. xviii. 23–35: M; Lk. vii. 41–43: L). In both cases the emphasis is on the fact that, even with the best will in the world, the debtors cannot pay what they owe. In the parable of the Vineyard we have a different treatment of the same theme of debt; in this case the debtors refuse to pay (Mk. xii. 1–11). The 'debt' consists in the failure to produce the sort of character and life that God requires, the things that St Paul describes as 'the fruit of the Spirit'. Under another figure the same point is made in the parable of the Barren Fig Tree (Lk. xiii. 6–9: L).

(b) The 'sinner' is 'lost': that is, he is, as a result of his own character and mode of life, estranged from God. This is the theme of the kindred parables of the Lost Sheep, the Lost Coin, and the Prodigal Son. The prodigal both rejects the duties and loses the privileges of the father's house. Somewhat similar is the parable of the Great Feast, where absorption in their own selfish interests deprives the invited guests of their share in the feast.

The question as to forgiveness, so far as the teaching of Jesus is concerned, is thus the question what is to be done about this debt or this estrangement. And the answer of Jesus is perfectly simple. Let the debtor realise that he is bankrupt and throw himself on the mercy of God. God will cancel the debt.[1] Let the prodigal return to the duties of his father's house. The father will receive him with open arms and restore him to the privileges also.

Forgiveness is thus a free gift of God. It is, however,

[1] It may be observed that there is no suggestion of the debt being paid by a third party. It is simply cancelled. Whatever view we may take of the Atonement, it must be confessed that the notion of the payment of man's debts to God by Jesus is one which finds no support in the teaching of Jesus himself. That teaching is perfectly plain, and it is that the debts are not paid by anyone, but wiped out by God's free grace.

neither indiscriminate nor unconditional. In order to qualify for it at all the sinner must realise that he is a sinner. The debtor must realise that he is hopelessly insolvent. The prodigal must realise that he has forfeited his sonship. And that is simply to say that a man must realise that the principle of self-love is the root of all his evils, and, as a consequence of that realisation, turn in repentance from the love of self to the love of God and his neighbour.

It is at this point that we touch what is one of the most remarkable points in the teaching of Jesus, and one which deserves much more attention than it commonly receives. This is the principle which may be briefly put: He who would be forgiven must himself forgive.[1] This does not of course mean that a man may purchase God's forgiveness by forgiving his neighbour. It means that a forgiving spirit in man is an essential condition of his receiving God's forgiveness. In other words there are two ways open to man: the way of estrangement from God and neighbour, the way of self-love; and the way of reconciliation, the way of love toward God and neighbour. The change-over from the one way to the other is what we call repentance; and this change-over is the essential condition of reconciliation or forgiveness. But the change must be complete in order to be genuine. It must be a change from self-love to love of God *and* neighbour; and the man who cherishes an unforgiving spirit against his neighbour proclaims by that the fact that his own repentance is not genuine, and that he is therefore himself unforgivable, unfit to receive God's forgiveness. The matter is put plainly in a few words in the First Epistle of John: 'we know that we have passed from death to life because we love the brethren'.

Always we are brought back to the same fundamental

---

[1] This principle is stated in Mk. xi. 25, Mt. vi. 14 f. (M); in the petition for forgiveness in the Lord's Prayer; and in the parable of the Unmerciful Steward, Mt. xviii. 23–35 (M). The idea was not a novelty. Cf. Ecclus. xxviii. 3–5.

principles: love to God and love to man. The moral ideal for Christians lies not in a code, nor in a social order. It lies in a life where love to God and man is the spring of every thought and word and action: and for Christians the sum of all morality is to have the same mind which was also in Christ Jesus.

DETACHED NOTE D.

Mk. x. 42–44

The meaning of this passage is obscured for us by the translations commonly given of the phrase οἱ δοκοῦντες ἄρχειν. The Vulgate gives 'hi qui uidentur principari': and this is the sense which is given to the Greek by Tyndale: 'they whych seme to beare rule'. The Authorised Version has: 'they which are accounted to rule' with the marginal alternative, 'they which think good to rule'. The Revised Version follows the Authorised with the exception that the second rendering is dropped. Dr Moffatt writes: 'the so-called rulers'. The modern German versions are to much the same effect. 'Die, welche für Fürsten der Völker gelten' (Wellhausen, *Ev. Marci*, 1903; *H.B.N.T.* 1919); 'Die, welche die Völker zu regieren scheinen' (*S.N.T.³*).

The objections to this way of translating the Greek are:[1]

(1) That it makes δοκοῦντες mean something which is quite pointless, not to say false. The kings and emperors in the first century A.D. did not *seem* to rule. They *did* rule, and usually with a heavy hand. No one who lived under the sway of Tiberius would have found anything illusory about his power.

(2) It throws the emphasis on to the question what the rulers of the Gentiles do with their power. That they exercised their authority in a despotic manner is no doubt true; but that fact has little or nothing to do with the matter which is under discussion in this passage.

(3) It destroys the contrast (antithetic parallelism) between *v.* 42 and *vv.* 43 f. The latter verses are concerned with the question how greatness and authority in the new community are to be *achieved*. The current translations of *v.* 42 make that verse deal with the manner in which greatness and authority among the Gentiles are *used* after they have been achieved.

In order to obtain a satisfactory translation it is necessary to take account of two factors: the circumstances in which the words were spoken, and the necessity of preserving the parallelism between *v.* 42 and *vv.* 43 f.

The circumstances are that two of the disciples, James and John, came to Jesus with a request that he would grant them

---

[1] These criticisms do not apply to A.V. margin.

whatever they should ask. Jesus refused to sign the blank cheque which they presented, and demanded what it was that they wanted. It then transpired that they desired the chief places in the coming Messianic Kingdom. Jesus reminds them that the immediate future contains not a throne of glory but a cup of suffering and asks if they are as ready to share the latter as they are to share the former. They answer 'Yes', and are then told that they will certainly share in the cup and the baptism, but that the assignment of the chief places is in God's hands alone.

So far two things are clear. The sons of Zebedee are set on getting the highest honours and the greatest authority possible in the coming Kingdom for themselves. And in order to attain their ambition they do not scruple to hoodwink their Master and to go behind the backs of their comrades.

This shabby trick naturally arouses the resentment of the rest of the disciples: and Jesus takes the opportunity to read them all a lecture on ambition and the ways men take to achieve their ambitions. He contrasts the way to greatness in the kingdoms of the world with the way to greatness in the Kingdom of God: and the implication is that the spirit displayed by all the disciples, but most flagrantly by James and John, savours not the things that be of God, but the things that be of man.

The cogency of this argument clearly depends on the force of the contrast between the way of the world and the way of the Kingdom of God: and this demands that οἱ δοκοῦντες ἄρχειν τῶν ἐθνῶν should be construed in a sense similar to that of ὃς ἂν θέλῃ μέγας γενέσθαι ἐν ὑμῖν. That is, the meaning required by the context for οἱ δοκοῦντες ἄρχειν is something like 'Those who aspire to rule': and this meaning the words may very well bear.

The sense of δοκοῦντες here has thus nothing in common with that in Gal. ii. 2, 6, 9[1]; but is akin rather to that in Mt. iii. 9. Closer parallels to this use of δοκεῖν in the sense of 'wish' or 'hope' may be quoted from outside the N.T. For example:

(a) From the classical period:

Aeschylus, *Agam.* 16: ὅταν δ' ἀείδειν ἢ μινύρεσθαι δοκῶ....

---

[1] In Gal. ii. 2, 6, 9 δοκοῦντες has reference to what was in the minds of other people concerning the leaders. In Mk. x. 42 as in Mt. iii. 9 it has reference to what the persons concerned think about themselves and their proper destiny or their origin.

Aristophanes, *Vesp.* 177: ἀλλ' εἰσιών μοι τὸν ὄνον ἐξάγειν δοκῶ....
    Idem, Eccles. 170: αὐτὴ γὰρ ὑμῶν γ' ἔνεκά μοι λέξειν δοκῶ.

(*b*) From the Papyri:

ὑπόμνημα ἀφ' οὗ ἔδοξεν δυνήσασθαι ἐμποδισθῆναί μου τὴν πρᾶξιν.[1]
A memorandum by means of which he hoped that my execution
might be prevented.

καὶ δο[κο]ῦσα ν[ῦ]γ [γ]ε σοῦ παραγενομένου τεύξεσθαί τινος ἀναψυχῆς.[2]
And expecting that now at last on your return I should obtain some
relief.

In view of these considerations we may translate our passage as *Mk 10 42-44*
follows:

You know that those who aspire to rule over the Gentiles subjugate
them[3] and the greatest of them (*sc. τῶν ἀρχόντων*) rule them des-
potically. Not so is it among you.
    But whoever wishes to become greatest among you shall be your
servant. And whoever wishes to attain the primacy among you shall
be the slave of all.

There was no lack of examples in the days of Jesus of men
who found the sword the readiest instrument to cut a pathway
to the throne, and to close it against rivals once the hazardous
journey was accomplished. And it requires no supernatural
insight to perceive in the request of James and John the same
spirit that prompted all the palace intrigues, the plots and
counterplots, that fill the pages of ancient history. In opposition
to this pagan spirit and the pagan way of winning honour and
power, Jesus sets up his own ideal, an ideal which would leave
no room in the community of his disciples either for the diplo-
matic overtures of the sons of Zebedee or for the jealous
resentment of the Ten.

DETACHED NOTE E.

Mk. vii. 6–13

The severe strictures passed by Jesus on the Scribes and
Pharisees in these verses have, not unnaturally, roused Jewish
scholars to defend the Rabbinical tradition and Christian

---

[1] P. Oxy. VII. 1027⁹ (first century A.D.) quoted by Moulton and Milligan,
Vocab. s.v. δοκέω.
[2] P. Lond. (I), 42¹⁸ (second cent. B.C.), ed. Witkowski, *Epp. Privatae Graecae*,
p. 63.
[3] Cf. LXX. Gen. i. 28; Num. xxxii. 22, 29 (Heb. כבשׁ); Ecclus. xvii. 4;
Acts xix. 16.

scholars to support the attacks made by Jesus. Consequently much has been written and said in a partisan spirit, without a proper regard for the realities of the case.

A vow may be defined as:

> A voluntary obligation solemnly assumed towards God to do something not otherwise required, but believed to be acceptable or influential with him. The promise may be either simple or conditional.... Vows of the latter kind were in ancient religions the common accompaniment of prayer and were believed to contribute greatly to its efficacy.... The vow being a solemn promise freely made, was a most binding obligation.... Even a rash vow or one which entailed unforeseen and terrible consequences, like Jephthah's (Judg. xi), must be fulfilled to the letter.... It is no sin not to make a vow, but being voluntarily made it must be fulfilled.[1]

The Pentateuchal laws in Num. xxx and Lev. xxvii. 1–29 deal with details. The former passage determines who can make a binding vow, the latter deals with the conditions under which persons or property vowed to God may be redeemed. These two passages do not, however, affect the main point, which is that the making of vows is not a religious obligation, but the fulfilment of a vow validly made is. This is the position as it is left by the written Law.

The problem with which the Scribes, as interpreters of the Law, had to deal was therefore: What constitutes a valid vow? The answers to this question are contained in the Mishnah tractate *Nedarim* and in later legal compilations. The result is that the definition given above is no longer wide enough to comprehend all the declarations which rank as vows in the Mishnah. It is not in dispute, for example, that the case adduced by Jesus would be considered a binding vow, although it is admitted that none of the goods upon which a *Korban* was placed would actually be given to God. As Dr Montefiore puts it,[2]

> 'Corban' does not mean that the property was dedicated to the use of the Temple. The word is used as a mere oath. When I say 'Corban, if you shall ever eat anything that is mine', this does not mean that my eatables are dedicated to the use of the Temple, in which case neither I nor you might eat them, but merely that, so far as you are concerned, they are 'dedicated'; you may never eat what is mine. I should sin in letting you eat any of my food so long as the vow stands, and you, if you ate, would sin also. The Temple does not come in.

[1] G. F. Moore, *Ency. Bib.* cols. 5252 f.
[2] *The Synoptic Gospels* (1st ed.), I. 164.

Now it may fairly be claimed that a vow of this sort is something very different from the kind of vow that is contemplated in the Old Testament. And the difference lies in the fact that 'the Temple does not come in'. In other words nothing at all is dedicated to God and nothing is given. The *Korban* is simply a legal fiction. A man goes through the formality of vowing something to God, not that he may give it to God, but in order to prevent some other person from having it. That such a transaction was allowed to rank as a valid vow and to share the inviolability possessed by vows in the strict and proper sense was the work of 'tradition'.

It is clear that this legal device could, in the hands of unscrupulous persons, lend itself to all kinds of abuses: and it is one of these possible abuses that is adduced by Jesus in the passage before us. Here a son is represented as making *Korban* everything of his by which his parents might be benefited. The question at once arises: If this is a valid vow, what becomes of the honour due to parents? The case from the side of Jesus might be put in this fashion. There is a positive command of God that children should honour their parents. There is no positive commandment to make vows, but only that if made they must be kept. It is only by the tradition that this travesty of a vow is allowed to rank as a valid vow. The Scribes are therefore responsible, as guardians of the traditional law, for allowing the state of affairs to exist in which the positive commandment to honour parents can be made of no effect by an easy legal device with no safeguards to prevent its abuse.

The situation having arisen, the next question is what the legal authorities are to do about it. According to Jesus they do not permit (οὐκ ἀφίετε) him to do anything further for his parents. This is not to be taken to mean that the Scribes were careless about the honour due to parents—the contrary is the case—but that, speaking as responsible lawyers, they were bound to say that the law did not permit the son to do anything for his parents so long as the vow stood. The only way out of the impossible situation was, therefore, the annulment of the vow. What provision did the Rabbinical system make for the annulment of a vow by which a man bound himself to do what was obviously wrong or to neglect what was an obvious duty?

It appears from the Mishnah (*Nedarim* ix. 1) that this question was engaging the attention of the Rabbis as early as the time of R. Eliezer (c. A.D. 90) and R. Zadok (prob. c.

A.D. 60) if not earlier. The decisions recorded are that if a vow made by a son affected adversely only the credit and reputation of his parents, it must stand; if, however, it caused them material damage, it could be annulled. That is to say, a son who had, say in a fit of temper, made such a vow as is described by Jesus, and subsequently repented of it, might go to the proper authorities and ask to have his vow annulled. If they were satisfied that the keeping of the vow would cause material loss or damage to the parents, they could and would grant the application. If, however, the son remained obstinate, it does not appear that there was anything that could be done. Unless the undutiful son himself came to a better frame of mind, the Law was powerless to help the parents.

This is not the view of Dr J. Klausner. Dealing with this passage from Mark he says:[1]

Of interest as explaining Jesus' argument is the following Mishnah: 'He saw them (certain men) eating figs, and said: it is *Korban* for you (i.e. his father and brother and certain others). The School of Shammai say, They (the father and brother) were permitted, but not the others: the School of Hillel say, All were permitted'. Hence the father and brother (and, therefore, of course, the mother) were not included within the scope of the '*Korban*' oath even according to the stricter interpretations of the Shammai School.

Dr Klausner's argument rests on a complete misunderstanding of the Mishnah in question (*Nedarim* iii. 2). The third chapter of the tractate begins by specifying four classes of vows which the Rabbis hold to be invalid. These are (a) vows uttered while bargaining (נדרי זרוזין), (b) vows in confirmation of an obviously exaggerated statement (נדרי הבאי), (c) vows made under a misapprehension (נדרי שגגות), and (d) vows which turn out to be impossible of fulfilment owing to pressure of other circumstances (נדרי אונסים). The Mishnah then goes on to give typical examples of each class: and the case cited by Dr Klausner is given as an example of class (c). It runs as follows:

A man sees certain people eating figs and says: 'Lo they are *Korban* for you'. It turns out that the people are his own father and brother accompanied by certain others. The School of Shammai say: 'They (the father and brother) are permitted (to eat), but those who are with them are forbidden'. The School of Hillel say: 'Both parties are permitted'.

[1] *Jesus of Nazareth* (trans. H. Danby, 1925), pp. 289 f.

The whole point of the example is that the son did not know the identity of the persons when he made the vow: and it is assumed that, had he known who they were, he would not have acted as he did. The stricter School of Shammai take it that he would at least have excepted his own kindred from the operation of the *Korban*; the less exacting School of Hillel assume that he would not have made the vow at all.[1] In any case the exemption given to the father and brother by both Schools rests on the fact that the vow is invalid because it was made under a misapprehension. There is no question here of annulling a valid vow on account of the honour due to parents.

[1] According to Strack-Billerbeck (1. 713) the School of Hillel in permitting all act on the principle that if a vow is cancelled in part, it is cancelled altogether.

APPENDIX I

Words and phrases characteristic of those sections
of the teaching addressed to the disciples (D).

ἀγρυπνέω, Mk. xiii. 33. (Cf. γρηγορέω.)

αἰτέω, of requests from man or prayer to God.

ἀνίστημι, of the Resurrection of the Son of Man. All cases fall
after P.C.

ἀνοίγω, all after P.C. Q passages only.

ἀπαρνέομαι, all after P.C. (Cf. ἀρνέομαι.)

ἀποκαλύπτω, Q and M.

ἀπόλλυμι ψυχήν, Mk and Q.

ἀρνέομαι.

βαλλάντιον. Luke only (x. 4; xii. 33; xxii. 35, 36).

βλέπω, in the following special senses:

(a) = beware. Mark only (viii. 15; xii. 38; xiii. 5, 9).

(b) Where the word contains the idea of seeing below the
surface of things or having insight. (Mk. iv. 24; viii. 18;
cf. Mt. xiii. 13 = Lk. viii. 10.) These cases are all D and all
before P.C. The demand in the first part of the ministry is
for insight and understanding.

(c) Where the reference is to keeping watch for something
specially important (Mk. xiii. 23, 33).

γινώσκω, in those cases where the verb connotes knowledge of
the inner meaning of things, secrets, in short all that may be
comprised under τὸ μυστήριον τῆς βασιλείας τοῦ θεοῦ
(Mk. iv. 13; Mt. x. 26 = Lk. xii. 2; Lk. x. 22).

γρηγορέω, Mk. and Q. All after P.C.

δέω = Rabb. אסר. Mt. xvi. 19; xviii. 18 (M).

διακονέω ⎱
διάκονος ⎰ All after P.C.

δίδωμι, in cases where heavenly gifts are the object of the verb.

δόξα, in all cases where the word has reference to the glory of
God or of the Son of Man. All after P.C.

δοῦλος, in all cases where the responsibilities of servants to their
master or to one another are in question.

ἐγείρω, of the Resurrection of the Son of Man. (Cf. ἀνίστημι.)
All after P.C.

ἔθνος, all cases are late in the ministry except Mt. x. 5, 18.

εἰσέρχομαι, into the Kingdom, Life, or the like. See the discussion in Chapter v.

ἐκκλησία. Thrice in Matthew (xvi. 18; xviii. 17 bis). All M.

ἔνεκα (-εν). See p. 203.

ἐξουσία, in those cases where it means 'power'; where the meaning is 'authority' it is P.

ἐργάτης, in a good sense. Q and M.

ἔσχατος, in contrast with πρῶτος. All after P.C.

εὑρίσκω τὴν ψυχήν; Matthew only.

ζωή, where αἰώνιος is expressed or understood or where ζωή is equivalent to ἡ βασιλεία τοῦ θεοῦ. All after P.C.

θησαυρός, of a treasure to be obtained at all costs.

θλίψις

θύρα

καλόν ἐστιν, Mark only. All after P.C.

κατανοέω, Q only.

καταφρονέω, Q, M.

κερδαίνω, all after P.C.

κλέπτης, Q only.

κληρονομέω, M only.

κρούω, Q only.

λύω = Rabb. התיר. M only (Mt. xvi. 19; xviii. 18).

μαμωνᾶς, all after P.C.

μέριμνα

μεριμνάω

μικρός, in the phrase 'one of these little ones'.

νοέω, cf. συνίημι.

νομίζω, Matthew only.

ξένος, Matthew only.

οἰκιακός, Matthew only.

οἰκονομέω (-ία, -ος), Luke only.

ὁμολογέω, Q only.

ὄνομα, in the phrase 'in my name'.

οὔπω

οὐράνιος, Matthew only, in the phrase ὁ πατὴρ...ὁ οὐράνιος.

παραδίδωμι, in those cases where the object of the verb is the Son of Man or Jesus or the disciples. These cases fall after P.C. except Matthew x. 17 which is probably out of place. Cf. Mark xiii. 9. This use of the verb is not found in Q.

παρουσία, Matthew only; in Q passages. All very late in the ministry.

πάσχω, of the suffering of the Son of Man or the Messiah or Jesus. All after P.C.

πατήρ, as a designation of God. This word is fully discussed above, Chapter IV.

περιζώννυμαι, Luke only.

πήρα

πίνω, of a cup of suffering, or of the Messianic banquet.

πίστιν ἔχειν is always D as are also ὀλιγοπιστία and ὀλιγό-πιστος.

πιστός, all after P.C. All cases are Q or L.

πόσῳ μᾶλλον, Q and M only. Rabb. קל וחומר. Cf. p. 74.

ποτήριον, in all cases where it means suffering or sacrifice. All such cases belong to the period after the journey to Jerusalem has begun. Cf. πίνω.

ποτίζω, where Jesus or the disciples are object of the verb. All after P.C.

προσέχω, not in Mark which has instead βλέπω (q.v.).

πρῶτος, see ἔσχατος above.

πύλη, cf. θύρα above. πύλη is found in Matthew only.

πῦρ. It will be convenient to give the examples of this word in full. They are:

Mark. ix. 43, 48, 49. (All D.)

Q. Mt. iii. 10 = Lk. iii. 9; Mt. iii. 11 = Lk. iii. 16; Mt. iii. 12 = Lk. iii. 17—all in sayings of John the Baptist. Lk. xii. 49; xvii. 29. (Both D.)

M. Mt. v. 22; vii. 19. (Sermon on the Mount.) Mt. xiii. 40, 42, 50; xxv. 41. (All D.) (Mt. xviii. 9 is a case of editorial alteration.)

It is noteworthy that the numerous instances of the use of the word in Matthew, where πῦρ signifies final destruction, find their natural parallel, not in other recorded utterances of Jesus, but in the teaching of John the Baptist. We may compare Mt. vii. 19 with Mt. iii. 10 = Lk. iii. 9; and Mt. xiii. 40, 42, 50; xxv. 41 with Mt. iii. 12 = Lk. iii. 17. It is curious that these pieces of teaching attributed to Jesus which tally most closely with the threats of John are all derived from M.

σκανδαλίζω. Mark has six examples all D. Of the five cases in Matthew, two are in the Sermon on the Mount (v. 29, 30) and are a doublet of Mk. ix. 42 f. (D). Mt. xi. 6 = Lk. vii. 23 is in a G context; but is probably addressed to the disciples of Jesus. The two remaining cases in Matthew are D.

σκάνδαλον, all D. Not in Mark.

συμφέρω, Matthew only. This word is the Matthaean equivalent for Mark's καλόν ἐστιν (q.v.)

συναίρω λόγον, Matthew only.

σύνδουλος, Matthew only.

συντέλεια (τοῦ) αἰῶνος, peculiar to M.

τάλαντον, Matthew only. All cases are D and after P.C.

ταμεῖον

τέλος, of the Final Consummation. All after P.C.

ὁ υἱὸς τοῦ ἀνθρώπου, see Chapter VII, § 7.

φοβέομαι, thirteen cases, of which all but Mk. v. 36 are D.

φρόνιμος (-ως) not in Mark.

ψευδοπροφήτης

ψευδόχριστος

ὥρα, all cases subsequent to P.C.

APPENDIX II

Words and phrases characteristic of those sections of the teaching addressed to the general public (G).

(Words common to the public teaching of John the Baptist and that of Jesus are marked with an asterisk.)

ἀνατέλλω

ἀποθήκη,* cf. Mt. iii. 12 = Lk. iii. 17 with Mt. xiii. 30 (M), and Appendix I, s.v. πῦρ.

ἐγγίζω,* in the phrase ἤγγικεν ἡ βασιλεία τοῦ θεοῦ. Cf. Appendix I, s.v. εἰσέρχομαι.

εἰρήνη, in the phrase ὕπαγε (πορεύου) εἰς εἰρήνην. All before P.C.

ἐκκόπτω,* of the unfruitful tree. Cf. Mt. iii. 10 = Lk. iii. 9 with Mt. vii. 19 (M).

εὔθετος

ζυγός

θυγάτηρ, in vocative.

κατακαίω,* cf. Mt. iii. 12 = Lk. iii. 17 with Mt. xiii. 30, 40 (M).

κοράσιον

κούμ (קום Cf. Dalman, Gramm.[2] p. 321 n. 1).

κυνάριον

ὅμοιος, introducing a parable. The adjective is peculiar to Q and M.

ὁμοιόω occurs once in Mark (iv. 30). Otherwise it is found only in Q and M.

For these two words there are a number of exceptions. Four cases are D and one P. Enough however remain to show the general nature of the use of the word—in public discourse. Parabolic teaching is, as a rule, exoteric in accordance with the dictum Mk. iv. 11.

οὖς, in the expression 'He that hath ears...let him hear'. The cases are: Mk. iv. 9, 23; [?vii. 16]; viii. 18 (all G except viii. 18); Mt. xi. 15 (G); xiii. 43 (D); Lk. xiv. 35 (G).

πίστις, in the expression 'Thy faith-hath saved thee'.

σῖτος,* in metaphorical sense. Cf. Mt. iii. 12 = Lk. iii. 17 with Mt. xiii. 25, 29, 30 (M).

σκοτεινός

σκότος, of the soul. Lk. xi. 35 = Mt. vi. 23.

σώζειν, of the cure of disease.

ταλειθά (טְלִיתָא).

APPENDIX III

Words and phrases characteristic of those sections of the teaching where Jesus is engaged in disputes with the Jewish religious authorities (P).

(New-Hebrew or Aramaic equivalents are given for technical terms.)

ἀκυρόω (בְּטֵל, הֶעֱבִיר or הִפְסִיק. Cf. Soṭa ix. 9, 10; S.B. i. 717).

ἁμαρτωλός in contrast with δίκαιος.

This contrast is one which first becomes prominent in the later books of the O.T. It is most frequent in the Psalter, where I have noted about a score of examples. It is also found once or twice in Prov., and in Ezek. xxxiii. In the LXX the two words normally represent the Hebrew רָשָׁע and צַדִּיק, which in the Targum are rendered by רַשִּׁיעָא (more rarely חַיָּיבָא) and צַדִּיקָא (more rarely זַכָּאָה). The contrast recurs in the Psalms of Solomon in Pss. iii. 13 f.; iv. 9; xiii. 5–7; xiv. 4 ff.; xv. 7 ff.

In Hebrew usage the contrast between רָשָׁע and צַדִּיק is:

(1) between Israel and foreign oppressors, e.g. Pss. cxxv. 3; cxxix. 4; or

(2) between Pharisees and Sadducees, e.g. in the Psalms of Solomon (Ryle and James, *Introduction*, pp. xlvi–lii); or

(3) the moral distinction between the good man and the bad, e.g. Ps. xxxii. 10 f.; xxxiv. 22; Ezek. xxxiii. 11 f., 18 f.

In all these cases it is the *torah* which is the decisive factor as (1) Israel's peculiar possession, or (2) the special possession of the Pharisees, or (3) simply the criterion of morality. So the צַדִּיקִים are the possessors of the Law, who cherish and study it and live by its ordinances; the רְשָׁעִים are those who fail in one or other of these particulars—Gentiles who have it not (cf. Gal. ii. 15), Sadducees who reject it in its fuller oral development, or simply the עַם הָאָרֶץ who cannot or will not observe it in all its details (cf. Duhm, *K.H.C.*, *Die Psalmen*[1], pp. 1, 4; S.B. 1. 50).

ἀναγινώσκω (קְרָא): the only exception is Mk. xiii. 14 (D) which is probably a marginal gloss.

ἀναίτιος (פְּטוּר—so Oesterley, *Tractate Shabbath*, p. xx; or זַכָּאי—Tg. for נקי has (דם זכי דם).

ἀνάστασις, of the Resurrection in general.

ἀνίστημι (*a*) of the Resurrection in general. (Cf. ἐγείρω.)

(*b*) ἀνίστημι ἐν τῇ κρίσει (Rabb. עָמַד בַּדִּין: *Sanh*. x. 3).
The expression goes back to the O.T. (Ps. i. 5; Is. liv. 17).

The reference of κρίσις is to the Final Judgement.

ἀποδεκατεύω (–όω) (N.H. עִשֵּׂר, *Shabb*. 11. 7; Aram. עַשֵּׂר, *Tg. Deut*. xiv. 22).

βαρύς, Matthew only. (יַקִּירָא, יַקִּיר, which has the two meanings 'heavy' and 'important'.) Mt. xxiii. 4; Lk. xi. 46 (δυσβάστακτα); cf. Ps. xxxviii. 5, מַשָּׂא כָבֵד; Tg. יקיר ממול; LXX φορτίον βαρύ. Mt. xxiii. 23; Lk. xi. 42, with which cf. *Aboth*, iv. 5 (ed. Taylor), בן עזאי אומר הוי רץ למצוה קלה.

διδάσκω: all cases are P except Lk. xii. 12 = Mt. x. 20 (D).

δοῦλος, where it is used of God's messengers inviting men or making demands upon them.

ἐγείρω, (a) in references to the General Resurrection;

(b) ἐγείρω ἐν τῇ κρίσει: cf. ἀνίστημι above.

ἐκδίδωμι

ἐντολή, all cases except Mk. x. 19 and parallels (G).

ἔξεστιν (Rabb. מֻתָּר).

ἐξουσία (Rabb. רְשׁוּת, רְשׁוּת; Aram. רְשׁוּתָא). Where the word means 'authority' the context is P. Where it means 'power', the context is D.

In Mk. xiii. 34 ἐξουσία seems to be almost equivalent to what we should call power of attorney. It is perhaps worth noting that the Old Syriac (Sin.) ܡܣܢܐ presupposes the reading οὐσίαν for ἐξουσίαν. Cf. the O.S. rendering in Lk. xv. 12 f.

τὸ ἔξωθεν, (Rabb. אֲחוֹרִים or בַּר).

ἔχιδνα, in the phrase γεννήματα ἐχιδνῶν: Mt. iii. 7 = Lk. iii. 7 (John the Baptist is the speaker); Mt. xii. 34; xxiii. 33. The two last cases are both P and both from M. Here as elsewhere the strong words of John reappear in the speech of Jesus as recorded by M only.

ζάω

ἱερόν

καθαρίζω, in those cases where ritual purification is meant (N.H. טָהֵר; Aram. זְכִּי or דְּכִי. Cf. Dalman, Words, 62 f.; Wellhausen, Einl. 27; Ev. Luc. 61). Where the verb is used for the cure of leprosy the context is G or D.

καλῶς (שַׁפִּיר).

κορβάν (קָרְבָּן. Cf. Dalman, Gramm. p. 174 n. 3).

κρατέω, of holding a doctrine (N.H. אָחַז or הֶחֱזִיק; Aram. אֲחֵזִק).

μανθάνω, in the phrase πορευθέντες μάθετε: Mt. ix. 13. The expression, which belongs to M, corresponds to the Rabbinic

צֵא (וּ)לְמַד of which numerous examples are collected in S.B. i. 499.

Μωυσῆς, all cases except Mk. i. 44 and parallels and Mt. xxiii. 2.

ναός, four times in Matthew only: xxiii. 16, 17, 21, 35. In the last case Luke in the parallel xi. 51 has οἶκος (cf. Dan. v. 2 O′ and Θ, MT. הֵיכְלָא).

νέος

νηστεύω (N.H. צוֹם, הִתְעַנָּה; a frequent paraphrase is
יָשַׁב בְּתַעֲנִית, Aram. יְתִיב בְּתַעֲנִיתָא—S.B. 1. 426).

ὀμνύω, M only. (N.H. שְׁבַע.)

ὀρθῶς, Lk. only. Cf. Rabb. שְׁפִּיר (ק) אמרת. S.B. II. 30, 177.

οὐδέν ἐστιν, Mt. xxiii. 16, 18 (M). (Rabb. לֹא אָמַר כְּלוּם, S.B.
ad. loc.)

παλαιός

παράδοσις, Mk. vii. 8, 9, 13. Here the 'tradition of men' or
'your tradition' is set in contrast with the commandment or
word of God. Cf. Detached Note E, above; Abrahams,
Studies in Pharisaism and the Gospels, II. 199 f. (Rabb. מָסוֹרֶת;
Aram. מָסוֹרְתָּא. Cf. Taylor, Sayings of the Jewish Fathers,
Excursus I; Aboth (ed. Taylor), III. 20. The remark of Wellhausen (Ev. Marci, ad loc.) equating παράδοσις with 'asch-
lamta' (אשלמתא) appears to be a slip. There is no trace of
such a word before the time of the Masoretes, who appear to
have coined it as a name for the prophetical books of the
O.T. (Buxtorf, Tiberias (edition of 1665), p. 223; Bleek-
Wellhausen, Einleitung in das AT. (1878), p. 547.)

σάββατον: all examples are P except Mt. xxiv. 20 (D), which is
a characteristic Matthaean interpolation. Cf. Mk. xiii. 18.

The word does not occur in Q, which does not record the
controversies about Sabbath observance.

ὥστε, with a following verb in the indicative, drawing an
inference from what has been said previously. Mk. ii. 28;
x. 8; Mt. xii. 12; xxiii. 31.

APPENDIX IV

Words and phrases common to the D and G sections
of the teaching.

ἀστραπή
εἰρήνη, cf. App. II, s.v.
καλός, excluding καλόν ἐστιν, for which see App. I, s.v.
μαθητής, cf. Detached Note C.
μακάριος, not in Mk.

μαρτύριον
μικρός, cf. Appendix I, s.v.
μισέω
ὅρα and ὁρᾶτε. Cf. Ex. xxxi. 13; Num. i. 49 (LXX), where the
    word ὅρα (ὁρᾶτε) represents Heb. אַךְ, which is rendered in
    the Targums by בְּרַם.
πετεινόν
πίνω, cf. Appendix I, s.v.
ῥίζα
σῖτος, cf. App. II, s.v.
σπείρω (σπέρμα, σπόρος).
σταυρός
συνίημι, all cases are in Mk. or M and prior to P.C.
σῶμα
φυλακή. Not in Mk.
φῶς
φωτεινός
φωτίζω

APPENDIX V

Words and phrases common to the D and P sections
of the teaching.

αἰών, not in Q. The phrase οἱ υἱοὶ τοῦ αἰῶνος τούτου is
    peculiar to L, and the phrase ἡ συντέλεια τοῦ αἰῶνος to M.
αἰώνιος, not in Q. (Cf. App. I, s.v. ζωή.)
ἀνομία, Matthew only.
ἀποκτείνω
βλασφημέω (-ία).
γέεννα
γραμματεύς, not in L.
διαφέρω, not in Mk.
ἐξουσία. Cf. Appendices I and III, s.v.
ἐπιθυμέω, not in Mk.
εὔκοπος
καρδία, the only exception is Mt. xi. 29 (G).
κατὰ c. gen.
κρεμάννυμι, Matthew only.
κωλύω
μαστιγόω

νυμφίος, Mk. and M.
οὐαί, not in L.
παρέρχομαι
πλανάω
πορνεία
σατανᾶς, Mk. and L.
χαίρω, Q and L.
χαρά
χριστός, not in Q. All cases fall after P.C.

APPENDIX VI

Words and phrases common to the G and P sections of the teaching.

Ἀβραάμ
γενεά, in those cases where the Jewish contemporaries of Jesus
   are rebuked.
δικαιόω
καρπός
κατεσθίω
λῃστής

ADDITIONAL NOTES

p. 36. On the animus of M against Scribes and Pharisees.
Bultmann (*Geschichte der Synoptischen Tradition²*, p. 54) remarks
that there is a tendency at work in the tradition to bring the
Scribes and Pharisees forward as the opponents of Jesus. This
contention is fortified by numerous examples (pp. 54 f.). It
is notable that the best and most convincing of his cases come
from Mt.: Mt. xv. 14 (M?), cf. Lk. vi. 39; Mt. xii 33–35 (M?),
cf. Mt. vii. 16–20: Lk. vi. 43–45; Mt. viii. 19, cf. Lk. ix. 57;
Mt. xxii. 41, cf. Mk. xii. 35; Mt. iii. 7, cf. Lk. iii. 7. The
strong anti-pharisaic tendency seems to belong both to the
first evangelist and to his special source.

p. 45. The view that Mk. was originally written in Latin
is as old as Ephrem Syrus: Matthaeus Hebraice scripsit Evan-

gelium, Marcus Latine ab Simone in urbe Roma, etc. (*Evangelii Concordantis Expositio*, Aucher et Moesinger (1876), p. 286). Cf. Couchoud in *J.T.S.* xxxiv. 115 f.

p. 45, n. 1. E. Littmann agrees with Wellhausen: *ZNW*, 1935, p. 34.

p. 46. Rabbinic Hebrew and classical Hebrew are both distinguished from the 'vulgar tongue' (לשון הדיוט or לשׁון לישׁן חול), i.e. Aramaic. Cf. Dalman, *Gramm²*., pp. 3 f.

p. 48. Jesus as a competent Rabbinical scholar: cf. J. Weiss, *Paulus und Jesus*, p. 38; and Bultmann, *Jesus*, pp. 55 f.

p. 51. Burney was anticipated by John Jebb, who applied Lowth's principles to the New Testament in his book *Sacred Literature* published in 1820. I am indebted for this information to Bishop Vere White. See his pamphlet, *Bishop Jebb of Limerick* (S.P.C.K., 1924), pp. 14 f. The phenomenon of parallelism had also been examined by R. Schütz, *Der parallele Bau der Satzglieder im Neuen Testament* (1920), before Burney's work was published.

p. 55. Possibly we should add to the list of twin parables those of the Ten Virgins and the Man without a wedding-garment (Mt. xxii. 11–14).

p. 78. On the ambiguity of the particle ד cf. Burney, *Aramaic Origin of the Fourth Gospel*, pp. 69–76; Wellhausen, *Einleitung²*, p. 15. See also C. C. Torrey, *The Four Gospels, a new translation* (1933), pp. 75 f., 299.

pp. 82 f. *Detached note A*. To the arguments given add:

(d) ἐν πνεύματι θεοῦ corresponds to the *Rabbinic* formula בְּרוּחַ הַקֹּדֶשׁ as Schlatter shows (*Der Evangelist Matthäus*, p. 405), and is another example of Matthew's tendency to prefer Rabbinical modes of speech.

pp. 89 ff. *God as Father*. Reference should be made to an important discussion by G. Kittel in *Die Religionsgeschichte und das Urchristentum* (1932), pp. 92–95 and *Lexicographia Sacra*, pp. 14 ff. He examines the usage of Palestinian Aramaic with regard to the word 'abba (cf. Mk. xiv. 36; Ro. viii. 15; Gal. iv. 6). His conclusion is that the determined form 'abba was originally vocatival and that in ordinary speech it had completely usurped the place of אָבִי. The result was that the Palestinian Jew in speaking about his earthly father, or to him, did not say 'my father', but simply 'father'. ''*Abba* says this' or ''*abba* does this' was understood to mean 'my father says' or 'does this'. That is, all the possessive suffixes were in use except that of the 1st person singular. Only when the reference was to the Father in heaven was this rule broken. The Jew would not use '*abba* for God just because he would not be too familiar with the Almighty. God is 'our Father' or even 'my Father', but not '*abba* 'Father'. The characteristic thing about Jesus is that he used just this familiar form, from which Jewish piety shrank; he used אַבָּא where others used אָבִי or אָבוּן. And he taught his disciples to do the same (Lk. xi. 2). Cf. John xx. 17.

These considerations shed a fresh light on Rom. viii. 15 and Gal. iv. 6; and it is possible that they may contribute something to the better understanding of those sayings of Jesus about the necessity of becoming like children if we are to enter the kingdom of God.

p. 89, n. 1. Add: W. Eichrodt, *Theologie des Alten Testaments* (1933), I, pp. 118 f.

p. 104, n. 1. The argument from the sleep of the disciples is still in use. See M. Dibelius in *ZNW*, 1931, p. 196; Ch. Guignebert, *Jésus*. pp. 211 f.

p. 106, n. 1. For H. B. Chajes read H. P. Chajes. The reference is to his *Markus-Studien* (1899), pp. 10 ff. That such a mistranslation as Chajes supposes was at least possible is shown by the Greek versions of Ezek. xix. 14. Cf. Field, *Origenis Hexapla*, II. 816.

p. 111, n. 2. Cf. Eichrodt, *op. cit.* I. 189 f. Knowledge of God in the Old Testament is 'Anerkennung, nicht Erkenntnis in neutralen Sinne' (p. 190).

p. 115, n. 1. Cf. W. Jaeger, *Paideia*[2], i. 65 f.

p. 124, n. 2. I am now disposed to withdraw this interpretation in favour of that defended by Otto (*Reich Gottes und Menschensohn* (1934), pp. 84 ff.).

p. 125, n. 1. Cf. I. Abrahams, *Studies in Pharisaism and the Gospels*, ii. 189 f.

p. 130. The passage quoted from *Sifre* has a parallel in

Gen.R. 59 (ed. Theodor, p. 636; translation in Strack-Billerbeck, iii. 196). The passage in *Gen.R.* does not use the word 'king'.

p. 131, l. 13. 'my Commandments'—גְּזֵרוֹתַי, cf. Bacher, *Terminologie*, pp. 12 f. *s.v.* גְּזֵרָה.

p. 135, n. 1. Cf. R. Otto, *Reich Gottes und Menschensohn*, pp. 26 f.

p. 142. It is held by some scholars that the national name Israel means 'God rules'. Cf. Eichrodt, *op. cit.*, p. 9 and n. 6.

p. 148, n. 1. See *Bel and the Dragon* for a third treatment. Cf. G. B. Gray, *Sacrifice in the Old Testament*, pp. 41–54.

p. 151, foot. Cf. K. Holl, *Gesammelte Aufsätze*, II. 3, where Judaism is defined as 'ein durch den Monotheismus begrenzter Dualismus'.

p. 172. On the oracle of Balaam cf. Galling, *Die Erwählungstraditionen Israels*, p. 8.

p. 174. Israel's king as Jehovah's viceroy: cf. I Chron. xvii. 14, 'I will set them' (David and his successors) 'for ever over my kingdom'. Note '*my* kingdom', and cf. Otto, *op. cit.*, p. 24.

p. 175. The Remnant: cf. art. λεῖμμα in *Theologisches Wörterbuch zum N.T.* iv. 198–221 (Herntrich and Schrenk); Eichrodt, *Theologie des A.T.* i. 188; H. Wheeler Robinson, The Hebrew Conception of Corporate Personality in *Beiheft* 66 *zur ZAW*, pp. 49–62.

p. 179. Israel as servant of Jehovah: cf. *Ps. Sol.* xii. 7; xvii. 23.

p. 182. The new community growing up around Jerusalem after the Exile: cf. Neh. x. 29 f.—the נִבְדָּלִים. Here G. Kittel (*Religionsgeschichte und Urchristentum*, p. 69) sees the spiritual ancestors of the later Pharisees.

p. 183. The 'I' of the Psalms: cf. H. W. Robinson, *op. cit.*, pp. 57 f. The 'saints' in the book of Daniel. These are also referred to in Daniel as 'The Covenant' or 'The holy Covenant'. See A. A. Bevan's commentary on Daniel, p. 187. In this connexion it is worth noticing that in Deutero-Isaiah the Servant of Jehovah is twice given the strange title בְּרִית עָם (Is. xlii. 6; xlix. 8).

p. 188. *Jubilees*, xv. 31 f. Cf. *Or. Sib.* v. 384.

p. 189. The name 'Remnant' is used explicitly for the Church by Paul (Rom. xi. 5), and that in connexion with the Elijah Remnant. Cf. LXX, IV Reg. xix. 4. The quotation from Canon Streeter should be supplemented by Harnack's *Mission und Ausbreitung*³, I. 231–267 and the early Christian literature there cited.

p. 195. I Macc. ii. 29–38. A similar case is related by Agatharchides ap. Jos. *c. Ap.* i. 209 ff. See further Jos. *Ant.* xii. 277 and *B.J.* i. 146; also *Ant.* xviii. 322; *B.J.* iv. 99; *Vita*, 161. Schlatter, *Theologie des Judentums*, p. 127.

p. 207. The use of 'Amen' by Jesus. An interesting contrast is furnished by the case of Mohammed. Strong asseverations are almost entirely confined to the earlier (Meccan) surahs of the *Koran*. Cf. Nöldeke-Schwally, *Geschichte des Qorans*², I. 75.

p. 227. See the important discussion of the topic 'Restgemeinde und Messias' by Herntrich in *Th. Wb.* iv. 215.

p. 228, ll. 4 ff. Cf. Origen's use of αὐτοβασιλεία as a name for Jesus. See G. Kittel, *Die Probleme des palästinischen Spätjudentums und das Urchristentum* (1926), pp. 130 f. We may add the scholion in Peter of Laodicea's commentary on Matthew (ed. Heinrici, p. 122). It is probably derived from Origen. ἡ βασιλεία τῶν οὐρανῶν ἐστι Χριστὸς Ἰησοῦς προτρεπόμενος πάντας εἰς μετάνοιαν καὶ ἕλκων εἰς ἑαυτὸν διὰ τῆς χάριτος.

p. 232. To the list of Pauline passages add II Cor. iv. 10. Cf. Feine, *Theologie des Neuen Testaments*⁵, p. 192.

p. 234. 'In the end the particularity of the Old Testament is only intelligible in the light of its narrowed fulfilment in Jesus, the Messiah, and of its expanded fulfilment in the Church.' Sir E. Hoskyns, in *Mysterium Christi* (1930), p. 89.

p. 263. In Mk. viii. 38 there is an interesting and important textual question. The word λόγους is omitted by W k Sah, and the shorter text ὃς γὰρ ἐὰν ἐπαισχυνθῇ με καὶ τοὺς ἐμούς is defended by C. H. Turner (*J.T.S.* xxix. 2 f.; see also his commentary on Mk. *ad loc.*). To the arguments advanced by Turner may be added that from Marcan usage. The only other example of ἐμός in Mk. is in x. 40: οὐκ ἔστιν ἐμὸν δοῦναι, where ἐμόν means 'mine' and not 'my'. For 'my' Mk. always uses the genitive of the personal pronoun (31 times). We may note particularly xiii. 31 : οἱ δὲ λόγοι μου οὐ μὴ παρελεύσονται (not οἱ ἐμοὶ λόγοι). It is therefore not unlikely that the shorter text should be preferred, and that we should read :

Whoever shall be ashamed of me and mine.

In that case 'mine' refers to the disciples of Jesus, and the case for the collective interpretation of 'Son of Man' is further strengthened. 'Me and mine' can also be added to the list given at the end of note 2 on p. 269. Finally there is in this reading obvious support for the interpretation of Mt. xxv. 31–46 advanced on pp. 264 f.

p. 270, n. 2. Cf. H. J. Polotsky, art. *Manichäismus* in Pauly-Wissowa, Suppl. Bd. vi. cols. 261 f. Manichaean eschatology, which, according to Polotsky, is based on the N.T., distinguishes three classes: the elect (zu Engeln verklärt), the catechumens (set on the right hand), and the sinners (set on the left hand).

p. 270, n. 3. Add I Cor. vi. 2 f., where a similar idea is present. It is also prominent in the Apocalypse (i. 6; ii. 26; v. 10; xx. 4, 6; xxii. 5). See E. Huhn's note on I Cor. vi. 2 (*Die messianischen Weissagungen*, ii. 170). Also *Enoch*, xc. 19 and M. R. James, *The Testament of Abraham* (*Texts and Studies*, ii. 2), pp. 52 ff.

p. 279, n. 5. Add Grotius, *Annotationes in Libros Evangeliorum* (1641). p 299; Sanday, *Life of Christ in Recent Research*, pp. 115 ff.

p. 285. 'Ethics of Jesus': cf. H. D. Wendland, *Die Mitte der paulinischen Botschaft*, p. 12.

p. 292. Divorce. On the Jewish view see G. Kittel, *Probleme*, 99 ff., and on that of Jesus, p. 127.

p. 292, n. 5. A similar transposition in the Greek text of *Ecclesiasticus* xi. 27, compared with the Hebrew: עֵת רָעָה and κάκωσις ὥρας.

p. 293. R. Akiba on divorce: cf. G. Kittel, *Probleme*, p. 100.

p. 303, n. 3. After 'note *i*' add:
Cf. also S.B. iii. 542 ff.; Bacher, *Pal. Amor.* i. 557 ff.

GENERAL INDEX

REFERENCE INDEX

I. OLD TESTAMENT

(References to Kittel, *Biblia Hebraica*, 2nd edition)

III. NEW TESTAMENT AND APOSTOLIC FATHERS

John

Acts

Romans

IV. RABBINICAL LITERATURE

A. Mishnah and Talmud

(Tractates in alphabetical order)

B. Midrashim

(Figures in brackets denote the passage of Scripture commented upon)

Reprinted by photo-offset by Percy Lund, Humphries & Co. Ltd.,
for the University Press, Cambridge.